THE CAMPER'S COMPANION

The pack-along guide for better outdoor trips

by

Rick Greenspan and Hal Kahn

Foghorn Press

San Francisco

51295

9 780935 701296

Art Direction and Design. . . .   I. Magnus
Illustrations. . . . .   Gordon Ohliger
                                         Ian Sandiland/I. Magnus
Editor. . . . .   Deke Castleman
Cover Photo. . . . .   David Stocklein/West Stock

Cover photo shows Scott and Sue camping in Boulder, Colorado.

Library of Congress Cataloging-In-Publication Data:

Greenspan, Rick.
The Camper's Companion:
The pack along guide for better outdoor trips
by Rick Greenspan and Hal Kahn.
p. cm.
Includes bibliographical references and index.
1. Camping – Handbooks, manuals, etc.
2. Outdoor recreation – Handbooks, manuals, etc.
I. Kahn, Hal, 1930- .   II. Title.
GV191.7.G74 1991   796.54–dc20   91–2784 CIP
ISBN 0-935701-29-X : $12.95

About the Authors

Hal Kahn and Rick Greenspan admit between them to over half a century's experience backpacking and camping. City boys, they took early to the country and its illimitable charms, and for many years have walked, wheeled, paddled, and feasted in the wilderness and campgrounds of the western United States. When they're not out "There," Rick is at the College of Alameda where he teaches auto mechanics, and Hal is at Stanford where he teaches Chinese history. Rick doesn't know a dynasty from a doughnut, but that's alright because Hal couldn't tell a carburetor from a condominium. The only thing they have in common is their love for the outdoors.

Their first book, *Backpacking, A Hedonist's Guide*, was inspired by the fun they've had putting the pleasure principle to work in the wilderness. This book takes off from there, renewing and expanding on that pleasure. If you have ideas and suggestions for them, or if you just want to communicate about camping and its delights, write them at their publisher:

Foghorn Press
P.O. Box 77845
San Francisco, CA 94107
Telephone: (415) 241-9550
Fax: (415) 241-9648

Acknowledgements

The people who made this book possible are the ones who have traveled with us, sharing our pleasure in wilderness camping and helping us test the depths of our ability to improvise and have fun. They are all in the book, mostly under their own names, though sometimes shaded by a "moniker." To them our thanks has often been spoken privately; here it is made public, and we hope they enjoy reading the words as much as we enjoyed writing them.

Deke Castleman can recite the entire text of the book by heart. That's because he's read it so many times, as one of the world's all-time tough and compassionate editors. He cast a cold eye on lyrical excesses and dumb diction. If you want bear stories and highfalutin' camping philosophy, you'll find them on the cutting room floor, victims of a conspiracy against Fluff and Solemnity. Karen Bernstein also slashed and burned, dismissing treacle and B-grade sunsets with a wave of her wand.

Gary Wendt-Bogier and Rob Kerson, experts on equipment, answered a barrage of questions, as did the incomparable staff at REI in Berkeley, California. Bonnie Lewkowicz introduced us to the problems and prospects for camping with physical disabilities. Helen and Rudy Kass shared canoeing lore gathered from many years on New England waters. Marianne Babal and Doug Nelson, who seem to have covered the world on their touring bikes, steered us in the right direction, as did Tom Pissarri. Beau Barnes, multi-media outdoor fanatic, fired advice at us from all quarters. And Joan Hamilton brought alive the joy and wackiness of backpacking with children. We've threatened to hold all these friends responsible for any mistakes in the book, but they don't scare easily, so we'll take the blame.

We are grateful to the editors of *Sierra* for permission to cite a passage from Joan Hamilton's lovely article on children, and to the International Mountain Bicycling Association for permission to reproduce their "Rules of the Trail." The American Canoe Association, American Hiking Society, American Red Cross, National Forest Service, National Park Service, and the Sierra Club kindly provided us with helpful information.

Finally, all those anonymous trail crews, rangers and strangers we've met in the mountains deserve a nod and a note of thanks as well. There is a great store of friendship in the backcountry, and we seem to have drawn on it more than most. Our book is a little gesture of repayment, and we hope our friends take it as that.

A Word to the Reader

This book appeared in an earlier, much different incarnation as *Backpacking, A Hedonist's Guide* (Moon Publications: Chico, CA, 1985). Upon publication it received instant critical acclaim and then, just as suddenly, disappeared from view. It became a rare book, hard to find and much treasured by collectors. Two things happened to make it a cult classic. First was its title. Polls show that three-quarters of the reading public think "hedonism" is either an incendiary political movement or a blood disease. And here we thought we were offering pleasures and delights! Second, the book was confiscated by the U. S. Customs Service. Yep. The same folks who defend our shores against drugs and subversive ideas fixed their steel claws and padlocks on our little guide to the backcountry. We had come afoul of an old (and since discarded) law about printing books abroad. Lawyers and depleted bank balances later, we sprung the book, but the season—our season in the limelight—had passed. Relatives and a few lucky outdoor fanatics got copies which to this day, it is whispered, are passed from hand to hand among the faithful. *The Hedonist's Guide* became the *samizdat* of wilderness literature.

In the meantime there was still an audience out there crying for a decent, all-purpose, wide-ranging, user-friendly how-to book about the outdoors. We harkened. And with feverish brows and quivering keyboards, we set out to fill the bill. The result, even as we speak, is in your hands.

Camping, hiking, canoeing, and biking now share the stage with backpacking. Our perspective on the outdoors has broadened. Our experience on land and water, on roads and trails has expanded. We still love to backpack. That is obvious in the book. But you'll find us as well with children in a canoe, with friends on the bike-touring routes, with a hammock and cooler in the campgrounds. Food preparation and the pleasures of eating still occupy hallowed ground at the center of our concerns. But now they're expanded, enriched, and garnished with years of experience and improvisation. If you can't discover the hedonist principle at work in this new book, we've failed. If you don't have the best camping trip in the history of the outdoors after reading this, we've gone astray. If you're an expert and can't learn anything from our book, we've done you wrong. If you're a novice and can't understand what we say, call us. We'll say it again.

Our new publisher has gone all-out to make this book the most functional of its kind ever published. Printed with a durable cover, constructed with clip-out packing lists and recipes for your camping convenience, equipped with the most thorough index since the variorum edition of Shakespeare hit the bookstalls, *The Camper's Companion* cries out to be used. We think it cries out to be *read* too, but that's our problem.

We're still waiting for a Nobel Prize in outdoor writing to be created. In the meantime, our reward will be your pleasure. Let us know what you think.

HLK and RG
San Francisco
February 1991

TABLE OF CONTENTS

CHAPTER 4 Food

CHAPTER 5 Lists: A Schlepper's Guide to the Universe

CHAPTER 6 Getting There

INTRODUCTION

Brooklyn Boy Meets Wilderness

Steve looks like a surfer but sounds like a mobster.   Behind the Dayglo tan and obedient muscles is a bookish film critic from Flatbush who'd never been closer to the wilderness than summer camp at Bear Mountain. The Great Outdoors ("outta daws") meant Belmont Racetrack and Shea Stadium. The only trails he'd ever hiked were asphalt; the only lonesome roads he'd traveled under his own power were the sidestreets off Queens Boulevard on a three-speed bike he had lifted from his cousin Jimmy.

But like many young city slickers, he craved the country. We'd never taken anyone camping who was so eager to "tame" the wilderness. He couldn't wait to strap on the pack and get started. He was strong and fit. He was ready for bear! He lasted about three hours. Several miles from the trailhead, he began to mutter and grumble. Howinhell could anyone enjoy schlepping a forty-pound pack uphill in 80 degree heat all afternoon toward some abstract promise of a cool mountain lake? The farther we got from the last beer, the darker became his mood. His boots were good looking but a size too small; long before we reached our destination they had rubbed his heels raw. His pack felt like some mythic burden of the

damned. The route was incomprehensible. By the time we
stopped for dinner, he was ready for a hotel. But a quarter-
inch foam sleeping pad was not his idea of the Waldorf Astoria.

The second day brought no relief. Up too early, we climbed
1,500 feet in the first mile, then set off cross country around a
mountain bowl strewn with rock slides, boulders and steep
pitches into space. The streets of Brooklyn seemed safe by
comparison. Steve's every muscle ached from yesterday. We
kept up a steady stream of encouragement, however, and by
mid-afternoon, Steve made a monumental discovery. You can
make the pack work *for* you, keeping the weight on the hips
and off the shoulders. He began to notice that the view before
him was improbably remote and beautiful, something he
couldn't see elsewhere. And when we finally climbed down to
a granite-girded lake, filled with trout and inaccessible
enough to promise a week of solitude, Steve remembered why
we came: five days of fishing, cooking, eating, and relaxing.

His contentment lasted till we set out to catch our supper.
Steve regarded the fishing rod with suspicion. We put a lure
on the line and taught him how to cast. But that did nothing
to dispel his skepticism. How could you catch fish with a
spoon-shaped piece of metal at the end of a nylon string? He
cast and cast—aspersions and oaths as well as lures and flies
and bubbles. Around the lake he went. No luck. He announced his early retirement from the game.

His mood blackened as the clouds rolled in, necessitating
another trauma—setting up his tent. He hesitated. We ca-
joled. He procrastinated. We insisted. He refused. We
quickly erected it. It began to pour. It rained all night. In the
morning, Steve's tent looked like a collapsed dream the day
the circus leaves town. Somewhere under that heap of netting, nylon, and wind-sundered rain fly lay a sodden camper
converted to the virtues of foul-weather protection. While the
sun dried his sleeping bag, Steve spent an hour erecting the
tent in the ideal place with geometric fanaticism. It looked
great, and he never spent another moment in it. But he was
glad it was there, waiting.

The next day Steve caught his first fish, an eight-inch
brown trout, with a grasshopper. Well, perhaps he'd consider
coming out of retirement. Two days later he returned with

seven little rainbows after a tough solo hike to a lake beyond
the razor-back ridge. And he began to *talk* fishing. He studied the "hatch" of flies on the water's surface, invented fishing
knots, and experimented with salmon eggs as extra entice-
ment on his lures. Trout with almonds, trout baked in soy
sauce, ginger, and garlic, fish grilled over red-hot coals at sunset—all helped make the talk better. Camping began to look—
and feel—like fun.

On our fourth day, Steve set out to bake a cake. He'd never
before baked anything, anywhere. He had, however, been impressed with the cinnamon nut bread and the chocolate cake
with icing we'd pulled from the coals. He hauled out flour and
baking powder, corn meal (which he mistook for milk powder),
RyKrisp, raisins, apricots and sugar; mixed them all in a pot;
added some margarine, sugar, an egg, then poured in just
enough water to make the batter run off the spoon like a ribbon. We reminded him to grease the pot before surrounding it
with hot coals, wished him luck and went fishing. When we
returned, an apricot cornbread awaited us and Steve carved
another notch on the stock of his outdoor knowledge.

After that, we had a wilderness fanatic on our hands. He
insisted on doing everything: fishing, sewing, cooking, gathering wood. We managed to keep busy swimming, sunning, eating and reading. Together we invented ways to cook fish, fry
corn cakes, and coin new names for constellations in the night
sky because we weren't sure of their classic names and didn't
care. By the time we walked out, Steve was a confirmed
camper and we were convinced that anyone could become
one too.

What This Book Is About

There are enough texts on hiking, cycling, canoeing, backpacking, car camping, mountaineering, survival and fishing to fill
a four-year curriculum on the fine art of leaving your house.
This book doesn't duplicate the other guides. Rather, it illus-
trates how imagination, improvisation, and commitment can
unfold the possibilities of the outdoors, whether you get there
by car, foot, bike, canoe, llama, horse or wheelchair. It takes
an agnostic view of what defines the outdoors. For some it is

a campground filled with RVs and barbecues, sort of a downtown with trees. For others it is a remote off-trail lake two days distant from the nearest human voice. For many it is somewhere in between—a state park, a river bank, a day hike away from the madding crowd.

This book recognizes that whatever the outdoors means to you, its pleasures can be enhanced by some common sense planning, a willingness to slow down and hang out, a disposition to indulge in minor adventures. The book is based on the Pleasure Principle: A camping holiday is neither boot camp nor a triumph of the will. It is not (necessarily) uplifting or ennobling. It is, or *should* be, more fun and less expensive than a motel tour of the world's Disneylands and watering holes. And this book shows you how.

This book is practical. It tells you four things: how to plan a trip; how to get where you're going; how to cook and eat as never before on a camping trip; and what to do in the long hours between sumptuous meals. If you're a novice we'll show you how to get started and how to finish gracefully, even if you've gotten egg on your face along the way. If you are an old hand at camping, we'll give you new and useful information about fishing, cooking, trail-finding, stargazing, family entertainment, and all-purpose, world-class hanging out. If you've ever come back from a camping trip bored or discontented, this is the book you need.

A book can't paddle a canoe, catch a fish or bake a cake. It *can*, however, provide the initial inspiration, point in the right direction and above all, cut the time, cost and hard knocks of learning. We'll show you how to stay dry, stay full, stay busy, stay friends. We'll run you through the basics—how to get the information you need, how to think about equipment, packing, maps, and trails. We'll then give you hints on improvising: drying food, fishing in the rain, repairing boots, entertaining children. We are equal-opportunity enthusiasts and want you to get a feel for the limitless possibilities of a camping trip.

We do make several assumptions: that you like to camp and love to eat; that you want a vacation, not a forced march; that you like to get away from the Grind. (Rick's grandmother used to kvetch, "If you've seen one tree you've seen 'em all."

This book is not for her.) We also assume that you are not necessarily a mountain climber, spelunker, Yukon guide or even a member of the Sierra Club. You may never have set foot in a national park or on a wilderness trail, or you may have been haunting them for years. You are reasonably fit but not a triathlete. You may be too young to read this book or too old to believe all its claims; you may be "abled" or disabled. You believe that locomotion by foot or boat or bike or wheelchair is an honorable and even enjoyable way to travel. And that financing a camping trip does not require a seat on the New York Stock Exchange.

The style of camping espoused in this book requires no exceptional skills. Getting a canoe across a lake or down a slow-moving river is not the same as taking a raft or kayak through white water with the family's Waterford crystal on board. Our book is about the first, not the second. Riding a mountain bike on a dirt trail or a touring bike into a campground does not require experience in the Giro d'Italia. We know something about the former, nothing about the latter. Backpacking in the wilderness, on or off trail, takes ordinary, not extraordinary know-how.

One of us is afraid of heights, but gets along fine even on steep trails. We've been lost and even without radar have managed to figure out where we were and how to get to where we were going. We don't have the newest, most expensive equipment. But we've lived on fish we caught, baked breads and cakes, read some of the world's longest novels, kept our clothes dry and spirits up in 48 hours of steady rain, and come back to spin tales that made our friends' feet itch and our own thoughts turn to the next trip out. Everything that we write about we (or our friends) have done ourselves, and most of it we learned by doing. All the stories are true. And if we haven't done something—for example, performed triple bypass surgery with a Swiss Army knife or coped with a serious injury—we don't write about it. We prefer to go easy on the detailed information you can get better elsewhere. But we make every effort to show you how to get that information (in Chapter 2 and in the Book List).

How to Use This Book

We've never met anyone who has actually read a camping book from cover to cover. Unless you can't bear to skip a single page, you'll want to cut in at functional points and then cut out again. To that end, we divide the book into four parts: Planning a Trip, Outdoor Basics, Cooking and Eating, and Pleasure Principle: Creative Loitering. Here's a brief summary of each.

Planning A Trip

Planning a camping trip takes time and energy, though the amount of each depends on your mode of travel. Car and canoe camping are relatively easy. Think of your "vehicle" as an extra-large steamer trunk. Toss in anything you want and get out of town before the IRS comes calling. Biking and backpacking take more planning. You need to consider total weight, packing constraints, route difficulty, number of people involved, distances. In all cases—however you travel—planning requires making lists, deciding where to go, when to go, how to get there, whom to go with. Then you have to assemble gear, maps, permits, more gear.

In Chapter 1, we show you how to plan trips by car, bike, canoe, horse, and foot, for one person, two, four, or more, for families and extended families—bringing babies and great-grandmothers and disabled friends takes only a little special forethought. We also discuss the great philosophical question, How far should one go? Not on the first date, but on the first day, and on subsequent days too. We have a formula that operates here and you're going to like it. It has to do with resting as much as moving, and will prepare you for the great culture shock of PHO (Planned Hanging Out).

Chapter 2 puts at your fingertips the kind of information everybody always asks for: Where do we get maps and permits, find campgrounds, get in touch with experts and guides and like-minded enthusiasts? Where do we find the right fix-it manual, the local or regional outdoor club or clinic, the best advice on equipment, the meaning of life? Let your ham-handed fists do the walking through its pages.

Chapter 3 is all about equipment—with a twist. We show you how to stay warm, dry, and comfortable, *without spending a fortune.* Canoeists, we argue, don't need the latest second-skin rain gear, bicyclists the newest genetically engineered light-weight frames, backpackers freeze-dried tent stakes. What everybody needs is a make-do attitude and a sympathetic sales clerk.

Chapter 4 concerns food: what and how much to take, where to buy it, how to weigh and pack it, what kind of utensils and stoves and pots you will need, even how to cache food on a long trip. Once you've got this part of the planning done, the cooking and eating will be a piece of cake! In short, it will take you an hour to read these suggestions, two hours to absorb them, and a few more hours to put them into practice. But we guarantee it'll save you countless hours and dollars and hassles.

So will Chapter 5, which is devoted to the exquisite art of making lists. We show you basic lists and arcane, Gothic lists. We'll help you make equipment lists, tool kits, and medicine chests. Even book lists! If after this chapter you forget something, don't call us, we'll call you.

Outdoor Basics

You've planned and prepared for your camping adventure for a week. You've got everything. You're in the saddle, on the dock, or at the trailhead. Chapter 6 takes you from there to your destination. It shows you how to read maps, load and adjust a pack, pannier, or canoe, and how to hike or bike a trail and negotiate off-trail terrain. It gets you through weather and around obstacles. It tells you how to get acclimated to altitude, heat, and cold. Above all, it stresses the importance of remaining flexible. A blister, a storm, or just a meadow full of wildflowers may slow you down and make you change your plans. This is a vacation. Look around, enjoy, take it easy.

Chapter 7 shows you how to choose a site and set up camp. If you don't know where to pitch your tent or stow your canoe, how to build a fire, protect your food from small and large creatures of the night (your partner excepted), stash your gear, enjoy or at least survive a storm, the information is there. Use it.

Cooking and Eating

Eating is at the heart—well, gut—of the outdoor experience. Our attitude is this: If you enjoy eating in your own kitchen, why deprive yourself of the pleasure just because you're three days and nine thousand feet away from a home with a range? Stick with us and you'll be able to have your cake and eat it too!

Chapter 8 tells you how to avoid the library-paste peril of freeze-dried foods by preparing your own dried meals at home, simply and inexpensively. It takes you through cooking basics with the expectation that even if you have never boiled an egg you can still bake a trout or make the best Brazilian black bean soup this side of Rio. Need to clean or bone a fish? Cook in the rain? Use a camp stove? Need to eat fast and travel light? Want to carry a forty-pound reflector oven and microwave blaster into a campground? We have answers to all these questions and more. We show you how to become an outdoor chef without burning yourself, the food or the forest.

Chapter 9 is the long-awaited clip-out collection of recipes that have made us famous from Kneejerk Junction to Toehold Lake, from Chez Panisse in Berkeley to the Oyster Bar in Grand Central Station: freshwater fish, homemade soups and sauces, stewed fruits, jams and chutneys, baked breads, cakes, pizzas. The recipes are keyed for time, ease, heat source (stove or fire) and perishability. Read 'em and drool.

Pleasure Principle: Creative Loitering

Bikers and canoeists sometimes want to take a day off. Day hikers and car campers have loads of time on their hands. And backpackers—at least those dedicated to the Kahn &

Greenspan school of sequential hiking and loafing—love long days wondering if it's worth getting up to bag a grasshopper as bait or read the world's second longest novel. Children need to be busy, amused, content, dirty, startled and entranced by the simple wonder of it all. This is the part of the book that caps the journey and makes it all worth while.

Chapter 10 pulls together all the good things to do on a lazy day (well, all the good things fit to print), whether you're in a paved campsite or stuck in an aerie below the summit of Mount Vertigo. This is a chapter dedicated, but not limited, to children. Whatever your age, if you don't know what to do with time on your hands 200 miles from the nearest game show, take heart. Help is at hand. Here. Now.

Chapter 11 is the amateur angler's guide to the briny deep. Some people fish for sport. Others fish to relax. We fish to eat. Here is the info on everything from gear to casting to landing the big cahoonga. You even get a fish-eye view of the whole thing: where they hang out and why, what they're looking for and at. We don't use the latest in laminated fly rods, and purists might cringe, but we've never gone hungry and never left a lake or stream dissatisfied, even when we didn't catch a thing.

Chapter 12 is an introduction to the heavens. Stars are just about the only nighttime viewing entertainment in the backcountry, and viewing them is the second most popular sport conducted in a prone position after dark. We have tried in this chapter to give you a couple of working methods for making personal sense out of the slice of sky above you; it is legitimate to see constellations with your own mind's eye. Just as ancient Greeks and Chinese discovered different formations in the same stars, you may rearrange the classical sky for yourself with much pleasure and no damage to the astronomical establishment. On the other hand, if you're a traditionalist and want to know how to read a star map, the information is here. But either way, you'll never know how bright the night sky is until you see it unobscured by city lights and a pall of smog.

THE CAMPER'S COMPANION

The pack-along guide
for better outdoor trips

by

Rick Greenspan and Hal Kahn

Foghorn Press
San Francisco

CHAPTER 1

Variables:
Who's Going Where
and How?

Getting Ready

Anyone who has ever camped out in the backyard as a kid or whose children have waved goodbye after supper and gone off down the back steps and disappeared into a tent knows that there are things to do to get ready. Complex things: Which cookies to take? Which friend? And simple things: Knowing the fastest, safest escape route back to bed in the event that the yard is overrun by goblins. A grown-up camping trip farther afield isn't much different. While you don't have to gird for battle to get ready, you do need to answer some fairly basic questions: Where to go? When? How far? How many? Who? And the answers depend in the first place on the great locomotion dilemma: To go or not to go by car, by bike, by canoe, by horse, by foot. Once you resolve that, proceed to the section which applies to you, and then browse the others. You may be persuaded to try another way another time.

Car Camping

We know two people whose names are Ed and Edna. They are not related. They have never met. They have nothing to do with one another. But combined, their stories ought to prove once and for all that car camping comes in as many hues as a smoggy sunset in Passaic or L.A.

Edna is a biker. She rides a 750cc Harley, wears leathers and a tattoo, and is, we swear it, sixty years old. She looks *bad* and we've heard teenagers exclaim, "Awesome, dude!" when she pulls into the parking lot. The parking lot in question abuts REI (Recreational Equipment Incorporated), the great western states' equivalent of EMS (Eastern Mountain Sports) and other outdoor provisioners. Twice a year without fail Edna shows up there to check out the latest in camping gear, everything from stoves to tents to orienteering compasses. She plunks down a bundle and leaves the staff agog from the tales she tells of her latest adventures on the camping trail. Edna and her women pals have been to every campground from the San Juan Islands in Puget Sound to Death Valley. She likes to keep moving, but she also knows how to hike, cook, fish, and strip down her bike and rebuild it in a campground. She rides for the feel of the wind and the speed of her wheels, and camps for the companionship and the beauty of the places she finds off the road. She's one of our favorite all-time campers, daring, eccentric, funny, and good at what she does.

Ed is a retired bodyshop owner whom we met in a campsite on the Oregon coast a couple of years ago. Every summer he takes off in his camper truck, fishing the coastal rivers and the ocean beaches for three months. But when we met him he was a shattered man. Hadn't slept for a week before he pulled into this particular campground. This was no insomniac. He told us he could sleep through a fender job on Al Capone's Packard. But he had made a mistake and tried the mountain campgrounds in the Cascade Range. They were clean, accessible, friendly, uncrowded. Still, he couldn't get to sleep. It was too quiet! He realized when he got back to the shore that what he had missed was the sound of the sea. It was part of his routine; it defined his environment, and he swore he would never leave the coast again. For him that was a blessing not a constraint. His vistas were bounded by tidewaters, but within them were unlimited expectations.

While few people can afford to take off three months to camp out of their cars, the number of people visiting parks and campgrounds for a few days alfresco is growing. And camping with your vehicle has a lot of advantages which other kinds of camping (such as backpacking) lack. You don't have to haul anything anywhere but out of the trunk of your car. (And if you have a motor home, you don't have to haul anything out at all!) Your tent can be old or new, heavy or light— or you can sleep in the back seat of your car. You can bring a lightweight backpacking stove or a four-burner extravaganza with a cantilevered oven or a ten-pound bag of briquettes for the campground grill. Car camping is great for small kids, who can't carry a pack or walk for miles. It's also just the ticket for disabled people if the campground has the necessary access facilities and construction. For campers who like conveniences like showers, flush toilets, picnic tables, and possibly a nearby Foster's Freeze, it provides a happy alternative to urban life.

Campground Reservations

Most campsites, whether in county, state or national parks, are available on a first-come, first-served basis, and it is possible and often necessary to reserve a site by mail or phone well before you leave on your trip. In the northern tier states and Canada, where the summer season is short, camping pressure is heavy and often campsites are sold out by January! The same is true in heavily populated or touristed parks (e.g. Yosemite, Yellowstone, Acadia). So:

- Reserve early.
- Call your local, county, or state Parks and Recreation Department for reservation information and requirements.
- Call the National Park Service (see Chapter 2 for numbers) for reservation info at specified parks. Many parks will not accept reservations before a certain date.

- Cancel reservations as soon as you know you can't use them. That's a courtesy to others on the waiting list.
- If you don't have a reservation, you may still get a campsite on a first-come basis at the park itself.
- Try to avoid the big holiday weekends if you don't have a reservation.

Once you get to a campground, you may want to hike the local trails for a day. That means you may need a map (and may want to know how to read it), a day pack, and some food and water to bring along. You may want to take your all-terrain bicycle for a trail ride. You may want to fish in a nearby lake or stream, spend some time cooking, or just sit in the shade and read.

Whatever your preferences, you can enhance your experience by using the sections below which apply to you and your particular needs. If you want to hike off the trail, read the section on topo maps; if you like to fiddle with the menu, go to the chapters on food and cooking; if you're bringing a bicycle, check your tool set against the list in Chapter 5. And if you're a first-timer, you'll want to know what equipment is necessary, what is optional, what can be rented, and what is useful to buy if you're on a limited budget. Check out Chapter 3 for hints and some unconventional wisdom.

Crime in the Campground

"They took my bicycle, my money and all my credit cards."
Jenn DeRosa, Westfield, N. J.
(*N. Y. Times*, August 21, 1990)

"It's no secret that national parks are ripe grounds
for larceny—autos, camera equipment, jewelry."
Ken Miller, Chief of Visitor Protection,
Grand Canyon, also in the *Times*.

Alas the age of innocence is over. It is a fact of life that crime is up in the outback. Reported burglaries in the National Parks are up from 717 in 1984 to 801 in 1989; reported assaults down from 527 to 300; reported vehicle thefts up from 178 to 313. Unreported cases would swell these figures. Car camping grounds are a lot safer than the mean streets you left behind, but still you need to take some common sense precautions to assure that your holiday remains a holiday.

- Ask the park rangers what the local safety protocols are. They know best.
- Don't assume that gear locked in your car or trunk is safe if you head off for a day on the trail. Leave as little behind as possible. Ditto your tent.
- Hike or travel in groups.
- Party in moderation. Park rangers report more assaults among people who know each other than between strangers.
- If you don't need your Kohinoor diamond, leave it at home.

Bicycle Touring and Mountain Bikes

A bicycle is one of the best ways to reach choice and remote camping spots. You move faster than on foot, but notice things that you would miss in a car. Bike touring is marked above all by self-sufficiency. You carry all your own gear in panniers, the cyclist's equivalent of saddlebags. You can cover a continent or your local neighborhood, cross Canada or mosey through the backroads of Denmark: As long as you are camping along the way, you'll find a great deal of useful information here.

Bike Touring for the First Time?

- Take day trips before trying an extended tour. Build your stamina.
- Take short "shakedown" tours *with all your gear* before trying a long one. These will accustom you to the feel of a fully loaded bike, allow you to iron out glitches in equipment, and probably persuade you to lighten your load!
- Plan to travel with someone else or a group.

- Take advantage of "walk-in" campsites. They are almost always available for cyclists (and hikers) without reservations. They're cheap, convenient, friendly.
- Learn basic repair skills for *your* bike: tire changing or patching, chain and cable repair. Or tour with somebody who knows how to fix your bike.
- Carry a lock and use it.
- Protect against sun and heavy weather.

Mountain biking means using your bicycle to travel on hiking trails or rough logging roads. As these are often steep and rugged, it's nearly impossible to carry a lot of weight on the bike. Furthermore, mountain bikes are heavier than touring bikes, for they have to stand up to the constant jolting of rough terrain. You don't take the Encyclopedia Britannica along on such a vehicle. Mountain bikers are essentially day-hikers on bicycles, and they need to have map-reading skills, adequate food and drink, and protection from sun and rain, just as day-hikers do. In addition, they have to deal with the possibility of breakdowns miles from the nearest shop. That often requires innovation and ingenuity, as well as having the proper equipment and parts in the toolbag.

Talk to touring cyclists or mountain bikers. You'll discover that most of them love and know the outdoors and take pride and pleasure in combining camping and cycling. Like canoeists and backpackers, some camp in order to travel and some travel in order to camp. Either way, its the combination that counts, and you'll find a wealth of valuable camping and traveling hints in this book, in addition to the specific sections which deal with bicycles and the outdoors.

Bikers and Hikers

A great trail-use controversy has surfaced in the past few years as more and more mountain bikers are beginning to show up on what once were exclusively hiking (or horse packing) trails. There are now 15 million all-terrain bikes in the U.S., and some experts estimate that between three and five million are being used in forested and mountain areas, along some of the 77,000 miles of trail maintained by the National

Forest Service outside of designated wilderness areas. Who has got the right of way? Does peace and solitude take precedence over equal access rights? Are the trails being ruined? The answers aren't in yet, and the partisans on each side still outnumber those who are trying to work out compromise solutions. Meanwhile bikers are beginning to learn the art of "soft cycling," walking their bikes over fragile terrain, slowing down on heavily hiked trail sections, making way for hikers and horses, learning trail etiquette. Here are the six "Rules of the Trail" put out by the International Mountain Bicycling Association (for address and phone, see Chapter 2):

- Ride on open trails only.
- Leave no trace.
- Control your bicycle.
- Always yield trail (to hikers and pack animals).
- Never spook animals.
- Plan ahead.

Canoeing

Helen Kass is a self-professed klutz. She insists that the genes for grace and athletic skill were removed surgically from her body by aliens at an early age. Yet she proudly points to almost 40 years of New England canoeing experience and insists with a kind of triumphant resignation that if she can do it, you can too. Helen thinks that it's the only way to travel on Maine's rivers and on the inter-island itinerary along the coast. She and her family have been at it for a couple of generations, and the first time you find yourself waking up unexpectedly in a field of wild strawberries (having disembarked after dark), or the first time you take a wrong turn up the local sewer outlet with a dachshund who abandons ship, you will not be a pioneer. They beat you to it and lived to tell the tale.

Canoeing is the nautical equivalent of cross-country skiing, an invitation to random discovery. In many areas you can combine hiking and canoeing, taking day trips on land and then heading out for another site down or up stream. In other areas you can combine river and lake canoeing and literally go on for weeks, portaging between launching sites. Canoeing is also one of the easiest ways to transport yourself, your gear, and the entire *mishpukheh* (family, to you) across a lake to your favorite campsite in the woods. A 70-pound, 16.5-foot canoe holds just about as much as a VW Bug, so you can toss in the lawn chairs and the old five-person canvas tent along with the spouse and close relatives. Made of everything from ye olde wood and canvas to hybrid miracle laminates, it is almost indestructable, and for class 1 (lake) and class 2 (slow-moving river) travel no special repair kit is necessary (see Chapter 5, pg 103). And because it's a shallow-draft craft, the canoe is ideal for exploring tidal waters. Other boats are at the mercy of the tides. Not the canoe.

Canoeing, like car camping, is a glorious way to travel with small children. You can stop as often as they like—to explore a tidal pool or mud hole, to examine a bird's nest, to romp and stretch, swim or pee. On a lazy river you can always have a hand free to get food, comfort a crank, play a game, steady a fussbudget, pet the dachshund. Children even love the tipover drills you put them through before their first trip, and the drills themselves help demystify water-borne transport. You can even let small children help paddle. They'll grow up to take *you* canoeing.

Experienced canoeists agree that the "tippy" issue is much exaggerated. Of course you can tip over a canoe. You can tip over a Volvo too if you're not careful, or fall off a bike or trip over your shoelaces while hiking. With a modicum of care and a sense of weight displacement that should come naturally, you'll board and exit the canoe, shift positions, pack, and paddle it safely and smoothly. If you've never paddled a canoe, take the Red Cross hands-on course, pass their test, and be on your way. Read their big book, *Canoeing* (see Chapter 2), and you'll get all the hard information you need, from loading a canoe on your car to portaging, from handling a canoe in rough weather or water or fog to stashing gear and dealing with emergencies. After that, come back to us here, for all the news you need to make a canoeing trip a fabulous camping

trip as well. What we say about backpacking below applies to
you too.

Whaddya Do With Your Car While Canoeing?

- Take a loop trip which brings you back to the car.
- Have friends or a canoe livery service (ask the park
  ranger station for information) drive your car to your
  destination point. Don't forget to take a set of keys for
  yourself!
- Hitch a ride back to the car while the rest of the party
  stays with the canoe. This only works on short trips
  and only where you feel safe hitchhiking.
- Sell the canoe to a passing farmer, walk into town, buy
  a new car, drive it back to your old car, sell it to a passing farmer, and drive off into the sunset.

Backpacking

Some years ago Rick discovered a gem of a lake in the high Sierras by just the method we want to get across to you here: a
combination of memory, guile, imagination, curiosity, map
reading, and schmoozing. Here's the story.

Back in college when he was young and spry (he is now old
and spry), Rick had a classmate whom we shall call Alice for
national security reasons. Alice came from one of those uncon-
scionably rich families that owned real estate—like half the
South Pacific. As a little girl she would be taken to the mountains by the family, its well-lardered pack train, a couple of
spare aunts and uncles, and of course its retainer, a grizzled
wilderness guide right out of central casting named Big Buck.
B.B. got them to this storied lake filled with giant golden trout
and pure water, and Alice's fragmented memory of it provided
Rick with the first shards of the information he needed.

The horses were left at a base camp, before the terrain got
rough. The party had to hike, climbing ridges and walking

through snowfields. "We hiked forever," Rick recalls Alice saying, "upwards, always upwards." (Alice, it must be noted, has never won a drama critics award.) The trail climbed a steep ridge over an 11,000 foot pass, and then at some predetermined point—there were no markers—Buck turned off the trail and began winding his way up a rocky streambed. The going was slow, steep, boulder-strewn. "I remember thinking that the top of the mountain was near, only to find that over each crest lay yet another rocky basin. And over the crest of that basin, there was still another."

Finally of course the party stopped at Big Buck's command and followed his gaze and ancient arm. There below, couched between snowfield and evergreen grove, lay Lake Nirvana, Buck's private Shangri-la, and the most beautiful place on Earth.

Years later Rick was determined to find that place. He knew the lake's name and its general location. He gathered up maps and guidebooks, checked indexes and keys, and finally found it on a topo map. It was several miles off a main trail, nestled in a bowl surrounded by steep pinnacles and spires. Big Buck's route was easy to spot, over one crest, then another, then another, climbing upwards from the main trail toward the single passable entrance among the tall crags. Even the snowfields were on the map.

The map told him even more. The stream flowed into the lake year round, providing fresh water even in the late summer when the trip was planned. Just below the lake there were several flat, meadow-like areas in the forest. These could provide a sheltered campsite with running water nearby. So Rick set off by himself for the lake in mid-September.

The trip itself was too good to be true: wonderful fishing, secure campsite, superb weather, and above all, a breathtaking panorama of domes, spires and steep crags burnished by the late summer sun. Using maps, a compass, planning and common sense, Rick had decoded Big Buck's secret. To this day he is touched by the memory of that experience. Before it, he had never left the trail with a pack. But his trip to Lake Nirvana gave him a new sort of confidence about backpacking. The wilderness beyond the trail was no longer a mystery.

Shangri-la was open for business.

Backpacking doesn't always take you to a special place like Lake Nirvana. We have hiked "off trail" all day only to come to a lake that recently had a logging road cut into it. Four-wheel drives and boom boxes greeted us at a shoreline fouled with soap suds, garbage, and dead fish. At that point, it was nice to know that we could keep on hiking—over another ridge, to another stream—to a campsite still untouched by civilization.

Like all the other forms of camping, backpacking requires planning, knowledge, practice and desire. But done well it confers special rewards: a feeling of independence as you and your pack comprise a total environment for survival and pleasure, an exhilarating sense of distance from the nervous noise and speed of the city, a knowledge that the only way into this arena of high mountain grandeur was by foot, and a total conviction that it was worth every hard step.

Horses, Mules and Llamas

Hal wouldn't get on a horse unless he lost an election bet; Rick's an old hand at packing into the wilderness on horseback. The point is that you don't need to be an expert equestrian to utilize pack animals and saddle horses to enhance the possibilities of a backpacking trip. Small children can be carried in the saddle with you. They love it. Disabled hikers, if secure in the saddle, can get farther into the wilderness than otherwise, and their special gear can be carried in on the pack animals.

Pack stations will help you arrange your trip (see Chapter 2 for information). If you're an experienced rider and have the facilities for transporting a horse, you may be able to rent a mount and take it on your own. If not, a station hand will accompany you and lead the mules and your horse to your destination. You can contract to be left off and picked up say a week later for the long trek out, or you can arrange to have the pack station "do" your whole trip, setting up camp, cooking, the works.

All National Forest Service and National Park trails are required to be maintained for horse travel. That means clearance for a mounted rider and secure footing on the trail. Don't expect horses or mules or llamas, also increasingly available as pack animals, to leave the trail when you want to go cross country. They can't and won't, so plan to have the animals tended during the time you are gone, be it hours or days.

Special Considerations

Camping with Children

Traveling with the very young—ages one to seven—has been a special and wonderful experience for us, and it can be for you. But it requires special forethought and follow-through. After all, *they* don't necessarily want to go camping; you do. They're following Mom or Dad or some other irrational parental figure who positively insists on getting back to nature. If they're too young to care, they're probably in a pack on your back, happy to be along for the ride. If they're old enough to think about it, they may have decided that they're doing you a favor. Hal's cousin Elizabeth remembers four things about her early days in a canoe: the black flies, the mosquitos, the dachshund, and the fanatical enthusiasm of parents who insisted that everyone was having a good time. Children are not necessarily born to the outback, littler versions of John Muir. They have to learn too.

Car and canoe camping are naturals for the very young. Horse camping can be too. In all of these cases, small legs don't have to go far, and big appetites and natural curiosities can be immediately satisfied. We don't know anyone who has ever tried long-distance bicycle touring with a young child, though it no doubt has been done too. Backpacking takes a little more care in planning, but we've done it pleasurably with infants, toddlers, and active five-year-olds. Special arrangements for sharing loads and responsibilities need to be worked out beforehand. *Really* worked out. Otherwise one or two peo-

ple will end up harassed, overworked, and unhappy. Throughout this book you'll find ideas and suggestions to make kid
camping so good that they'll want to come back for more. And
that's the point, isn't it?

Camping with Kids: A Starter Set

- Keep car travel brief. Break up the journey with frequent stops. A highway rest area may be the highlight
  of a young child's trip. Enjoy it.
- Car games. Keep a good supply in your head: license
  plate lotto, road-sign alphabet, story telling, songs, rid-
  dles. (See Book List for references.)
- Special equipment: favorite games, toys, teddy bears.
  (See Chapter 5 for packing for babies and the very
  young.)
- Food. Take what they *like* to eat, not what you think is
  good for them. Children, like adults, will not expire of
  malnutrition if they eat nothing but marshmallows (or
  carrots!) for three days. (See Chapter 4 on food planning for children.)
- Keep things simple. A one-mile camping trip over two
  or three days may be just the ticket. Hal's first trip
  with his daughters covered two miles in two days. On
  the way back (downhill), it took only two hours! Rick
  has spent the past two years traveling all of 3/4 of a
  mile (the *same* 3/4 mile!) with his very young daughters.
- Play while hiking. Walking can be fun or a bore. Make
  it fun. Play "ambush"; stop to check out a mud puddle
  or a bug. Catch a toad. Get to camp before your nerves
  and inspiration give out.
- Play while canoeing.
- Let kids participate. Let them help set up the tent,
  light the fire or stove, mix the batter, bake the cake,
  lick the pot, lead the way, paddle the canoe, hold the
  reins. Figure in extra time for all this, so you're not
  fuming when you put up the tent at midnight.

- Put on their rain suits at meals. Saves clothes; makes cleanup a snap.
- Wrap sock-clad feet in plastic bags before putting on tennies. Keeps feet dry when shoes get soaked by rain or puddles.
- Hang a whistle round their necks. They blow when lost. You find.
- Use a mix of diapers: disposables for inclement weather, cloth for sunny days.
- Give adolescents and teenagers lots of leeway but assume that they may need and want to learn how to do things too (but may not know how to ask without seeming "dumb").

"Camping With Kids": A Sampler

"...around Katie's third birthday, we discovered pack goats. An eight-year-old nanny goat...carried 30 pounds with faithful devotion over the course of two summers...We formed an odd but able pack string in those days: mother, child, father, grandfather, dog, and goat, united in common endeavor."

"The hike becomes a game. You walk for half an hour and get a lemon drop, some raisins, or a chocolate square. It takes us 45 minutes to fit in half an hour of pure walking, since we often stop for birds, bugs, and berries...But Katie never lags behind. In fact she brags about her prowess....After those grim first steps, there is astonishingly little grumbling."

"'Horsey!...Horsey!' shrieks Pat [the two-year-old]. We peer into the woods to find a small mule deer just 20 feet away....We watch quietly until the deer crosses the trail and heads downhill. The kids are quiet and big-eyed with their new knowledge: The woods are alive!"

[As they reach the trailhead and the car at the end of the journey:] "'There's the outhouse, Mom...There's the sign....There's the cars! We're home!'....'Aren't you glad, Mom?' Katie asks. 'Not really,' I say. 'It was a wonderful trip.' 'It was a stupid trip,' Katies says. 'No garbage cans, no picnic tables, no bathrooms. When I get home I'm going to stay indoors for a

*long time.' I have no rejoinder. Preaching wilderness apprecia-
tion to Katie is futile....She's young...stubborn. [But] she's deter-
minedly on the way to discovering hiking, camping, and
snooping around the woods for herself."*
Joan Hamilton, "Camping with Kids", *Sierra*, July/August 1986.

Camping with the Disabled

Bonnie Lewkowicz, an experienced outdoor hand, recently
took 30 Japanese disabled persons on their first camping trip.
There were the usual language and first-timer problems but
everyone muddled through. There were also the usual *unusual* problems which disabled people have to deal with all
the time: inadequate transportation and assurances of campground accessibility by operators who don't understand what
"accessible" means to disabled people. For example, a sandy
campground, which on the surface looks comfy, may be so soft
that a disabled person can't get enough purchase to turn over
at night, or can't negotiate a wheelchair sunk to its hubs in
the sand. One wheelchair-accessible restroom is better than
none, but is so inadequate for large numbers as to render "accessible" meaningless. Some trails are in fact wheelchair accessible—for example some old fire roads; some are accessible
to the blind and are known as "braille trails."

Things are getting better, if all too slowly, and for any disabled person who wants to participate in outdoor activities, including all the forms of camping we talk about here, there are
a growing number of resources—organizations and publications—to turn to for assistance and advice. Need to know
about adaptable equipment? About the kinds of questions you
should ask of a campsite—food-storage lockers reachable? Pic-
nic-table extensions available for wheelchair access? About
rafting and canoe gear? About transportation? About clinics
and clubs? About the "rails to trails" conversion program to
make old railroad beds suitable for hiking by those with disabilities? See our resources list in Chapter 2. Disability need
not be a constraint on outdoor enthusiasms. Don't take our
word for it. Take Bonnie's. Though she uses a wheelchair, she
hasn't let the barriers overshadow the joy of being outdoors.

Agenda for Improvements

- A new classification system of "accessibility."
- Federal legislation requiring wheelchair lifts on major transportation carriers.
- Adequate as distinct from token facilities in publicly maintained campgrounds.
- Less expensive conversion equipment.
- A change of mind among the "abled." The outdoors belongs to all of us. Lend a hand.

Where to Go

The absolutely best way to find a destination for a camping trip is by word of mouth. Ask your friends. Ask their friends. Check with salespeople at the outdoor outfitters, seek out local photographers, ask old-timers. Get in touch with the Sierra Club, local outdoor clinics and clubs, even the Boy and Girl Scouts. Check with resort owners, guides, and camp counselors.

Another way to choose a camping destination is through a book or magazine. Check the library, bookstore, or camping store for trail, stream or route guides and commentaries. Local newspapers, newsletters and magazines often describe campsites and trails. See Chapter 2 and the Book List for suggestions. Be careful to notice the difference in difficulty between outings for beginners and those for experts. Don't start toward a scenic wonderland only to discover that you overlooked the section that mentioned the white water you have to negotiate, or the cliff face.

The precision of the answers you get from your research will be determined by the precision of the questions you ask. Figure out in advance how far you want to drive, and how far you want to hike, bike or paddle. Do you expect to hang out in a campsite or pile up the miles? Do you expect to catch fish? Need firewood? Well-defined trails or routes? Then hit up the experts with, "We're looking for easy paddling downstream for a four-day trip with really good fishing, and no portages."

Don't worry if the answers are vague, and don't limit yourself to one or two suggestions. Any spot you might choose has its advantages and disadvantages. Keep checking out people, places and possibilities. If you're car camping, call the campground authorities for this kind of information: campsite availability, fire restrictions, entrance and overnight fees, opening and closing dates, fishing, swimming, boating info (boat ramps closed/open?). Collect people's secret spots like a CIA agent collects microfilm.

Then locate the spots on a map. If you can't find them on paper, there's no sense setting out into the wilderness to look for them. Figure the distances and elevations; study the maps for possible difficulties: obstructions, streams to ford, logging trucks to avoid. (See Chapter 6 for a short course on how to read maps.) Once you've had a little practice, this will be easier than you think. Once you've figured out where to go, you can start thinking about how far to go, and for how long.

How Far Can You Go?

It's one thing to return from camping feeling exercised and healthy; it's quite another to limp home with blisters and sore muscles. A slow pace starts you off, so to speak, on the right foot.

A lot of people, especially beginners, take off after work on Friday, fight traffic on a long drive to a trailhead or campsite, and start out bright and early Saturday morning after five hours of sleep toward a destination that is just beyond their ability. By the time Saturday evening rolls around, they're exhausted, blistered and cranky. Whether you head for your campsite via bike, canoe, horse or foot, it's important that you don't overextend yourself, especially in the first day or two. The muscles you use on your daily job and those you use on a camping holiday are very different.

Long uphill grades can be disheartening if you're on foot or on a bike, and you should plan to stop often. If you're riding horses, remember that they need rest too. If you're canoeing upstream or against the wind, you'll work harder and need more rest. Make time for it.

Backpacking is a little more complicated because pack weights vary according to the length of a trip. A half-day of hiking is plenty on the first day, regardless of how much ground you cover. Most people can cover three to five miles uphill with a heavy pack in that time, usually at a rate of about 45 minutes per mile (about four hours of hiking). Reach your destination in early afternoon, have a swim, lunch, and then hang out for the rest of the day. You'll be able to hike farther as you acclimate to the altitude and as the pack gets lighter. If time permits, try a day or two of rest and relaxation after two days of hiking. And don't even think of the hike home. It's always easy. Most of the food is gone, the packs are light, and it's mostly downhill. That's the day you can expect to cover 10-12 miles, back to the trailhead and the ride home.

A Guide to Moderation

- Almost every morning of travel, whether by bike, canoe or foot, deserves an afternoon of rest.
- A full day of travel deserves a full day of rest.
- The first day: by bicycle, no more than 30 miles in distance and 750 feet in elevation; by canoe, no more than four hours of paddling; by foot (backpacking), no more than five miles in distance and 1,500 feet in elevation.
- On succeeding days, no more than 50 miles/1,000 feet by bike; five hours by canoe; seven miles/2,000 feet by foot.
- The last day: Go for broke! Vacation's over, and you can sleep at work the next day.
- On horseback: Know your horse's limits and don't exceed them. Follow the advice of the pack station or your leader.

How Many Are Going?

There are no rules about the number of people that can go on
a trip, but you should have some idea of what the different
numbers mean. Going alone is a lot different from going with
one other person, or with two or 20. We once met a party of
15 far off the trail in the Sierra wilderness who seemed content and happy. We never figured out how such a large group
could hold together, and we shudder at the thought of having
to organize such an expedition, but clearly it can be done.
However, if the object is to recapture a bit of solitude and to
relax, keep your forces down. We've traveled alone, as a pair,
in a threesome, with four and with six.

Soloing

Solo camping is a special and satisfying art, though going one-
on-one with nature has its own requirements. Four or five
days is a long time to spend by oneself. And while being alone
is not the same thing as being lonely, it does call for a good set
of inner resources in top working order. Keeping busy isn't
hard, but since the kind of trip we're describing isn't a 20-
mile-a-day grind, if you don't like tinkering with fishing lures
or boat repairs, devising new ways to cook trout or just sitting, you may get antsy. That's OK, you've got plenty of room
in which to be restless and plenty of space to pace. When solo
camping, all your emotions become more intense: the questions, worries, phobias, as well as the rewards, highs and joys.
Also, you alone get to make and unmake all the plans. And
the only problem you'll have with "human dynamics" is figuring out how to get along with yourself.

If you go solo on foot, you'll have to sacrifice some weight
that would otherwise be shared. The inflatable raft you might
want for those lazy days on the lake will stay behind. The
extra cooking pot, set of lures, roll of film, cinnamon container—may have to go as well. But for almost everything
you leave behind, you can improvise with what you've got.
You can make a raft, roast fish in the coals, sketch instead of
taking pictures, fashion lures with your hooks, or substitute
flaked chocolate for cinnamon.

The more experience you have camping with others, the better equipped you'll be to go it alone. The same is true of solo hiking off the trail: Experience *in a group* is a prerequisite. Any kind of hiking is safer, more fun and more confidence-building when done at first with others.

With Others

But how many others? First, it's useful to understand that camping is not a personality-altering experience. For all the solace and rejuvenation that a trip in the backcountry provides, you're apt to take in and bring out the same likes, dislikes, habits and concerns that you carry around every day. The same is true of your friends. What pleases you or irks you about them will tag along, and may well be heightened by the unfamiliar environment.

The more people there are, the harder it is to achieve compatibility, and the more time and patience are necessary to make the trip work well for everybody. With larger groups, decision-making takes longer and is more emotionally draining. There are more ideas and opinions to deal with. Complications increase exponentially. A six-person trip is not three times as complex as a two-person trip: it's nine times as complex.

Try to straighten things out as much as possible beforehand. Talk over what you each like to do and eat, and what you can't stand. Discuss relative experience, physical fitness, allergies and ailments. Figure out who knows what. Share any information you can. The expert who makes you feel like a fool is dispensable; leave him or her home. The one who makes *you* feel like an expert is, at 9,000 feet, the most wonderful human being on Earth.

There are other advantages and disadvantages to numbers. The more people, the more you can bring—an extra book, additional chocolate bars, a tripod. Tasks can be shared and loads lightened. On the other hand, some lakes you want to camp at have only one small campsite, barely room for two. And the bigger the party, the harder it'll be to concentrate on the sounds of silence.

Count animals in your calculations too. Dogs are wonderful companions in the wilderness and can carry their own food on the trail, but off-trail you must carry it for them: The probability of their tearing a pack on rough terrain and losing the food is high. And remember, unless you have a Siberian husky, Malamute or some other pooch who is happiest in inclement weather, you'll share limited tent space with wet fur on those rainy nights. But as long as the trail is not too rocky for their footpads or off-limits to pets (as in National Parks) they're great to have along.

Traveling with Dogs

- Prevent dehydration. Carry water in the car for them.
- Exercise dogs if confined to a campground or a long canoe ride.
- Keep 'em on leash in cattle or sheep country. A dog that starts a stampede is fair game for ranchers.
- Keep 'em on a leash if they're carrying their own food. They can lose their packs if they go off-trail chasing local wildlife.
- Don't overload a dog's pack. They get tired too.
- A name-and-address tag is essential. Dogs lost in the wilderness *have* been found and returned. Ask Rick: He lost Punkie in a thunderstorm. She was carried out by campers who found her, paws cut to shreds. (Great campers!!)
- Protect a dog's feet above tree line. Pads are easily cut on the granite high ground, and easily burned on extremely hot terrain.
- Dogs are *Not Allowed* in National Parks.

Regardless of the number of people and pets, there are several useful rules to go by:
- The slowest person sets the pace. Plan distances for the day or week with this in mind. If you have to stop short of those goals, well—it just doesn't matter. This is particularly important with children.

- Stay together. This is crucial if you're going off the trail ("cross country") or into new waters by canoe. If there are four of you, you can go in pairs, but even then all four should follow the same route. Most serious accidents occur when one person goes off alone.

- Cater to individual needs. If people hate to cook, don't make them feel they must. This isn't a test, it's a vacation. If others don't know how to cook but want to, help them out, but let them do it. This isn't a three-star French restaurant, and if the bread burns or the fish falls in the fire, so what? You'll still eat and you'll go home with a funny story.

- Share leadership and decision-making as much as possible. Let everyone take the lead on the trail. This is a matter of courtesy, and it's important. Many guidebooks suggest appointing a leader, someone who knows in advance he or she will have the final say in any difficult decision. This is good advice in emergency situations. The person with the most experience might be best to lead you up a mountainside or through rough water, but in most cases, there doesn't need to be much structure. Most decisions are better made by consulting everyone and finding a common denominator. Flexibility is the key: stay loose and happy.

CHAPTER 2

Resources and Guides: Getting the Information You Need

Yellow Pages and Hot Lines: Working the Local Angle

The most frequent question we're asked is, "Where do I find out?" Instead of leaving you in the dark till you get to the "end matter" of the book, we want to answer the question now, when you need it. Here's where you'll find the addresses and telephone numbers of the people or organizations that can help you plan a camping trip and find your way. If you learn to use a phone strategically, you can get information fast and reasonably cheap. If you have more time, write and get the same.

Rather than try to be comprehensive and definitive, we give you here a finder's guide—sort of a Camper's Yellow Pages. One call or letter will lead to others till you have the information you need.

Look for local help first, then regional or national. Sometimes the fastest way to that end, however, is to start the other way round. Example: You want to find out local canoeing information: clubs, routes, trips, tips. Yet you don't know any local outlets and the phone book is no help. What to do? Call or write the American Canoe Association and ask for the names, addresses and phone numbers of their local affiliates, sometimes it will be a club and sometimes an individual (the local "commodore"). Now you're back to square one, and in a few minutes ought to have the information you seek.

You may need help on several fronts at the same time. The format here lets you package information. Example: You want maps, consumer guidelines for buying a mountain bike, park access and reservations info, and some literature to read on hiking and biking. Scan the categories and subcategories. No use writing away for a Forest Service map if what you need is a topo map. No use calling the bike shop in East Missoula if you live in Rattler Bend 2,500 miles away. Identify the park or parks you intend to visit then go to the information here on the national, state, or county agency which administers those parks. Check our Book List if you don't find the book or magazines you need here. Assemble *all* the information first, then make your calls or write your letters. Do it early. You'll be surprised how helpful people are.

Local Clinics, Clubs and Bulletin Boards

Experienced backcountry types tend to congregate at local outfitters and outdoor clinics or clubs. Local outdoor stores often serve as the hot-stove leagues for their immediate areas. They'll have bulletin boards announcing all sorts of information—second-hand equipment for sale, offers to join a trip or expedition, learning clinics, rides to share to Mount This or River That. Store staffers are more often than not outdoor fanatics themselves and will give you enthusiastic and usually sound advice. And there will always be a couple of grizzled experts just hanging out swapping lies and tips on their own particular Thing. They're human resources. Use 'em.

If you live near a college, community college or university, look up the name of the appropriate club—mountaineering, river/water sports, hiking, environmental concerns—and give a call. You may not be able to join such a group or get paid service—many are limited to staff and students—but almost certainly you'll get friendly advice as to where to turn for the information you need. Some of these services are run by professionals, some are co-ops, some student-operated. Most will let you run at the mouth with questions and let you look at their bulletin boards and brochures. It's a small community, after all, and they like interested people whatever their connections.

If none of the above exist in your immediate neighborhood, get in touch with the local environmental organization. They usually have reliable and helpful advice on outdoor recreation: trips and activities for members (and non-members), local clubs or private groups, names of individuals or organizations you can call, pamphlets on the National Parks and trail systems, and the like.

Where are the Forests, Where are the Parks?

Recreation follows politics, and thus parks, forests, and wilderness areas are administered under different and sometimes competing jurisdictions. You don't need to be a Washington lobbyist to find out what you want to know, however, you just need an up-to-date phone book. Once you get someone on the line, you'll get friendly, informative service. We've dealt with federal and state agencies, departments, offices, field headquarters, and ranger stations, and over the years they have been almost uniformly helpful. The fat cats are in Washington or the state capital; the outdoor experts are in the local and regional offices.

National Parks are administered by the National Park Service, a branch of the U.S. Department of the Interior. The country is divided into 10 regions, so if you know the rough location of any National Park you might be planning to visit, call the appropriate Regional Office:

National Park Service Regional Offices

Alaska Region
(Anchorage)
(907) 257-2690

Mid-Atlantic Region
(Philadelphia)
(215) 597-7013

Midwest Region
(Omaha)
(402) 221-3431

National Capital Region
(Washington, DC)
(202) 433-1185

North Atlantic Region
(Boston)
(617) 565-8800

Pacific Northwest Region
(Seattle)
(206) 442-5565

Rocky Mountain Region
(Estes Park, Colorado)
(303) 586-2371

Southeast Region
(Atlanta)
(404) 331-5185

Southwest Region
(Santa Fe)
(505) 988-6388

Western Region
(San Francisco)
(415) 556-4196

Can't get no satisfaction? Write or call:

U.S. National Park Service
U.S. Department of the Interior
Washington, DC 20240
(202) 208-6843

National Forests are administered by the National Forest
Service, a branch of the U. S. Department of Agriculture. Wilderness areas are specially designated areas *within* National
Forests. For information about trails, maps, permits, location,
availability, rules and regulations in your state or local region,
check the U.S. government pages in the phone book. First
find "Department of Agriculture." Under that heading locate
"National Forest Service." And under that heading locate the
office of "Recreation." Then go to work with your questions.
Otherwise write or call:

U.S. Forest Service
Washington, DC 20240
(202) 655-3706

State and county parks are administered by their respective Parks and Recreation Departments. If you're not sure who oversees which park, call the state offices. They will tell you the park's status and refer you to the proper office and phone number.

Printed Trip Guides

The National Parks and Forests are huge recreational areas, big management complexes. They don't look like Wall Street, but they're run by agencies that want the paying public to spend time and money in them. Hence they produce publicity and detailed information. Want descriptions of their facilities and camping possibilities? Write for their printed matter. Get the Sierra Club's booklet on the National Parks. Check your local library for literature. State parks also have printed brochures. Regional and state guidebooks are often complete, entertaining, and filled with the kinds of information you need: route information, number of campsites, recreational facilities (swimming, boating, fishing, trail hiking), amenities (showers, laundry facilities, cabins, shops), maps. Don't buy a guidebook that doesn't have this kind of information. (See Book List for partial guidebook list.)

Trail guides are indispensable for trip planning. Most of the major forest, park and wilderness areas are now covered by convenient individual hiking guides. For example, Wilderness Press (2440 Bancroft Way, Berkeley, California 94704, [415] 843-8080) produces detailed trail descriptions, itineraries, suggested number of days needed for round-trip hiking at various levels of expertise, altitude changes, flora and fauna to be seen, camping and fishing possibilities for almost all wilderness areas in the western United States. Similar guides exist to other wilderness areas. And mountaineering guides, which grade peaks by their climbing-difficulty, make the high country accessible and safe. See our Book List at the end for a selection of such *Tote Books* put out by the Sierra Club. Ask your local camping store to show you what they have or tell you what they know about.

Maps and Permits

Maps

There are four types of maps you may need to plan a camping trip: road maps, Forest or Park Service maps, topographical maps, and, if you're canoeing in coastal or large lake waters, nautical charts.

Road Maps

Reliable road maps are updated every two years or so and will distinguish, by color, various road types: interstate highways, state highways, county roads, paved and unpaved local roads. Wherever you get your map, from the supermarket or the local auto club or map store, check the date of publication. A state road map may serve you best for long-distance driving; a sectional map (part of a state) may be drawn on a larger and hence more readable scale. If you are traveling through several states, try to collect similarly printed and scaled maps for the entire trip. Check the Yellow Pages for map sources. Call the state automobile association. Or ask Aunt Phionia, whose cross-country trip was planned by the swank travel agency you can't afford, if you can borrow the maps they gave her.

Forest and Park Service Maps

The National Park Service, and National Forest Service, and some state park services put out maps of specific parks and forest lands, updated every ten years or so to show changes in access roads, jeep trails, campgrounds, parking areas and new hiking trails. If you're serious about getting access to the wilderness, you'll need such a map. Otherwise, you won't know how to navigate to the trailhead, which may be miles up a warren of logging roads and washboard tracks. These maps can be obtained from the appropriate agency office. Often this can be done with a phone call, and the maps will be sent to you free of charge, though sometimes you have to send a

check or money order. You'll find that the more camping you
do, the less you'll need to send away for maps. Not because
you use them less, but because you'll keep returning to the
same parks and forests year after year.

It is one thing to get to the trailhead, another to walk the trail
or climb the mountain. Hiking requires topographical ("topo")
maps, which bring you face to face with the lie of the land.

Topographical Maps

Mountains and valleys normally don't change as fast as roads
and other human structures. True, Mount Saint Helens can rearrange things dramatically. So can the San Andreas Fault.
But by and large the topo map drawn thirty years ago will
still represent physiographic reality pretty accurately. Unfortunately, it won't show the latest trails and may show trails
long since abandoned. That's why you should work with a combination of topo and Park/Forest Service maps. They'll allow
you to chart a trip with reasonable accuracy.

Topo maps are obtained from the U.S. Geological Survey,
which is also a sub-unit of the U.S. Department of the Interior. Check in the phone book to see if there is a Geological
Survey office in your area. If so, go down and get the maps
you need from them. If not, try the local map vendors or camping stores. More and more of them sell the USGS maps. The
maps for any area in the U.S. are also available by mail,
though you'll first need to send for a free "key" or index map if
you don't know the name of the particular quadrant (of the entire area of a state) you want. The key divides the whole land
area of the state into small squares. Each of these squares is
numbered and titled, representing one topo map. After you
pinpoint the area(s) you want, order the relevant maps by
number and name. If there's not a USGS office, map source,
or camping store in your area, write or call:

U. S. Geological Survey
Federal Center
Denver, CO 80225
(303) 236-7477

Nautical Charts

Most river canoeing can be done with Forest/Park Service maps and topo maps. Coastal canoeing, island hopping, and large lake travel may require nautical charts. These you obtain locally through map stores or independent dealers who specialize in nautical travel (salt-water fishing specialists, boat dealers, tour operators). Or write to:

> Distribution Branch (N-CG 33)
> National Ocean Service
> Riverdale, MD 20737-1199
> (301) 436-6990

Permits

Permits are gatekeeping and safety devices, similar to campground reservations for car campers. They allow local forest or park rangers to keep track of the number of people entering each part of their jurisdictions each day, and to control the use of campfires in hazardous conditions. One permit that grants access and states fire conditions usually serves the two purposes. The idea is to maintain a balance between nature and human visitors to the maximum benefit of each. And while evidence shows that fewer people are backpacking in the wilderness, more people than ever are car camping, and hiking the most popular and accessible trails. It's not unusual for 200 people a day to pass some scenic spots on the John Muir Trail in Sequoia National Park, for example. Trails are fragile; numbers need to be controlled. Fire rangers also need to know where you are in case of an emergency, such as a forest fire.

It's best to apply for a permit after you've had a chance to look at the maps and decide exactly where you want to go. Call or write the appropriate ranger station, which issues the permit. Addresses and phone numbers are available from the National Park or Forest Service office nearest you. Get the permit early. Along with it, you'll get any information that the rangers feel is important to pass on to hikers. This includes warnings about bears in the area, cautions involving drinking water and possible disease transmission, notices of areas closed to camping and rules regarding firewood, fires and fishing. These are all important to know about before you arrive on the scene with your backpack bulging, only to discover, for example, that you've mistakenly forsaken the campstove, expecting to cook with firewood.

It's possible to get permits at the last minute, but rules differ depending on the area. Sometimes, you can arrive at a ranger station, get a permit immediately, drive on to the trailhead and begin hiking. Sometimes you can telephone ahead and have the permit waiting for you in the "night pick-up" box outside the ranger station door for late-night arrivals. Other times you'll find that the trail is full for the day; permits will be issued for the following day only. It pays to have alternate routes and destinations in mind for just such eventualities. One year, we drove to a National Forest area in the evening, planning to get a permit the following morning. A sign in front of the ranger station said that half the permits were issued in advance by mail (only until the end of April). The rest were issued that day, with the last few to be distributed the next morning at 6 a.m. We got to the door of the ranger station at 5:45, to find ourselves behind nearly 40 other early risers. Our first choice was booked solid, and we had to settle for a second-choice route. Plan your trip well in advance. Make campground reservations early. Start ordering maps during rainy winter afternoons; send off for July and August permits in March. Especially if you're planning a week-long trip, the more time you give yourself to plan, the smoother it will go. It's possible to camp "spontaneously," but trips invariably work out better if they are thought out and arranged months in advance.

Pack Stations

If you want animal transport into the mountains, call or write the pack stations closest to your destination. The National Forest Service requires all pack trains which enter National Forests to be licensed by them, so you can get a list of accredited pack stations from the appropriate regional National Forest office or its field station. The National Park Service runs its parks through concessionaires which either directly provide pack service or lease it out to local pack stations. Check with the National Park of your choice for information.

Equipment

If there isn't a good camping, biking, or boating store in your area, use the mail. The number of excellent illustrated catalogs of camping, biking and canoeing equipment is growing, and the information in them is reliable, often accompanied by expert technical advice, and the prices are usually fair and competitive.

REI Co-op Catalog
Seattle, WA 98138-2125
1-800-334-547

REI Cycle Source
Box C-88125
Seattle,WA 98188-0125
1-800-426-4840
(outside Washington)
1-800-562-4894
(inside Washington)

REI stands for Recreational Equipment, Inc., one of the country's oldest outdoor suppliers. Meets all the outdoor needs covered in this book. Expert advice. Buying made easy through the mail. REI is a co-op, and holds regular clinics, talks, and demonstrations for the public.

Eastern Mountain Sports (EMS)
1 Vose Farm Road
Peterborough, NH 03458
(603) 924-9571

The equivalent of REI in the eastern part of the U.S. Equally expert and reliable. They do not have a mail-order service, but have 43 stores. Call or write them for the nearest to you.

L. L. Bean, Inc.
Freeport, ME 04032
1-800-221-4221

Old favorite, though has gone awfully upscale in recent years. Even sells its own brand of bicycle and cycling accessories, as well as its old line of standard camping equipment. Threatens to become the Abercrombie and Fitch of the late 20th century. Still, they know their stuff and it's good.

Mad River Canoe
Annual Catalog
Box 610
Waitsfield, VT 05673
(802) 496-3127

A comprehensive, superbly illustrated catalog with enough technical information and non-technical advice to appease the appetites of beginners, experts and everybody in between. Mad River people also travel, giving demonstrations at outdoor stores all over the country. The catalog contains a calendar of appearances. The same people also issue a brochure on inn-to-inn canoeing vacations.

Voyageur's Definitive
Action Gear
PO Box 207
Waitsfield, VT 05673
(802) 496-3127

The Mad River folks under a different label. They hold a lock on waterproof storage bags and flotation systems for canoes and other water craft. You want dry sacks, sea sacks, fanny thwarts, portage harnesses, tandem end-bag flotation systems, lash kits? These are the folks to write. Their catalog is, well, definitive. And easy to read.

Rhode Gear
765 Allens Avenue
Providence, RI 02905
(401) 941-1700

High-quality cycling equipment including parts, clothing and other specialized and useful gear.

Bikecology
1515 Wilshire
Santa Monica,
CA 90403-3900
(213) 451-9977

Catalog of bicycles, frames, parts, components, clothes, exercisers and more.

Performance Bicycle Shop
Box 2741
Chapel Hill, NC 27514
(919) 933-9113

Prices for quality equipment—bicycles, accessories and clothing—are considerably cheaper than those offered by some of the glitzier places.

The Third Hand
Box 212
Mount Shasta, CA 96067
(916) 926-2600

Every bicycle tool known to man, plus a wide assortment of spare parts not generally available elsewhere, such as derailleur bolts and nuts, seatpost binder quick-releases and much more. If you do your own repairs and maintenance, you need this catalog.

*The Complete Book of
    Bicycling*
by Eugene A. Sloane
Simon & Schuster, 1985

An encyclopedic book which includes the names and addresses of almost every reputable mail order or catalog dealer.

Outdoor Services for the Disabled

The number of resources for disabled campers is growing exponentially, and we list here only those most readily available, or those which are resource guides themselves.

Contacts

Environmental Traveling
  Companions
Fort Mason Center
Building C
San Francisco, CA 94123
(415) 474-7662

Whole Access
517 Lincoln Avenue
Redwood City, CA 94061
(415) 363-2547

SOAR (Shared Outdoor
  Adventure Recreation)
PO Box 14583
Portland, OR 97214
(503) 238-1613

Wilderness Inquiry II
1313 Fifth Street SE
Box 84
Minneapolis,
MN 55414
1-800-728-0719

P.O.I.N.T. (Paraplegics on
  Independent Nature
  Trips)
3200 Mustang Drive
Grapevine, TX 76051
(817) 481-0119

C. W. Hog
  (Comparative Wilderness
  Handicapped
  Outdoor Group)
Idaho State University
PO Box 8118
Pocatello, ID 83209
(208) 236-3912

Bay Area Outreach
  Recreation Program
605 Eschelman Hall
University of California
Berkeley, CA 94720
(415) 849-4663

Physically Challenged
  Access to the Woods
  (PAW)
1810 Quail-Unit C
Lakewood, CO 80216
(303) 328-6582

*Local chapters throughout the
country offering camping and
backcountry information.*

National Sports Center
  for the Disabled
PO Box 36
Winter Park, CO 80482
(303) 726-5514, Ext. 179

Printed Information

Spinal Network
Box 4162
Boulder, CO 80306

*Spinal Network is a major
publishing source for the
physically disabled. It puts
out books and a magazine.
This "Extra" issue of the
magazine has a comprehen-
sive annotated listing (pp. 26-
29) of resources and
suggestions for outdoor activities, such as hiking and camping, fishing, kayaking and
canoeing, biking, and other
summer sports. An indispensable guide. For an even fuller
listing, see Spinal Network's
big book of the same name.
On pages 114-173 you'll find
information on sports of all
kinds. On pages 324-366 listings of resource connections.*

*Access America, An Atlas
and Guide to the National
Parks for Visitors with
Disabilities.*
National Cartographic
Box 133
Burlington, VT 05402
(802) 860-2886

*Also available through Spinal
Network Bookstore. This is
the latest on accessibility in
the park system, with information on travel, parking,
restrooms, medical facilities,
dining, campgrounds and
everything else you can think
of. Expensive ($45) but a
valuable resource.*

Sports & Spokes
5201 N 19th Avenue
Suite 111
Phoenix, AZ 85015
(602) 246-9426

*A magazine largely devoted to
cycling sports.*

Palestra
Challenge Publications
Box 508
Macomb, IL 61455
(309) 833-1902

*A research-oriented magazine
covering sports and recreation
for a wide range of disabilities.*

*Disabled Outdoor
Magazine*
5223 South Lorel Avenue
Chicago, IL 60638
(312) 284-2206
(708) 366-8526

*Specializes in outdoor recrea-
tion, with useful information
on access, wilderness possibilities, fishing, etc.*

Adaptive Equipment

If you're looking for adaptive outdoor equipment or information on how to get it made, try:

Access to Recreation:
  Adaptive Recreational
  Equipment for the
  Physically Challenged
2509 E Thousand Oaks
Boulevard, # 430
Thousand Oaks, CA 91362
1-800-634-4351
(805) 498-7535

*This is a free mail-order
catalog. Illustrated.*

International Directory
  of Recreation-Oriented
  Assistance Devices
by A. Lazerow
(Lifeboat Press: Venice,
California, 1986)
PO Box 11782
Venice, CA 90295

A comprehensive catalog.

ABLEDATA
  Adaptive Equipment
  Center

Newington Children's
  Hospital
181 E Cedar Street
Newington, CT 06111
1-800-334-5405
(203) 667-5405

*This is a computer database
which indexes products useful
for people with disabilities.
An electronic Yellow Pages for
adaptive equipment. For-
merly associated with the National Rehabilitation
Information Center.*

Bicycling

Touring Information and Organizations

Bicycle Institute of America
1818 "R" Street NW
Washington, DC 20009
(202) 332-6986

Bikecentennial
Box 8308
Missoula, MT 59807
(406) 721-1776

Excellent maps, clothing, camping gear and a great tour organizer.

British Cycling Federation
26 Park Crescent
London, W1
England

Maps, hostel info, advice on touring British Isles and Europe.

Canadian Cycling
 Association
333 River Road
Vanier
Ontario K1L 8H9
Canada
(613) 748-5629

Cyclists' Touring Club
69 Meadrow
Godalming
Surrey GU73HS
England

Touring info on British Isles and Europe, including a handbook with cyclist-friendly lodging information.

International Bicycle
 Touring Society
846 Prospect Street
La Jolla, CA 92037
(609) 459-8775

International Mountain
 Bicycling Association
 (IMBA)
Route 2, Box 303
Bishop, CA 93514
(619) 387-2757

Fosters mountain biking as an environmentally sound and sustainable activity. See their Rules of the Trail, Chapter 1.

League of American
 Wheelmen
6707 Whitestone Road,
Suite # 209
Baltimore, MD 21027
(301) 944-3399

Oldest bicycle organization in the U.S.

On the Loose
1030 Merced Street
Berkeley, CA 94507
(415) 527-4005

U. S. Cycling Federation
Route 1, Box 1650
New Tripoli, PA 18066
(215) 298-3262

Publications

There are so many cycling publications now that any listing will necessarily be incomplete. In the Bibliography, we note some of the more useful books. Here we list the major magazines, many of which are the house organs of the groups listed above. Thus the name in parentheses here means "Publication of (this group)."

Bicycle Forum
(Bikecentennial)
PO Box 8311
Missoula, MT 59807
(406) 728-4497

Bicycle Rider
29901 Agoura Road
Agoura, CA 91301
(818) 991-4980

Includes articles on bike touring worldwide.

Bicycle USA
(IMBA)
6707 Whitesone Road
Baltimore, MD 21207

Bicycling
33 E Minor Street
Emmaus, PA 18098
(215) 967-5171

This is the oldest U.S. bicycling magazine.

Cycling USA
(On the Loose)
1750 E Boulder
Colorado Springs,
CO 80909
(303) 531-0177

Land Access Alert
(International Bicycle Touring Society)
Route 2, Box 303
Bishop, CA 93514

Excellent information on trail biking, including articles on sharing trails with horse riders, hikers, campers. Its land-access concerns are international.

Mountain Bike
Box 989
Crested Butte, CO 81224
(303) 349-6804

Emphasis on off-road touring.

Outside
1165 N Clark Street
Chicago, IL 60610
(312) 951-0990

One major cycling piece per issue.

Hostels

Still called "youth" hostels, these organizations house cyclists and other travelers of practically any age. The two listings here will point you to hostel resources in the areas you expect to be cycling through.

American Youth
  Hostels
132 Spring Street
New York, NY 10012
(212) 431-7100

Canadian Youth
  Hostels Association
1515 Discovery Street
Vancouver
British Columbia V6R 4K5
Canada
(614) 224-7111

Canoeing

Organizations and Informal Groups

American Canoe
  Association
Box 1190
Newington,
VA 22122-1190
(703) 550-7495

This is the godfather of canoeing organizations in the U.S., over 100 years old. It's the place to call or write for information on clubs and groups in your area. Its club membership list is huge, so there will be something for you unless you live in the desert. It has a book service with over 250 publications on canoeing, river guidebooks and maps, and instructional manuals. Also videotapes and films on canoeing. *And, of course, it publishes its own magazine,* The American Canoeist.

American Red Cross

Contact your local chapter for training programs. See also the comprehensive illustrated book, Canoeing *(Doubleday, 1977), which the Red Cross put out as the "compleat" manual of canoeing. It's invaluable.*

American Whitewater
  Affiliation
146 N Brockway
Palatine, IL 60067
(312) 359-5047

Canadian Recreational
Canoeing Association
Box 500
Hyde Park
Ontario NOM 1Z0
Canada
(519) 473-2109

National Organization
for River Sports
314 N 20th Street
Box 6847
Colorado Springs,
CO 80934
(303) 473-2466

Friends of the River
Fort Mason Center
Building C
San Francisco, CA 94123
(415) 771-0400

United States Canoe
Association
2509 Kickapoo Drive
Lafayette, IN 47905
(317) 474-9391

Canoeing Magazines

There are not as many as the bikers have, but still more than
you might expect. We list only three more here (see American
Canoe Association), and expect that will keep you afloat during the long dark winter nights.

Canoe Sport Journal
Tanis Group
Box 697
Fallbrook, CA 92028
(619) 723-3633

Canoe Magazine
10526 NE 68th Street
Suite # 5
Kirkland, WA 98033
(206) 827-6363

River Runner
Same address and phone as:
Canoe Sport Journal
(above)

Camping, Hiking, Backpacking Resource and Advocacy Organizations

The following organizations focus on efforts to maintain and
enhance the outdoor environment through national and local
political efforts, trail development and maintenance pro-

grams, national park maintenance, hands-on environmental work, information resources. These are the real good-hands people.

Alpine Club of Canada
Box 1026
Banff
Alberta T0L 0C0
Canada
(403) 762-4481

American Alpine Club
113 East 90th Street
New York, NY 10028
(212) 722-1628

American Hiking Society
1015 31st Street, N W
Washington, DC 20007
(703) 385-3252

An advocacy group which seeks to protect, maintain, and develop trails on federal land, organizes volunteer opportunities for trail development, campground posts, archaeology work on public lands. Has listings of trail clubs and organizations in almost any area. Want to learn how to build a horse trail, stop erosion, clear a trail? They'll tell you who to see.

American Walkers
 Association
6221 Robinson Road
Cincinnati, OH 45223

Appalachian
 Mountain Club
5 Joy Street
Boston, MA 02108
(617) 523-0636

This is a big New England organization that helps to maintain the northeast portion of the Appalachian Trail.

Appalachian Trail
 Conference
Box 807
Harpers Ferry, WV 25425
(304) 535-6331

The umbrella organization that oversees maintenance of the Trail. Its members are the various Appalachian Trail clubs.

The Green Mountain
 Club, Inc.
Box 889
43 State Street
Montpelier, VT 05602
(802) 223-3463

Like the Appalachian Trail Conference, helps maintain the Appalachian Trail. Also the Long Trail which runs between Canada and Vermont.

Mazamas
909 West 19th Avenue
Portland, OR 97207
(503) 227-2345

Activities oriented. Mountaineering.

The Mountaineers
300 Third Avenue W
Seattle, WA 98119
(206) 284-6310

National Campers and
  Hikers Association
7172 Transit Road
Buffalo, NY 14221
(716) 668-6242

Activities oriented.

New York-New Jersey
  Trail Conference
232 Madison Avenue
New York, NY 10016
(21) 696-6800

*Maintains and develops
trails. About 5,000 members.*

North American Family
  Campers Association
Box 328
Concord, VT 05824
(802) 695-2563

The Prairie Club
10 S Wabash Avenue
Suite 603A
Chicago, IL 60603
(312) 236-3342

*Instrumental in developing
the Prairie Path, a long trail
across the Great Plains.*

Sierra Club
  National Headquarters
730 Polk Street
San Francisco, CA 94109
(415) 776-2211

*The great environmental
organization also provides
outdoor recreational activities
for its members, including
national and international
outings. Local chapters—57
main chapters and 382 clubs
in the U.S. and Canada—put
on local activities often open
to non-members too. Also publishes books and pamphlets
on all aspects of the outdoors,
including information on
the National Parks and the
National Trail System, and a
bimonthly magazine, Sierra.
If you don't know where the
nearest chapter is, call or
write the national headquarters.*

Wilderness Training

Leadership and survival training is another way to "do" the outdoors. It's not quite the laid-back experience you'll get from our kind of camping, but it's compelling, challenging and an altogether legitimate alternative to the "one-step-at-a-time" camping which most of us do. People who have gone through these programs feel themselves special.

National Outdoor
  Leadership School
PO Box AA
Lander, WY 82520
(307) 332-6973

Outward Bound
384 Field Point Road
Greenwich, CT 06830
(203) 661-0797

CHAPTER 3

What to Bring

_____

Danger! Big Bucks

Those faded photographs of the early mountaineers like John
Muir and his pals are probably banned in better camping
stores. There's not enough equipment in them: no aluminum
frame wraparound packs, self-standing dome tents, color-coor-
dinated climber's shorts, not even sleeping bags. Just wood
and wool. In those days, goose down was still the underside of
Christmas dinner. Nylon and Gore-Tex were not even a gleam
in an inventor's eye. Nevertheless, those pioneer trekkers
were well prepared and equipped. They just weren't fashion-
able.

We don't subscribe to the "old is beautiful" or "back to
basics" nostalgia. The revolutionary lightweight equipment is
breathtaking and extremely valuable—sleeping bags weighing
as little as three-plus pounds and efficient at zero degrees
Fahrenheit, five-pound tents with archery-shaft poles, featherweight self-inflating ground pads, Kevlar canoes. But that
doesn't mean you have to go broke using it. Camping and
cycling have become big business, and it's easy for ads and

sales pressure to convince you that you'd better buy a lot of costly equipment in order to safely, comfortably or competently hit the trail.

The way out of this financial bind is through "functional shabbiness," with the emphasis on functional. Hal is a classic practitioner. He began hiking in a pair of work boots, which he repaired at every campsite. After they fell apart on the trail, he bought a pair of irregular hiking boots on sale at a factory outlet, and has worn them ever since. He used a Taiwan-made sleeping bag for eight years until there was no loft left, then got a PolarGuard bag. He bought his used 12-speed bike for $76, and though it looks like it was built by committee, it's just fine for day touring and local camping trips. He's never owned a backpack, preferring to borrow a 19-year-old model with a re-welded frame, so disreputable that a shoe store, asked to replace a pouch zipper, refused to work on it. Hal isn't very pretty on the trail; but he does keep safe and solvent.

Like most people, you don't have a lot of money to spare, but you can manage by scavenging, improvising, borrowing and renting. An old shower curtain can become a tarp or tent (wash it first!); a padded book mailer can serve as a camera case. You'd be surprised at the number of ways to recycle plastic, wire or bits of material into functional camping necessities. Rick, for example, developed a list of 47 different functions for a bandana with a safety pin! And the more familiar you become with the routines and rhythms of camping, the more inventive you'll be.

If you plan to borrow, some rules should be followed carefully. Make an accurate list of everything you need to borrow. Then make duplicate lists of everything you *do* borrow. Keep one and leave the other with each lender. Make sure you both agree on its contents. Check the condition of the borrowed gear with the lender. Know what shape it's in before you use it. Return all items clean. Replace and repair (or have repaired) every piece of lost or damaged equipment, even if the damage is minute or superficial. Don't assume that the owner won't notice a missing strap, torn parka, clogged fuel vent or a half-empty Band-Aid box. Finally, make a voluntary cash contribution to the lender when you return the equipment. This is both a gesture of thanks and a way to let the lender add a little something to the equipment stash. Gear is expensive and anyone who lends it to you is a real friend. If you use care and consideration, you'll maintain the friendship and be able to borrow again.

Renting equipment is useful for testing items you're considering buying, or for things you use infrequently. Renting also makes sense if you aren't sure how much you'll like camping in the first place, or if seven avid first-timers show up on your doorstep ready to head into the Great Void with nary a kerchief to their names. Many camping and recreational stores have rental services from which it's now possible to get almost everything you need for a trip.

If you have some money to invest, it's worthwhile to buy equipment that will last. Plan to assemble a set of decent equipment over several years. Shop slowly and carefully. Get advice from friends, experts and sales people. Also, study the semi-annual catalogs of the great outdoor stores such as L.L. Bean, Mad River Canoe, and Recreational Equipment, Inc. (REI). Their information is reliable, fastidious and based on expert experience and testing. Their prices are competitive and fair (see Chapter 2 for catalog addresses). Remember to bargain!

Sandwich of Warmth

Clothing

Car campers and canoeists don't have clothing problems. They can take the entire summer wardrobe and a full-length mirror if they want. All they need to do is stay dry and, if elevation is a factor, warm. Cyclists and backpackers need to pack with an eye to weight and space. That wrinkled, drip-dry camper next to you at Ranger Ron's fireside chat is probably the world's bicycle touring champ just off the road for a night in the woods. She discovered years ago that Levis were too heavy and parkas too bulky to pack and went for thin cotton polyesters and a wool sweater. She's spent *her* extra cash on Gore-Tex raingear and maybe a pair of cycling shorts to prevent chafing during all those hours in the saddle. Hikers don't need to make a fashion statement either. Tastes will vary. Some people are cool and comfortable in shorts; some hate having their bare legs covered with dust and sweat. Some women swear by halter tops, others by T-shirts to keep pack straps from rubbing the skin raw. Hats and underwear are as much articles of faith as clothing: "To wear or not to wear?" is thus a religious question. Follow your conscience. And check the clothing lists in Chapter 5 for variations and suggestions.

Our English friend Claire began her first backpacking trip in white shorts. Five minutes after we hit the trail, they were no longer white. And eight days later, they were nearly ready for the dumpster. Another friend discovered after four days that his three ragged woolen sweatshirts were too heavy to carry and unnecessary for summer weather. He burned them one afternoon while baking bread, along with his "spare" hiking boots, thus anticipating the latest innovation to hit the outdoor showrooms, lightweight throwaway backpacking clothes. Don't get too attached to your camping togs. They're going to go sooner or later.

The minimum hiking kit goes something like this: two T-shirts, a warm shirt, a sweater or sweatshirt, a pair of jeans, a pair of long johns or light pants (sleepwear on cold nights), a pair of shorts, as much or little underwear as you like, three pairs of heavy socks, a warm jacket (down or fiber-filled are lightest), a wool hat, a sun visor or baseball cap, and a rain poncho that can double as a ground cloth. We'll discuss boots below. If you can get everything in a normal sleeping-bag-sized stuff sack and it weighs no more than twelve pounds, you're in business.

There are several extras that we always take along backpacking: a pair of gloves for warmth, wood gathering and pot holding; a bandana for the brow, nose, and neck; a pair of light-weight moccasins, old sneakers or thongs for the campsite (and crossing streams); extra poncho(s) in order to fish in the rain without taking the groundcloth out from under the tent; and a small towel. Remember that even damp towels are heavy. Take only one and share it.

After that you're on your own. If something gives you particular pleasure—a wash cloth or party hat, a tallis or a cummerbund—take it. A couple of years ago, we were startled to see, across a wilderness lake, a woman standing on a rock, dressed in a full karate outfit with a *kendo* stick in hand. Colored by the setting sun, she was an unexpected and picturesque sight. Her whim had cost extra weight, but was worth it in charm, and, we suppose, in self-satisfaction.

Layering: Defense Against Heat, Cold, and Rain

Temperatures in the mountains often vary radically, from 80/90+ degrees at noon to subfreezing at dawn. Your body temperature, however, needs to stay constant, so dressing right is important.

Loose, absorbent clothing allows air to flow next to the skin in hot weather, and keeps you cool and dry. Natural fibers like cotton and wool insulate best against the heat.

As the air cools, add layers of clothing. Polypropylene underwear is the space-age answer to longjohns, lighter and "breathable." Skiers and mountaineers use it (though Hal won't wear

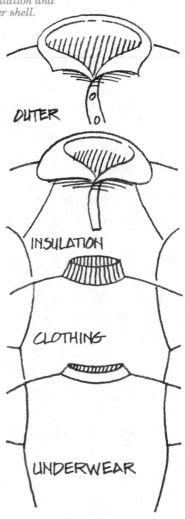

Layering is important to trap air and create layers of insulation around the body. The basic layers are: underwear, clothing, insulation and outer shell.

OUTER

INSULATION

CLOTHING

UNDERWEAR

anything he can't spell). Wool or cotton pants and shirt or sweater come next, absorbing sweat and retaining warmth. As the sun sets add a light-weight insulated parka against the cold, filled with goosedown, duck feathers, or a synthetic fiber. Most parkas are rated for weight and warmth. Down is the lightest, most efficient and most expensive. Synthetics are non-allergenic and mildew-resistant, and dry faster when wet.

Finally, if it's wet you'll need an outer layer of protection—anything from a plastic garbage bag to the latest "breathing" fabrics such as Gore-Tex, which permit sweat to escape but are impermeable to rain. Top of the line gear, featuring sealed needle holes on the seams, guarantees to keep your powder dry in a three-inch-per-hour rainstorm. It costs, but is worth it on Mount Arrarat and other storm centers. Short of that, go plastic. You'll shvitz but stay dry (if that's not a contradiction) and debt-free. Canoeists, incidentally, do better in rainsuits or garbage bags than in ponchos, which transform them into human sails in a high wind.

Sweat, above all, is a pain in the foot. Dry feet don't burn or blister; sweat-soaked feet do. Changing socks is a form of layering, and can save your day. Carry three pair, one to wash (and dry on your pack while hiking), one to wear, one to change into as your feet get hot and wet. Some hikers wear a light silk or polypropylene sock next to the skin. This transports the sweat into the woolen hiking sock, keeping the foot dry.

Layer at night as well. Wear longjohns and a shirt to bed if your sleeping bag is too light: Hell, wear *all* your clothes if need be. And if you're stuck in a bag that's too efficient, wear a thin layer of clothing to absorb the sweat and avoid a clammy wake-up call. Wear a wool hat when it's cold. It'll prevent major heat loss, something that skiers know and hikers ought to.

If it starts to rain on the trail or in camp, make sure that both you and your clothes and sleeping bag are protected. Some people, like canoeists, carry an extra set of clothes in a plastic bag, especially if they're camping in rain country. Remember also that synthetic fibers dry faster than down and, like wool, keep you warm when wet. If you fall in a river, take time to dry your clothing or hang it from your pack as you hike. If you're sleeping in the open, keep tomorrow's clothes in your sleeping bag, or in a stuff sack which can double as a pillow. It's not exactly wash 'n wear, but remember that a combination of wet, cold and wind can cause hypothermia (lowered body temperature), which can be fatal (see Chapter 6, under "Hiking in the Rain").

Keeping Clean

One year, four of us were climbing down a steep bowl to Dead Man's Lake, several miles off the trail. Rick looked, as usual, like a peddler from the lower East Side, socks and pots dangling from his pack and belt, his Levis caked with sweat and dirt. First-timer Essie's clothes, new three days before, would have been rejected by Goodwill and the Salvation Army. Karen resembled a misplaced Bedouin, swathed in tattered gauzes of her own devising to shield her sensitive skin from the sun. Hal brought up the rear, the Pig Pen of the group and living proof that there is a difference between dirt (what humans create) and earth (what nature creates).

We weren't alone. Coming from the other side of the bowl was another party of four. When we eventually met, we were astounded. They were a nice nuclear family: mom, dad and twin boys, aged 11. They were clean and tidy. In fact, they were fastidious! Mom's hair looked as if it had just been set; Dad was ready for church; the boys were exemplary behind the ears and, one supposes, everywhere else. Their clothes fit well and were spotless. We still remember Mom's lipstick, make-up and manicure. Yet these were no fancy dude-ranchers. They were experienced backpackers, had been over this arduous terrain before, carried plain efficient packs and wore modest clothes that never saw the inside of a posh sporting goods shop.

The point is, you can be as clean or as "casual" as you want. One is not better than the other. Just be sensitive to the preferences of others in your party.

If you intend to keep your clothes washed, take precautions to keep the wilderness clean, too. Don't wash clothes in a lake or stream. Don't use soap: it's the sweat you want out; dirt can wait for the laundromat. Even without soap, clothes often contain detergents from previous washes. They also spew dirt into the water. Wash in pots and discard the laundry water at least 300 feet from the water source. Otherwise seepage will carry suds and dirt back to the stream or lakebed.

Odds 'n Ends

Individual precautions are vital. Karen is allergic to the sun. A long-sleeved cotton shirt, light-weight long pants, a visor and lots of super sun-screen are necessities to keep her on the trail and in the canoe. Hal's thinning hair recently reached the point of no return; after a blazing sunburn on his balding head, he now wears a cap instead of a visor. Our friend Don, who carries baby Julia, the hair-pulling champ, has discovered a foreign legionnaire's hat with a neck piece that protects what's left of his locks from the dreaded one-year-old cling and jerk.

We always leave a clean shirt and underwear, fresh socks and pants in the car while we hike. They do wonders for morale when we're driving through 95-degree heat toward home. And we need hardly mention what they'll do for the staff of the roadside beanerie where you stop for your first indoor meal in a week.

Sleeping Bags

A sleeping bag is nothing more than a heat-retaining sack to keep you warm while horizontal and snoozing. It needs to be efficient: the temperature of the body drops when it's at rest, and the higher the elevation, the colder both the air and the ground will be. But a sleeping bag doesn't need to be so efficient that it would keep a climber cosy on Everest; it doesn't need to be so expensive that it would make a night at the Ritz a bargain by comparison. It should be light (five pounds or less; ultralight for summer cyclists), warm and affordable.

Sleeping bags are generally filled with either down (goose or duck) or synthetic fiber. Down is warmer, lighter, and more expensive. But when wet, it loses its insulating abilities. Fibers—Quallofil, Hollofil, PolarGuard, Polysoft—come out of the test tube, are cheaper, and increasingly challenge down's warmth/weight ratio. Combined with heat-reflecting bag liners, fiber bags are becoming lighter than ever. These fibers dry faster than down and are warmer when wet, because they maintain their loft. Unless you're off to Annapurna, a down/fiber mix or a 100 percent fiber bag will easily suffice.

Sleeping bag ratings indicate the lowest temperatures at which they'll keep you warm. Going to be in high alpine country? Use a bag rated at 10-plus or 20-plus degrees Fahrenheit. Camping on the bayou? A thin shell should do.

Now consider construction of the bag. As always, quality costs. You pay more for better nylon, closer stitching, high-quality zippers, and fancier insulation systems which promise to stay in place over the years. To reduce weight, newer bags concentrate the insulation over your head, chest and feet, where you need it the most. Another innovative design has no bottom insulation at all, providing instead a slot for a sleeping pad which thus becomes part of the bag. As a bonus, the pad stays under you all night!

The sleeping bag is only one part of the "sandwich of warmth" you need to create. If other parts of the sandwich are missing, you'll be in exactly the kind of trouble one encounters trying to eat peanut butter and jelly without any bread. Think layers. On the bottom is a groundcloth, poncho, or rein-

Sleeping bag and pad

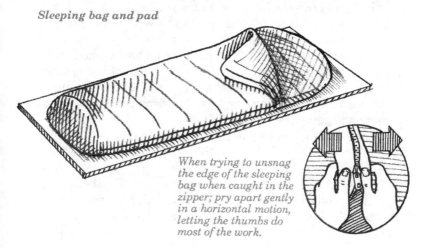

When trying to unsnag the edge of the sleeping bag when caught in the zipper; pry apart gently in a horizontal motion, letting the thumbs do most of the work.

forced tent floor.

Then comes a thin sleeping pad, available in a wide range of materials, lengths and thicknesses. The old standby is Ensolite, a blue foam roll-up pad. The latest and lightest, such as Ridge Rest, are made of closed-cell foam, molded into a series of ridges (for comfort) and valleys (for trapped-air warmth), and flexible (for packing ease). Direct from aerospace comes a remarkable self-inflating pad called Therm-A-Rest. It's a foam mattress that refused to grow up. Covered in a nylon fabric with a valve at one corner, it deflates as you roll it up, squeezing the air out of the foam pockets, and inflates as you unroll it, the air seeping back into the foam. Car campers and canoeists can use the 3 $^1/_2$-pound model or regular 1 $^1/_2$-pound or 2 $^1/_4$-pound (long) pads; cyclists and backpackers the ultra-light models (1 $^1/_{16}$ pounds and 1 $^3/_4$ pounds). They're not cheap, and it's easy to slide off them, so if you're a poor and restless sleeper go for something simpler.

Next up is the sleeping bag. Inside that is a clothed body if the bag is not very warm: the warmer the bag, the fewer the clothes. As Hal's bargain-basement bag got older, the more clothes he wore. Finally, he was forced to make a choice: Get a raccoon coat or a new bag.

Finally comes the roof of the tent, with a rain-fly as another layer just above. Properly arranged, this sandwich is guaranteed to keep you warm and dry.

Unless you have the habits of a nocturnal arctic animal, a cold, sleepless night isn't much fun. And a wet sleeping bag almost assures a grouchy morning. If it does get wet, however, you have several options, depending on how soaked the bag is and what it's made of. If you're sleeping out in the open and wake up with a dew-drenched bag, it'll often dry out an hour or two after the sun rises. If a thunderstorm catches you en route and your bag gets partially wet before you batten down the hatches, you can usually get through the night comfortably: the wet spots will be on the surface and won't penetrate the fill. If a sleeping bag really gets soaked, you've got troubles. A hot sun will dry out any bag eventually, though down takes considerably longer than fiber. But bad weather may cut off that option and the only alternative may be to share the other bags in shifts or pack up and head out. So take every precaution to keep the middle layer of your sandwich of warmth dry.

Sleeping Bag Tips

- Some sleeping bags can be zipped together to make one double bag. When buying or borrowing bags, make sure that you come away with both a left-hand and a right-hand zipper. Otherwise, even if you're with your mate, you'll be sleeping alone.

- Carry a couple of repair patches. Nothing is quite so discouraging as free-flying goose or duck down. Band-Aids or adhesive tape will also do the trick in a pinch.

- Be sure the stuff sack you use actually accommodates the bag. In fact, if the sack is a bit bigger, you can fit a down jacket, wool hat and flashlight—all your nighttime gear—with the sleeping bag in one convenient place.

- Follow cleaning directions carefully or you may end up with a ruined sleeping bag. Hang bags on hangers or keep them on shelves when not in use. Kept in stuff sacks, they lose their loft.

- Expect to spend anywhere from $80 to $160 for a good sleeping bag. Warmer, lighter bags with better zippers, materials and construction cost more; it pays to shop around.

- Finally, be patient when trying to unsnag the edge of the sleeping bag if it's caught in the zipper. It will get caught often, especially when you need to zip up or down in a hurry. To unsnag, pry apart gently in a horizontal motion. The thumbs do most of the work as they move away from each other. Don't try to unzip the snag. You'll only snag it further, or rip the material.

Tents

On the afternoon of the fifth day at North Lake, it began to rain. Our old, two-person, A-frame tent was set under a tree on a slight incline. By 9:00 p.m. water was seeping through the tent floor. Rain was dripping through the makeshift rain-fly we'd rigged from two ponchos, then through the roof of the tent. Add two wet and affectionate dogs atop our sleeping bags, and by morning, our tent would have made even Buffalo attractive to W.C. Fields.

The rain continued for the rest of the second day and all that night. Though wet, we kept warm and active, and by nightfall were steeled for another eight hours of marine life inside the tent. We finally dozed off around dawn. Later, we peeked out. It had stopped raining. Now it was snowing! We made a quick decision. Forty-eight hours in a wet tent, half-frozen as well, was enough. We headed out. In fact, we headed straight for the tent section of the camping store, determined never to be evicted again.

Tents, like sleeping bags, come in many varieties. But there are three basic variables: utility, weight and cost. A tent does two things: It keeps out the weather and keeps out the bugs. If it accomplishes both those tasks but weighs in the neighborhood of Barnum and Bailey's Big Top, it's fine for the county campground but next to useless on the trail. And if it's the right weight (no more than seven pounds, about three-and-a half pounds per person), but costs as much as the bridal suite at Claridge's, it'll never leave the display window. You can spend as little as $40 or as much as $200 for a two-person tent (see Chapter 2, for a catalog which rates and compares tents).

The hottest new tents, now arriving at a showroom near you but too expensive for most mortals, are "self-pitching" tents. The poles or "spines" are internal to the design: almost no tent assembly necessary! A miniature version of the "pop-up" tent is now made for infants—perfect for naps along the trail and as a tent-within-a tent at night, allowing Mom and Pop to get some sleep while little Julia has a room of her own just a cuddle away. It comes with a pad for the tent bottom.

Of the affordable designs, the freestanding dome or geodesic tent is one of the best. It can be erected effortlessly without pounding stakes or poles. The dome is suspended on two
or more spines made up of collapsible fiberglass or aluminum
poles, and unless there's a high wind, the tent doesn't have to
be staked. That means you can pick up the whole tent, with
sleeping bags inside, and move it into the shade for a mid-
afternoon nap, then return it to its original site for the night.
Also, you can sit up and even kneel in it comfortably, a
decided advance from the old horizontal squirm required in
the A-frame.

Even lighter and more compact than a dome is the "tunnel"
or covered-wagon tent. It also uses "spines" to give the tent its
shape. This design creates the most usable floor space in relation to tent size, but is usually not free-standing and must be
staked.

Make sure you've got enough tent pegs to secure tent and
rain fly. Plastic tent pegs are useless in the high granite country; we prefer to carry metal ones. Often a tent peg is useless
no matter what it's made of. Don't fret: Wrap the tent line
around a heavy rock or tree trunk instead.

*Tents are available
in a variety of styles
and sizes. With the
application of modern
materials and engineer-
ing, the A-frame tent
has gone the way of the
dinosaur.*

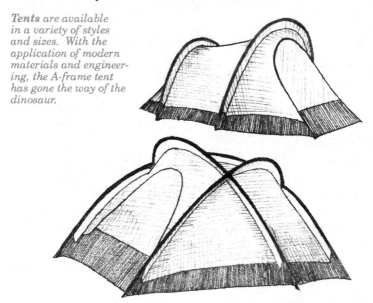

Be careful of fiberglass tent "spines." While lighter and less expensive than aluminum, they get brittle with age and may break. The break is often "clean" and hard to splint; and replacements cost as much as the tent itself. Aluminum poles seem to last forever, bend when they fail, and are much easier to fix.

The tent roof is *not* waterproof. Made of breathable rip-stop nylon it allows the moisture in your sweat and breath to evaporate. That means you *need a rainfly*. It *is* waterproof, fits over the roof of the tent and is meant to carry rain water off and away from the tent sides. Beware rainflies which can't be extended several inches beyond the lower tent walls: A steady downpour will seep through the tiny seam holes of the "waterproof" sidewall. Everything will be soaked. It's a good idea to apply a sealant to the tent seams at home, but sealed seams won't make up for a scrawny rainfly.

The rainfly makes the tent hot. Many people leave the rainfly off until they sense rain. But sudden storms have a way of sneaking into camp unannounced. So give yourself a break and leave the rainfly in place even on clear nights. You won't regret it. As a bonus, it will protect the tent nylon from overexposure to the sun and hence prolong the life of the tent. The rainfly thus doubles as a sunfly.

Tents are susceptible to fish hooks, knife blades, sharp edges, red-hot pans, burning cigarettes and importunate dogs wanting in. The more holes in your tent, the more moisture and bugs, so it's useful to keep some patches on hand to repair damage immediately. At home, the tent should be thoroughly dried, then brushed or shaken clean and stored on a shelf or a hanger rather than in its stuff sack.

One final word of advice. Make sure everybody who's using the tent knows how to set it up. Let everyone take a turn at it on sunny days, so they're ready during that sudden hailstorm. Manufacturer's directions usually get lost, so learn the tricks yourself and pass them on by the old show-and-tell method.

The Versatile Garbage Bag

One more item that'll keep you dry is the garbage bag—the big garden-sized, plastic sack that you stuff fallen leaves into once or twice a year. No longer does a backpack or food stash have to be crammed into your tent during the rain; the garbage bag is a perfect protective fit. It is the functional equivalent of an inverted canoe! Take along as many bags as there are packs on your trip. In a pinch, if you run short of rain gear, punch some holes in one to wear for upper body protection. We always buy ours as thick as they come (they're measured in "mils"). Special backpack covers are also available for very wet climates.

Boots

When our London friend, Brian, arrived for a quick trip to the Yosemite backcountry on his way to Alaska, we were not surprised that he had no boots. He'd just come from hiking all over Europe—*sans* boots. And he was too broke to even think about getting some. We tried to convert him: he could use good boots in Alaska. He agreed to think it over, even went out and tried on a pair. And a day before we were to leave, he came back all smiles from a shopping spree. He'd made the plunge. Out of a huge box he pulled a beautiful, pristine white pair of high-top basketball sneakers. He was ready for the Himalayas.

Brian made a Class 2 ascent of an 11,600 foot peak ("Class 2" is mountaineering for moderately difficult), took two rough cross country trips, went off on a four-hour solo adventure down a tributary of the local river, carried a heavy pack, and got nary a blister or sore foot from his high-tops. Hal's daughter, Annika, did a five-day trip in a pair of boots meant for city wear in the snow. And her friend Kelly, loath to shell out too much money before she knew if she'd really like backpacking, hiked comfortably in tennis shoes.

It's possible to hike seriously in rough terrain in almost any kind of comfortable footwear that has some sort of rubberized sole and a modicum of support. Good mountaineering boots are used—and useful—because they're sturdier than other kinds of shoes, last better under the punishing treatment they receive in mountain terrain, give support to ankles and feet that are subjected to heavy loads and unexpected twists and turns, prevent frostbite and falls during freak snowstorms, and provide better traction on steep rock faces and other quirks of nature not found on Main Street. Brian, for all his agility, came out of the mountains minus those new sneakers—they'd been ripped to shreds. Kelly will never play tennis again in her tennies, and Annika is hard put to keep the snow out of those poor over-abused boots.

The message is: don't be intimidated if you don't have and can't afford a pair of super-ace Mountain Goat expedition

Boots, a glossary:

Full grain is the outermost part of the cow's hide; it is the stiffest, most waterproof type of leather. It is sometimes turned inside-out (rough-out) so the smooth, outer layer won't get nicked or scratched. The **upper** part of the boot should have as few seams as possible. A one-piece upper is more water resistant. A **gusset** is a thin piece of flexible leather sewn to both the tongue and the upper. It keeps out water and stones. A "bellows" tongue has wide gussets, allowing it to open further so it is easy to put on. Some boots have two "overlapping" tongues, each connected to one side. The **back-stay** is a strip of leather sewn over the back seam. If it gets torn or chafed, it is almost impossible to replace. For that reason, it should be as narrow as possible.

A **welt** is the stitch which connects the upper to the sole. A Norwegian welt is doublestitched, strong and stiff. Other welts (Goodyear, McKay, etc.) are not as strong but allow more flexibility. A **rand** is a wide rubber strip protecting the stitching that holds the upper to the sole. The **sole** has three parts: a padded "footbed" just below your foot, an "insole" below the footbed and an "outsole" on the bottom. The insole can be soft and flexible for light hiking,

or it can be stiffened with a half- or full-length "shank" (sheet) of plastic or steel for added support. The sole is made of rubber (Vibram is a type of stiff, hard rubber) with a "lug" pattern designed for gripping the path. Deep lugs are best for steep, rugged terrain, while shallow lug patterns are lighter and more flexible.

FULL-GRAIN UPPER
BACKSTAY
GUSSET
RAND
WELT
SOLE

boots. Don't stay at home just because you feel unshod. However, if you can afford decent hiking boots, you won't be throwing away mutilated sneakers every year after five days in the wilderness. You'll be more confident in off-trail situations where traction is vital, safer in inclement weather, and probably more secure with a heavy pack. Cared for properly, good boots will last a long time—often five to ten years, depending on how hard you and the terrain are on them.

On the Trail of a Good Boot

It's one thing to "talk" boots, another to buy them. Consider the following:

- Leather or lightweight? Leather is strong, tough, durable, heavy. Great for serious mountaineering. Lightweights are made of plastics, nylon, other synthetics. They literally take a burden off your feet. Sturdy, flexible, comfortable. Perfect for hiking and most backpacking.

- Soles. The thicker the Vibram rubber sole and the deeper the treads or "lugs," the greater the traction but the heavier the boot. Likewise, the stiffer the "midsole" layer above the rubber sole, the stronger but less pliable and comfortable the boot. Day hikers don't need steel/plastic mid-soles; mountaineers do.

- Welt-anschauung. Welts are stitching systems that join boot to sole. The better the welts, the stronger the join. Hence more water-tight, more durable, though perhaps less flexible. Lighter shoes use bonding-cement joins.

- Cycling shoes. Try touring in soft running shoes. Your toes will go numb. Cycling shoes with stiff soles distribute pressure evenly over more of your foot, preventing numbness, encouraging comfort. But at a price. Weigh cost and comfort in the balance.

- Canoeing shoes. No such thing. Wear whatever pleases short of high-heel stillettos or baseball cleats, as long as they're tied to your feet. Otherwise you'll lose 'em during a spill. Cut several holes in old sneakers: provides instant drainage.

Aside from the appropriateness of the boot (you don't want technical mountaineering boots, unless of course you are a technical mountaineer) and the cost, the all-important consideration is size. Get it right. You and your hiking mates, will regret it if you don't. Unless ordering by mail, try on boots with a knowledgeable salesperson to help determine choice and fit, and wear the same socks (or two socks) you'll be wearing on the trail. Boots are one of the few items that are hard to rent. So the money you spend—not less than $65 and more likely over $100—is a long-term investment. Plunge wisely, watch for sales, and see if the salesperson will bargain.

Install fresh, strong laces before the trip. If a lace breaks on the trail, knot it and carry on. If the whole thing shrivels and dies, rig up a lace out of a length of that nylon cord you're carrying.

When you get home from each trip, clean your boots and treat them with a conditioner. Be careful: leather boots need oil- or wax-based conditioners; composite boots (fabric plus leather) silicon-based conditioners. Store in a cool, dry place with crumpled up newspapers inside to absorb any moisture. Before going out on the next trip, treat them again with conditioner and perhaps coat the seams with seam-sealant to protect the stitches from mud and rain.

Never dry your boots by a fire, stove or heater. Excessive heat cracks leather, destroys cement, and generally shortens the life of boots. Let them dry gradually in warm, dry air.

The subject of boots inevitably leads to the subject of blisters. No matter how perfect the fit of the shoe or how expert the wearer, blisters can strike anyone, anytime. New boots, an extra-long day of hiking, a continuous downhill stretch, wet or dirty socks, an inadvertent abrasion on the heel or toe— the causes of blisters are endless. To be prepared, carry enough Moleskin (the trade name of a lightly padded adhesive plaster) to service everyone on the trip. One pack of several strips per person is generous. To cut moleskin to the desired shapes, a scissors far surpasses a knife. Some people prefer their moleskin doughnut-shaped, with the blister in the center. Others use Band-Aids, or gauze and tape.

Packs

You can day hike with a gunny sack or a Gucci bag over your shoulder. You can't backpack that way. That requires a pack on the back. To do this efficiently and with reasonable comfort, you need an external frame pack. Such a pack consists of a lightweight frame, usually made of aluminum or an aluminum alloy, from which is suspended a large nylon bag, often divided into compartments and pouches. The frame goes on you, via padded shoulder straps and waist bands. The load, packed in the bag, goes on the frame and is separated from you by a back band. No part of the load should touch any part of you. The principle is to distribute weight evenly between shoulders and hips, and a good pack will permit you, by strap adjustments, to shift weight from your shoulders to your hips in varying degrees.

External-frame packs put the weight over your hips and let the load sway slightly as you walk. But if you try to climb or ski with such a rigging, you'll be thrown off balance. Look up as you climb? Your head hits the back of the pack. Shift your weight? The pack may shift it too far.

Internal-frame packs by comparison lower the center of gravity of the pack and "hug" your body. All gear is stowed snugly inside the pack. You can turn around and maneuver without losing balance. But hiking long distances with heavy loads in an internal frame pack will be hard on your back.

Outfitters stock a bewildering variety of packs: top-loading and back-loading backpacks with single-compartments, divided compartments, adjustable hip arms, quick-release compression straps, and on and on; babypacks with canopies and windshields (!) to protect the sole heir from inclemencies; travel packs, rucksacks, daypacks, fanny packs; duffels; packs that convert to luggage. Know what you'll use the pack for. Be guided by weight, utility, comfort and cost. Research and shop carefully. Most adult packs weigh from 4 $\frac{1}{2}$ - 5 $\frac{1}{2}$ pounds. (The latest models, barely in the stores, are constructed of super-light fabrics—Spectra, for example, a bulletproofing synthetic—and titanium stays, resulting in expedition-size packs weighing only a little over three pounds! If you're a rich, class-one climber, you'll be able to afford one.)

External frame packs consist of a rigid frame made of aluminum or aluminum alloy, from which the bag is suspended. Sleeping bags are strapped to the frame.

With ordinary materials, however, anything lighter means either the frame will be weak (poor welds, cheap alloys), or the pack will be made of material too fragile to sustain a heavy load. Anything much heavier you won't want to carry.

Try on several packs. Frame sizes differ. It's important to get the frame that's made for your height and build. Most packs come small, medium, large or extra large. Make sure the frame has room below or above the pack for strapping on a sleeping bag, tent, ground pad, and other gear. Think also about how much you plan to carry. A three-day trip requires a pack capacity of 3,000 to 3,300 cubic inches on an external frame. For the same purpose an internal frame needs 4,000 cubic inches to accommodate a sleeping bag stowed inside.

Weight also counts. It won't make sense to buy a huge 5,000-cubic-inch pack if you can only handle the weight that would fit into a 2,500-cubic-inch pack. Ask the salesperson to load up the pack so you can test it for weight. See how it feels on your shoulders. Check out the number of compartments and side pouches. A single-compartment top-loading bag may be the one you like, but if it doesn't have a back-loading zipper panel as well, every time you want some-

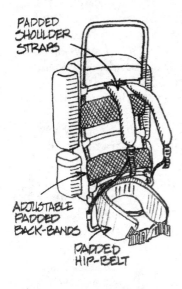

PADDED SHOULDER STRAPS

ADJUSTABLE PADDED BACK-BANDS

PADDED HIP-BELT

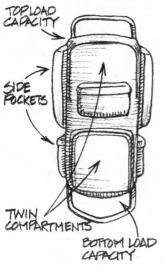

TOPLOAD CAPACITY

SIDE POCKETS

TWIN COMPARTMENTS

BOTTOM LOAD CAPACITY

thing stashed down at the bottom, you'll be pulling everything out. Look at the suspension system, how the bag is hung on the frame. Can the bag be moved for body adjustments? Can the hip or waist bands be altered? Can a missing part (pin, bolt or back band) be fixed or replaced? Check for soft padding on shoulder straps and hip belts. And expect to pay, unless you rent, $100 and up for a good pack. Among the brand names you can trust are Kelty, Camp Trails, Jansport and REI.

Wear and tear on packs show first in the fastenings. Zippers and their fittings fray; D-rings and tie-cord loops disappear; key wires work loose from clevis pins; nylon bags rip. With some care, however, a good backpack should last for years. Hal's 19-year-old loaner looks forlorn and much amended, but there it is, on his back, on the trail, hauling and carting as bravely as ever.

Necessary repairs can be made cheaply. A little WD-40 lubricant (or a silicon-spray equivalent), available in auto parts stores, should be applied to all zippers before leaving home. Frayed nylon strands that get caught in zippers can be trimmed with scissors or sealed with a match flame. Rings and wires can be fashioned out of everything from

Internal frame packs employ a semi-rigid support system. All gear, including a sleeping bag, is stowed inside the pack

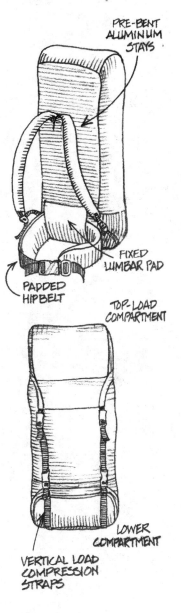

PRE-BENT ALUMINUM STAYS

FIXED LUMBAR PAD

PADDED HIPBELT

TOP-LOAD COMPARTMENT

LOWER COMPARTMENT

VERTICAL LOAD COMPRESSION STRAPS

Dog Packs

Bicycle Panniers

bailing wire to paper clips. Bags can be patched and sewn. Weakened or broken frames can be rewelded ("heliarced" with aluminum alloys); on the trail they can be patched together with cord, fishing line and ingenuity.

Packs for the Pooch

Let your dog do its part of the work when backpacking. If weight is evenly distributed over its sides, most dogs can and will pack a modest amount, at least as much as they'll eat. Thus they can carry their own food into the wilderness and, as it diminishes, can take out your supplies (garbage, shoes, whatever can be symmetrically distributed). Dog packs cost between $25-$55 depending on size and padding. They consist of two oblong carrying sacks made of treated nylon with a tough canvas or leather underside fixed to a strong nylon "saddle" that fits on the dog's back. The sacks are suspended over the dog's flanks in a manner that will not chafe its legs or sides while on the trail. Straps fit around the chest and under the belly.

We use home-made versions of the commercial model for our small dogs. Two rubberized can-

vas sacks or small reinforced stuff sacks from an army sur-
plus store, two lengths of strap and four large safety pins are
all that's needed, plus the patience to sew the parts together
with heavy carpet thread. The safety pins are used to close
the sack openings.

Rover doesn't need special training to carry a pack, though
a dry run helps get the pooch used to that strange unseen burden. Remember to keep the dog on a leash whenever the pack
is on, even when you are stopping to rest. Otherwise, on the
first scent of a deer or chipmunk, dog and pack will disappear.
Dog will most likely return, but pack almost assuredly will
not. If it does, it may be minus its contents: rocks and brush
can rip it to shreds. Off the trail, remove the dog packs and
carry them yourself. And unless your pooch's pack is water-
tight, expect the bottom of the pack and its contents to get wet
when crossing shallow streams and rivulets.

Bike Packs: Panniers

A bicycle is more stable if its pack weight is low and evenly
distributed. With a sleeping bag and tent strapped *above* the
rear wheel the bike may start to shimmy uncontrollably while
braking. Panniers keep everything close to the ground and
allow even weight balance. If you plan to tour on a bike, you'll
need at least two, and probably four, panniers.

High-quality (and expensive) models have better rain protection systems (flaps or special covers), better or quicker at-
tachment systems (remember that panniers tend to fly up
each time your bike goes over a bump), more pockets, and interior straps to keep the load from shifting around inside the
pannier.

Loaded panniers require a strong bike frame and carrier
racks to take the extra weight stress. After investing a lot in
the former be sure you've invested enough in the latter. Otherwise *you'll* be carrying the panniers *and* the bike.

Panniers demand the same care and feeding as backpacks.
Mend the tears, lubricate the zippers, and patch the holes.
Also add reflective striping if the panniers don't come with it.

Canoe Packs and Racks

The great canoe pack controversy was resolved 1,500 years ago when someone observed, "The canoe *is* your pack." A sensible argument if not absolutely watertight. As a concession to inept paddlers, card-carrying splashers, rain and wind, stow your gear in "dry bags." Use that old rubberized duffel in the attic, wrap and tie your gear in a heavy-duty garbage bag, or buy a spiffy polyurethane duffel designed specially for water sports. They're oval top-loading bags that come in all sizes and designs. A portaging bag, for example, has backpack and hip straps. Others have duffel straps, shoulder straps, load-compression straps. You'll spend up to $35 to $40 for a bag big enough to hold sleeping bag, tent, clothing and food.

The canoe as a luggage carrier on water is matched by its facility on a car rack. Lash all your gear inside the canoe, load it on the rack upside down and there you have it—a rain-proof, space-efficient packing system.

Bicycles

Remember when running was easy? Put on a pair of high-tops, old shorts, and place one foot in front of the other quickly? Then the marketing boys took over and now we have therapists to see us through the ardors of shoe selection. Cycling's the same. Cycling's worse.

Confused about the kind, make, efficiency, and cost of cycles and accessories? Don't know the difference between racers, all-terrain bikes, hybrid touring models? Between chromoly steel, titanium, carbon fibers, aluminum? Beween 17 kinds of gearing and braking systems? Getting the answers to these and other arcane cycling trivia is easy. Adopt your local bike store staff. Get to know them on a first-name basis. Their wheels may cost a few bucks more but they'll pay you back in knowledge and guidance. They'll help you select the right bike for the right occasion, make adjustments and modifications, and service your machine like a pit crew.

If you're buying, do some homework. Rent and test-ride several kinds of bike. Ask questions of experts. Tell them what you want it for: day touring, casual tour camping, group touring where you don't have to schlep any gear, serious long-distance touring and camping, trail and off-road riding.

Once you determine how bikes and camping fit together, you'll begin to understand the possible trade-offs in weight, strength, cost and reliability. As with other expensive camping equipment, start modestly, with a used or rented bike. By the time you're hooked, you'll know exactly what you want. That's the time to plunk down $600 for the Hell's Fury of your dreams. In the meantime see Chapter 2 for assigned reading on cycling, bikes, and buying.

Canoes

Boats are bigger than bikes and even more expensive. If you're prepared to walk in and buy a canoe before you've ever been water camping, you're reading the wrong book. Don't kid yourself. First of all, these things are big—averaging 15 to 17 feet—and expensive. And once you own one you need a car rack, tie-down material ($\frac{1}{4}$-inch nylon rope), paddles, PFDs (personal flotation devices: lifejackets to you), kneeling pads, towing or tracking line, perhaps a carrying yoke for portages, and (you forgot?) a place to store it! Rent, borrow, or join a club outing first. And second. Then perhaps invest in a used canoe. Tinker with it and your camping technique for a couple of seasons. Then go get a new one. It'll cost between$850 and $2,000.

Length, weight, capacity, construction, and design will vary according to performance need and cost. Whitewater canoeists and duck hunters speak different languages and paddle different canoes. Lake campers require good tracking (straight-line) ability and load-carrying capacity. River campers need moderate speed and maneuverability. Both need their craft to be durable, especially if heading for remote wilderness waters. Most manufacturers offer both versatile (multi-purpose) and specialist craft, and choices are no more (or less) complicated than buying boots.

Buying a Canoe? What to Consider

- Solo or partnered canoeing?
- River or lake? Both?
- Day trips or camping trips?
- Durability or lightweight? Both?
- Versatility?
- Maneuverability? Speed? Stability?
- Capacity?
- Easy maintenance?

The aerospace industry has touched canoeing as it has camping and biking with lightweight, durable plastics and bonding agents. Top of the line are Kevlar (grandson of fiberglass) and the hybrid laminates which draw on miracle resins, airex foam, high-tech fibers and gel-coats. Heavier are Royalex, ABS plastic and fiberglass, all also tough in the crunch. (See Chapter 2 for explanatory catalogs and reliable manufacturers.) Weightier still is aluminum, whose most fetching quality is its indestructability. You could enter a demolition derby and still sail away. But not quietly. Aluminum's noisy,

Personal flotation devices are available in five U.S. Coast Guard approved types. One PFD per person is mandatory.

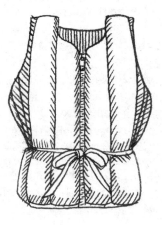

an irritation to some. Advanced flotation chambers make canoes bouyant, stable, safe. Inflatable craft may be the wave of the future, so to speak. New models, constructed of heavy-duty hypalon-coated synthetics, make for easy stream and lake paddling and are convertible into kayaks for white-water running.

PFDs are *legally mandatory*. You need at least one life-jacket in the canoe, preferably one for each passenger. They come in five U.S. Coast Guard-approved types having to do with bouyancy and function (floating conscious or unconscious persons; use in water-sports, etc.). Your local canoeing expert and the Red Cross will recommend the most appropriate for you—probably Type III, the kind water skiers wear.

Paddle selection depends on level of skill and the water conditions you expect to encounter (think of the unhappy marriage between a long paddle and shallow water), but almost anything reasonable will do. Cheap is beautiful. Here's the old standard measure: place the paddle on the ground; the grip should come to eye level. Should you carry a spare? Probably, though your chances of losing a paddle in the water are less than on the top of the car. Figure costs and take it from there.

Knee pads are a blessing. So are cushions for the kids. Make 'em at home out of old lawn-chair cushions or cut down ensolite pads. If you need anything else, call your banker. Anchors aweigh!

Stoves and Fuel

Among the several basic types of backpacking stoves, white gas, kerosene, and bottled gas (propane or butane) are the most popular. Alcohol stoves are cheap, but so inefficient they're not worth it, and Sterno, which is light, is impossible to control. Since there's a wide and technical range to choose from, we suggest you study the literature, get face-to-face advice from someone who has actually used these stoves, then check them out in person. If possible, rent and use one before buying. Some questions to consider:

- What kind of fuel?
- How complicated to use?
- Can you trim it to a low flame for simmering?
- How much fuel does it consume?
- How much does it weigh?
- What is likely to go wrong?
- Can you fix and clean it with the tool(s) you have along?

The best news for campers is the new generation of multi-fuel stoves. They burn white gas, kerosene, even diesel and gasoline! The fuel tank is external to the stove, doubling as the pump and carrying bottle, thus eliminating messy and dangerous fuel transfers. Priming, which we explain below, is easy and doesn't require separate primer fuels. Most of them come with efficiency-enhancing wind baffles. Drawbacks? They're next to impossible to control for simmer, burning at only one intensity. To overcome that defect, slip a coffee can lid between burner and pot to disperse the heat, thus lowering it.

White-gas stoves are popular because the fuel ignites fast and burns hot. They're easy to use. Many require no pumping to vaporize the fuel, which can be carried in easy-to-pack aluminum or plastic containers. Its disadvantages? White gas is volatile, which is what makes it ignite so easily. It needs to be handled with care so it doesn't burn unexpectedly, and fuel containers need to be vented periodically so that pressure doesn't build up. Also, white gas may be difficult to find, though hardware and camping stores stock it or a substitute called camping or Coleman fuel, known also at gas stations as "Blazo."

Kerosene ignites more slowly but burns hotter. It's thus potentially safer and more efficient. It is also almost universally available and cheap. On the minus side, it stinks, it stains and it's hard to start in the cold. Furthermore, it usually requires another fuel, such as denatured alcohol, for priming, and needs to be pumped up to obtain vaporizing pressure in the fuel tank. In short, kerosene stoves are rarely worth the hassle.

Many white-gas and all kerosene stoves need to be primed to start. This means that the stove must be pre-heated with some extra fuel so the gas in the tank will vaporize, expand and force its way into the burner in a steady flow. To prime a stove, extract some fuel from the fuel container—*not the stove's tank*—with an eyedropper or plastic tube. Place it in the bowl of the stove beneath the vaporizer. Light it and, as it burns, open the control valve. This starts up the burner—or it's supposed to. If it doesn't, begin the whole operation over again. Don't overfill the bowl. And remember, cold weather inhibits vaporizing, so it may be harder to start your stove in the mountains than in your backyard.

Bottled-gas stoves are so easy to use that you'd think they'd have long since replaced all the others. The fuel— propane or butane or a mix of the two—is purchased in a pressurized cartridge. When it's attached to the stove, all you do is turn on the valve, light up and cook. No pumping, no priming, no muss, no fuss. The flame is more finely adjustable than on the liquid-gas stoves. However. The fuel can be hard to find and is more expensive. It doesn't burn as hot, which means you need more of it to get the same amount of work done, and the

Stoves are available in many styles and burn a variety of fuels. Here are some typical examples.

Optimus 111B (white gas)

Bleuet S200S (butane)

MSR WhisperLite (multi-fuel)

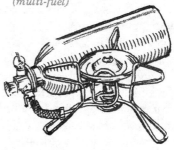

stove's efficiency decreases in direct proportion to the amount of fuel left in the cartridge. Four days into the mountains you'll have to cook longer and longer to get a meal done. Propane and butane also have an embarrassing tendency to revert to liquids when it's cold, or freeze solid if the temperature really hits bottom. Butane liquifies at 10 degrees Fahrenheit, propane at -45 degrees Fahrenheit. If the weather threatens to turn you blue, it will turn your gas blue too. Take a fuel cartridge to bed; sleeping-bag warmth will help keep it in firing condition. The recent propane/butane mixes overcome a lot of this problem and work well at high altitudes and in extremely cold weather. Two final things: Once a butane fuel cartridge is attached to the stove, it can't be removed until it's empty; a puncture hole in the cartridge allows the gas to escape into the stove. It will escape all over the environment if you remove it. Yet hiking on with a half-empty cartridge attached to the stove can be cumbersome. And of course you have to pack out the used cylinders.

Your actual "mileage" may vary, but with a little basic math you can get a ballpark estimate of how much fuel you'll need. First, count the meals. Say you're going for seven days. On the first and last days you'll need only one hot meal, on the other five, you'll need two. Altogether twelve hot meals. Assume you use a half-hour of fuel for each meal. That's extravagant, for at least some of your meals will be those "add-hot-water-and-serve" affairs. But better to have more fuel than less, especially for that last unforeseen banquet of six big trout and trimmings. So in all, six hours of cooking. If you're using a small multi-fuel stove, say an MSR X-GK which burns very hot, the pump/fuel bottle will hold 22 fluid ounces, enough for the entire trip. Say, on the other hand, that you're using a butane-burning Bleuet Gaz C-206. Six hours will use most (or all) of two cartridges.

Ever notice that the people in those rosy-hued camping stove ads are always smiling? That's because their stoves work! It'll be cold comfort in the mountains if you can't get your Promethean Mountain Model going when you need that hot cup of brew to get *you* going. Know how your stove works. Practice starting it at home. Take it completely apart and put it together again. Bring along the tools you might need to tinker and clean. Stove repair people say that over 50 percent of "defective" units work just fine—the problem is the camper and not the stove.

Learn to save fuel. If the recipe calls for a cup of water, don't boil two cups "just for good measure." The most efficient and brilliant menu in the world won't warm the cockles of anybody's heart if you can't heat the pot. And don't fire up till you see the whites of their eggs!

Essential Stove Lore

- Fuel contaminates food. Pack it separately from edibles. Wrap the fuel container in a plastic bag or two. Then if it seeps, or cracks when your pack drops on the ground, the food stays safe.

- Fuel is volatile. Keep it away from extraneous heat sources. Release the vapor pressure in fuel containers and the stove's tank occasionally as you hike. Never refuel a stove while it is hot.

- Stoves need ventilation; give them air. A large pot on a small stove may prevent proper ventilation and cause overheating. So can cooking in a closed space.

- Be careful cooking in a tent. Many tents are flammable; only recently have laws required that tents be made of flame-resistant materials. Make sure yours has been treated before cooking inside it. Even then, open tent flaps and keep the stove near an exit. Check out the new hanging stoves for tent use; they're designed to prevent spills.

- Stoves work best when set on a flat surface and protected from the wind. Cook on a flat rock or smooth ground in the lee of a tree or boulder or make a wind baffle out of a circle of rocks or aluminum foil fashioned into a cylinder that fits around the stove with enough ventilation space.

- Oh, and one more thing. Don't forget your matches.

Water filters are a wise investment since all wilderness water should be considered contaminated, any stream can be infested with Giardia or bacteria. Boiling and chemical treatments are effective but not always convenient–filters are compact and reuseable.

Water Purifiers

The question is no longer, "Should you treat water?" but "How to treat water?" Disease-bearing microorganisms thrive in "pure" mountain lakes and streams, and the cramps, vomiting and diarrhea they visit on the system are enough to strike fear in the bowels of any camper.

Treatment systems vary in method and effectiveness. Iodine crystals or tablets are light and easy to use. They kill microorganisms. But they take from 20 minutes to an hour to work, a long time if you're thirsty, and make the water taste worse than the stuff you left behind in the city plus iodine is not a guarantee against Giardia.

Boiling water—a full, rolling boil for three to four minutes—is another alternative, but doesn't eliminate debris, takes forever to cool, uses up fuel and may taste "smoky."

Filtration systems are expensive and heavy. But they're quick, safe and nonintrusive. The water tastes as if it actually came from a mountain stream. You pay in increasing weight as the filter retains liquid and clogs with use. Ceramic filters can be cleaned and reused, but cost $180 and may crack if dropped. Paper-type elements are cheaper, about $35, but not renewable after clogging. They can, however, be back flushed (pumped in reverse) with a supply of pure water and reused for a total life of about 400 quarts.

Plan ahead for your drinking-water needs. Mix and match. Cook with boiled water, use the filter till it clogs, and keep a tiny bottle of pills in reserve for emergencies.

Adaptive Equipment for the Disabled

The number and types of adaptive aids for disabled campers are growing exponentially. So are prices. But everything from adapted fishing rod holders and electric reels to swimming frames, all-terrain wheelchairs, accessible rafts, kayaks and canoes, and hand-powered bikes are out there. Availability is often haphazard and geographically limited, but resources and references are varied and plentiful. See Chapter 2 for listings.

Fixing Things and Mending Bodies

Repairs

If all that expensive gear breaks down on the trail, the one-year guarantees won't be worth the proverbial paper. You either live with the problem or fix it. We've never seen or heard of a camping trip where everything worked right; something invariably breaks, tears, rips or malfunctions. A good repair kit is essential.
- Vise Grips
- Needle and thread
- Safety pins
- Spare clevis pins and key wires (for the backpack)
- Spare flashlight batteries and bulbs
- 50 feet of nylon cord

- Roll of half-inch adhesive tape
- Swiss Army knife ("Tinker" model)

Patience and ingenuity are also required to make adequate repairs; these are both a matter of attitude. Make the job challenging and fun. Sit in a shady place, unpack the repair kit and ponder the problem. Take frequent breaks if the job is tedious. Once Hal's boot sole started to come apart. He got out the large needle, pushed it through the rubber and leather with a rock, then pulled it the rest of the way with the vise grips. On another trip a backpack frame broke in two. We trimmed a tree branch to fit inside the hollow tubes, butted the broken pieces against each other with the branch acting as a reinforcing rod, then taped and tied the frame back together. Another time, a low-hanging branch snapped Rick's fishing rod in half. He found that one section of the hollow fiberglass tubing slid right into the other. So he looped the thick carpet thread around the break to keep the pieces together. Using only the Swiss Army knife and vise grips, we've even disassembled and reassembled our backpacking stove. Ripped packs, broken sunglasses, sticky fishing reels all have been repaired. Finally, don't worry if you make something worse by trying to fix it. Even the most ingenious jack- or jill-of-all-trades occasionally packs out a broken article. If, however, you work slowly and carefully and have some basic tools and supplies, you can usually do an adequate job.

Bike Repairs

If your fishing reel jams or your stove conks out, you don't have to pack up and go home. If your bike breaks down miles from the nearest shop and you don't know how to fix it, you may not be *able* to get home. The moral? Learn how to troubleshoot and make simple repairs before you leave home. Carry a basic tool kit in a seat pack. Attach or tape a pump and spare spokes to the bike frame. Or else!

Unless you're a mechanic or a genius, you're not going to repair any bike but your own and maybe your partner's. Take a maintenance course at a local bike clinic. Buy a maintenance manual written a couple of years *after* your bike was built. That way it's liable to cover the new systems which are actually on your bike: derailleur, freewheel removal, brake and gear adjustment. Buy the tools which *your* bike requires: the laser widget for Greg LeMond may be useless for you (see Appendix for a clip-out tool list).

What are your basic repair needs on a touring or mountain bike trip? You should know how to do four things: mend a tire (patch or replace a tube); replace broken spokes; repair a broken chain; and adjust brake and gear cables. Each requires practice and the right tools (listed in Chapter 5). None is so hard that an amateur can't do the repairs.

Bike Repair Hints

- Tube and tire repair. Make sure pump fits tire valves. Dust spare tube with talcum; carry in a plastic bag. Use duct tape to reinforce torn tubes and to wrap cut tires.

- Broken spokes. Improvise: loosen brake to provide clearance for the wobbly wheel. Brake on the one good wheel. Slow down and carry on till you're in camp. Then replace the spokes. A "pocket vise" (see Chapter 5, third list) provides the best leverage to remove the freewheel nut. Spare spokes can be taped to the bike frame.

- Broken chain. Be sure spare links fit *your* chain. Know how to use the chain tool to remove and install pin.

- Cable repair. Carry spare rear brake and derailleur cables with one head removed to allow threading through housing. Front cable breaks: coil excess cable and trim later.

Canoe Repairs

Bikers need wrenchs. Canoeists need glue. Or a facsimile thereof. The best all-purpose facsimile is ordinary heating duct tape. In an emergency it'll patch and fill till you get to camp. Then haul out the canoe and make a mend with the epoxy kit you've brought along. Use a torn-up kerchief as stuffing. Serious repairs—of dents, splits, loose rivets, damaged fiberglass—can be made at home or in the shop. A little seepage never hurt anyone; a lot could sink your trip.

First Aid Kit

Our first-aid kit has never really been tested. We've never had a major medical or first aid problem on a trip. All we can tell you is what we take and what we've used. There are good books on outdoor and wilderness first aid which you may want to look at (see the Book List). Beyond that we suggest you get in touch with local authorities regarding any special medical precautions for your trip (for example, preventive measures against Lyme disease or against contaminated water).

We routinely use lots of aspirin on hiking trips. It relieves headaches caused by sun, lack of salt, altitude or fatigue. It also helps aching muscles. Band-Aids and moleskin, both of which may be found liberally attached to our feet, are the other two items always in high demand from the first-aid kit.

The rest of our first-aid supplies are rarely touched but they're there, just in case. We bring several square gauze bandages; strong tweezers for splinters, ticks, and porcupine quills in the dog's nose; adhesive tape and needle (from the repair kit), codeine or its equivalents for serious pain, decongestant, Lomotil for diarrhea, antacid for upset stomachs and antibiotic pills in case of a strep throat. A salve, first-aid cream or disinfectant is also useful. Some people bring Ace bandages for strained or swollen ankles or knees. When backpacking alone, add a mirror in case something gets in your eye. Mountain bikers, who live more dangerously, should add butterfly bandages and hydrogen peroxide for the inevitable scrapes and cuts, and an "instant cold" pack against swelling in the first 30 minutes after a sprain.

Individuals should carry whatever medicines they need. Karen wouldn't be caught in Carlsbad Caverns without a good sunscreen, while Hal would sooner go into the mountains without boots than leave his back pills behind. Mary brings sulfa drugs in case of a urinary infection and Rick is addicted to Vitamin C. Don't skimp on what's necessary for you.

There are two other necessary items: lip balm and hand lotion. Hot weather, cold winds, and constant exposure to the elements really dry out face, hands and lips. A nightly application of lotion goes a long way toward preventing that loss of moisture, as does a daily dose of Chap-Stick. After one trip when it becomes painful to move your hands or lips, you'll never forget either of these items again.

The great snake-bite question inevitably arises. We can give you a few hints. In twenty-five years of backpacking in California, the Rockies, the Ouintas and the Southwest, we've never seen a poisonous snake nor heard one rattle. Snakes are as terrified of you as you may be of them. Statistically, the number of fatalities from snake bites in the U.S. is so small as to be almost negligible: about 30 people, mostly small children, die each year from snake venom.

The snake-bite kit itself (razor blade, tourniquet and disinfectant) is a double-edged sword. "Authorities generally advise carrying a snakebite kit, but in unpracticed hands of semi-hysterical first-aiders, the kit can be more dangerous than the bite; the rule is to seek instruction before entering an area where it may be needed." (Harvey Manning, *Backpacking, One Step at a Time*, pg.52). We used to carry a bite kit, but it seems to have disappeared in recent years and we haven't replaced it. There are very few snakes over 7,000 feet (where we backpack), but rattlesnakes might be a danger in other areas. Check before you go. If in snake country, be sure to wear long pants and heavy boots.

Likewise, in deer tick country, wear long pants tucked into hiking socks or taped closed against these Lyme-disease carriers.

What about serious injuries exceeding CPR and first-aid skills, such as a broken leg, near drowning, a wound needing sutures? In the first place, these are most dangerous when alone. If you and your gear fall into an icy river late one rainy, windy afternoon, there is a real danger of hypothermia. Alone, you're in the same fix as a solo climber who falls and breaks a leg. Anytime you go off by yourself, whether exploring or cycling, be sure someone knows exactly what your plans are and where you'll be. And come back on time, even if that means not making it to your destination.

The second rule is not to move seriously injured victims. Set up a campsite that is as warm and dry as possible. Then go for help. Canoeists can often make good time to a trailhead and help. Most ranger stations have helicopters available for life-threatening emergencies. Rangers are rarely more than two or three slow hiking days away (one long hiking day without a pack). If the injured person can be left in comfortable surroundings, you can usually have a doctor there within 24 hours. Don't try to carry anyone out over rough terrain.

Weight

Weight watchers—cyclists and backpackers—need to fuss. If all that nicely assembled gear is too heavy to move out of the living room, you might as well stay home. Just how much you can carry depends on your own weight, height, physical condition and state of mind, and on the facilities you have for carrying a load: a strong and big pack, a strong and little pack, two panniers, four. It also depends on how long the trip is and how many people will be sharing the load. Putting all these ingredients in the hopper and shaking, we've come up with the "average load" for an "average adult" for a four-person hiking trip for six days, door to door: 34 pounds. Of this, food will weigh about 7 $^1/_4$ pounds per person (1 $^1/_2$ pounds/person/day, excluding the first and last travel days). Non-food weight—clothing, equipment, personal accessories—will be about 26 $^3/_4$ pounds, including water and the weight of the empty pack itself. As trips get longer, food takes up a greater percentage of total pack weight, and other things, like the inflatable raft, 35mm camera, or the frying pan, may have to go.

If you take along something extravagant, like the inflatable raft and paddles, each person needs to add a little more weight to the pack load. That doesn't mean everyone will carry equal weight. On a four-person excursion, somebody will haul nearly 45 pounds and someone else closer to 25 pounds. That's OK. If there are only two of you, you'll each carry a lot more (excluding the raft), for a minimum total of just over 39 pounds.

How much can one person carry? A good guide is to begin with 20 percent of your body weight. If you're in good shape, you can raise that to 25 percent. A group of 160-pound joggers can easily carry 40 pounds each. But if three of your four-person group weigh less than 120 pounds, you might have to start cutting corners to reduce their packs to 25 pounds or so.

Much the same applies to cyclists. When push comes to shove, you have to be able to lift the bike off the ground if it falls over! Figure 40 pounds maximum for four fully loaded panniers; figure a lot less for your biking pleasure. Unlike backpackers, you can always replenish supplies en route.

Anticipation

With equipment in order and maps and permits in hand (see Chapter 2), you're ready to head for the market. The following chapter will get you there.

CHAPTER 4

Food

Food Weights and Planning

Our friend Lowell used to be an ace backcountry hiker. Then he became a letter carrier on the hills of San Francisco. He soon grew weary of his busman's holidays and retired from backpacking in favor of his work. But on the trail he was good, and often did things his own way. Where others wore the latest hiking boots, he'd lead the way down rock falls in a pair of battered basketball hightops. When others pressed grimly toward the destination in afternoon's hottest sunshine, he'd find the deepest shade available, unroll his Ensolite pad and sleep out the heat, often arriving at the campsite by flashlight. And where the rest of us were satisfied with dried foods and soup packets, he insisted on packing in fresh onions, potatoes, carrots, turnips and other weighty produce for his cherished stews.

Then there's Rob, who lives on rice and oatmeal cooked in a coffee can, raisins, seeds and other bird food so he can carry along his camera and telephoto lenses. The message? If you really want to bring something badly enough, you'll bring it and enjoy it, even though it seems to defy all the logic of backpacking. This logic insists that food is heavy. Especially food with a high water content. If you filled your pack with onions, you'd need a forklift to get it up on your back. Food is also bulky and packs have just so much space.

Car campers and canoeists need not attend class today. Unless planning a multi-day hiking trip from the campground, take granny's entire larder for all we care. Cyclists, like backpackers, however, need to be minimalists or plan to shop on a daily basis.

Unless you pump iron for a living or are related to a burro, weight and space will dictate how much and what kind of food you can take on a camping trip. So will distance and taste. When all the variables are considered and combined, the figures work out something like this. An average pack loaded with everything except food will weigh in the neighborhood of 27 pounds. To this will be added about $1\frac{1}{2}$ pounds of food per person per day, the accepted median limit of food weight in most backpacking circles. Jewish mothers, a stable of sumo wrestlers, and Lowell with his stews may insist on two pounds per day, but any more than that and you'd better start pumping iron for a living or take up with a burro.

Actually, we begin with the goal of a pound a day and grudgingly go up the extra half pound when we can't part with the Kahlua or matzoh meal. If you go exclusively with freeze-dried foods, of course, your cooking utensils will be cut to one pot, plus stove and fuel, which permits greater food weight. Anything much below a pound a day verges on nuts and berries—the school of caloric deprivation.

For the sake of argument and a contented after-dinner glow, let's take $1\frac{1}{2}$ pounds and see how it adds up. A five-day trip will mean a $37\frac{1}{2}$-pound pack; an eight-day trip, a 42-pound pack and two weeks, a 51-pound pack. That's a lot to haul up a hill. Beyond that, plan to cache some food or get resupplied. If you don't believe us, put 50 pounds of rocks (or onions, we're not fussy) in a backpack and walk up two flights of stairs. Welcome to the reality of weight watching.

Those $1\frac{1}{2}$ pounds a day include everything you'll ingest—staples, ready-to-eat foods, spices, cooking oil—as well as the packaging containers. Thus, another law of backpacking logic is: the lighter the container, the more food you can carry. Check out the *net* weights on food packets when you shop. That gives you the amount of actual food in a package, as distinct from total shelf weight, which includes wrapping, cardboard, plastic and puffed-up space. With few exceptions, everything will need to be repacked in the lightest wrapping anyway, so the net weight becomes the operative figure in calculating those 1 1/2 pounds.

Before going to the market or camping store, figure out how many meals you'll be having and where you'll be having them: on the trail (simple and quick) or in camp (complex and leisurely). You needn't know precisely what you'll be eating for every meal, just what will be available for as many hot meals as you'll need. Of course, if you like to plan menus, do so; lots of suggested meal plans appear in the literature. Since we're never sure if we'll want minestrone on Tuesday or lunch (at all) on Wednesday, we fudge on the menus and prepare with an eye toward improvising. That, however, does not mean spur-of-the-moment.

To illustrate the food-planning process, we show you how we planned two six-day trips, each with four people. For both trips, the total *on trail* food weight was about 30 pounds (i.e., 1 1/2 pounds per person per day, *not including* car meals). But that does not mean that each group carried the same food.

A couple of years ago we went on one of those literally breathtaking trips in the high Sierra—five days at about 11,000 feet, above the tree line where no fires are permitted. The four of us were (still are) what can only be called competition eaters: The technical term is fressers. We intended to eat well and nutritiously with a one-burner MSR X-GK stove and a 22-ounce fuel bottle—enough gas to cook two hot meals a day for five days for a small bar mitzvah party of 30, though light enough to justify the extravagance. We didn't even contemplate taking freeze-dried foods. We brought fishing rods for day hikes at lower altitudes, but didn't like our prospects and, anyway, knew better than to count our fishes before they're caught. So, our 1 1/2 pounds-per-day specs didn't include the trout flambé des Alpes Maritimes.

Take a look at the Food Planning Table that follows. Let your eye run down the first column. There is enough variety

to provide for quick but filling meals (an important consideration at that altitude) and a few improvisational licks. (See
Chapter 8 for all the dishes described here.) We ate straw-
berry pancakes, having dried plenty of strawberries at home
and let them soak in cold water overnight to rehydrate; also
fruit crepes, the mixed home-dried fruits reconstituting
quickly in water boiled at high heat for a few minutes.
Nobody could face the instant oatmeal plain, so we concocted
a pan-fried "polenta," mixing the oatmeal with cornmeal,
margarine, sugar, and eggs.

Suppers were super. Pasta with homemade spaghetti
sauce, dried and reconstituted, topped with parmesan cheese,
which is one of the best hiking cheeses because it's hard and
doesn't spoil. Homemade minestrone, also dried and reconstituted in a few minutes; Indian fried rice with raisins, nuts,
coconut, sprouts and chicken, spiced with garam masala. And
three providential trout caught on the last day sautéed with
almonds, and served with stir-fried vegies. Karen insisted as
a finale that we have her famous chocolate mousse a la Red
Peak Pass, and she used up enough of the remaining fuel to
lighten the packs for the hike out. On day six, we ate a quick
oatmeal breakfast and hot chocolate, snacks for lunch and
reached the car with just enough left over for an emergency
that never happened.

The second trip couldn't have been more different: Rick,
Hal and two ravenous adolescents, intent on several days of
hiking, fishing, cooking and general relaxation. We camped
at three successive lakes, all well stocked with small brown
trout. Firewood was plentiful. Most afternoons, while the
girls were swimming or reading—or noshing on the snack
food—we invented new ways to bake breads, cake, pizza, and
the thousand and one other recipes you'll find in Chapter 9.
A couple of things went wrong. Stanya decided after catching
her second fish that she was a vegetarian, and Annika
stunned us with the announcement that she loathed cheese.
Rick, ever resourceful, said "Let them eat cake." They did.
And loved it. We ate the fish and cheese, and loved it.

Food Planning for Two Six-Day Trips

	Trip One Min. Cooking (weight = lbs.)	Trip Two Max. Cooking	Weight Difference (2nd trip)
Ready-to-Eat Foods:			
Dried fruit, Raisins	3.0	3.0	
Chicken/Beef Jerky	1.8	1.8	
Dried Vegetables	1.5	1.0	0.5 less
Cheese	3.5	2.5	1.0 less
Nuts	0.8	0.5	0.3 less
Cookies	1.5	1.5	
Crackers	1.5	1.5	
Chocolate	2.0	2.0	
Granola and Coconut	0.8	0.5	0.3 less
Sprouts	0.1	0.1	
Rice, Pasta, Soups:			
Minute Rice	1.0	0.7	0.3 less
Dried Minestrone	0.8	0.8	
Dried Pea Soup	0.8	0.0	0.8 less
Spaghetti Sauce	0.8	0.8	
Spaghetti and Ramen	1.2	1.0	0.2 less
Flour, Sugar, Cereals:			
Instant Oatmeal	0.4	0.0	0.4 less
Flour	1.5	3.0	1.5 more
Yeast, Baking Powder	0.0	0.3	0.3 more
Cornmeal	0.3	0.3	
Sugar	0.5	1.0	0.5 more
Dairy, Oils, Spices:			
Powdered Milk	0.5	0.8	0.3 more
Eggs	1.0	1.7	0.7 more
Hot Chocolate	1.5	1.5	
Tea/Coffee	0.2	0.2	
Cooking Oil	0.0	0.5	0.5 more
Margarine	0.5	0.5	
Spices, Condiments, Syrup	2.5	2.5	
Total Weight	30.0	30.0	

The interesting thing about these two radically different trips is the similarity in their food lists. Most of the items are exactly the same. They diverge—in quantities— where considerations of fuel use and food-preparation time are paramount. Neither of these factors appears on the food lists, but they cannot be ignored when planning a trip.

One last piece of advice: many wilderness hikers recommend having extra quantities of emergency high-protein food: milk powder, soup or bouillon cubes. Should you get caught in an early snowstorm for two unexpected days, that could be vital to pull you through.

The more you know about your appetites, abilities and the conditions at your destination, the better you can plan a food inventory. You're already familiar with the first two: you know what and how much you like to eat, and can gauge your physical ability to carry weight. Conditions, however, are likely to change. Someone may get sick and not be able to eat what's available. The fishing may be lousy. The salami may be left in the fridge at home by mistake. The bears may get to dinner Number Three before you do. By assessing the knowables, and expecting the variables, you're better prepared to improvise.

Food Planning: What You Need to Know

- Fires permitted? Check *before* you go.
- Fishing prospects? *Never* assume you'll catch fish. Accept them as a bonus.
- Dietary considerations? Check likes and dislikes before you go. Likewise special needs. Vegetarians won't eat jerky; carnivores won't eat vegetables.
- Taking the dog? Plan food weight for the pooch as carefully as you would for yourself. Size and weight of dog make a difference. Average: two packets moist food per day. Plan to carry dog food over rough terrain.
- Fuel consumption? Stove campers: Learn the cooking capacity of your particular stove before you go. Fire builders: Leave axes at home. Use only free fall wood.

- Low-impact camping? One hot meal per day rather than two. Take more snacks, less cooking food.
- Plan car meals separately, but *don't forget them*. The fried chicken, macaroni salad, fresh fruit and juice to be taken in the cooler go on your shopping list. Likewise the small juice packets for the ride home.

What To Bring?

It's finally time to shop. You've discussed likes and dislikes, determined how much or how little cooking you'll do, how much money you can spend, what kind of hot meals you want, what munchies are absolutely indispensable. You've made a preliminary shopping list, then checked off what items you already have at home. Your first target is the supermarket. It's cheaper than specialty stores and carries all kinds of heat-and-serve foods. If there's a bulk-food store in town, you'll probably shop there for grains, flours, dried fruits, nuts and the like. If there's a camping store, you may head there for the latest in freeze-dried foods. If you do, bring along a shopping bag full of money.

You won't be Ace Market's favorite customer if you ask for "1 pound $11^1/_2$ ounces of cookies, please, and throw in $7^1/_2$ ounces of flour, will you?" Weigh out the amounts at home after you've done the shopping (see Weighing Food in this section). If you buy too much, save it; it won't spoil.

Cooking and Eating Utensils: What We Bring

Spartan backpackers hell-bent for distance can make do with a pot and a spoon. Add a pocket knife to skin a bear or fell a tree and they are content and at peace with the world. Cooking in the wilderness, after all, is no exercise in elegance. However, if you prefer Athens to Sparta, you may want to add just a couple more pots and maybe even a fry pan. The goal is to keep things few and light, but as you'll see from our recipes

(Chapter 9), it's possible to satisfy most hedonistic impulses with a minimum of hardware. Here's what we take for two to eight people on our longer trips.

- A set of three nested pots and tops with capacities of one quart, two quarts, and two-and-a-half quarts. Weight: 1 pound, 13 ounces.

- A flex-grip metal pot holder, a pliers-like tool that grips the rim of a pot, one tong fitting under the lip of the rim, the other fitting over it. Weight: 2 ounces. If the pots have bails (wire handles), use a heavy pair of gloves instead. Steadier and more efficient than the flex-grip.

- An $8^1/_2$-inch teflon-coated aluminum fry pan. It's old enough so that we don't worry about scratching the surface. Otherwise, use a spatula made of wood or plastic instead of metal. A teflon-coated pan requires less shortening, saving weight in the cooking oil department. And it's easy to clean in case of burning on uneven heat. Weight: 1 pound.

- A small aluminum spatula. Weight: 3 ounces.

- A light-weight three-pronged backpacking grill in its own protective sack (to keep soot off other things in the pack). Weight: $4^1/_2$ ounces. If we're going where the fish are, we often take along a 14" x 10" wire-mesh grill (a cake rack works fine) which makes grilling fish a breeze. Weight: 7 ounces.

- A plastic egg container (one dozen). Weight: $5^1/_2$ ounces.

- A small wire whisk. Weight: 3 ounces. Alternatively, a small spring-loaded swizzle stick (like an egg-beater). Weight: $3^1/_2$ ounces.

- Pocket knives, one each person. We use Tinker model Swiss Army knives, which substitute a Phillips screwdriver for the more common corkscrew. Weight: 3 ounces.

- Two boxes of sulphur kitchen matches packed separately in water-tight Ziploc bags. Weight: 4 ounces (both boxes).

- Two small plastic garbage bags for packing the pots and fry pan—for soot containment.
- Extra Ziploc bags for food storage: Weight: 1 ounce.
- Eating utensils: 1 Sierra cup ($3^1/2$ ounces), 1 tin plate ($3^1/2$ ounces), 1 fork ($1^1/2$ ounces), and 1 spoon ($1^1/2$ ounces) per person. The forks are optional; chopsticks are lighter. The pocket knife completes the set.
- An MSR X-GK multi-fuel stove. Weight: 1 pound. Plus 22 ounce fuel bottle/pump (need not be filled to capacity). Alternatively, a Bleuet C206 camping stove plus one butane cartridge. Weight: 1 pound, $7^1/2$ oz. These are only taken if camp fires are not permitted.

The total weight (not including the stove equipment) is 5 pounds, 14 ounces. The MSR stove and its accessories add 2 pounds, for a grand total of 7 pounds, 14 ounces. Clearly there are expendable items here. Consider how much time you want to spend, and what kind of cooking you plan to do. Then adjust the utensils accordingly.

Shopping

Light and Quick Foods

In the above trip plans, freeze-dried foods are conspicuous by their absence. After many years of sampling, we found we didn't really need them. First and foremost, our budget never allowed it. Freeze-dried foods aren't cheap. Second, we prefer to dry our own. Third, we don't need their convenience. With a fire, our rice, beans and dried veggies do just fine. Where a stove is required, home-dried meals, soups and noodles work as well and are a lot cheaper.

Nevertheless, freeze-dried foods *are* remarkably convenient. Light in both bulk and weight, they're quick and easy to prepare. Supermarkets carry some, but the largest selections are found in camping or specialty stores. And many people find them quite palatable.

Bulk Foods

Bulk foods include rice, beans, pasta, lentils and peas, nuts, raisins, dried fruits. They're cheaper than packaged varieties, are bought in just the weights you want, rather than what the processor wants to sell you, and exist in enough varieties to satisfy just about everyone. Brown sugar, brown rice, rye or soy flour, 57 varieties of noodles—most bulk food stores have what you need.

Alternative Foods

A world of other possibilities exists out there in the market-place. One friend, after spending nearly 10 years as a reporter in Tokyo, relies almost exclusively on Japanese food products. He takes Japanese buckwheat noodles (*soba*); he also carries seaweed (*nori*), which he wraps together in a flexible bamboo square used in rolling rice for Japanese sushi (raw fish and rice delicacy). He also relies on soybean soup bases (*miso*), dried fish, and, unaccountably, popcorn. Others carry falafel mix, a practical and delicious Middle Eastern grain and chick pea combination. And for the sentimental mid-Americanist, there are always instant mashed potatoes and Rice-a-roni.

Extravagances

If backpacking were a science, there'd be no room for frills. We'd have to leave fresh eggs at home, along with mustard powder and sesame oil. But backpacking's an art, subject to (some) whim and a (little) fancy, and that allows for incorpora-tion of particular idiosyncrasies into the overall weight limit. If you absolutely cannot do without some Granny Smith ap-ples, or a watermelon, pare down the weight elsewhere. Your extravagance becomes a working part of your inventory. You have turned a frill into a necessity.

Dog Food

Dry dog food is too bulky to take on a mountain trip. Canned dog food is full of water *and* prohibitively expensive. That leaves moist dog food, which is not as bulky as the dry, nor quite as expensive or heavy as the canned. And, according to the makers' claims, it's more nutritional per unit of weight. It's also conveniently packaged. We always allow our pooches a little more than the minimum requirements, but never so much that they can't carry most of it. For our (medium-sized) dogs, eight packets are sufficient for a four-day trip, 12 packets for a seven-day trip. The only other thing to remember is that dogs, like humans, can carry only so much weight. Make appropriate allowances for your dog's size.

Weighing, Packing, Transporting, and Caching Food

Weighing Food

Virgil, a fanatical solo backpacker who goes out for six weeks at a time without resupplying, refuses to weigh his food. He just eyeballs the amount, tests the "feel" of his pack, and goes off. He hasn't starved or expired of muscle fatigue yet. The rest of us mortals need reassurance that we have the right amount of food for the finite number of days we'll be on the trail. It need not be exact. If you've gone rigid with anxiety over our fine-tuned weighing in those food lists above, relax. You needn't be a charter member of the U.S. Bureau of Standards to camp, hike or backpack. The important number is the total weight—that's what you'll carry. To determine this, a bathroom scale will work just fine.

When you get the food home from the market, eliminate all extraneous packaging. The aim is to get as close to the net weight as possible without sacrificing freshness or protection against breakage and spillage. You may want to keep the Ry Krisp in its cardboard box to prevent crumbling, the soup powder in its packet to save cooking instructions, or the baking chocolate in its box for shelter against the sun. But as a rule, repack almost everything in plastic bags. Then fetch the bathroom scale. Weigh yourself. Now weigh yourself holding all the food in a cardboard box or brown paper bag. Don't forget the eggs, cheese, salami and other things stashed in the fridge. You won't be able to read the scale because the food box will be in the way. Ask a friend to read it for you. That's what friends are for. You now have an idea of the total net weight. If it much exceeds your expectations ($1\frac{1}{2}$ to 2 pounds per person per day), start cutting and paring. Some of the flour can go. Put some of the maple syrup back in the cupboard. On second thought, who needs that many almonds? Now get back on the scale. If you're a couple pounds over or under, it's close enough. When you reach the trailhead, you can cut or add again.

If you own a small postal scale, the kind that weighs packages up to about four pounds, you can fine tune by weighing individual items. And if you're a classic anal compulsive, you can even get a letter scale that is calibrated to half-ounces. That way you can be content in the knowledge that exactly $3\frac{1}{2}$ ounces of cinnamon and sugar are nestled against the $1\frac{1}{2}$ ounces of nutmeg and cloves. Authors of camping books somehow always feel obliged to know such things; no one else we've ever met on the trail has known or cared.

Packing and Transporting Food

Don't knock plastic. The Ziploc bag just may be the most important advance in hiking since the invention of the foot. We sympathize with those who hate Ziplocs; we often can't get them closed either. If you're a Zipophobe, pack your food in sturdy plastic bags and secure them with wire ties. If you can deal with Ziploc technology, buy several boxes and use them liberally. So liberally in fact, that you'll double-bag many items. Always carry out the used bags with you. Burning plastic is a foul(ing) deed.

In the off-season, collect plastic bottles. Small ones are perfect for vinegar, sesame oil and hot sauce; large ones for cooking oil, maple syrup and brandy. Compartmentalized pill boxes, obtainable in drug stores, are great for carrying spices.

On the trail, carry extra plastic bags. They'll come in handy to replace torn ones, or for caught fish, map cases and garbage bags.

Individual foods should be packed separately. Cookies, nuts, dried fruit, etc. get their own bags. Liquids such as syrups and oils should be kept in well-sealed containers and carried upright. Don't put them vertically in a backpack which you then lay on its side for a five-hour drive to the trailhead; you may find a syrup-soaked pack when you arrive. Keep liquids upright in a box in the car and transfer them to the pack before you start to hike.

Eggs should be placed in plastic containers you can buy at camping stores. They come in half-dozen and dozen sizes and keep the eggs from breaking even if the pack gets dropped or slammed around. Some people prefer to keep breakfast, lunch, and dinner foods separately, each in their own section of the pack. Others, like ourselves, prefer to organize the staples apart from the ready-to-eat (trail) foods. Whichever system you use, what's important is that it works for you.

Once everything is swathed in plastic or secured in containers and bags, you need to get it into the packs. It's common to pack at home and transport the filled packs in your car to the trailhead. But loaded backpacks take up lots of space in a car. Especially if you drive a compact, you could leave the final packing for the trailhead and transport the dry food in boxes and the perishables in a cooler. Then tie the empty backpacks on the roofrack, or under the canoe.

Be sure you know where in the pack your food is. If you dive in searching for gorp and cheese for lunch and can only come out with cornmeal, you might be nettled. So do a little planning. Someone might carry the lunch foods; someone else the staples, liquids, and dinners. If you're a large party, two people can carry the ready-to-eats and two the staples. Within any pack, try to be consistent, so nuts and raisins are in the same place every day and are not crushed by, say, that watermelon you couldn't leave behind. And while in camp, where most cooking, baking and eating are going on, system becomes crucial. We try to arrange the packs in camp so all the baking gear is in one place, all the condiments and spices in another, the jerky, salami, cheese and crackers in the left upper pocket, the chocolate in the fridge, the cookies in the cupboard, and so on. If two packs will accommodate all the food in camp, it becomes more efficient. Only those two packs have to be moved periodically to keep up with the shade.

Caching Food

We'd never made a food cache until we met an old-timer some years ago who convinced us that it was easy and efficient. The simplicity was at first unbelievable. He took the food he wanted to stash, stored it in plastic containers stuffed in a green plastic garbage bag and thrown on the floor of the forest. Nothing more. He insisted that bears and other cognoscenti rarely disturbed the sack. Were we being taken? We'll probably never know, because we take a few more precautions with our own cache.

Old coffee cans and plastic half-gallon ice-cream containers with tight lids make up our inner defenses, in which we pack and tightly seal 10 pounds of extra food. We then stuff them in a garbage bag, and bury the stash under a canopy of rocks under a low-spreading tree high in a mountain meadow. We've never retrieved a cache in less than perfect condition.

A couple of hints. Store relatively dispensable food: extra flour, dog food, supplementary sweets. Make sure the cache is out of the sun. Make even surer you can find it again. That particular tree might not look so particular from a mile away. Or the meadow may be shin-deep in water when you get back and look very different from your last view. Sight your cache from different angles. You don't need a compass, just a sense of proportion and a good memory.

Allow space in your pack for the cache food and its large containers when you leave the trailhead. You may have to hang the empty containers from your pack until you get to the cache site, or stow them in the pack already filled, if there's space.

Finally, grin and bear it if the bears or squirrels get what you've squirreled away. Besides, you may catch enough extra fish to compensate for your losses. Anyway, it's not that awful to hike out a day or two early.

CHAPTER 5

Lists:
A Schlepper's Guide to
the Universe

Out there somewhere may be a monster of total recall who
can keep in mind everything necessary for a camping trip.
But that's not us. We keep lists. Lots of lists. Lists for food
and equipment. Replacement items within the equipment list
(such as the first-aid kit and repair kit). We even make a list
of the lists we need to make. That sounds like a lot of trouble,
but since our requirements don't vary much from trip to trip
or year to year, once one is made it can be used almost forever.
Just keep a master list in reasonably good shape in your map
drawer. Lists will grow and shrink occasionally, according to
group size, needs, new discoveries or tastes and discarded or
obsolete items. It's a good idea to keep a spare list handy to jot
down details as you think of them before, during and after
your trips.

The lists in this chapter should make it possible for you to
create a set of master lists—combinations which work best for
the particular kind of trip you have in mind. Tear the copies
out of the Appendix, apply scissors and tape, mix and match.
Then, when you've got the right package, xerox it in multiple
copies. That way you won't have to start from scratch two
years from now when you set out on a similar camping trip.

Never mind that you no longer need the baby-wipes or tire patch kit or that you no longer "do" sugar and polished rice. Cross out what's obsolete—the ear spoon and fog horn, the training wheels and fire axe—pen in the sketch pad, bird book and mosquito net, copy again and you're ready for the last half of the last decade of the twentieth century. Use three copies of the list for each trip, the first while assembling gear, the second when loading the car, the third at the trailhead. After that it's best to forget what you forgot.

We begin with the car and proceed through canoes and bicycles, ending with the kinds of planning lists which multi-day hikers and backpackers need to get them well-provisioned on the trail. The Food Planning List for Two Six Day Trips (Chapter 4) is not reproduced here, however, all lists are reproduced in the Appendix for your clip-out convenience. Note that some items are duplicated as we try to make each list comprehensive in itself.

List of Lists:

The Before-Leaving-Home-Did-I-Turn-Off-the-Gas Checklist

☐ Leave a schedule/map/itinerary with someone to call out the Mounties if you don't return on time. Include name and phone number of nearest ranger station.

☐ Get neighbor to watch the house and take in newspapers, take out garbage, feed the pets.

☐ Leave written instructions on plant care.

☐ Leave adequate pet food, and name and phone number of the vet. Alternatively, take pets to the boarding kennel.

☐ Camping equipment:

    ☐ Lubricate all zippers—on tents, sleeping bags, packs—with silic one lube or a light oil (WD-40).

    ☐ Waterproof boots. Use only recommended agent for your particular footwear.

    ☐ Repair/replace damaged or missing parts. *(A leaking inflatable raft can ruin a fishing trip. So can a missing tent pole.)*

☐ Check car:

    ☐ Tires, belts, hoses, and battery cables

    ☐ Wiper blades. Fill windshield washer reservoir with a mixture of Windex and water.

    ☐ Vital fluids: gas, oil, automatic transmission fluid, brake fluid, coolant

    ☐ Tire-changing equipment: jack, lug wrench, spare tire

    ☐ Roof rack: All parts present?

☐ In car:

    ☐ License and car registration

    ☐ Credit cards and cash on board

    ☐ Fire/wilderness permits, fishing licenses

    ☐ Road maps and directions to trailhead or campground

    ☐ Ranger station address and telephone number

    ☐ Sunglasses

    ☐ Accessible rain gear

    ☐ Cooler/ice chest with perishable foods

    ☐ Car meals and snacks

    ☐ Drinking water

    ☐ Dog food and water bowl

    ☐ Litter bag

    ☐ Games, toys, stuffed animals, books, distractions

    ☐ Personal needs: music/story tapes, Walkman, pencil, paper

    ☐ Clean clothes for return drive home

☐ Did I leave the gas on, the toilet running?

Bicycle Touring/Mountain Bike List

- [ ] Bicycle in top running order
- [ ] Cycling shorts
- [ ] Helmet
- [ ] Cycling shoes
- [ ] Shoe covers
- [ ] Cycling gloves
- [ ] Rain gear
- [ ] Sunglasses *(shield type)*
- [ ] Safety glasses *(for mountain biking)*
- [ ] Shoulder strap *(for carrying a mountain bike up or over rough terrain)*
- [ ] Rear-view mirror
- [ ] Horn/bell
- [ ] Panniers
- [ ] Pannier rain covers. *Alternatively, plastic garbage bags in which all gear is stowed.*
- [ ] Lock
- [ ] Headlamp plus extra batteries
- [ ] Fold-up reflective triangle
- [ ] Water bottle(s)
- [ ] Litter bag
- [ ] Talcum powder *(for saddle sores & flat tires)*
- [ ] Optional: *(for high-tech cycling)*
  - [ ] Small radio *(for weather reports)*
  - [ ] Cyclometer *(indicates speed, distance traveled, etc.)*
  - [ ] Two-way radio that fits in helmet *(lets you chat with a partner while biking)*
- [ ] Tool and Repair Kit
  - [ ] 6" crescent wrench
  - [ ] Folding Allen wrench set *(metric/standard)*
  - [ ] 2 four-way cone wrenches *(metric/standard)*
  - [ ] Small vise-grips with wire-cutter built in
  - [ ] Swiss Army knife *(Tinker model includes Phillips and standard screwdrivers.)*
  - [ ] Paper towels and hand cleaner
  - [ ] Pump *(does it fit your tire valve?)*
  - [ ] Spare tube *(right size?)*
  - [ ] Talcum powder *(to dust spare tube before wrapping in a plastic bag)*
  - [ ] Plastic bag
  - [ ] Patch kit: fresh, unopened tube of glue plus several patches in a plastic bag
  - [ ] 2-3 tire irons *(plastic, aluminum or steel)*
  - [ ] Duct tape
  - [ ] Pocket vise
  - [ ] Spoke wrench *(does it fit your spokes?)*
  - [ ] 3-4 extra spokes taped to frame
  - [ ] Chain tool
  - [ ] 4 spare chain links
  - [ ] Chain lube
  - [ ] Extra rear brake cable *(cut off one end)*
  - [ ] Extra derailleur cable *(cut off one end)*
  - [ ] Extra nuts and bolts *(for all-purpose emergencies)*

Canoeing List

- ☐ Canoe *(a very hard item to forget, but we know people who've had to go back for it)*
- ☐ Roof rack and tie-down line
- ☐ Paddles and one spare
- ☐ Personal Floatation Device: one per person
- ☐ Dry sacks. *Alternatively, duffels lined with plastic garbage bags.*
- ☐ Waterproof map case. *Alternatively, large Ziploc bag.*
- ☐ Portage harnesses *(to convert duffels, sacks into carrying packs)*
- ☐ Knee pads plus cushions for children
- ☐ 50-foot length of 3/8" line: one per multi-canoe party *(for rescue, etc.)* *Note:* Plastic lines float.
- ☐ Two 15-foot end lines *(bow and stern)*, 3/8" diameter
- ☐ Foul-weather gear

- ☐ Sneakers with drainage holes cut in them
- ☐ Watertight food containers
- ☐ Large sponge *(your handy "bilge pump")*
- ☐ Bailer
- ☐ Portaging yoke *(if required)*
- ☐ Optional
  - ☐ Extra flotation *(styrofoam inserts)*
  - ☐ Thigh straps
  - ☐ Extra tie-down straps
  - ☐ Spray skirt
- ☐ Repair kit
  - ☐ Duct tape
  - ☐ Patch material *(appropriate to canoe-type, e.g., epoxy plus glass cloth scraps)*
  - ☐ Swiss Army knife *(with scissors, sharp blades)*
  - ☐ Small putty knife
  - ☐ Sandpaper
  - ☐ Paper towels
  - ☐ Lacquer thinner
  - ☐ Small paint brush

Group Accessories, Individual Needs, Optionals

Group accessories

So many things on a camping trip can be shared that they become group accessories rather than private necessities. Some things everyone should have while other things individual members of the party may want. Here's a list of items which we take as shared goods on backpacking trips:

- [ ] Maps and permits
- [ ] Compass
- [ ] Star chart
- [ ] Tree guide/bird book/wildflower guide
- [ ] Two boxes kitchen matches with sulphur heads (strike anywhere). Everyone carries some in Ziploc bag.
- [ ] First-aid kit
- [ ] Drugs and medicines
- [ ] Repair kit *(see itemized list)*
- [ ] Tooth paste, dental floss
- [ ] Small towel
- [ ] Liquid (biodegradable) dish soap and pot scrubber
- [ ] Lantern *(car / canoe / horse camping only)*
- [ ] Mosquito repellent (two bottles)
- [ ] Plastic spade *(to bury human waste)*
- [ ] Paper and pencil
- [ ] Camera, film, extra battery
- [ ] Extra pack straps
- [ ] Garbage bags (one for each member of the party)
- [ ] Extra Ziploc bags (10-12)
- [ ] Extra tent pegs
- [ ] Extra ground cloths/ponchos (one for each tent)
- [ ] Backpacking (Sven) saw
- [ ] Book for reading aloud
- [ ] Two-person inflatable backpacking raft plus paddles *(when other weight considerations permit)*

How Much Toilet Paper

This is the most poignant question of all. The answer is, "enough to satisfy everybody's expected needs." This includes cleaning pots, polishing glasses, sometimes lighting a fire, as well as the manufacturer's recommended use. We've found that two rolls are adequate for a six-day trip for two. Others require two or three times as much. This is a touchy point. Don't argue. Nobody's right; everybody's right.

Individual Needs

Everyone should have the following:

☐ Pocket knife

☐ Sunglasses *(in hard case)*

☐ Matches
(from Group Accessories list)

☐ Flashlight
(such as Mallory AA compact flashlight or another weighing about 3 ounces with batteries, *and which can be held in the mouth when both hands are needed)*
Caution: Remove batteries before storing for winter. This will avoid a corroded, ruined flashlight six months later.

Optionals

Other things are optional in the eyes of some, but essential in the eyes of others:

☐ Ring clip to carry the car keys

☐ Fishing license

☐ Camera and film

☐ Binoculars

☐ Paperback book

☐ Toothbrush, toothpaste, comb, barrettes, ponytail bands

☐ Towel and bar of (biodegradable) soap

☐ Sanitary napkins, tampons, sponges, etc.

☐ Birth control devices

☐ Glasses case and extra glasses

☐ Contact lens solution

☐ Personal medications or prescriptions

☐ Nail clippers

☐ Playing cards, chess set, etc.

☐ Security blanket, stuffed animal, etc.
(Rick's daughter Sheri does not travel without her miniature pink plastic ponies and a generous selection of bath toys. They're always necessary.)

Tips on Sunglasses

- Ultraviolet rays (UVA/UVB/UVC) are dangerous. Protect your eyes in strong light.
- General-use sunglasses should pass no more than 5-percent UVB and 8-percent UVA. Check labels; ask questions.
- Sports sunglasses should pass no more than 1-percent UVB plus equal amount UVA and visible light. Check labels; ask questions.
- Cyclists should wear shield-type glasses; *never* wrap-arounds which impair peripheral vision.
- High-altitude hikers (in bright sun/snow) should wear very dark wrap-arounds for full protection.
- Lens color: neutral gray or green yield least color distortion.
- Use retainer straps if engaged in strenuous activity. *Canoeists note*: some retainer straps float and will prevent glasses from being deep sixed.

Leave-at-Homes

Some things, however desirable, should not be brought into the wilderness:

- deodorants, perfumes and other scented cosmetics, which all attract insects and some of which attract bears
- cassette recorders and other machines which don't come with headphones (why disturb other campers' searches for solitude?)
- guns, which are not permitted in designated wilderness areas and which can be dangerous in the close quarters of a camping trip.

Backpacking List: Equipment

Tent and Sleeping Gear:
- ☐ Sleeping bags
- ☐ Ensolite, Ridge Rest, or Therm-A-Rest pads
- ☐ Tent, rainfly, stakes, poles. *(Note: a two-person tent will not sleep three. Add another tent, rainfly, etc.)*
- ☐ Spare tent stakes
- ☐ Ground tarps/ponchos: one per tent

Packs and Protection:
- ☐ Backpacks
- ☐ Four straps per pack
- ☐ Four extra pack straps
- ☐ Large green garbage bags. *Alternatively, pack covers.*
- ☐ Ponchos/tarps *(as rain gear in addition to ground tarp for tent)*
- ☐ Stuff sacks for clothes and personals
- ☐ Day-pack. *Alternatively, a strap-rigged stuff-sack to double as day-pack.*
- ☐ Flashlights plus new batteries and bulbs
- ☐ Dog packs, as necessary
- ☐ Child carrier, as necessary

Cooking, Fire, Water Gear:
- ☐ Three nested pots and lids
- ☐ Sierra cups
- ☐ Tin plates
- ☐ Spatula
- ☐ Forks and spoons. *Alternatively, chopsticks.*
- ☐ Frypan
- ☐ Backpack grill
- ☐ Camp stove plus fuel and funnel
- ☐ Matches (two plus boxes; strike-anywhere type)
- ☐ Lighter fluid/fire starter paste in tube or cubes
- ☐ Candle
- ☐ Scouring pad/sponge
- ☐ Aluminum foil (two folded sheets for baking)
- ☐ Light mesh bag *(as dish drainer, suspended from tree)*
- ☐ Pair of garden gloves *(for cooking, wood gathering)*
- ☐ Sven saw *(for gathering dead wood)*
- ☐ Canteens/water bottles
- ☐ Water-purifier system
- ☐ Food storage:
  - ☐ plastic egg carton (half dozen or one dozen sizes)
  - ☐ plastic pill box *(as "spice rack")*
  - ☐ plastic bottles, jars *(as condiment, syrup, oil, margarine containers)*
  - ☐ spare Ziploc bags (10 each small & large)

Backpacking List: Clothing, Boots

For high altitude temperatures: 90s-20s Fahrenheit

- ☐ One pair pants
  (jeans or cotton / canvas)

- ☐ One pair shorts
  *(light weight; doubles as
  swim suit)*

- ☐ Three pair socks
  (inner and outer)

- ☐ Three underwear

- ☐ Two cotton shirts
  *(one long-sleeved,
  one short)*

- ☐ Long johns
  *(cotton / polypropylene /
  wool)*

- ☐ One sweater or
  sweatshirt

- ☐ Down parka.
  *Alternatively, Gore-Tex
  shell and layered
  sweaters.*

- ☐ Baseball cap or sun visor

- ☐ Wool (ski) hat

- ☐ Sunglasses
  (with UV protection)

- ☐ Boots

- ☐ Moccasins/tennies/
  reef slippers
  *(for stream crossings,
  fishing, in camp)*

- ☐ Mosquito-netting "hat"
  *(slips over visor; indis-
  pensable for "that" time
  of year)*

- ☐ Pocket knife

- ☐ Personal toiletries:
  (mandatory)

  - ☐ toothbrush
  - ☐ toothpaste, dental floss
    (Group Accessory)
  - ☐ toilet paper
    (Group Accessory)

- ☐ Personal toiletries:
  (optional)

  - ☐ comb/brush
  - ☐ barrettes/ponytail bands
  - ☐ razor
  - ☐ glasses case
  - ☐ small towel *(share)*
  - ☐ birth control devices
  - ☐ contact lens solution
  - ☐ nail clippers
    (Group Accessory)

First Aid and Medicines

Quantities for Four-Person Trip

First Aid:

- ☐ Moleskin
  (one or two packets)

- ☐ Adhesive tape
  (one small half-inch roll)

- ☐ Band-Aids
  (12 assorted sizes)

- ☐ Gauze pads
  (six assorted sizes)

- ☐ Ace bandage (one)

- ☐ Butterfly bandages
  (four)
  (Attention: mountain bikers)

- ☐ Hydrogen peroxide
  (Attention: mountain bikers)

- ☐ Instant cold pack
  (Attention: mountain bikers)

- ☐ Tweezers/surgical locking hemostat (one)

- ☐ Small mirror
  (for shaving, inspecting eyes, signaling)

- ☐ Baby-wipes or similar
  "dry washes"
  (four unless there's a baby aboard, in which case thousands!)

Drugs and Medicines:

- ☐ Aspirin or its equivalent

- ☐ Mosquito repellent
  (two for four people)

- ☐ Sunscreen

- ☐ Lip balm

- ☐ Hand lotion

- ☐ Optional:

  - ☐ Vitamins
  - ☐ Neosporin/Bacitracin
    (first-aid ointment)
  - ☐ Caladryl itching lotion
  - ☐ Antacid pills
  - ☐ Snake-bite kit
  - ☐ Aspirin with codeine
  - ☐ Lomotil diarrhea medicine
  - ☐ Athlete's-foot treatment
  - ☐ Desitin/Zinc ointment
  - ☐ Talcum powder
    (Attention: cyclists)

Repair Kit

- ☐ Swiss Army knife
- ☐ 50-foot length of nylon rope
- ☐ Small vise-grips
- ☐ Heavy duty *("carpet")* thread plus two large needles
- ☐ Light nylon thread plus two small needles
- ☐ Nylon patch material *(called "ripstop" tape)*

- ☐ Patch kit for rubber raft
- ☐ Extra flashlight bulb(s) plus batteries (two per flashlight)
- ☐ Safety pins
- ☐ Spare clevis pins and key wires for backpacks
- ☐ Roll of half-inch adhesive tape *(see First Aid and Medicine List)*

Maps and Permits

- ☐ Spare change for phone call
- ☐ Campsite reservation
- ☐ Fire permit
- ☐ Wilderness permit
- ☐ Fishing license
- ☐ Driver's license
- ☐ Automobile registration
- ☐ Road map

- ☐ Trail map
- ☐ Topo map
- ☐ Sea chart *(Attention: canoeists)*
- ☐ Waterproof map pouch or Ziploc bag
- ☐ Compass
- ☐ Star chart

Traveling with a Dog

- ☐ Check that dogs are per- mitted at your hiking venue
- ☐ Dog pack
- ☐ Dog food (minimum two packets moist food per day)
- ☐ Leash
- ☐ Flea collar

- ☐ Name tag with address, phone number
- ☐ Water bowl for car
- ☐ Extra food for car
- ☐ Tweezers/hemostat *(to extract porcupine quills etc.)*

Kiddy List: For Babies and the Very Young

- ☐ Whistle
  (hang a loud one around child's neck)
- ☐ Extra clothes:
  (depending on ages and affinity for dirt)
  four pair of pants, three shirts, four pair of socks for one-week trip
- ☐ Diapers:
  (mix of cloth and disposable)
  one dozen each for one-week trip. Cloth for sunny weather, disposables for inclement weather
- ☐ Diaper-washing gear: two plastic buckets, biodegradable soap, clothes line
- ☐ Baby-wipes

- ☐ Tie-on hat
- ☐ Rain suit
  (for use at meals as well)
- ☐ Plastic bags as "outer" socks *(quart / gallon size depending on size of foot)*
- ☐ Life jacket
  (for swimming, boating, canoeing)
- ☐ Syrup of Ipecac
  (induces vomiting)
- ☐ Fever-scan forehead-type thermometer
- ☐ Zinc oxide / Desitin
- ☐ Games
- ☐ Books
- ☐ Favorite toys
- ☐ Comforters: stuffed animal, favorite blanket, etc.
- ☐ Edible hiking incentives!

Fun and Games

- ☐ Paper & pencil
- ☐ Playing cards
- ☐ Star chart
- ☐ Tree guide
- ☐ Wildflower guide
- ☐ Bird book
- ☐ Binoculars

- ☐ Books
- ☐ Camera, including extra battery and extra film
- ☐ Musical instruments
- ☐ Pocket chess/checkers
- ☐ Lightweight games
- ☐ Frisbee

Fishing List

Quantities for Two Anglers, Five-day Trip;
Spinning Tackle Only

☐ Fishing license
☐ Telescoping rod
☐ Rod case
   (to prevent snapping in backpack)
☐ Spinning reel, lubricated and in good working order
☐ Fresh 4 lb. test monofilament line on reel
☐ Spare 4 lb. test line (one small spool)
☐ Spare 2 lb. test line (one small spool)
☐ Six bubbles
☐ Eight flies
☐ 10 lures
   (vary by weight, size, color)
☐ Two bottle corks
   (to carry lures, five per cork)

☐ Eight snap swivels
☐ Two packets No. 12 hooks (six per packet), for 8"-15" fish
☐ One packet No. 14 hooks (six per packet), for 8"-12" fish
☐ Eight weights: split shot, egg sinkers
   (vary in size, weight)
☐ Bait
   (bottled salmon eggs; power bait; cheese; worms)
☐ Worm threader
   (optional)
☐ Net
☐ Large Ziploc bags
   (the "tackle box")
☐ Swiss Army knife

Food Shopping List

No quantities given here.
See Food Planning list in Chapter 4.
If drying food at home, purchase fresh fruit and vegetables up to a month in advance of trip; purchase meat and poultry no more than a week before trip.

☐ Flour
☐ Cornmeal
☐ Sugar
☐ Yeast

☐ Baking powder
☐ Baking soda
☐ Powdered milk

- ☐ Semi-sweet baking chocolate
- ☐ German sweet baking chocolate
- ☐ Instant hot chocolate
- ☐ Tea
- ☐ Coffee
- ☐ Rice
- ☐ Beans
- ☐ Mung beans
- ☐ Pasta: spaghetti
- ☐ Soba
- ☐ Instant ramen
- ☐ Chinese noodles
- ☐ Nori *(Japanese seaweed)*
- ☐ Raisin cookies
- ☐ Ginger snaps
- ☐ Ak-Mak crackers
- ☐ Saltines
- ☐ Instant soups
- ☐ Instant oatmeal
- ☐ Cooking oil
- ☐ Sesame oil
- ☐ Rice vinegar
- ☐ Soy sauce
- ☐ Maple syrup
- ☐ Brandy
- ☐ Hot sauce
- ☐ Lemon/lime juice
- ☐ Salami
- ☐ Cheese
- ☐ Margarine
- ☐ Dried fruit/fresh fruit for drying
- ☐ Vegetables for drying

- ☐ Dried meat (jerky) or turkey/chicken for drying
- ☐ Nuts: almonds, cashews, filberts
- ☐ Eggs/powdered eggs
- ☐ Raisins
- ☐ Powdered ginger
- ☐ Garlic
- ☐ Cinnamon
- ☐ Cayenne
- ☐ Paprika
- ☐ Tarragon
- ☐ Basil
- ☐ Thyme
- ☐ Curry powder/Garam Masala (pepper, cumin, cinnamon, cardamom, coriander, cloves, mace, nutmeg)
- ☐ Salt
- ☐ Pepper
- ☐ Car food
- ☐ Chicken
- ☐ Salad stuff
- ☐ French bread
- ☐ Cheese
- ☐ Juices
- ☐ Fresh fruit
- ☐ Dog food
- ☐ Baby food

Your Master List

- Select from the lists only those appropriate for your trip (See Appendix for clip-out lists.)
- Eliminate duplications
- Add individualized items
- Combine into handy packet. Our own master list for backpacking trips consists of three pages:

Equipment:

- ☐ Cooking Equipment (pg. 107)
- ☐ Camping Equipment (pp. 107, 110, 111)
- ☐ Dog Equipment (pg. 110)
- ☐ In the Car (pp. 101, 104-106)

First Aid, Clothing, and Fishing:

- ☐ First Aid & Repair (pp. 104-106, 109, 110)
- ☐ Clothing (pp. 108, 111)
- ☐ Fishing (pg. 112)

Food:

- ☐ Food Planning and Shopping (pp. 89, 112-113)

CHAPTER 6

Getting There

Packing Your Car

Six hours in a car headed for that dream wilderness vacation
can be hell on wheels. You know the feeling: too many bodies,
not enough space, sticky buns melting down the dashboard,
maps misplaced, a couple of wrong turns and a flat at high
noon. Welcome to the Great American Highway.

Is there any relief in sight? Yes, as a matter of fact, if you
plan the car ride the way you would the rest of your trip. For
one thing, if you pack that old Ford Fairlane right, you'll save
a lot of grief. The cooler with lunch and snacks belongs right
there within hand's reach—especially little hands. Stowed in
the trunk, it's useless. The maps need to be in the navigator's
general vicinity, not on the kitchen table or in the duffel
lashed to the canoe on the roof.

A little foresight goes all the way to the ranger station.
Got cash for tolls and the last roadside hash house in northern Minnesota? Credit cards for the tow truck? Games and
books for the kids? A big litter bag? It all seems obvious, but
we've found over the years that a car checklist gets us off with

most of the Absolutely Indispensable Items on board. (See Chapter 5, List 1.) It's amazing how comforting it is to know that the car jack is in the trunk and actually works. That the dog has a water bowl which can be filled at gas stations and rest areas. That stick-on window shades will protect the sun-ward passenger(s) from drowning in a sea of sweat before the last K-mart passes from ken. That a small pillow, strategic seating, and sensible packing may let someone actually get some sleep.

OK, that's the inside of the car, where cabin fever and expectations of the wide open spaces vie for attention over the long haul. What about the other places? Up on the car rack is the gear that can't fit in the trunk and that you don't need till you arrive at the final carpark. Once off the main highway, it's going to get coated with an archaeological layer of dust if it's not covered with a tarp. Once it starts to rain....Obvious, isn't it? But one piece of advice. Secure the tarp carefully before heading out of the driveway. Loose ends or edges soon begin to flap maddeningly on the freeway, sounding like an awning shop in a hurricane.

In the trunk will be the other stowables, including most of the food for your camping trip. All of the liquids— cooking oil, soy sauce, syrup, hot sauce—will stand upright in their containers, packed securely against leakage. Otherwise they'll come up empty by the time you pack the backpacks at the trailhead. And since it'll get colder as you gain altitude and night falls, warm clothing should be easily available.

A car packed properly is a lean, mean pleasure machine. Enjoy it. But don't make the trip into an endurance contest. Rarely are wilderness trips tied to deadlines. If you need to make 14 pit stops rather than the planned three, because someone wants out of the car, make 'em. And let the dog out each time. Instead of eating lunch in the broiling sun on some highway turnout, check out the local park in the little town just off the road. (A good travel guide should have that kind of information. Take one along.) A 10 minute detour may rescue nerves and flagging humor. Lunch under an old New England elm at midday in early August will soothe a savage breast, or at least let the driver snooze in the shade. Properly rested and fed, the car crew will waltz through those final dusty miles up the old logging road to the trailhead or put-in point along the river.

Packing Your Pack

We usually arrive at the trailhead after dark. We crawl into our sleeping bags, and the next thing we know, the sun is coming up. Time to hit the trail. Half awake, we squint mournfully at the little Datsun station wagon that brought the four of us here. The seats are piled with coats and parkas, the back is full of food boxes, and strapped to the roof rack is a monstrous heap of packs, ponchos, and stuffsacks. How will we ever fit all that gear into our packs? And how much can we possibly pack into the backcountry on our backs?

Everything seems so disorganized the first morning that it's a miracle when we square things away. But somehow it all fits into the packs, and somehow we contrive to pack it into the mountains. We just keep telling ourselves that the packs are always heaviest and the hike always hardest this first morning. And each day, as we hike farther away from civilization, the load gets lighter, our bodies get stronger, and the packing gets easier.

How should you pack a backpack? First decide what you'll need during the day. What does the weather look like? Will you need easy access to rain ponchos and plastic garbage bags to cover the packs? Or will you want to change into shorts at midday? Change of clothes, along with sunglasses, suntan lotion, maps, candy bars, and other small essentials need to be within easy reach. Lunch and munch food should also be easily accessible. Plan to take pictures at every scenic point? If so, keep your camera in a handy pouch.

After the small, reachable pockets have been filled, the main compartments can be packed. It may sound obvious, but keep in mind that whatever goes into the pack first will come out last. Also, heavy items should go next to your back and as high in the pack (between shoulders and waist) as you can get them. (The latest packs have compression straps which allow the load to be pressed toward that ideal carrying point on the back.) The pots and pans, stove and fuel go in first. Heavy food packages, such as flour, rice and beans, go next. That two-pound block of cheddar cheese (less some for lunch) falls in the "heavy" category too, as does Charles Dickens.

Once those are packed, separate the rest by function. We usually make one compartment the "drug store/emergency room." Another is the "hardware/fix-it shop." You might designate a "candy store" as well. Save the lightest items—ponchos and Ensolite pads—to strap onto the top of the packs.

Organizing by function lends itself to packing as a group. One person may have the cheese, another the utensils and spices, and a third might end up with two sleeping bags and an inflatable raft. One person could be responsible for all liquid containers: cooking oil, maple syrup, vinegar, etc. Make sure this pack always stays upright. No one carries more than he or she feels capable of. And if a shoulder or neck begins to ache after two miles, we reorganize, trading a heavy sleeping bag for a lighter ensolite pad.

There's room to strap things on the top and bottom of most packs. A stuffed sleeping bag, rolled-up poncho, tent, or stuffsack full of clothes are easy to trade if one person's pack is too much for weak knees or a bad back. But be careful. A rule of thumb is that anything hanging below your waist "feels" about 50 percent heavier than it would up next to the middle of your back. Anything strapped to the top of the pack feels about 75 percent heavier than it really is. And whatever hangs behind you in the middle of the pack gains a good 100 percent because it is so far behind, swinging as you walk.

When strapping on pads, tents and stuffsacks, it's important to double-knot everything. Each stuffsack gets tied into a double-bow. Each strap gets wrapped back around itself, then knotted. Never leave anything that might work loose as you hike. This is especially important if you're the last person in line. We've had a few instances where things fell out of stuffsacks or off packs, but usually the person immediately behind noticed. If you're last, the wool sweater you drop will probably stay lost. And when you're shivering at night, you'll become a life-long convert to the double knot.

A couple of other tips from the school of hard knocks. Don't keep your maps or permits in your pants pockets. They'll invariably get wet from sweat, fog or rain. Once that happens, and the colors and lines start to run together, they become difficult to use at all. In fact, most books recommend keeping maps in a plastic bag inside the pack so they won't get wet in a sudden downpour (or if they're below a cracked bottle of vinegar, a leaky tube of suntan oil or a broken egg).

Take care packing your fishing rod too. On Rick's first backpacking trip, the rod stuck out a good 18 inches above his pack. While he managed to avoid low overhanging branches for the first two days, he accidentally knocked his pack over during a rest stop on the third day, and the top 18 inches of his rod snapped off. The rest of the trip he fished with a "splinted" fishing pole.

Most "backpacking" rods come apart in small sections or collapse ("telescope") to a small size. They can simply be placed in the main compartment of your pack. But many spinning and fly-fishing rods don't break down small enough to be protected inside the pack. They need to be secured to the outside of your pack, enclosed in a hard case or tube.

If the weather's been wet, try to keep the waterlogged rainflies and ponchos separate from the tents and sleeping bags

Packing the pack.

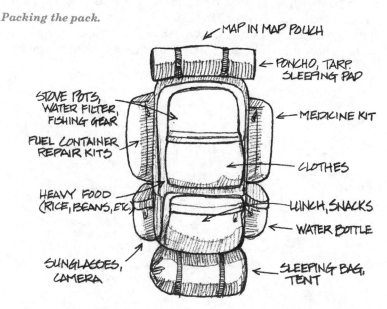

MAP IN MAP POUCH

PONCHO, TARP, SLEEPING PAD

STOVE POTS, WATER FILTER, FISHING GEAR

MEDICINE KIT

FUEL CONTAINER REPAIR KITS

CLOTHES

HEAVY FOOD (RICE, BEANS, ETC.)

LUNCH, SNACKS

WATER BOTTLE

SUNGLASSES, CAMERA

SLEEPING BAG, TENT

when heading out the next day. The tents and sleeping bags may be damp in the morning, but they won't be nearly as wet as the rainflies. Pack them separately, even if it means breaking up a logical pair, such as tent-and-rainfly or sleeping-bag-and-ground-cloth. You need not pack everything in the same manner each day, or even from morning to afternoon. Also, remember that your backpack is a natural drying platform. Wet socks? Dripping poncho? Hang them securely from the pack as you hike, rotate them occasionally to get the sun on all sides, and by the end of the day, they'll not only be dry, but fresh and aired too.

Finally, your belt or belt loops can act as an extension of your pack, though don't forget to secure things on your belt—knives, gorp pouches and compass—with the same care you take with things hanging off your pack.

Adjusting the Pack to You

Three things connect you to the pack: two shoulder straps and a hip strap. All three should be padded. Unpadded straps tend to cut into clothes or skin. It's best to have someone help you with the initial adjustment. Then, when the straps are right, you might want to put in a safety pin or tie a knot to prevent

Fitting the pack.

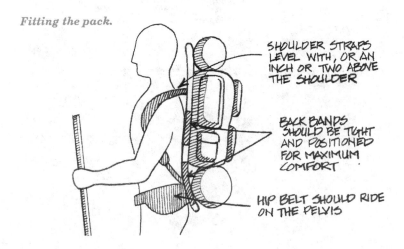

SHOULDER STRAPS LEVEL WITH, OR AN INCH OR TWO ABOVE THE SHOULDER

BACK BANDS SHOULD BE TIGHT AND POSITIONED FOR MAXIMUM COMFORT

HIP BELT SHOULD RIDE ON THE PELVIS

them slipping as you walk.

Adjust the hip belt first, with someone holding the pack against your back. The belt should rest on your hip bones tightly enough to hold the pack there. Then, tighten the shoulder straps so the pack is held upright but doesn't pull on your shoulders. The pack should actually ride on your hips, which support most of the weight. The shoulder straps are meant to take very little weight. They mainly keep the pack in position, straight up and centered over your hips.

As you hike, the pack should not cut into your back. Sometimes a misplaced belt buckle or stove piece will protrude and become a pain. Sometimes shoulder straps cut into shoulder bones. They can usually be shifted sideways to get a better fit and temporary relief. Also, the spots on each hip where the pack makes contact might get a little sore.

Occasionally you'll want to shift weight to rest your hips. Simply loosen or release your hip belt. The pack will drop about an inch, your shoulder straps will tighten and the weight will now be on your shoulders. Experiment as you walk—more weight on the hips or shoulders—until you find the right distribution. After a day or so, pack, back and hips all seem to mesh comfortably into an incredible walking machine.

Packing Your Bike

Load panniers bottom to top, heavy to light. Whether you have two or four panniers, they need to be symmetrically balanced. To get this right weigh each pannier load and make fine adjustments. No sense falling into the canyon because your port side panniers are hauling you off the track.

The front-to-rear load should be balanced as well. One way to do this is to set the bike on two bathroom scales, one under each tire. Lean the bike against the wall, load the panniers, then climb on. Have a friend read the two scales, then make weight adjustments between rear and front till the readings on the two scales are close.

Some mountain bikers prefer to use a tight-fitting, internal-frame backpack rather than panniers. That results in a higher center of gravity, but you'll be less likely to snag, rip or tear the pack on rocks or logs.

Packing Your Canoe

Like bicycles and dogs, canoes yearn for low, even weight displacement. If you lean the old Philco radio against one gunwale, lean the laundry hamper against the other. Steady as she goes. Pack the dry sacks or duffels as you would panniers— vertically, heavy to light. Set them, balanced like panniers, at midships, offset by passenger weight. The aim is to trim the canoe so that neither bow nor stern are too high out of the water. Weight displacement figures, telling you how much the canoe will safely carry, vary according to size and design of the craft and you should know them.

As with backpacks, stow stuff you'll need while paddling in easy-to-reach places, and keep the map and compass (and your powder) dry. Tie fishing rods and other non-floatables securely to the canoe, and spare paddles lightly to same. You may need them in a hurry. Bon voyage.

Packing and loading the canoe. All items should be packed in waterproof dry sacks or plastic garbage sacks. Heavy items should be centered on the bottom of the canoe with lighter items stowed above and around them. Necessity items should be stowed on top for easy access.

LIGHTWEIGHT & NECESSITY ITEMS

MEDIUM WEIGHT ITEMS

HEAVY-SOFT ITEMS

HEAVIEST ITEMS ON BOTTOM

LIGHT

HEAVIEST

LIGHTEST

Tips on Getting Acclimated

The week before your trip, you run around like the proverbial headless chicken, lists in hand, trying to arrange every detail while working an eight-hour day. You're up half the last night trying to finish packing. You leave early the next morning, drive hours to the trailhead and immediately begin to hike. You're at 7,000 feet, walking uphill, with the pack at its maximum weight. Your body is not accustomed to so much strain. All day you feel dizzy, nauseous, achey. That night your brain feels like it's trying to come out of your ears. You're camped at a beautiful lake at the top of the world, and all you want to do is crawl head first into your sleeping bag until the pain goes away.

Luckily this isn't inevitable. It needn't happen to you. With a little forethought and a few precautions, you can avoid Early Trip Discomfort (ETD). Here's how:

- Even if you have only a week for your trip, plan a whole day to drive to and sleep at the trailhead. That first night in the thin air will help acclimate your body to the first hard day on the trail.

- Eat breakfast. Anything which gives you protein, fat, and carbohydrate is adequate. Cheese and crackers, a granola bar, or peanut butter and jelly make a fine beginning. Most of your initial hiking will usually be over by early afternoon, so breakfast is the main source of energy for the day's challenges.

- You might want to use salt and aspirin. (This applies only to people not adversely affected by either of these substances. Salt can cause nausea; aspirin can upset the stomach.) The salt can be in food, such as salami, jerky or crackers. Some people take it in pill form or direct from the container. We also often take one or two aspirin first thing in the morning of a long hike.

- Start early. This is hard for the leisurely breakfast junkies, but that's invariably the most pleasant time to hike. The cool air is refreshing and you don't lose a lot of water through sweating. The sun isn't blinding, the rocks aren't hot, and by the time the afternoon thundershowers begin you've arrived at your destination and set up camp.

- Wear sunglasses and a hat or visor. You've heard of snow blindness, caused by the intense glare of the sun off a white snowfield. The same problems can be caused by reflections of sunlight from gray granite boulder fields. The mountain air is thin and the mountain sun is bright. While hiking, it's best to keep your eyes and face covered, especially for the first few days.

- Drink plenty of water. Stop on the trail when you get thirsty. Drink a few cups before the steep uphill climb. We carry a minimum quart of water for every two people, but it's not a bad idea start with even more. You can always pour it out if you're sure that the streams you expect to cross are running full, and you have the time to filter or purify the water. Several times we planned to fill the canteens at a stream which was running on the map but dry as a bone on the trail. That meant several miles of dry throats. In the spring, there's water everywhere. In the fall, however, be careful. Extra water is heavy, but it's much more uncomfortable to hike when you're thirsty.

- Don't be afraid to stop and rest, or vary your pace, which often accomplishes the same thing. The destination is rarely over that next rise. A steady slow pace will get you there with fewer problems and less pain than the sprint-and-collapse method. Remember the tortoise and the hare.

- Keep the carbohydrates coming. Stop for energy food about mid-morning, or carry a pouch of gorp to munch as you hike. We like semi-sweet baking chocolate, raisin cookies and ginger snaps. Sweets give you that instant pick-up you can use along the trail. If you know your limits and don't push too far beyond them, and if you're not afraid to stop and relax, you'll do just fine. Two days into the trip, you'll be hiking farther, breathing easier, resting as often as you like without fear that you won't get "there," and carbo-loading like a champ.

Crossing Streams

Many trails are constructed so that horses can cross streams. The trail crosses a stream at a level, wide area with a rocky bottom. A horse doesn't care about stepping stones. A horse also doesn't care if the water is one or five feet deep. Unfortunately, it's not as easy for a human to wade across in three feet of freezing, rushing water. A stream is always a wise place to take a break. Make it a point to ponder before you ford. Make it another point to scout the stream up and down for the best crossing.

One spring Rick and a friend were among the first backpackers on the trail after a wet winter. About halfway to their destination, they came to a stream running high, fast and cold. Sam, a first-time backpacker, took one look and decided that wading was not part of the original contract. So they renegotiated. Rick would wade across with both packs, one at a time. Sam would head a few yards upstream to a stretch of water which was deeper, but strewn with enough high boulders to let him step across. Sam balanced gingerly on the first boulder. He hopped to the next, then the third. Two more to go. The second-to-last boulder was unsteady. So was Sam. With arms flailing and eyes wide, he plunged into the foaming torrent. Luckily he only got a few bruises and soaked clothing. Had he decided to boulder-hop with his pack on—including his sleeping bag and all his extra clothes—it would have been a lot worse.

Late in the summer, when there's not much water flowing, you can hop from boulder to boulder without much trouble or danger of getting everything wet. But early in the spring, it's better to wade. You'll have to get wet. It's that simple.

Well, hopefully it's that simple. A pair of sneakers or tennies, which you've brought along to use in camp, come in handy here. The water is usually so glacial and the bottom of the stream so rocky that going barefoot is painful and dangerous. Just remove your socks, sling your boots around your neck, don the Converse and head in. If you didn't bring any sneakers, wear your boots, sans socks. Once across, drain your boots and put on a pair of dry socks, which will soak up most of the moisture as you hike on. At your next rest break, change into a second pair of dry socks, and by the time you get to camp your boots will be dry.

During the spring, the level of a stream rises noticeably during the day as the sun melts snowfields high above, and falls again each night as snow refreezes after sundown. The best time to cross a stream is early in the morning; the worst time is late in the afternoon.

Be especially careful of stream depth: *do not* confuse clear water with shallow. Mountain streams are often so crystal clear that what looks like a two-foot bottom might actually be six feet deep. It's a good idea to cross once without a pack to be sure you won't encounter any dangerous flows or depths. It's much easier to bail out and turn back with nothing weighing you down. Caution is the key.

It helps to carry a big stick or wading staff when crossing. You can distribute weight more evenly on three points than on two. As long as you walk slowly and carefully, with the staff downstream, and don't mind numb feet and legs, you'll get across safe and sound.

What about using a rope? It's possible, of course, and sometimes necessary. But our own rule of thumb is: if a crossing is so dangerous that it *requires* using a rope, don't do it unless it's *more* dangerous to stay where you are. In an emergency, a two-person party with about 150 feet of five-millimeter climb-

Crossing a stream with two people.

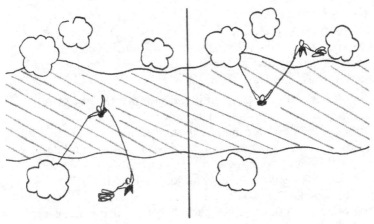

ing rope can ford a stream, as follows.

Step one. The rope is tied to a tree, wrapped once around the forder, then held by the anchor-person who stands downstream of the forder and pays out rope from the coil. The anchor person is *not* tied to the rope. The forder always faces upstream while crossing. If she/he falls, the anchor-person hauls her/him in. Once across, the forder waits while the anchor-person unties the rope from the tree. The length of free rope is then hauled over and tied to a tree on the far side.

Step two. The rope extends from the tree to the original anchor-person, who wraps it once around the waist and then tosses the remaining coil to the first forder. First forder walks downstream of the second forder and pulls in slack as the second forder, also facing upstream, makes her/his way across.

It may take two trips to get a single backpack load across a stream, because the stuff sacks which hang from the pack can't be left in place if the water is deeper than about two feet. When you're wading with a pack on, it's advisable to unbuckle the hip strap. That way, if you fall, you can release the pack easily and not get swept under or downstream by it. Once you've safely negotiated the stream and carried all the gear over, dry off, take another rest, repack, put the return crossing out of mind, and head up the trail.

Crossing a stream with three people.

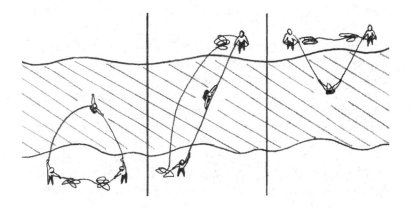

If a log happens to be across the stream just where you want it, don't let such luck go to your head. Take your time. Log walking above a rushing stream can feel like walking a tightrope. And like tightrope walkers, you may want to use a long stick or staff as a balance rod. Ideally it should be longer than you are tall, but it doesn't have to be. Hold it even with your waist as you cross the log. Also, beforehand, come to terms with everybody's sense of balance in your party. The surest-footed member should take the packs over. The unsurest should sit, straddle the log and inch across. And if you're traveling with dogs, one of you may have to wade across with them on a leash. We've never been able to persuade our pooches to walk the log.

Summing up, when wading across a stream, 1) wear sneakers or boots but not socks; 2) check depth; 3) use a big branch as a wading staff; 4) face upstream when crossing; 5) unbuckle your hip belt.

Hiking in the Rain

We once made a list of "Things to Do When it Rains," and hiking was at the top. That's because huddling in a tent or under a poncho can get awfully boring, and keeping everything in a campsite dry *without* cramming it all into the tent with you is a practically unattainable goal. If you can keep dry, hiking in the rain is fun, pretty, and actually easier than hiking in very hot conditions.

There are many "systems" for keeping yourself and your pack dry in the rain. We prefer to wear short ponchos designed to cover a person without a pack on. These can be used around camp without dragging in the mud, and while fishing in the rain. The special ponchos designed to cover you and your pack are so long they can be unwieldy. If the weather is warm, a short poncho and a pair of hiking shorts are ideal for a walk in the rain. So are plastic bags as foot protection for very young children who don't wear boots. They go over the socks and into tennies, cheap protection against soaked socks and feet.

Special backpack covers are sold at outdoor stores, but garbage bags are a lot cheaper and just as light. Punch two holes and feed the shoulder straps through before hoisting the pack onto your back. The garbage bags flap a little in the wind, but they keep the packs very dry. Buy the thickest ones you can find and carry one or two extras.

Sometimes there may be no getting away from a prolonged spell of foul weather. However, many summer rains are of the "afternoon thundershowers" variety. They come on fast, last a short time, then move off. Often, the mornings are gorgeous, and at 2 p.m. there's not a cloud in the sky. But by 4 you find yourself huddled in a forest as the thunder crashes around you and huge hailstones bounce off your head. From the comfort of a cottage a thundershower can be spectacular; at 8,000 feet, near the timberline, however, it can be terrifying and dangerous. You need to keep dry and stay safe—if possible among the smaller trees. Easy access to the plastic garbage bag and a poncho will let you stay dry and cover ground at the same time. Or, if you prefer to sit it out, protect your pack while you watch the thunder and lightning roll across the mountain tops. The poncho will keep most of you dry, and while you end up with wet boots, socks, and maybe pants legs, it's rarely enough to worry about.

However, when it rains, beware of hypothermia! It needn't be cold out—even wind and rain at 60 degrees Fahrenheit can make you dangerously chilled. The symptoms are uncontrolled shivering, followed by the inability to think clearly. Don't wait to reach your destination to deal with this. Get out of the wind and your wet clothes. Start a fire or crawl into a protected sleeping bag. Drink something hot. Huddle close to others who are dry. Rest and get warm.

If you're going to an area where it rains hard or for days at a time, this may require serious preparation. "Foul-weather gear" (like that used on sailboats), special backpack covers, boot covers, Gore-Tex wool parkas (which ingeniously keep the rain out while letting your sweat escape)—all or some may be necessary. Check out the weather conditions before you leave home. Most camping trips, however, are predicated on sunny weather, and wet ponchos or socks can usually be dried out in the warm morning sunshine.

Mud and Snow

From the hillside above, a lush Sierra meadow looks like a golfing green. But trying to hike across it in the first few weeks after snow melt is like trying to run through tapioca. Each step is an effort. Your boots get stuck in the mud. We've known people to lose their boots entirely in the slimy goo, pulling up their feet to find nothing but a sock on. If there's an alternative trail which skirts the springtime meadow, take it. It will save time, physical effort and mental exhaustion. It will also save the ecologically fragile meadowland.

Snow is normally considered a problem for winter backpackers, but it can stay on the ground long into the spring and summer. The trouble is, snow can be hard or soft, icy or slushy, sticky or slippery. It can be a pleasant stroll or a dangerous slide, and you need to be careful on it.

Mornings, snow is usually icy and slick. A very slight gradient can send your feet from under you. Even worse, it might start you sliding down an icy slope into a freezing river or lake. As the day progresses, the snow begins to melt. By late afternoon it may have turned into sticky slush. Like mud, this kind of snow is a disheartening inconvenience. It slows you down but isn't likely to hurt you. Beware, however, of "snow bridges" which may collapse during hot afternoons. A snow bridge is a layer of snow—perhaps a foot or more in depth—over a large hole caused by flowing water (from melted snow) underneath. Step on the bridge in the morning, and it will hold you. Do so in the afternoon and you'll fall through. A likely spot for snow bridges is next to large rocks, which absorb heat and melt snow from below at the same time the sun melts it from above. The result is a sort of ice cavern whose sides are prone to collapse when weight is put on them.

Our advice is try to avoid hiking over more than short stretches of snow. If you must, hike early. When you get to the snow line, don't plan to go much farther. If you know in advance that there will be a lot of unmelted snow on the trail, bring a pair of crampons to strap onto your boots. These are spikes which allow you to walk on icy or slippery snow with out much danger of falling. They won't help in very soft, powdery snow, for which you need snowshoes or cross-country skis, but they will get you safely through most springtime snow conditions with a minimum of bruises and sore muscles.

The other thing to consider before you tromp off above the snow line is that firewood up there is probably buried beneath a foot or two of wet slush. That makes cooking and warming a great deal more time-consuming and complicated. If you have to be up there, bring a good camping stove and fuel that works efficiently in cold weather. (See Chapter 3 for tips.)

Biking Tips: On Road and Off Trail

Cyclists need rest breaks, carbohydrates, liquids, and common sense, just as hikers do. Biking with a heavy load, even on flat, well-paved stretches, is a lot more strenuous than the day-biking you may be used to. Take a break. It can be short and sweet (if you let the chocolate melt in your mouth, not in your pannier). It's also restorative. Toes, hands, and butt go numb if you're too long in the saddle. Stop and walk some circulation back into these useful body parts. In fact, walk the bike up steep grades when the going gets too hard. Nobody's timing you. You can't come in last.

Like hikers, bikers need to have warm clothes and foul weather gear close at hand. The speed of a bike increases the wind-chill factor impressively. A 15-mph wind blowing in the face of a bicyclist traveling at 25 mph downhill is the equivalent of a 40-mph wind chill. Lesson? Dress warm in these conditions. And remember, as wind causes a bike to yaw with a heavy load, rain makes brakes less efficient. Steering feels sluggish, and sudden stops on steep grades can be dangerous. Hard weather makes a bike hard to control. It also cuts down visibility—yours and passing motorists'. Take it easy. Stay warm, dry, keep a helmet on and, where appropriate—on mountain trails or dusty roads—use safety glasses against dirt, twigs and bugs.

Up the Creek with a Paddle

Unlike most hikers and bikers, canoeists can arrange to go in one direction only. Downstream, for example, or (with a streak of masochism), upstream, or across a lake or inlet. With a car pickup at the end of the route, canoeists are the wilderness equivalents of Charley of the MTA—the paddlers that never returned. This means that the work load can be regulated more easily, or at least predicted with more certainty.

Predictability goes only so far, however, and you need to take basic precautions whether headed down the Grand Canal or across the local duck pond.

- Boarding and exiting the canoe are the choicest times for tipovers. Learn the proper techniques before entering the millrace.

- Prepare for rough water even if you don't expect to encounter any. When the wind comes up on a lake, things can get dicey. You can get swamped. Pull into shore, paddle in the lee of the land, take time out on an island. Turn *into* swells rather than taking them broadside.

- Learn (from a Red Cross course, a guide, or an experienced partner) how to "read" a river. The current usually flows faster in midstream and does tricks (which only physicists understand) at sharp bends. Stick to

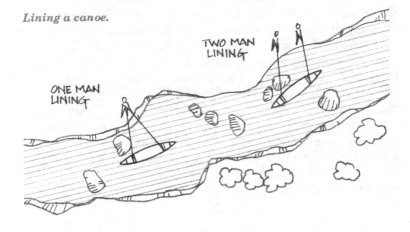

Lining a canoe.

TWO MAN LINING

ONE MAN LINING

the inside rather than the outside of a big bend for safer, easier handling. Ledges, rocks, "holes," falls all create flow problems which can be solved by proper handling techniques. We are not talking about *The African Queen* or riding Niagara in a barrel, but foreknowledge is a useful "hiking" tool on the river. Even then be prepared to get lost on occasion. The current is not always the surest guide to the main channel. Rainwater may obliterate a familiar river bank; drought may turn a navigable passage into marshland. When you dead-end up the Blackstone River, take a nosh break, scratch your head, mull over the situation, sigh, backtrack, and be comforted by the fact that your second cousin Rudy and a lot of other experienced deck hands have been here before you.

Use your ears as eyes. You can often hear a waterfall long before you can see it. At that point be prepared to pull in and portage around the fall. Unless you're Humphrey Bogart or Katherine Hepburn.

Boarding a canoe.

- Island hop at high tide. You don't want to return to shore when the tide's out for the simple reason that you'll have to schlep the canoe over hundreds of feet of mudflats.

- A rain poncho worn in high wind becomes a sail. Beware!

- As backpackers need to learn how to cross a stream, canoeists need to know how to walk a canoe through passages too rough or swift for paddling. You may have to use end lines attached to bow and stern to "track" a canoe upstream (or "line" it downstream) around obstacles. This can be done from shore, if not too impassable, or in wading water along the shore.

- Portaging engages the same techniques and attitudes as backpacking: slow and easy, lots of rest breaks, have a bite to eat. A portaging yoke allows one person to portage a canoe, but beware of neck injuries if you don't know how to use one. Two persons can easily carry a 70-pound canoe over the portage. You may have to go back for the packs if the load is too heavy, but call it a day-hike and enjoy. Local up-to-date printed guides may indicate portage trails, while older trails may still be marked by blazes. If you're unsure of where you are, take five and reconnoiter. Land bridges between bodies of water are usually accessible and short. Get a fix on the easiest route first and then heft the canoe and packs.

Dealing with Fears and Phobias

As we noted earlier, you take all of yourself into the mountains when you go backpacking. It's impossible to leave the bad parts behind. This means that your whole party has to deal with anyone's particular hang-ups, and you should know what they are before you go. But you should *not* let them stop you from going. Hal, for example, is scared of heights. Really scared. He learned it to his surprise about 20 years ago when he was half-way up a Mayan temple pyramid in the Yucatan.

Convinced that he was about to pitch backwards into space, he clung for dear life to the safety chain, inched to the top, sat down in a cold sweat, fantasized helicopter rescues and other humiliations, and eventually invented one of mountaineering's newest and most useful (if less graceful) techniques: "rappaporting."

Rappaporting is a play on the word "rapelling" and has nothing in common with it. To rappaport is to get from Point A to Point B *very carefully*. That's it. Any way you can do it, do it. It usually involves a good bit of frantic caution, inelegant clambering, and the use of the "sidle," as you inch your bottom and those jellied appendages called legs over the loose shale toward the haven of a firm root or branch or a six-million-year-old boulder. You can tell you're rappaporting when other members of the party, no more experienced than you, move confidently, even nimbly, on two sure feet over the same terrifying terrain.

In short, it's perfectly possible to live with a fear of heights in the mountains and enjoy the trip thoroughly. It's OK to laugh *with* the person who makes fun of his or her own phobia. It's *not* OK to laugh at them. A foreknowledge of the problem, a helping hand, plus a whole lot of support and common sense gets one, and therefore everyone, through.

The same is true in camp. One of our friends has an abiding fear of spiders. It means taking extra care that tent flaps and mosquito nettings are *always* tightly secured. And it means doing a careful spider search for that friend whenever the request is made. A little extra effort and support makes enjoying the outdoors both possible and fun for someone whose fears might otherwise preclude it.

Support for somebody's fears doesn't mean going gooey with concern or "manly" with false bravado. The person who is scared of heights more often than not doesn't need your hand, just a little more time. And the person who's scared of the dark or of mountain thunder doesn't need to be surrounded by firm shoulders to rest on. Unaffected presence is usually enough. In any case, let people know before you set out what may bother you; and let other people know also that it's all right to have their own bothers.

Mosquitos

In late spring, mosquitos can literally drive a hiker crazy. It's not so bad when you're camped, as you can escape into your tent and close it up. But when you're hiking through a meadow with a cloud of mosquitos buzzing around your ears and eyes, and sometimes up your nose or into your mouth, you will devoutly wish to be anywhere else on earth. Repellents, such as Cutter's or one of the war-surplus "jungle juices," will stop the little critters from biting, but it's the humming and buzzing that makes you want to throw yourself off the nearest cliff. Rest stops are pure purgatory, and it's not unusual for you to hike twice as fast and far as planned on total insane energy.

Two suggestions besides the repellent: mosquitos like grass, forest, water, and deep shade. So when you stop to rest, pick a spot as high, barren, rocky, and windy as you can find. Second, if you hear rumors in advance of a particularly bad mosquito plague in the area you're headed for, you can get lightweight mosquito-net hats which drop a circular netting from a round hat to your shoulders. This will keep the mind-wrenching buzzing away from your ears, eyes, and nose. A long-sleeved shirt and some repellent on your clothes will allow you to hike through even the worst mosquito-infested marshes.

Maps

In Chapter 2 we showed you how to obtain up-to-date Forest and Park Service and topographical maps. The first kind, which show distance and direction but not elevation, are fairly easy to read. Trails are marked by broken lines, roads by unbroken lines, unimproved dirt roads by double hash marks, marshes by grass clusters, that sort of thing. The symbols are standardized and you can learn them fast. Best of all, the symbols lie on a flat-plane surface (hence the technical name of the maps: planimetric) and are easy to locate and follow. Topographical maps, which show distance, direction and elevation, require some explanation.

A topographical ("topo") map does for the backcountry traveler what a street map does for the urban visitor. It helps in the planning of your trip: what's the safest and most convenient route between the trailhead and final destination, how far you want to hike each day, how high you want to climb, which day trips are possible and which aren't worth the effort, what kind of scenery you're likely to encounter—shale and rocks, long vistas, lakes and streams, high mountain meadows, granite passes. They're a little harder to read than the handy street plan of the South Bronx, but you won't, repeat *won't*, want to be without one in the wilderness.

How To Read a Topo Map

The most noticeable things on a topographical map are the thin brown lines running in circles and arcs and squiggles all over the place. These are contour lines, lines corresponding to a specific elevation above sea level. Here's how they work. Imagine a small island in the ocean. At low tide we might draw a line around the island where the water meets the shore. At high tide we might draw another line around the island. Perhaps high tide is 10 feet above low tide. So we now have two contour lines, one drawn at low tide, one 10 feet higher drawn at high tide. Imagine next a super high tide 10 feet above normal high tide. We draw another contour line around the island. And then a fourth, fifth and sixth line each where the water meets the shore if the water level keeps rising at 10-foot intervals. (See next page for chart.)

If the lines were large and distinct enough, we could draw the island as it looks from an airplane. Six lines, each representing the shape of the island at a specific height above sea level, would be visible from the air. Now, suppose one side of the island is a sheer 50-foot cliff. All the contour lines will converge on this side when viewed from above, because they are nearly on top of each other. The opposite side of the island might be a wide sandy beach. Our first contour line rings the beach at low tide. Much of the beach is underwater at high tide. So our high tide line (10 feet above sea level) appears far from the first line, nearly at the edge of the jungle. And our line 20 feet above sea level does not touch the beach at all; it's a line through jungle and rocky cliffs.

The lines are widely spaced on the beach area of the island and close together where there are cliffs. This is our first clue to reading topo maps. Two or more lines very close together mean a very steep grade or cliff. Two or more lines wide apart mean a gentle slope or relatively flat area. Thus, for example, a trail that crosses contour lines is a steep trail and one that runs parallel to the lines is level.

Our illustration below demonstrates this. There are places where the lines form Us, Vs and figure-eights. Whenever the contour lines form Us or Vs, they indicate either a ridge or a gulley/streambed. A ridge is indicated on the map by a set of U-or V-shaped lines pointing toward lower elevations. A streambed or gulley is marked by a set of U- or V-shaped lines pointing toward higher elevations. On the illustration, our ridge ends in a cliff overlooking the sea, and our streambed/gulley begins high up, at the 60-foot line, and descends to the sea in a series of inverted Vs. Imagine the view from the air. When the 60-foot line describes an inverted V—facing into the island center—it is traveling along the walls of a streambed. So are the other, lower lines. When the lines describe a V pointing out to sea, they are running along the slopes of a ridge. The figure-eights, observed from above, describe two mountain peaks separated by a fairly gentle slope in one direc-

How to read a topographical map.

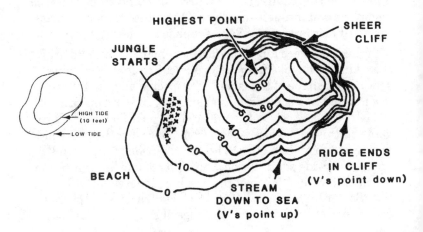

tion (east-west on our illustration) and by fairly steep gulleys in the other direction (north-south). This gives the contours a kind of pinched waist effect which translates into a figure-eight. (If you want some practice reading contour lines, see Bjorn Kjellstrom's *Be Expert with Map and Compass.* He even provides a couple of quizzes.)

The following four simple rules explain the contour lines on a topo map.

- Lines close together mean steep gradients.
- Lines farther apart mean gentle gradients.
- V-shaped sets of lines pointing to higher elevations mean gulleys or streambeds.
- V-shaped sets of lines pointing to lower elevations mean ridges.

Scales and Distances

A topographical map has two scales shown at the bottom margin of the map. One indicates distance as the crow flies, the other elevation between contour lines. The distance scale is called SCALE, and is represented by a ratio number, such as 1:24,000, meaning one inch on the map represents 24,000 inches (or 2,000 feet) in real linear space. Under that notation are usually three calibrated line figures which represent distance in miles, feet and kilometers. The elevation scale is called Contour Interval and tells you the vertical distance between the contour lines, such as Contour Interval 40 Feet. To make all these squiggles easier to follow, most topographical maps give real elevation readings along darker-brown contour lines every 100 or 500 hundred feet. Thus, for example, 7,500 will be marked along a dark brown line. There will then be several light brown contour lines and then another dark brown line with an 8,000 on it. You can figure out how hard or easy it'll be to climb up or down those 500 feet by reading the contour lines in between. Close together means tough going; far apart, it's a piece of cake. In either case it'll certainly take you longer than walking 500 horizontal feet along a dry meadow. By interpreting distance and elevation readings, you can plan how long and how far you can go in a day.

Topo maps come in different scales. If you see a map with a scale of 1:250,000, (meaning one inch on the map represents 250,000 inches or 20,833 feet in real linear space), a large distance can be crammed onto it—a whole national park, for example. That's great for a panoramic view of where you are in relation to the rest of the world, but it won't have the kind of detail you want for backpacking. Thus it is called a small-scale map: it contains a large amount of space but a small amount of detail. Always try to get the map with the most enlarged detail. Even if you have to carry two or three high-detail, large-scale maps to cover the distance you want to go, it'll be worth it. They foretell all the nooks and crannies, spurs and outcroppings, feeder streams and marshes you'll encounter, something to be thankful for.

How to Interpret Map Dates, Colors, and Symbols

Many maps, as we've noted, are outdated. Topo maps, mostly made in the 1950s from aerial photographs, then verified by survey teams, are great on permanent features such as mountains, but often not so great on impermanent roads and trails. Check along the lower border for the date of the map, and if necessary, try to locate a more up-to-date Forest or Park Service map to use in conjunction with it.

The picture from which a topo map is made supposedly was taken in a year of average rainfall during the dry season—late autumn in most parts of the country. The map should show all lakes and rivers at their driest stage. Still, there's no guarantee they'll be the same size or shape when you arrive. Much depends on the season and the latest annual rainfall. When you hike in the spring, that small creek marked on the map by a dotted blue line may be a raging torrent, too tough to cross. That same creek in the fall may be bone dry just when you were planning to stop for some fresh water. On the other hand, large lakes, rivers, meadows and most physical contours on the map will be just as they're supposed to be. Occasionally a flood or avalanche will have rearranged the topography, but on the whole you can rely on the topo map for contour accuracy.

Maps also show structures visible from the air when the area was photographed. Some are houses, cabins, ranger huts, or run-down old barns. Some may have rotted away completely. Take care not to depend on the topo map to find shelter from a storm. Those structures—even bridges—may no longer exist.

Finally, map colors are important. Gray represents treeless, rocky areas. White signifies snow or glacier. Green means forest. Mottled green or green-white shows meadowland. These colors help you hike by describing the terrain. Thus when you plan to leave a marked, manicured trail, it's important to consider not only contour and streams but also the *kind* of terrain you're heading into. A nearly flat manzanita forest is impassable. But the next hillside, while steeper, may be a pine forest crisscrossed with deer trails. Rocky areas are the easiest to cross but may take some climbing to get to. They're found mainly above the treeline at higher altitudes. Some terrain must be analyzed on the spot, but a great deal can be learned from the topo map's colors and symbols.

Bicyclists' Maps and Routes

Most people who tour on bicycles use automobile road maps and bike tour guides which include maps, elevation changes, distances and campgrounds. Here are a few hints if you are planning a bike tour without a guide book.

- Try to stay on the smallest rather than the newest or widest roadways. Local county roads are quieter, safer and more interesting than state highways (interstates don't permit bicycle traffic). Color- or letter-coded maps distinguish road size, paving, and jurisdiction.

- If there are no elevation markings on your map, look for mountain peaks and rivers. Once you determine which way a river's flowing, you can usually figure out how the road will run, uphill or down.

- Topo maps allow you to plan routes and adventures much more accurately than road maps. Large-scale, 1:250,000 topo maps of National Park or Forest Service lands are great supplements to up-to-date road maps.

- It is as important for a mountain biker to learn to use a compass and topo map as it is for a hiker or back-packer. Covering ground is one thing, knowing where you are is another. Get lost once and you'll become a convert to orienteering, the art of reading maps and compass.

Canoeing with Map and Sea Chart

Canoeists use topo maps too. The larger the scale (1:24,000 is a *larger* ratio than 1:240,000) the better, for what's at stake is the ability to pinpoint bends in the river, inlets, shoals, eddies, falls, flats, swamps and marshes. The curse of the back-packer is shared by the canoeist: a topo map seems never to be new enough, even if printed yesterday. Nevertheless a river- or lake-borne camper without a topo map is a camper in trouble. Streams can degenerate over the years into swamps. Small lakes can dry up. In tandem with a good, current local canoe guide, a topo map and the ability to read it will get you in and out of the wilderness in high fashion rather than high dudgeon.

What the topo map is to the land, the sea chart is to the water. In fact a sea chart is nothing but a topo map turned on its head. It reads the elevations and declensions under water. Coastal and island canoeing, large-lake canoeing require some ability to read sea charts and usually tide charts too. The big problem here is fog. It's the great disorienter, and without a compass and sea chart, you may be in the pea soup longer than is healthy. Get your bearings before the fog rolls in. Fix your destination on the compass and chart. Stay calm, take frequent readings, and trust the needle, not your nose.

Trails

A trail is constructed to certain specifications. It must be a certain width and level across its span. It must have drainage ditches or gutters to channel run-off rain water. Tree branches have to be cleared to a certain height above the trail to allow horseback riders to pass unimpeded. Also, a trail is allowed only a limited angle of inclination. If the grade is too steep, the trail must switch back and forth (hence "switchbacks") so it doesn't exceed the angle at which a horse can comfortably walk up or down. Of course not all trails comply at all points with all rules. But the vast majority of park trails were built with these standards in mind.

Trails are also maintained regularly. Trees are cleared, brush is trimmed, paths are rerouted on a regular basis in areas of flood damage or avalanche. Trail crews are hired or volunteer to bring the original trail back up to specifications and are paid by the mile. The work is checked by rangers who simply hike the trail behind them, and most parks keep records of trail maintenance. Occasionally a park will abandon a specific trail because it is used so rarely, or to give that particular sector of the backcountry an opportunity to regenerate. Sections of an unmaintained trail will disappear almost completely in three to five years. If you're planning to take what looks like an "out of the way" trail, it might be a good idea to check that it's being maintained before you begin. Any trail shown on the topo map but not on the more up-to-date Forest Service map should be regarded with suspicion. It may not be there any more.

Don't Cut Corners: They'll Wash Away!

It's difficult to construct switchback trails which won't wash out in the rain. To do this, the trail needs to have drains and run-offs in fixed places. When hikers decide it'll be faster to avoid the switchbacks by going straight up or down the slope, their footsteps tend to dig new drains across the switchbacks. When the rain begins to follow those new, irregular paths downward, the trail quickly erodes. The message, therefore, is clear and simple. When hiking switchbacks, don't cut corners. It'll be easier on your knees and feet to avoid a steep descent with a heavy pack and, more important, it saves the trail for those who come later.

Losing a Trail

Short Cuts

Short cuts are highly unpredictable. The terrain can be tricky or thick with vegetation. There's also the danger of getting lost. Short cuts often take longer than the route you're "cutting short."

On one of our first mountain trips we decided to take a short cut. It looked easy on the map: half a mile saved and all downhill. When we started out, we immediately ran into almost impenetrable brush—six-foot-high manzanita—solid and prickly. We couldn't see where our feet were landing. We got poked in the eyes. At points it was so steep we had to hang by the nearest branch, then slip and slide our way down. When the grade leveled off, we found ourselves over our heads in bush grass. The going was muddy, hot, slow, frustrating, and just plain dumb. We reached our destination more exhausted and tattered than if we had stuck to the trail. Luckily, we weren't hurt or lost.

Lost and Found

Even if you avoid shortcuts and have the right maps and a compass, it's still not hard to lose a trail. Trail markers may have been destroyed, junctions and turn-offs may be indistinct, or the trail may simply peter out at points. Finely crafted drainage ditches or dry streambeds might look more like the trail than the trail itself. Deer paths in the woods may seem to be the main one till they cross others that look exactly alike, at which point you begin to wonder where your partners went.

On a recent four-person trip we found ourselves lagging while our two companions wanted to hike faster. It was decided that they'd wait for us at the signpost to "Silver Lake" or at a trail junction. They bounded off without any maps, while we plodded slowly. About an hour later we realized that there'd been neither a sign nor a trail junction, and that we were well beyond Silver Lake. Doubling back, we found the signpost, broken off and obscured by brush, next to the junction,which was in an area too rocky and sandy to be seen. Meanwhile we had no idea if our companions had found the lake or not. So Hal sat at the junction with the packs while Rick hiked a mile to the lake, found no one there, and returned. Then Rick sat with the packs while Hal hiked down the main trail until he found our friends drying off after a trailside swim in a tiny lake they assumed was Silver Lake. Soon we were back together, but not without relearning a couple of lessons. First, never assume trails or crossroads are well-marked or marked at all. And second, never split up in unfamiliar territory.

There are several other things to keep in mind too. The most important is that as long as you have drinking water, food, and the shelter you carry on your back, you can make camp almost anywhere. If you can't find the trail, simply hunker down, take time to mull things over and meanwhile, enjoy your surroundings. Also, never let that pack out of your sight as you wander around in the woods looking for Route 66. And, for that matter, instead of plunging blindly ahead into the unknown, try to backtrack; that'll usually return you to square one and get you safely on your way again.

Often even a well-maintained trail can disappear as it crosses granite faces or other rocky terrain. There are no trees with blaze marks or ribbon markers to keep you on course, no boot prints in the dust. No dust! Only rock. You've stopped without a clue. Go back to where the trail is last visible. Check on your map how far you'll be walking over the rock face. Maybe it doesn't make any difference exactly where you walk if you can key in on your destination, and if the terrain is equally safe in the approximate vicinity of the trail. Above all, look for cairns (sometimes called "trail ducks"): three rocks set one on top of the other by some thoughtful hiker who knows the route. They are usually at regular intervals along the rock face or through an open, trackless meadow. Anyone who has ever lost a trail will be grateful to those anonymous friends who took the time to stop and build a cairn.

Other hikers not only sometimes mark the trail, but also often have advice that keeps you on course. Ask lots of questions of those coming from the opposite direction. Where are they coming from? How far is the nearest lake, campsite or watering spot? Where's the best fishing? Does the trail become hard to follow or is it well-marked all the way to your destination? Then *offer* information. Sit down, pull out maps and go over routes. Tell them which way to go. Remind them that a trail marker a mile back was hit by lightning and is no longer visible. They'll be as grateful to you as you are to them.

If, after all your efforts, you can't find a decent, well-marked trail, turn back. You may be on an unmaintained track. An alternative may have been constructed since your map was made. If you go on, assume that things may get worse and that for all practical purposes you will be doing a "cross-country"—that is, an off-trail hike.

Off-Trail Hiking

Slow and careful are the keys to cross-country or off-trail hiking. Cross-country hiking never works out exactly as planned, and you need plenty of time to stop, figure, and rest—off trail "bushwhacking" tires you out faster than on-trail hiking. Give yourself as much time to hike cross-country as you can. To do this, stay on the trail as long as possible before leaving it for the off-trail leg of your trip. Never start out late in the day if

Trail ducks.

you have to be somewhere by nightfall. You might need a whole day to negotiate the rock fall or steep ravine that stands between you and fabled Lake Mooselookmeeguntuk. Reaching your destination is always very slow; the return trip over now familiar terrain will be much faster.

We usually average a quarter mile per hour off the trail in the High Sierra or Rockies, half a mile or more in the Alaskan tundra or the high desert of Nevada. We never plan to cover more than one or two miles in a day. To start as early as possible, we camp near the point where we leave the trail. We *always* lay out our route in advance using the topo map, which is not difficult for such short daily distances. Just look for a route between two points that involves the least change in elevation. Try to avoid places where contour lines run close together. Even if only two lines seem to converge, that's a sheer 40-foot cliff—too steep to climb without experience, confidence and the proper gear. Keep the contour lines as far apart as possible when you plan a cross-country trek.

You must be careful with every step when off the trail. You can't let your mind wander to the scenery or to the snows of yesteryear. Eyes must stay on the ground just ahead, checking every footfall. There's lots of balancing to do, especially when hiking through brush. It saps strength, tears stuffsacks, snags fishing rods and anything else not properly battened down on your pack. If you have to go through brush, make sure all ties are double-knotted, all zippers fully zipped. Fishing and tent poles must not stick up above your pack or they will be broken by low-hanging branches. You might fall. In that case fragile objects inside your pack—camera lenses, eggs—may break unless they are properly cushioned. Liquids not tightly contained and encased in plastic will run all over everything.

Keep your hands free to clear brush or grasp at branches to pull yourself along. Mark your route if possible with bits of colored cloth or rope tied to branches so you don't get turned around or lost. And stay together! It's too easy to get separated and lost in thick growth.

Hiking over boulder fields is more common in the high mountains than crashing through brush. It helps to wear hiking boots (rather than tennis or jogging shoes), so the soles are not torn up by walking and balancing on the corners of large boulders, and the ankles aren't twisted by the precarious angles. Again, keep your hands free; use them to hold on when you can. Try to test each rock or boulder with light foot pressure before putting all your weight on it. If the rock is wobbly, be careful. It can send you and your 40-pound pack tumbling down a field of granite boulders.

It's generally easier to hike uphill than downhill when you're making your way off the trail. You can plan an uphill route from below, with a good view of the entire hillside. Going down, you're likely to come to a steep gradient you couldn't see from above. Suddenly you're staring down at what seems a sheer cliff.

Never assume a straight line is the safest or easiest way from here to there. Use the topo map wisely. Once you figure out the best route try to stick to it closely so long as it proves safe and feels right. The important thing is not to walk yourself into a place you can't return from.

If the going gets too tough, you can stop, turn, or go back. There's no requirement to get anywhere by any time. Never feel pressured to continue even your own pre-planned route. Stay flexible, stay cool, and don't be afraid to change plans and routes. There are other lakes to fish, other streams to camp along, other routes to the same place. There's no need to do something you're afraid of off-trail. Knowing that is the difference between a novice and an old-timer.

Getting Your Bearings Off-Trail

How do you prevent getting lost off the trail? Plan well, stay highly alert and observant, and keep track of both what's ahead and behind you.

First, pre-plot your route carefully. Know, for example, that it will take you over a ridge, along the flank of a 10,000-foot peak, down a granite field, then up a stream and through a meadow toward the lake. Keep these features on the surface of your mind. Before you leave the trail, take a hard look around for all distinctive landmarks: a strange rock outcropping, a tall barren tree once struck by lightning and thus black against the green forest, a distant mountain peak.

Note what lies in the direction you're headed. Think how the appearance of these landmarks will change as you hike cross-country. And look for features you know are on your route.

You may or may not plan to return by the same route. Nevertheless, you may *need* to get back to the trail at this same spot, especially if your route proves impassable and you must turn around. Thus, you might want to mark your trail. Cairns, colored ribbons strung on branches and retrieved if you return, green vegetation hung on a barren branch—all give you a sense of confidence that is more than worth the additional time you spend doing it. Also, if you do intend to come back the way you went in, a marked course will save you one final embarrassment—walking right past the maintained trail. It's surprisingly easy to miss an "obvious" trail, and frustrating, doubling back till you do find it. If you mark everything from the start, you can avoid that problem on a day when you may have to hike out, drive home, and get to work.

More precise than sighted landmarks or marked routes is a combined use of the topo map and a compass. They can help you decide where you are and where your destination is relative to you. There are whole books on the use of compass and maps (see the Book List); what we give you here is a quick digest of the main points.

Whether you have a compass or not, practice with the topo map on the trail, before you really need it. When you reach

The compass.

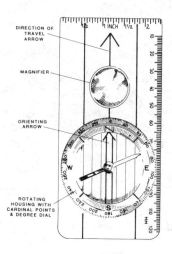

DIRECTION OF
TRAVEL
ARROW

MAGNIFIER

ORIENTING
ARROW

ROTATING
HOUSING WITH
CARDINAL POINTS
& DEGREE DIAL

open places, try to locate where you are on the map by observation alone. Do this by orienting the map to two or more ob-
servable landmarks, then draw imaginary (or real) lines from
them back toward "yourself." Where the lines intersect is approximately where you are. (See below.)

Now do the same thing with your compass. First orient the
map. That means getting it aligned with the real world out
there. Set the map on a flat rock, placing the edge of your compass on the magnetic north (MN) declination line marked on
the bottom margin of the map, and twist map and compass together until the north-pointing needle is lined up with the 360
or 0 degrees mark on the compass. (See pg. 151.) Now your
map is properly aligned and you're ready to go to work. Take
sightings on two or more identifiable landmarks, the farther
away (though still represented on your map) the better.

Here's how you take a sighting. Hold the compass in your
hand. Point the Direction-of-Travel arrow toward the landmark. (The assumption here is that you have an "orienteering" compass, see pg. 149.) Now twist the compass housing till
the north-pointing needle is lined up with the orienting arrow
at the bottom of the housing. That's all. Just read the number
of degrees which come up on the edge of the housing facing
the landmark.

If you don't have an orienteering compass, face the landmark, holding the compass in front of you. Slowly rotate the

Plotting position by observation.

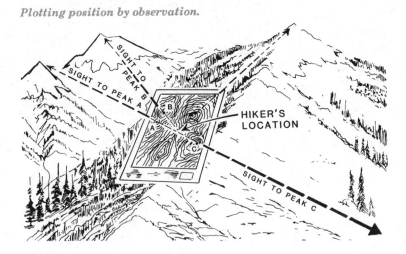

SIGHT TO PEAK B

SIGHT TO PEAK A

HIKER'S
LOCATION

SIGHT TO PEAK C

compass till its north-pointing needle lines up with the N on the housing. Don't rotate yourself! Now read the number of degrees facing the landmark.

Say the reading is 330 degrees. Once you have a first reading, take a second or third on other landmarks, the farther from each other the better. In the illustration below, the second reading is 32 degrees. Now go back to your oriented map, set one edge of the compass on the first landmark and then rotate the compass, still keeping the edge in contact with the landmark, till the north-pointing needle again lines up with

Map orientation with a compass.

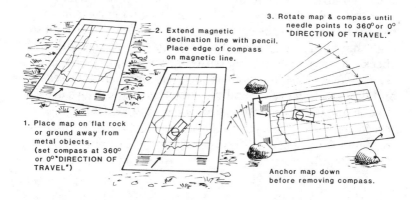

Map orientation without a compass.

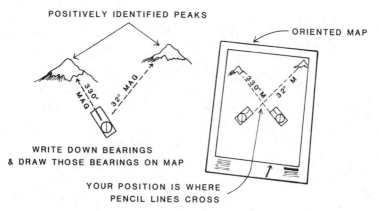

the orienting arrow, giving you a 330-degrees reading on the map. Draw a line along the compass edge back toward yourself. Repeat for the second landmark and maybe a third. Where the lines intersect is where you are. You can now determine from the map how much farther it is and how rough the terrain will be between your present location and your destination.

A final word of caution. Your sightings, readings and orientings may be correct but there is still a chance you'll end up with approximate, rather than pinpoint, locations. You may trudge on for an hour, reach the top of a rise and expect to see the promised lake. Instead you see another rise, like the bear that went over the mountain. You take more readings and bearings and come up with the same results. You have moved, but those distant peaks on which you sighted are so far and so high that to them you haven't moved at all. Keep the faith, check your progress vis-a-vis closer landmarks, and take it slow and easy. The lake is there, over one or two more rises, and if the footing is sure and the sun is up, you'll arrive in time to unpack, set up camp, drop a line and cook a fine trout supper.

CHAPTER 7

Setting Up Camp

Choosing a Campsite

A campsite must meet two minimum requirements to provide
the kind of comfort you've promised yourself after all those
miles on the trail. It has to have access to water and offer a
sheltered place to sleep. You usually find those essentials
where the trail crosses a stream or meets a lake. Ideally what
you want is a level, sheltered area, complete with fire ring and
tent sites. Often you'll get just that, because the people who
build or maintain trails have been there first and know that
people and pack animals require these amenities. Try to stop
at a site that's been used before rather than hew out a new
one from scratch. You'll do less harm to the environment and
work a lot less hard as well.

Canoeists want the same sort of deal—convenience, shelter,
comfort, a great view. But they need one other thing as well:
access *from* water. It's hard as hell to haul a 70-pound canoe
up a vertical incline to Pocahontas' Boudoir, and you may
have to settle for Joe Sixpack's favorite inlet and pool hall.
Nose around and ask questions aforehand.

Be forewarned that campsites vary with the season. That babbling brook you had your heart set on may have withered away late in the season, leaving you with a waterless gully. Mapmakers draw stream lines to conform to springtime reality. Check water sources as you hike. If the map shows blue and you find sere dust or a mud flat, suspect that other streams in the same area will be dry as well. Ask the local rangers about drought (or flood) conditions before heading into the backcountry. Choose your campsites accordingly.

Our favorite campsites are high mountain lakes, full of fish but not full of campers. Most picture-postcard lakes—the kind you see on the cover of Sunset Magazine—have wide and well-maintained trails to them. They're accessible to large groups, either on foot or horseback. The crowds at these lakes can get oppressive, especially on weekends and holidays. We like to get off privately to swim, sun and have fun. Usually this means scouring the map for a mountain lake off the trail, one we can call our own, if only for a few days.

We also love to catch, cook and eat trout—another consideration when seeking an off-trail lake on the map. Trout require a lake deep enough that it won't freeze solid during the winter. Lakes at or near the tree line get colder sooner and remain frozen longer, and cannot support the insect life that fish need to survive. In addition, the higher the lake the less firewood there is for our cooking projects. You'll find the best fishing at a lower-elevation lake with water flowing through it. If it's surrounded by meadows, don't plan on catching anything but mosquitos. In fact, you might find nothing but mud if you get there late in the year. Steep cliffs and sheer rock walls rising from one bank are an indication of a deep section, which may contain fish.

At times you'll want to spend a night on a ridge or peak—without access to running water. There's nothing so spectacular as the night sky seen from a summit. Sunsets and sunrises alone make it well worth the inconvenience of carrying water up there. We figure about a quart per person will get us through dinner and a morning hike down without doing any dishes. We wash them later when we get to the next water source (though never in it).

Once you've arrived at fabled Lake White Fish, choose a campsite with care. A free-running stream or wilderness lake requires a light touch and distance. Foul it and the whole idea of backcountry camping goes down the drain. Locate tent, fire ring and washing-up areas at least 100 feet away from the water, and even farther if it's safe and convenient. That way, spills will be filtered somewhat should they get back into the water. Remember too that any water you drink should be treated, boiled or filtered first: giardia stalks even the clearest springs.

Many hikers bring a collapsible, two-gallon container for storing water at the campsite. This is especially convenient if your camp is some distance from your source—for example, if the mosquitos are swarming down near the lake. In the absence of such a container, make do by filling all your pots and canteens, then covering them with lids or metal plates. Do this before dark. It's hard to carry two pots of water and hold a flashlight as you scamper up a steep grade to your campsite.

Tentsite

The sole requirement for a tentsite is that you can sleep there. This means different things to different people. We knew one old-timer who never carried an Ensolite pad. Instead, he'd stop early in the afternoon and work for at least two hours preparing his sleeping site. He meticulously smoothed the earth, picked out all the rocks and twigs, then laid down a soft bed of pine needles and fallen leaves. Finally he spread his sleeping bag down on the soft bed just in time to go fishing.

Before you choose a tentsite, look carefully at the drainage system of the surrounding hills. More than once we've set up in a likely looking area, flat and sandy, near a lake, only to discover it turned into a large mud puddle in the rain. Mountain rains often come suddenly and hard. Flat sandy areas can become Lake Superior in 20 or 30 minutes, putting you and your tent under two or three inches of water.

Another consideration in choosing a tentsite is the ability to stake your tent. While newer dome-type tents do not require stakes, most small tents need secure staking in the ground. This makes them difficult to set up in granite or sandy areas. In such spots, lay the stake flat on the ground and pile rocks on top of it, or wedge it in a granite rift. Sometimes you can tie the tent ropes to boulders or tree branches instead of to stakes. Sandy campsites present similar problems: the stakes shift easily or pull out. Every time the tent is bumped, the stakes slip a little and pretty soon the tent sags like a suspension bridge. Both rocky and sandy areas require extra care when you enter or leave the tent.

In foul weather, stake both rainfly and tent. The rainfly should completely cover the tent in order to shed water several inches away from the base of the tent, beyond tarp or groundcloth. Even then, you may still be in trouble if the uphill side of the rainfly funnels the water against the tent side or onto the groundcloth. The telltale sign will be a puddle inching across the floor of the tent in mid-storm. At that point, your options are cut to the bone. Use the small towel or sponge you've brought along to sop up the water. Wring out and repeat. This will keep you busy and your mind off murder. Get out and fix the rainfly's drain-off system. Or slosh around till the rain passes, make do as well as you can for the rest of the night, and hope for warm sunshine in the morning to dry you out. Next time site the tent farther from that potential Victoria Falls.

A rainfly should also be stretched or staked so that it clears at least an inch of the tent itself. If the rainfly simply lies on top of the tent, internal moisture from breath and sweat won't be able to escape, and by morning, you'll be cold and clammy even if it's warm and dry outside.

Finally one word about digging drainage ditches around your tent: *Don't*. They scar the land and, when filled with runoff water, erode the earth. You won't stay dry, but you'll literally diminish the wilderness.

Many people camp with only a sleeping bag and poncho or tarp. The poncho can be rigged up between or under trees or bushes to form a roof and keep you out of the rain. The canoe turned over can shelter you from a light rain, and rigged with a tarp can provide adequate protection if the wind is not up. If you use a tarp, carry some light nylon cord to secure the ends.

Some tarps have grommets or reinforced holes; otherwise use Visclamps (purchased separately) which act as portable grommets. Also useful are four metal tent stakes, which can anchor a tarp to the ground.

As long as the ground stays fairly dry, such shelter is adequate for most summer showers. A tentless pack is that much lighter, but it takes a fair amount of ingenuity to stay dry in really stormy weather (to say nothing of mosquito-proofing). And a wet sleeping bag can take days to dry out. Even if you plan to sleep under the stars, put up your tent (or tarp) as a precaution. Nothing changes faster in the mountains than the weather.

Campfires

Campfires have a magic all their own. Staring into the fire late at night gives you a sense of peace and security that is hard to match at home. Our trips into the mountains center around hot meals, which invariably center around the campfire. Cooking, baking, sipping hot chocolate, heating water for dishes or washing all require a well-tended hearth.

Wilderness campfires consume tremendous quantities of wood, however. In many areas of the mountains that wood is becoming very scarce, and fires are not permitted. This is particularly true at high elevations and along well-traveled trails. Even where it's legal to gather wood for a campfire, follow your conscience rather than the letter of the law. If you see that there's little deadfall wood left, leave it. Give nature a breather. Sacrifice the fire. Use the stove instead and cook your meals quickly. Or eat cold food on evenings when you camp in impacted areas. You may be rewarded for your fireless evening by a host of interesting sights and sounds usually obscured by the light and crackle of the fire.

Let's assume though, that you're camped at a lower elevation lake or stream, a couple of miles off the trail. There's plenty of dry wood on the ground. You plan to stay here a couple of days and your mouth is already watering with culinary intentions. First you need a fireplace.

A backcountry fireplace is nothing more than a circle of rocks with earth in the middle. Fires feed a constant shower of sparks into the air. While there's little wind, these are entirely harmless. But a sudden gust can blow the sparks toward combustible material, and you can quickly have a forest fire on your hands. If your campsite already has a fireplace, use it. Just be sure to clear the ground for four or five feet in all directions and check for dead, dry branches hanging less than 10 feet directly over the fire area.

For cooking and baking, we usually modify existing fireplaces, or construct from scratch new ones of our own design. The back of the fireplace is made narrow to support a small camp grill. The front of the fireplace has one or two rocks that are easy to remove. We clear an additional area in front of these for baking, and surround this area with a ring of stones. At baking time, we remove both rocks, and rake hot coals into this ring. Meanwhile, we can heat dishwater or stir-fry vegetables on the back grill.

As you construct different campsites, you'll get different ideas on how to modify the basic fireplace to meet your needs. If a wobbly rock sends a full pot of water tumbling into the fire, you won't let that happen the next night. You'll firm up the rocks to make a more stable base for the impending souffle. Next you may discover there isn't enough draft the way this fireplace is constructed, and you'll need to build the back higher than the sides. And you'll doubtless find that the artistic fireplace you come across at the Arcadian lake of your dreams is just too big for your one pot. It would be fine for U.S. Steel or a party of 30 with mules, but... So you hack and haul, sculpting a new, smaller, lighter and more efficient version on the same site.

It's useful to collect firewood in a variety of sizes. Small dry twigs are great for starting fires, but burn too quickly for cooking. Large, long logs burn for hours, but won't fit under the grill for heating a pot of water. We bring a camp saw to cut large logs into shorter, easy-to-use lengths, which can last longer. The saw is lightweight, folds into itself for safety, and can be sharpened at a saw shop between trips. It is *never ever* used on living trees, only on uprooted deadfall wood.

If you have to go far to gather the wood, bring a poncho to carry extra smaller pieces back to camp in fewer trips. But don't use it as a sack; it's guaranteed to tear. Rather, wrap the wood in the poncho and cradle the whole load in your arms. We also take a pair of garden gloves which help save the hands when we gather firewood. They also double as pot-holder mittens. In the cooking chapter, we tell you how to use the fire most efficiently.

Starting a Fire

Late in the summer, in a forested campsite, you'll find plenty of dry kindling. If you can bend a twig back against itself without breaking it, it's too wet for kindling. The best kindling will snap in two with a loud crack as soon as you bend it.

Start with the smallest, driest kindling you have. Keep a pile of it in reserve to add to the first flames. Remember that fires need lots of air. Too much fuel creates too much smoke which keeps the air away, so the fire goes out. Start your fire with a small, well-ventilated flame at the bottom, a space for

air, then another layer of wood. You can shape this like a tepee, a lean-to, or a log cabin. Make sure the kindling is burning well before adding larger pieces of wood.

So far so good. It's easy to start a fire with good dry kindling. But what if it's wet? Old-timers may tell you to break lower branches off live trees for kindling. These lowest limbs are actually deadwood and, if they fan out into small twigs, are fine for starting a fire even in rain or snow. But the idea of breaking dead branches from living trees is ecologically repugnant. Most campsites are surrounded by stripped trees for a 100 yards in all directions. It looks like the area was bombed from the bottom up. Don't break branches off trees *except in an emergency.*

We often use the pages of our paperbacks to start fires. We usually read 30-70 pages a day, between trailside rest stops and afternoon cooking sessions, so we have plenty to burn. Paper or cardboard from food containers is also great for starting fires.

Another easy way to start fires is to use a flammable liquid or gel. If you have a kerosene or alcohol stove, the fuel can start wood burning in wet conditions. Some people bring a small can of lighter fluid for emergency fire starting. If you do use a flammable liquid, *never* pour any onto a fire that is already lit or smoldering. It may ignite the can you're pouring from! You can also buy fire starter in a tube, like toothpaste.

OK. The kindling is burning, whether it's dry or wet. Now for the larger pieces. The point is to build a fire gradually. Onto the kindling go larger dry branches. When they're well lit and flaming (not smoking), place a log or two gently on top, leaving plenty of air space between the pieces of fuel. Larger logs are likely to be dry inside. Once you get them burning, they'll keep burning even in a drizzle or mist. If there's protection above them, they'll burn in the rain. We often place a layer of rain-dampened logs about three feet above the fire between two piles of rocks. This wooden roof protects the fire from rain and dries the logs at the same time. When these logs get dry enough to burn, they can be pushed into the fire and replaced. With a little ingenuity, you can cook and eat in the rain without much trouble.

One last word on fire-starting frustrations. The fire has started. The cardboard is burning. You add some more wood, but it's wet and the fire starts to go out. Frantically, you squeeze some fire starter onto a stick and throw it into the embers. It flares up, flames for a minute, then dies again. What now? Our advice is to stop, let it go out and start over from the beginning. We've seen novices waste reams of paper and tubes of fire starter trying to burn wet wood. Remember, a good fire starts with good kindling. For the second attempt, gather drier twigs and branches, even if you have to walk deeper into the forest or desert to find them. Keep a larger supply of dry twigs to add to the fire as it starts to burn. It will work: guaranteed! And at the next campsite, you'll gather the right combination of wood sizes and dryness to start the fire easily the first time.

Food Storage

Little Critters

The squirrel family is undeniably cute. All of them: chipmunks, prairie dogs, ground squirrels. They are positively Disney Worldish in their lovability. They'll approach fairly close, stand up on hind legs, rub front paws together and chirp. It's tempting to reward them with a morsel or two. Squirrels are also smart and voracious. They're world-class experts at stealing your stash. Chewing through a pack and several layers of plastic and cardboard is child's play for them, leaving you with a shortfall of precious food.

A cardinal rule of backpacking is *never feed the animals.* It is unfair *and* dangerous. Instead of applying themselves to their natural food, they've discovered an easier, tastier way to fill up. If you feed them, or leave leftover food behind, it makes them dependent and renders them less able to survive in their natural habitat. That's the danger to them. The danger to you, aside from the loss of some closely budgeted food, is a possible bite, which can be painful and sometimes septic.

A family or two of rodents living in or near any well-used campground is inevitable. They come out mostly at night and look for food. They are so used to finding food in backpacks that they will often chew through your pack even when all food has been removed and hung high in a stuffsack. All edibles should be hung up at night, if possible (see illustration, pg 164). Should you find rodent toothmarks on your cheese, just cut off the chewed portion and eat the rest. We've never heard of anyone getting sick by eating the untouched part. And a nibble-sized hole in a pack or pouch is easily sewn up.

We react similarly to ants and bees, brushing off those in the packets and eating the food. These insects can be kept out by packing food in tightly sealed plastic bags. Another common problem is food spilled inside the pack. The pack was set flat on the ground rather than upright, and the maple syrup, like flowing water, sought and found its natural level. Clean up as you might, the ants and bees will love that pack even when it's empty. But they never seem to do any harm.

The Long Hot Summer

Our worst problem with food is storage on hot days. Keeping your stash out of the mid-summer sun in a rocky campsite can be a 14-hour struggle. Not all food is harmed by excessive heat, but such things as cheese, eggs, and chocolate are. At the beginning of the trip you tend to throw chocolate bars into nooks and crannies of the pack to save space. But if they're not double-bagged in plastic, and if you set your pack down in the blazing, afternoon sun, a melted chocolate mess will be oozing through your pack. If you're in the desert or there are no deep-shade trees around camp, you have to figure out other ways of keeping food out of the sun. Don't try leaving food in the tent all day. Tent fabric is so thin it works more like a greenhouse than a refrigerator. Sometimes the side of an old tree trunk or a rock ledge may have a shady spot at its base. Or you might rig a poncho or tarp to block the sun from the food pack.

Bears

We've heard lots of bear stories: automobile trunks ripped open by powerful paws; mama-and-cub teams getting to "bear-proof" bags hanging high on guy wires strung between trees; meeting bears on trails; and even "playing dead," hoping that a bear wouldn't maul a camper after it ate all his food several feet away. We even have a few stories of our own, but like taxi stories—driver *and* passenger!—enough is enough. The point is that if you take a few precautions, you can share the wilderness safely even with the big critters.

The most important rule for dealing with bears is to be forewarned. Find out about them and plan a strategy before you reach bear country. Ask the ranger when you apply for your permit. Consult with the guard at the park entrance. Try to plan your trip to avoid campsites that have a reputation for bear troubles, such as Troublesome Creek Campground in Denali State Park—named for bear encounters!

Bear-Proofing the Food Stash

If you'll be camping in problem areas, learn if there are bear-proof wires at any of the campsites. These are steel cables, about 3/8 of an inch thick, strung about 20 feet off the ground between two stout tree trunks. If there are wires, you only need 50 feet of rope and two stuffsacks. Here's what you do.

Divide your food between the stuffsacks. Throw one end of the rope over the wire (tying a rock to it will help). Tie a stuffsack to the other end. Hoist the stuffsack about 20 feet into the air. Tie your other stuffsack to the rope as high as you can reach. The two sacks should roughly balance each other, one about six feet off the ground, the other about 20 feet up. Don't leave any extra rope hanging; stuff it inside the sack. With a long stick, raise the bottom sack as high as you can. Raising it to about 15 feet will lower the other sack to about the same height. And there you have it: two food-laden stuffsacks suspended about 15 feet off the ground. The wire is too thick for a bear to cut or tear and the sacks are too high for mom or her cubs to reach. You can sleep soundly. In the morning you'll need a pole long enough to push one sack up until the other is low enough to grab. Usually such a pole sits next to the wire and is easy to recognize.

If rangers or other campers tell you of a bear problem and there are no bear-proof wires in the area, you have several options. The first is to camp elsewhere. Bears don't *naturally* bother people or eat their food. They learn over time, like squirrels, that it's easier than foraging. They tend to have a territory that they regularly patrol in search of campers, food-sacks and garbage. If you're on their route, they'll try their luck with your goods. The farther away you get, the less likely they'll come to your campsite. An extra afternoon of hiking

Hanging foodstuffs.

will often give you enough room that you needn't worry. Hiking three miles from that scenic lake and camping along a stream might save a week's food.

A second option is to rig up your own bear-proof system of hanging food sacks. Getting a tight line 20 feet off the ground between two trees isn't easy, but it is possible if you persevere. Or you might just hoist the food 15 feet up by looping it over a single high branch. Another plan is to use a cliff ledge. While bears can climb trees, they cannot climb rock faces. If you find a cliff or ledge 12 to 15 feet up, and if you can reach it, the bear won't be able to.

The third choice is just to leave the food in your pack or in a stuffsack on the ground. You might fasten some cups or forks or spoons onto the drawstrings. Then go to sleep and hope that: 1) no bear appears, 2) failing that, you hear it beginning to rustle your food, and, 3) you are in the presence of one timid enough to be scared away by a furless, clawless and fangless human being banging pots and throwing rocks. We've done it and it's worked. But be careful. It's better to lose your food or your pack than to tangle with an angry bear.

Grizzlies

Outside Glacier and Yellowstone national parks and Alaska, most of the bears you'll encounter in the wilderness are black bears. They're interested in your food, but aren't intent on doing you any harm. What if you meet such a bear on the trail? If you remain calm and back off, the bear will probably do the same. Never get between a mama and her cub though. Don't surprise or scare a bear. And never back one into a corner. If you're worried about bumping into bears on the trail, make a lot of noise as you hike. Forewarned, the bear will avoid you.

Grizzly bears (and their relatives, brown bears) are something else. The only major grizzly populations in the Lower 48 are in Glacier and Yellowstone. Here the bears are very dangerous, being garbage-fed and unpredictable. They have been known to hurt people, seemingly for no reason. When antagonized (and just entering their territory can be antagonistic), it's possible they'll attack instead of waddling off. If you're entering grizzly country, you have to be much more careful. One veteran put together these rules:

- Make a lot of noise as you walk, especially when you're in thick forest or tall brush where visibility is limited.
- Try to hike with others. Numbers sometimes discourage bears.
- Leave the dogs at home. They can rouse a grizzly to a fright and fury.
- Camp, when possible, near a climbable tree. (Grizzlies don't climb trees. Though they can shake the hell out of 'em!)
- Try to cook (and hang your food at night) 200-300 yards downwind of your sleeping area. Have a separate set of "cooking clothes" and hang them up also with your food at night.
- Never bang a pot or throw a rock at a grizzly.
- Carry a spare stuff sack. If the grizzly gets your food, you'll still have a sack for your sleeping bag.

Stormy Weather

Most first-time backpackers have a negative attitude about rain, considering it "bad" weather. At home, you don't go out into the rain or cold for fun. You stay indoors, turn the thermostat up, and watch TV. The backpacking equivalent of that attitude is to set up the tent, put on the rainfly, and curl up in your sleeping bag until the sun comes out. But it doesn't take long to realize the quarters are a lot more cramped in a puptent than in your living room. You get claustrophobic. You want to stretch. Every time you go out for a snack, you track water back into the tent. Soon, you start to get depressed about the weather.

There is a different attitude toward stormy weather, however, one worth cultivating. The rain is another mood of the mountains, creating a unique beauty in altered sounds, smells and perspectives. Get out of your tent and enjoy it. In fact, we often take our tent down when it starts to rain and use the ground cloth and rainfly to make a porch and covered cooking area. We store the packs under plastic garbage bags. Once the clothes and sleeping bags are secure, we can go about our business. We read in the rain, cook in the rain, fish in the rain (often the best fishing), and sometimes just sit and watch the lightning in the distance, listen to the thunder as it rolls closer, and view the rain-washed lake and mountains.

Then the storm is past and the skies begin to clear. As long as you stay warm with several layers of clothes, and dry with a poncho on you or strung up above you, you can weather bad weather in good spirits.

There is no such thing as "normal" mountain weather. The hottest days often come in September. July thundershowers can turn to hail and snow at upper elevations. A clear morning can be followed by a wet, miserable afternoon. You have to be prepared for it all. Our guidelines are:

- A poncho for every person.
- A rainfly and groundcloth for every tent.
- A garbage bag for every pack.

These are admittedly conservative. Many people do it with less. The more experience you have, the better you can manage with less protection. It's frustrating to pack rain gear around for nine or ten days and never use it. On the other hand, people who pack in less rain gear often plan to do a lot of hiking each day. Since it's more likely to rain in the afternoon in the mountains, they plan to hike through the storm and need only keep themselves and their packs dry. Our idea of backpacking, however, stations us at a campsite most afternoons, either because we hike only in the morning or because we stay in one place for two or three days at a time. So when we see that first hailstone bounce off the ground, the extra gear is suddenly worth its weight in gold.

Washing Up

Pollution in the high country is disheartening and unnecessary. If you find a gum wrapper on the trail, you can pick it up and carry it out yourself. But if you see soapsuds along the shore of a lake, it's too late to do anything about it. Don't let detergent get into the water in the first place—that's the only time to stop it.

Never wash dishes in a lake or stream. Carry them and a pot of hot water at least 100 feet away into the woods or sage. Put two drops of biodegradable liquid soap in a small pot, then add about a third of the hot water. Wash each dish or pot with this until the food particles are gone. Rinse out the sponge, then rinse each dish with the clean sponge and the remaining hot water. One pot is plenty for all the washing up after a four-person meal. If even that amount of soap offends you, do without it. A good scrubbing with a "Tuffy" or even pine needles gets utensils clean. Use the same washing spot for several days, 20 or 30 yards from camp. Though it will attract flies and bees, it will impact the environment less and make campsite clean-up easier and more thorough.

Do your laundry the same way. One pot for soapy water and one for rinse water are enough for two people to wash shirts, socks and underwear. Often, a good rinse without soap will get socks or shirt ready for a morning hike. Even then, the dirty water shouldn't go into the lake or stream. Dump it onto the ground.

Cleaning yourself should also be done away from the stream or lake. Heat a pot to a comfortable temperature. Find a scenic spot back in the forest, away from the lake. Then soap and rinse. You can even do a fine job of washing your hair. Just have someone help you with the rinse.

Don't soap up and jump into the lake or stream to rinse off. Even if the label says "biodegradable," the suds will be around killing fish and insects until next spring. Rinse yourself thoroughly so the soap soaks into the ground. When you go for a swim, leave the water as unpolluted as you found it.

Finally, there's the matter of a toilet. Rule of thumb is 100 *yards* from any water; the farther the better. Dig a hole at least four or five inches deep. Cover thoroughly when you're finished. Pack it down. Don't bury toilet paper. While organic waste will decompose quickly, toilet paper may take years. Bring it back to camp and throw it into the fire (if lit), or put it in the garbage bag to burn later. The same rules apply to tampons and sanitary napkins: burn or pack along, but don't bury.

Breaking Camp: The Low-Impact Way

A "low-impact" wilderness ethic has developed in recent years, which is typified by the motto, "Take only pictures, leave only footprints." The wilderness is a fragile place and visitors, however careful, leave a permanent imprint. When you break camp, clean up. Repair any damage you've done. Take apart fireplace additions and thoroughly douse the fire. Comb the area for scraps of paper or plastic which may have blown into the brush while you were cooking or eating. Pack out found garbage as well as your own.

If you camp at a pristine, never-before-used site, leave it as you found it, without a fireplace or stacked kindling, without a path to the lake, a naked patch of earth where the tent was sited, or that overturned stump you made into a chair.

And in return for the joy you get from the wilderness, put some energy into its maintenance and preservation after you get home. Spend a weekend on a local cleanup crew or trail maintenance work group. Join environmental and outdoor organizations. Become involved in the legislative process that helps preserve and protect the wilderness.

CHAPTER 8

Home Cooking: Using a Dehydrator

Two Cooking Strategies

Our friends know us as "discriminating fressers." (To "fress" means "to eat like a pig.") If that conjures up an image of a couple of slobs shoveling ballpark franks washed down by a chilled Chateau Lafite Rothschild, forget it. We can't tell Ripple from Manischewitz. But we like—we love—to eat, and on a camping trip, we have the best of both possible worlds: great food and world-class outdoor living. And as everybody knows, great food tastes even better outdoors. That's why you're here, to rip out the recipes in the Appendix and learn to live without them at the same time.

We operate on two levels here, careful home preparation of foods that can be pre-dried, and carefree improvisation around the campfire or stove out in the wilderness. In this chapter, we introduce the versatile dehydrator, essentially a blow drier for food. We assume you understand or have access to the lore of the kitchen—measurements, proportions, definitions, directions.

In the next chapter we show you how to play riffs on the available food in your pack. We assume you have nothing at hand except your imagination and a couple of pots and pans. Hence we explain a few basics and show you how to free yourself from the iron law of precision. Either way is right. Both are easy and fun. Neither has the remotest resemblance to institutional cooking or assembly-line freeze-drying. Stop, look, and listen to the cries of joy emanating from the kitchen.

The Dehydrator: How It Works, What It Does

Hal recently came upon four old timers in a wilderness campsite stocked with three cases of beer, countless cans of beans and spaghetti sauce, an old iron reflector oven, sacks of flour and cornmeal, and two cast iron skillets. They didn't appear to be weight conscious, probably because they'd used two llamas to haul in all that stuff. Most of us, however, have to watch our pack weight, and that's where dehydrated food comes in.

There are lots of ways to preserve food. You can pickle it, conserve it in sugar in air-tight jars, salt it, freeze or vacuum dry it, and dehydrate it by the application of slow heat. The last three of these methods remove the water content of food, leaving a dry shell which can be reconstituted by those immortal three words, "Just add water." And while modern technology has made it possible to freeze and vacuum dry food at home, it still has the feel (and expense) of a physics experiment. That leaves the modest fan-driven dehydrator as the best home companion for wilderness cookery since Irma Rombauer stopped making air drops.

The home dehydrator is no industrial-strength giant. Its five or six stacked, slotted trays sit on a base, also slotted, which houses a small electric motor. This motor drives a fan which forces air over a heating coil—sort of like a four-sided toaster coil—and thence up through the trays encased in a perforated plastic cover. Some of the air recirculates down and over the trays, as the rest escapes to maintain an even temperature. Food placed on the trays loses much of its moisture within 24 to 48 hours. The electric motor is energy inefficient but it gets the work done and saves on camp stove and natural fuels in the wilderness. Some models have temperature settings, but ours doesn't, and we've never missed them.

If you don't have or want a dehydrator or can't afford one (between $60 and $90 at camping stores and "whole food" outlets), you can use the kitchen oven as a drier. To achieve the slow, circulating air effect of a dehydrator, run your oven at its lowest temperature setting and keep the oven door propped open. Don't look too closely at your next gas or electric bill. That's the price you pay for "saving" on a dehydrator.

Endless Possibilities

About a month before our backpacking trips we crank up the dehydrator and keep it running twenty-four hours a day till there's enough camping food to feed us and several waves of hungry in-laws or bears, whichever show up first. It's possible to dry food much farther in advance—in late winter or early spring, for example—and pack and store it securely till needed in summer. Dried thoroughly and double bagged in airtight Ziploc bags, stored in cool, dry, dark containers (again the trusty black garbage bag will do in a pinch), most fruits and vegetables will be edible for half a year or more. Meals containing meats and other perishables—milk, eggs, cheese— can be similarly packed and stored in the freezer. But summer fruits and vegetables are too good to miss, so we wait till the first bloom is off the peaches, and the apricots and eggplants are in the markets and then get to work.

Home drying allows hikers and campers to do two things: prepare in advance lightweight snack foods and full-course hot meals. Fresh fruit and vegies dehydrated become instant *nosherei* (snacks and trail food) as well as potential ingredients for hot meals made in camp. Soups, stews, sauces, ragouts, desserts allow for one-pot cooking in the wilderness and more free time to catch the fish or bake the bread that will accompany them on day three up the Housatonic.

Food Drying Tips

- Dehydrator trays should be washed and dried before beginning the drying season and when it's over.

- Line the dehydrator base with aluminum foil or plastic wrap to catch drips from the trays. *Don't* cover the air slots in the base.

- Spray a light coating of Pam or any of its anti-stick relatives on the trays before each drying. More things stick than don't, and to pry dried watermelon off a dehydrator rack requires the patience of an archaeologist.

- The thinner the fresh food slice, the faster the drying process, but often the less satisfactory the eating. Experiment with the thickness of slices. Medium cuts seem best. Example: Slice a medium-sized peach into eighths; a small plum into fourths; a large banana or zucchini into 10 to 15 slices.

- Food is done when it feels leathery. Don't expect to match the commercial driers. You're going to end up with chewy banana slices, not banana chips. Apricots will shrivel but never look like those sun-dried or sulphur-treated beauties in the produce store.

- Dried fruit will be as sweet as the fresh product you started with. Dehydrating concentrates natural sugars; it doesn't supply them. A tart pineapple is going to taste tart dry or moist; sour grapes will stay that way.

- Line trays with plastic wrap or aluminum foil when drying liquids such as sauces, soups and stews. Spray the lining with Pam too! Some dehydrators come with one or two plastic inserts as liners for trays. Spray those as well.

- All uncooked fruits and vegetables dry well. But some do not reconstitute well. Carrots and (fresh) tofu, avocados and eggplants end up hard as coprolites and don't take kindly to water. Broccoli disintegrates into green dust. Citrus fruit is a bust: it's made up essentially of water and tough fiber. You end up with fiber.

- Almost anything you cooked in thickened liquid form— sauces and soups, for example—will dry *and* reconstitute well.

- Unless marinated fresh meats (jerkys) are thoroughly dried, they will deteriorate faster than other foods. Dehydrate them last, closer to departure time, and give them 48 hours on the drier.
- No need to turn food over, despite directions to do that in other books.

Recipes

Fresh Fruit

Ripe summer fruits are the best candidates for drying. The following are among our favorites:

Mangoes	Cantaloupe
Nectarines	Strawberries
Papayas	Bananas
Peaches	Blackberries
Pineapple	Apples
Plums	Raspberries
Watermelon	Figs (though it seems criminal to tamper with a fresh fig. Eat
Apricots	them while drying lesser items.)

Slice six to eight pounds of summer fruit into moderate sections. Remove papaya and watermelon seeds. Peel mango. Core apples, and pare at your discretion (we don't). Spread directly on lightly "Pammed" trays. Dry for 12-24 hours. Pack in large Ziploc bags. Yield: about 3.5 pounds dried fruit.

CAMPING USES:

- Eat as is.
- Filling for fruit crepes. See recipe, Chp. 9, pg. 238
- Chutney for Indian meals. See recipe, Chp. 9, pg. 257
- Filling for chocolate cake. See recipe, Chp. 9, pg. 251

Fresh Vegetables

All vegies contain water and hence can lose it through dehydration. But like fruit, some rehydrate better than others, a consideration for the campfire cook. Some need first to be blanched (plunged into boiling water for a minute or two, no more). Others require thorough cooking before dehydrating. Some can be treated like fruit and tossed directly onto the drying trays.

No preparation required:

Onions	Leeks
Summer Squash	Mushrooms
Zucchini	Bell Peppers
Tomatoes	
(OK, they're fruit, so sue us)	

Blanching helps:

Cauliflower	Broccoli
Green Beans	Eggplant

Cooking required (*see dinner recipes below*):

Potatoes	Beans (dried)
Tofu	Carrots

Cut into medium slices four pounds fresh vegetables. Blanch those requiring it. Place directly on lightly "Pammed" trays. Dry for 12-24 hours.

Note: Onions *smell* while drying. Place dehydrator outdoors on an extension cord in good weather to keep smell out of house.

Note: Marinate fresh tofu in soy sauce/tamari and rice vinegar and only partially dehydrate, on Pam-treated plastic lining, about six hours. Done when chewy; overdone when rock-hard. This will *only keep* a few days. Dehydrate two days before your trip; eat on first day.

CAMPING USES:

- Eat as is. Peppers, tomatoes, onions are sweet, delicious snacks.
- Reconstitute for in-camp recipes.
- Reconstitute for sauces.

Soups

The single requirement for any backcountry soup is that it fill you up. It is *the* meal, not a foretaste of things to come. It must be hearty, thick, tasty, even nourishing. If successful, it evokes memories or images of great cauldrons bubbling over fires in open hearths: Breugel and barons, late autumn chill and a hint of snow. There's no room at the campfire for a deli-cate clarified consommé, a thin, consumptive chicken soup. Make a big soup or no soup at all. The following recipes are some of our favorites. The point is that you can make any of yours too.

Black Bean Soup

This is a great Brazilian recipe that delivers on its promise of being a meal in a meal. No known life form has ever eaten a second course after this one, not even the legendary John Israel, a gourmand in gourmet's clothing.

1 lb. black turtle beans
1/4 c. olive oil
1/4 lb. raw cured ham (Smithfield/country) cut
*   into 1/2" cubes*
1/4 lb. salt pork cut into 1/2" cubes
4 c. finely chopped onions
1/3 c. finely minced garlic
14 c. fresh or canned beef broth plus salt (optional) & pepper
*   to taste*
1/4 tsp. cayenne pepper to taste
2 tbs wine vinegar
1/4 c. dry sherry

Soak beans in cold water overnight. Render salt pork of its fat; discard fat. Cook the onions in oil in a deep kettle till translucent. Add the cubed ham, salt pork, garlic, and con-tinue cooking, about five minutes. Drain beans, add to kettle. Add broth, bring to boil. Add salt, pepper, cayenne. Partly cover and cook, stirring occasionally, about four hours. Put half the soup with beans through sieve or use a blender. Re-turn to kettle, stir to blend with remaining soup and beans.

Add vinegar and dry sherry.

Ladle onto lined "Pammed" drying trays. Each tray should be just covered with soup. Dry 12 hours or until thoroughly dry. The texture, when done, will be crumbly, resembling a thin, loosely structured peanut brittle. Store in Ziploc bags. Figure three trays for four adults. Reconstitute by adding water to cover and bringing to boil. Serve very thick over cooked rice, with flaked dried onions and a dash of lemon or lime juice. Expire with pleasure.

VEGETARIAN VERSION:

In place of salt pork and ham, substitute two cakes of tofu, cubed and sautéed in oil till lightly browned. Add to kettle with onions and garlic. May need more salt to replace that in the salt pork.

Dutch Split Pea Soup

Don't plan any strenuous paddling or cycling after this one. Dutch burghers have infarcted just reaching for their pipes after two helpings.

1 lb. Split peas
2 1/2 qts. Water
1/4 c. Diced salt pork
1/2 c. Chopped leaks
1/2 c. Chopped celery
1/2 c. Celery root
1/2 c. Chopped onions
1/2 Bay leaf
2 tsp. Salt (optional)
1 Pig's knuckle
1 Smoked Dutch ring sausage sliced, or
1 c. Sliced Polish sausage
Chopped parsley

Soak the peas overnight in a large kettle. Do not drain. Sautée the salt pork ina large pan for about seven minutes or until rendered of fat. Add the vegetables and cook till tender. Add the salt pork and vegies to the peas with a bay leaf, salt (optional), and the pig's knuckle. Bring to a boil, reduce heat to simmer, cover and cook for about two hours or until meat on the pig's knuckle falls from the bone. (If foam forms on the top of the soup during cooking, remove with a slotted spoon.) Take the pig's knuckle from the pot, dice the meat and re- serve. Discard bone and bay leaf. Purée vegies in a blender. Return them and the meat to the soup, add the sliced sau- sages and simmer five minutes longer.

Ladle onto "Pammed" lined trays. Dry 7-12 hours or until dry, flaky. Store in air-tight bags.

VEGETARIAN VERSION:

Omit salt pork, pig's knuckle, sausage. Flavor with $\frac{1}{4}$ cup sherry, 3 tablespoons hot sauce, lots of black pepper to taste.

Minestrone

An Italian regiment in the Val d'Aosta on the Swiss alpine frontier mutinied when they couldn't get their promised ra- tions of this great vegetable soup. We don't blame them; it's cold up there. Don't worry about the long list of ingredients. It's easy to assemble, inexpensive, and worth the effort.

1/2 lb. dry white beans soaked overnight in water
3 qts. water
1 tsp. olive oil
1/8 lb. salt pork, diced (vegetarians omit)
1 clove garlic, chopped fine
1 small onion, chopped
1 leek, diced & washed
1 tsp. chopped parsley
1 tsp. chopped basil
1 tbs. tomato paste
3 tomatoes, peeled, seeded, chopped
3 stalks celery, chopped
2 carrots, sliced
2 potatoes, diced
1 small turnip, peeled, diced
1/4 small cabbage, shredded
2 zucchini, diced
1 1/2 qts. water or soup stock
Salt (optional)
Ground black pepper to taste
1 c. elbow macaroni

Drain the beans then boil about 1 hour or till tender. Drain. In a large kettle render the salt pork, about 10 minutes, then add olive oil and brown the following: salt pork, garlic, onion, leek, parsley, basil. Add tomato paste and a little water to thin it. Cook five minutes. Add tomatoes, celery, carrots, potatoes, turnip, cabbage, zucchini, water, salt (optional) and pepper. Simmer slowly about 45 minutes to one hour. Add the beans. Add the elbow macaroni and cook 10 minutes more or until tender.

Ladle onto lightly "Pammed" lined trays. Dehydrate 7-12 hours or until thoroughly dry. Seal in air-tight plastic bags. Three trays serves four adults. Four trays serves four adults in the Val d'Aosta. Reconstitute by covering with water and boiling. Serve topped with lots of grated (or finely sliced) Parmesan cheese, a great backpacking cheese: hard, good on its own or in dishes, won't spoil.

Leek and Mushroom Soup

Make this soup as thick as a vegetable purée. Eat it with fresh bread baked at the campsite (See recipes, Chapter 9, pg . 240)

2+ lbs. leeks, sliced, washed, drained
3 large celery stalks with leaves, chopped
2 large carrots, sliced
1 small summer squash or zucchini
4 tbs. olive oil
1 1/2 qts. vegetable stock
6 fresh basil leaves in season or 4 sprigs parsley
2 tbs. flour
1/2 lb. mushrooms, chopped
3 tbs. margarine or butter
Lemon juice
Salt (optional) plus ground pepper to taste

Sauté the celery, carrots, squash and leeks in the olive oil till just tender (five to seven minutes). Sprinkle with flour and cook three minutes more. Add chopped basil or parsley, pepper and salt. Barely cover with some of the vegetable stock, lower to simmer, cover and cook 15 to 20 minutes till soft. In the meantime sauté the mushrooms in the butter or margarine till barely soft, about three minutes. Drain on paper towels. Place the leek and vegetable mixture in a blender. Add the mushrooms. Add a ladle of vegetable stock and blend till puréed. Return to clean pot and add just enough of the vegetable stock to make a thick soup to serve four. Add lemon juice and pepper to taste. The thicker the soup, the better it will dehydrate.

Ladle onto prepared, lined trays. Dehydrate 7-12 hours or until thoroughly dry. Reconstitute by covering with water and bringing to a boil.

VARIATION WITH TOFU:

Cut a half-cake of tofu into small cubes. It can be either hard or soft, Chinese or Japanese. Brown on all sides in peanut oil with a dash of sesame oil. Add ground black pepper to taste. When ready to purée other ingredients in blender, add the cooked tofu. Run the blender at high speed for at least two minutes. Otherwise the tofu will give the soup a grainy texture. Blended properly, the tofu adds a rich, creamy taste and texture to the soup.

Vegetable Stock

Stores used to sell soup greens, basically a little of "This" and a little of "That": celery leaves, spinach, chard, turnip or carrot tops. They don't anymore, so you have to buy the whole vegetable these days and make do. Vegetable stock is the generic home of leftovers. Don't worry about proportions or niceties. All you need is a big stock pot and lots of vegetables which have seen better days. If you need to clean out your fridge, you're on schedule for a great vegetable stock. Here's a recent one we managed out of necessity—it was either make a soup stock or appear at a hearing before the health inspector. The proportions below are arbitrary.

1 large onion, left whole
4 scallions, chopped
4 garlic cloves, crushed
2 leeks, washed, including green tops, chopped
2 large carrots, sliced
3 large celery stalks, with leaves, chopped
1 small turnip, with top, left whole

¹/₂ bunch spinach
¹/₂ lettuce
Mixed fresh herbs: bay leaves, oregano, parsley, basil,
thyme,tarragon.
10 peppercorns, whole or slightly crushed
Olive oil or butter

Lightly brown the vegetables in olive oil. Then season and cover with cold water in a large stock pot or kettle. Bring to boil, lower heat and simmer two hours. Strain through a colander. Discard vegetables. Return soup stock to pot, reduce under high heat to concentrate flavor. Cool in pot. Freeze in air-tight containers till ready to use. Keeps for months if properly frozen.

Stews

Anything thick enough to stick to your ribs can be pre-cooked and dehydrated, then reconstituted in a single pot by adding water, thus becoming a homemade entrée away from home. It will be as good as the ingredients you use to make it. That's its advantage over commercial freeze-dried dinners. You don't have any control over them, just faith, which is probably misplaced, but that's our particular axe. Like the soups, the following recipes are meant to inspire your imagination, not exhaust it. Add to the list, send us your ideas, and we'll add them to the next edition.

Chicken Casserole

A confession is in order here. We've never actually tasted this dish reconstituted. That's because it's so good dried that we ate all of it as trail nosh before we ever got it to the dinner pot. What can we say? We've eaten it often at home and guarantee it's a winner. If not, tear out the recipe and send it with an irate letter to our publisher. She will personally reimburse you with a plastic replica of a two-pound vegetarian burrito. She says you'll know what to do with it.

4 lb. chicken, cut up as for frying
1/4 c. seasoned flour [flour mixed with finely sifted bread
crumbs and mixed herbs: savory, chervil, chives, basil,
tarragon, pepper, salt, paprika]
1/4 c. olive oil
1 small onion, sliced
1 clove garlic, sliced
3-4 celery stalks, chopped
1 medium carrot, sliced
1 1/2 c. hot chicken broth
1 c. sliced, sautéed mushrooms
12 stuffed olives, sliced

Dust the chicken parts with the seasoned flour, then brown chicken in olive oil in large Dutch oven or fireproof casserole. Remove. Brown the onion, garlic, celery and carrot in the oil. Return chicken to pot with vegetables, pour the broth over all, barely to cover. Bake covered in 350 degree oven 1 1/2 hours or till tender. Five minutes before it is done, add the sautéed mushrooms and olives. Allow to cool.

When cool remove and debone the chicken parts, discard bones and return chicken to pot. Mix with vegetables. Spoon onto lightly "Pammed" plastic sheets covering the dehydrator trays. Dry for 12-20 hours. The texture will be crumbly, with chicken pieces dried like jerky. Pack in Ziploc bags as air-free as possible. Reconstitute by adding water barely to cover and bringing to boil. Serve over boiled rice.

Burgundy Beef

This famous dish (Boeuf Bourguignon) started as a peasant stew and graduated to the high table by the kind of culinary magic only known to the French. The first thing you're going to say is "Why go to all the trouble?" The second thing, "Oh man, am I glad I went to all the trouble." It's one of the best stews you'll ever eat, which is more than you can say for Ranger Ron's freeze-dried Mulligatawny.

1/2 lb. bacon, diced
3 lbs. lean beef chuck, cut into 1" cubes
1 c. chopped onion

Salt (optional) & pepper to taste
3 tbs. flour
3 c. dry red wine, burgundy if possible
3 c. beef broth
2 tbs. tomato paste
1 tbs. chopped fresh rosemary leaves
3 carrots, sliced
2 c. small pearl onions
1 tbs. butter/margarine
1 c. mushrooms, sautéed
1 tbs. red currant jelly

Sauté bacon till crisp, in a big flameproof pot then remove and drain on paper towels. Brown the cubed beef on all sides in the bacon fat, then remove. Brown the chopped onion and carrots in the fat, then return the bacon and beef to the pot. Add the flour, stirring to coat all ingredients and continue browning for about five minutes. Add wine, broth, tomato paste, rosemary, salt and pepper. Bring to boil. Cover and place in 325 degree oven. Bake till meat is tender, about two and one-half hours. Boil the pearl onions till just tender, and when cool, peel and reserve. Sauté the mushrooms in the butter or margarine. Reserve. When meat is done, transfer casserole to stove top, add the onions, mushrooms and currant jelly. Mix in very gently. Cook till hot, about five minutes.

Spread on dryer trays lined with plastic wrap and lightly "Pammed." Dehydrate 12-24 hours, till thoroughly dry. Pack tightly against air. Rehydrate by barely covering with water and bringing to boil. Serve over rice.

Squash Stew with Chilies and Almonds

This is a vegetarian stew created by the famous Greens Restaurant in San Francisco. We simplify and corrupt it here for plainer, easier cooking, and no doubt they would disown the whole thing. That's OK, they're not going camping, we are.

3 tbs. sesame seeds, toasted in a dry pan till lightly browned
2 dozen whole almonds, toasted in a dry pan till browned,
*   then coarsely chopped*

2 tbs. chili powder (less or more to taste)
1 1/2 tsp. ground cumin
2 tsp. dried oregano
2 tbs. olive oil
2 onions, roughly chopped (1/2" squares)
2 cloves garlic, finely chopped
3 c. squash (winter / summer) cut into large chunks
1/2 lb. mushrooms, halved or quartered
Salt (optional)
3-4c. vegetable stock heated
1/2 cauliflower, broken into florets
1 small can hominy, drained
2 lbs. tomatoes, fresh or canned, seeded, puréed
1 c. peas, fresh or frozen
2 tbs. chopped cilantro leaves

Grind the toasted almonds and sesame to a fine meal in a coffee grinder. Heat oil in fireproof casserole. Cook onions till just soft, then cook another minute with the garlic, cumin, oregano and chili powder. Add squash, mushrooms, salt (optional) and stock. Bring to boil, lower heat, simmer till squash is tender, 15 to 20 minutes. Add more liquid as necessary. Add the ground almonds and sesame seeds, cauliflower, hominy, puréed tomatoes. Continue cooking until cauliflower is almost tender, then add peas and chopped cilantro. Let cook a few more minutes.

Spread on prepared, lined dryer trays. Dry 7-12 hours. As this dissipates most of the liquid, the remaining ingredients will look pitifully few. Don't worry. Pack all five trays' worth. Reconstitute by adding water barely to cover, boil and serve over rice or with fresh baked camp bread (see recipes, Chapter 9, pg. 240).

VARIATION:

To cooked stew, add 2-3 large tablespoons sour cream or yogurt. Mix. Dehydrate and rehydrate as above. Remember that sour cream and yogurt are perishables, so make this variation no more than a week before leaving. Pack tightly and keep in shade.

Eggplant and Tomato Casserole

This recipe is brought to you directly from a hippie commune, vintage 1972. The flower children did a lot of nice things, and this is one of them. It reconstitutes more as a stew than a casserole, but who's going to quibble about niceties on a soft rainy evening deep in the Boundary Waters Wilderness?

1 large eggplant
1 tsp. salt (optional)
2 eggs, beaten
2 tbs. melted margarine/butter
Fresh ground pepper
2-3 tbs. chopped onion (or more!)
1/2 tsp. oregano
1/2 c. bread crumbs
2 large tomatoes, sliced in thin rounds
2 oz. grated cheddar or Edam cheese
1/4 c. grated Parmesan cheese
Paprika to taste

Peel and slice eggplant. Place in pot with salt and cover with about one inch of water. Cover and cook about 10 minutes or until eggplant is soft. Drain and mash with potato masher. Add the beaten eggs, melted butter, pepper, onion, oregano, breadcrumbs. Butter a 1 ½-quart baking dish or casserole. Cover bottom with half the sliced tomatoes. Spread in all of the eggplant mixture. Put rest of tomato slices on top. Mix together the grated cheeses and sprinkle on top. Then sprinkle with paprika. Bake in 375 degree oven about 45 minutes.

Spread on drying trays lined with plastic wrap and lightly "Pammed." Dehydrate 7-12 hours. Texture will be dry, crumbly. Pack in Ziploc bags. Eggs and cheese are perishable, so store in cool, dry place; keep out of direct sunlight while in camp. Rehydrate by adding water to moisten. Reheat slowly to prevent burning. Serves two fressers or four courteous adults.

Indian Cooking

For reasons we can't explain, almost all wilderness campers and canoeists we've met like their food highly spiced. Maybe it's a reaction to years of bland "Y" cooking, watery soups, peanut butter 'n jelly on Wonder Bread, K rations. Maybe it's a function of hard exercise, cold nights, and a need for a jolt and a kick from the menu. Whatever the reason, we've perfected the art of spicing over the years, though the only other person able to match Rick's tolerance for hot sauce is a Dravidian wise man we once met in southern India. He was impressed. Here are some of our favorites.

Zucchini Curry (Goodhi bhajji)

2 ^{1}/2 lbs. zucchini (or summer squash), sliced into ^{1}/4" rounds
^{1}/4 c. sesame oil
1 tsp. mustard seeds
1 tsp. ground turmeric
^{1}/2 tsp. chili powder
^{1}/2 tsp. black pepper
1 tsp. onion seeds (optional)
1 large onion, sliced into thin rounds
4+ oz. raw, unsweetened coconut
1 tsp. garam masala
^{1}/2 tsp. salt (optional)

Heat the sesame oil in a deep sauce pan or flameproof casserole. Add mustard seeds, which will sputter and pop. Add turmeric, chili powder, pepper and onion seeds. Stir over gentle heat for two minutes, then add sliced onions and sauté till just soft. Add zucchini, turning gently, cooking five minutes. Add coconut, garam masala, salt. Cover pan and simmer gently about 10 minutes or till zucchini is soft. Add a little water if zucchini is sticking to bottom of pan while simmering. That's it. Simple. Superb. Promise.

Spread on lightly "Pammed," and lined drying trays. Dehydrate 7-12 hours or till dry. Pack in Ziploc bags. Rehydrate by adding water to moisten. Heat and serve with rice (Basmati rice is great here; so is brown rice). A great complement to this dish is a campground chutney (See recipe, Chapter 9, pg. 257)

Garam Masala (1)

Garam masala literally means "hot spice" and is your basic homemade curry powder. There are as many varieties as there are Indian dialects, so you can tinker after your own tastes. It's so simple to make that we bet you never go back to store-bought curry powder. Here are two variants, the first "hotter" than the second.

4 oz. coriander seeds
5 bay leaves
4 oz. white cumin seeds
1 oz. cardamoms
1 oz. cloves
2" stick cinnamon
2 oz. chili powder
2 oz. black pepper
1 tsp. grated nutmeg

Mix and spread on a cookie tin or baking pan the coriander seeds, bay leaves, cumin seeds, cardamoms, cloves and cinnamon stick. Roast in a hot, 400 degree oven for 20 minutes. Remove and place in coffee or food grinder. Grind to a fine powder. Mix with the chili powder, pepper and nutmeg. Store in an air-tight jar. Will keep for months. On camping trips, put a few teaspoons in a Ziploc bag, small plastic bottle, or a plastic pill box.

Garam Masala (2)

Follow same procedure for (1) but omit the chili powder and black pepper. This makes a lighter curry powder, more aromatic than spicy. In both cases, add the garam masala to recipes close to the end of the cooking. This brings out the flavors and kicks in the spicing just before it hits the back of your throat. It'll bring tears to your eyes, a delicate emotion as you scarf down a third helping the night before the ascent of that 13,000-foot pass you promised yourself.

Spiced Cauliflower (Gobi musallum)

Read this one and weep. Well, eat it and weep.

1 large cauliflower
1 tbs. tamarind extract
1 c. boiling water
2 oz. cooking oil
2 tsp. chili powder
2 tsp. ground coriander
2 tsp. ground cumin
2 tsp. ground turmeric
2 tsp. black pepper
1 tbs. vinegar
1 tsp. salt (optional)

Break the cauliflower into florets, discarding the central stalk. Heat the oil, add the chili powder, coriander, cumin, turmeric and pepper. Stir two minutes, then add cauliflower, turning to coat with the spices. Add tamarind extract and the boiling water, then the vinegar and salt. Continue to cook over moderate-low heat about 15 minutes or until cauliflower is just tender.

Spread on prepared, lined trays, and dry for 7-12 hours. Pack in air-tight bags. Rehydrate by adding water to moisten over moderate heat. Serve with cooked rice.

Lentils with Cauliflower (Gobi dal)

If there is a vegetarian heaven, this dish is served there every other day. It's to die for.

1/2 lb. pink split lentils (masoor dal)
1 small cauliflower, broken into florets
2 medium onions
4 oz. cooking oil
1 tsp. chili powder
2 tsp. black pepper
1/2 tbs. ground cumin
1/2 tbs. ground coriander
2 tsp. ground turmeric
1/2 lemon

2 c. chicken stock
2+ oz. raw, unsweetened coconut
$^1/_2$ tbs. flour
$^1/_4$ lb. cashew nuts

Wash and drain lentils; peel and finely chop onions. Heat oil in a large saucepan or flameproof casserole, and sauté onions till translucent. Add chili powder, black pepper, cumin, coriander and turmeric. Stir and cook for another 30 seconds. Add lentils. Stir vigorously. Add lemon juice, then cauliflower florets. Pour chicken stock over all, sprinkle on the coconut. Bring to boil, lower heat and simmer 20 minutes. Mix flour with small amount of the cooking liquid to make a smooth paste. Add to pot. Now toss in the salt and cashews. Cook five to 10 minutes longer till lentils form a thick sauce and cauliflower is tender.

Spread on Pam-prepared lined drying trays, and dry for 12 hours or until thoroughly dehydrated. Pack in airtight bags. Rehydrate by adding water barely to cover; heat to boiling. Serve with plain cooked rice and a campground chutney (See Chapter 9, pg. 257)

Steamed Yam (Dum arvi)

Once you eat this dish you may never go back to granny's Thanksgiving candied yams. Tough luck, granny. See ya' down at Man Eatin' Lake. A great filler-upper.

2+ lbs. yams, peeled and cut into large (1 $^1/_2$") chunks
$^3/_4$ c. cooking oil
1 large onion, thinly sliced into rounds
3" piece fresh ginger peeled and cut into thin strips
2 tsp. ground coriander
2 tsp. garam masala
1 tsp. chili powder
1 tsp. black pepper
2 tsp. ground turmeric
2 tsp. salt (optional)
4 green chilies, topped and tailed

Heat oil in large ovenproof saucepan or fireproof casserole and brown the yams gently. Remove and set aside. Sauté the onion with the ginger; add, stir in well, and cook for two minutes the coriander, garam masala, chili powder, pepper, turmeric. Now add the yams and salt, and stir to coat. Cover casserole and place in 350 degree oven. After 30 minutes add chilies. Bake another 30 minutes or until yams are tender.

Spread on Pam-prepared lined trays. Dry 12 hours or till yams are thoroughly dehydrated. Pack in Ziplocs. To rehydrate, add water to moisten, and stir while heating. Serve with campsite chutney (See Chapter 9, pg. 257).

Indian Lentils (Masoor dal)

Take the lowly lentil, dress it up with aromatics and coconut, serve it with rice, and watch contentedly as the hikers in the next campsite fumble with the library paste they've made out of their Space-Shuttle beef stroganof.

1/2 lb. pink split lentils, washed, drained, boiled gently
  with water to cover, till soft
1 medium onion, sliced thin
2 cloves garlic, chopped fine
1/4 c. cooking oil
2 tsp. ground coriander
2 tsp. ground cumin
2 tsp. ground turmeric
1 tsp. chili powder
4 cardamoms
4 cloves
2" stick cinnamon
1 tsp. salt (optional)
4 oz. raw, unsweetened coconut
1/2 c. water or coconut milk

Heat oil in pan, sauté onions and garlic, then add coriander, cumin, turmeric and chili powder, stirring well. Cook two minutes, then add cardamoms, cloves, and the cinnamon stick. Add to the cooked lentils (and their liquid), mix well, sprinkle with salt, cook for five more minutes, adding a little water if necessary. In blender mix the raw coconut with ½ cup water or coconut milk till smooth, then add to lentils and stir.

Ladle lentils onto "Pammed" plastic-lined drying trays and dehydrate 12 hours or until dry. To reconstitute, add water to cover, boil down till thick. Top with dried tomato bits, and serve with rice.

Spaghetti Sauces

It's inevitable that you're going to eat pasta for one of your camping meals, so you might as well enjoy it. It doesn't make sense to haul whole tomato sauce into the backcountry if you have to carry it in panniers or backpacks. It makes a whole lot of sense to prepare your own favorite sauces at home, dry them, and carry the lightened load into the mountains. They reconstitute perfectly and really taste like home cookin' because they are!

Tomato Sauce

1 large can whole tomatoes
1 small can tomato paste
2+ tbs. sun dried tomatoes
1/2 lb. mushrooms, halved or quartered
1 bay leaf
3 sprigs parsley
Ground black pepper to taste
6-8 fresh basil leaves, finely chopped, or 2 tsp. dried basil
1 c. boiling water
1 c. dry red wine
3 tbs. olive oil
1 large onion, chopped fine
1 large clove garlic, chopped fine
1/2 lb. ground country sausage, or
1/2 lb. fresh Italian sausage

In a large saucepan put the tomatoes, tomato paste, sun dried tomatoes, chopped mushrooms, bay leaf, parsley, pepper, basil leaves, boiling water and wine. Bring to a simmer, cover and cook while preparing other ingredients. In a frying pan sauté the garlic and onions till translucent. Add to tomato pot. Sauté the sausage over medium heat, drawing off the fat as it accumulates. Add the sausage to the tomato pot. Simmer for 2 to 4 hours, adding wine/boiling water as necessary. Stir occasionally. Adjust seasonings. The sauce when done should be thick.

Spoon or ladle onto "Pammed," lined trays. Dehydrate 12 to 24 hours until a dark-red tomato "leather" has been formed. Peel off the plastic tray liners and store in air-tight bags. Two full trays will yield enough sauce for four; three trays will feed two adolescents.

To rehydrate, add water to cover, heat, stir, and if too watery, boil down. Serve with spaghetti or any other pasta and top with finely sliced or grated Parmesan cheese.

Eggplant and Walnut Sauce

This is so good that you may want to retire the more familiar tomato sauces you've grown up with. The combination of tomato, eggplant and walnuts is surprising only to us outlanders. The Sicilians have known and loved it for centuries.

2-3 large eggplants
3 eggs
15 walnut kernels
Quick tomato sauce (pg. 194)
Salt and pepper to taste
Olive oil

Place the eggplants whole on a cookie sheet or baking pan in a hot, 425 degree oven, and roast for about 35 minutes. You'll know they're done when they're wrinkled and soft. Meanwhile make the tomato sauce and hard boil the eggs till the yolks are firm and creamy, not hard, about four to five minutes. Run the eggs under cold water, shell and separate yolks from whites. Reserve. Grind the walnuts in a coffee or food grinder. Cut the roasted eggplants in half, scoop out the pulp and mix with the walnuts. Add the egg yolks and mix thoroughly. Now add the tomato sauce, salt and pepper to taste and a few drops of olive oil.

Spoon onto "Pammed," lined trays and dry for 12 hours or until thoroughly dry. Store in Ziploc bags. To reconstitute, add water barely to cover, stir while heating. Serve over pasta of your choice. Kvell.

Quick Tomato Sauce

2 tbs. olive oil
1 medium onion, chopped
2 cloves garlic, chopped
1 large (14 oz.) can whole tomatoes
1 tsp. sugar
Salt and pepper to taste

Sauté the chopped onion and garlic in the olive oil till soft. Add tomatoes with their juice, sugar, salt and pepper. Cook over moderate-high heat uncovered for 20 minutes, stirring occasionally. When thickened, puree in an electric blender. Finito. Use by itself with pasta or in other recipes.

Spoon onto treated plastic wrap on the drying trays and dehydrate 12 to 24 hours till a tomato "leather" is formed. It will feel like a fruit leather. Peel off and store in Ziploc bags. To rehydrate, add water to cover, heat and stir till hot and thick. Serve over pasta topped with Parmesan cheese.

Other Sauces

White and brown sauces and gravies can all be made in advance at home like spaghetti sauces, and successfully dehydrated. Follow your own recipes and remember that any sauce or gravy that contains butter, milk or eggs should be carefully packed and stored after thorough drying to prevent spoilage. Try to avoid storing them in direct sunlight while in camp.

And if, after all of this, you just want to go down to the neighborhood Mom & Pop store, buy a jar of spaghetti sauce, and dehydrate it, that's OK too. It works. We'll be busy for dinner that night, but we sure would've liked to be there. Bon appetit.

Desserts

If the super incredible, once-in-a-lifetime on-site campfire baking offer made in Chapter 9 isn't enough for your sweet tooth; if the semi-sweet baking chocolate, raisin cookies, ginger snaps, lemon drops and hard candy aren't enough on the trail; if honey drips and you don't "do" plain sugar—then here are a couple of ideas for the kitchen and dehydrator. Forget the cakes and homemade cookies. They'll be too heavy and bulky to carry, quickly go stale, and disintegrate under the pressure of a compressed backpack. On the other hand, call a pudding by any other name—"mousse," "flan," or "creme brulée"—and you'll transform the canoe ride, even if it's up the sewer outlet, into a gourmet tour of the old country.

Indian Pudding

What more appropriate dessert to eat around the campfire on a moonlit night, even if it isn't New England? We didn't promise you sugarless, but this comes pretty close.

1 qt. milk
1/2 c. yellow cornmeal
2 tbs. melted butter or margarine
1/2 c. molasses
1 tsp. salt (optional)
1 tsp. cinnamon
1/4 tsp. powdered ginger
2 eggs

Scald the milk, pour over cornmeal, stirring constantly. Cook over hot water (in top of double boiler) for 20 minutes. Combine butter, molasses, salt, cinnamon, ginger, and add to well-beaten eggs. Add all to the cornmeal mixture. Pour into greased baking dish. Place the baking dish in a larger pan of hot water. Bake in a 350 degree oven for one hour.

Spread on Pam-treated plastic-lined trays. Dry 7 to 12 hours. Store in cool dry place in airtight containers till you're ready to hit the trail. Rehydrate by adding a spoon of dry, powdered milk to water to moisten. Heat slowly. Serve plain or with stewed-fruit compote (See Chapter 9, pg. 238)

Rice Pudding

You're going to want rice one way or another on a camping trip, so why not in its sweetest, most inviting form?

1 qt. milk
4 c. uncooked long-grain rice
1/2 c. sugar
1/2 tsp. salt
1/2 c. raisins (optional)
1 tsp. vanilla or rum
1/4 tsp. nutmeg

Mix the milk, rice, sugar, and salt in a buttered casserole. Bake at 300 degrees uncovered for two hours, nice and slow. If you use raisins, soak then in water (or rum!) to soften; drain and add with the vanilla (or rum) and nutmeg to pudding after the two hours and bake another half-hour without stirring. The rice should be very tender. If not, bake on.

Spread on treated, lined trays and dry thoroughly, about 7 to 12 hours. Pack tightly against air and keep in cool, dry place. Rehydrate by adding a spoon of dry milk powder to water to moisten. Heat slowly or eat cold.

Chocolate Pudding

When we're backpacking, we fake a chocolate pudding by doing This and That with a couple of leftover ingredients (See Chapter 9, pg. 253 for slightly more precise directions). Everybody (except Jessie, who's allergic to chocolate) loves it, so we decided, why not make it at home? As the Chinese would say, "Shuo shi chi, na shi kuai!" —no sooner said than done.

1/2 c. sugar
1 egg, beaten till light
1 c. coffee
1 tbs. melted butter/margarine
1 1/2 oz. melted semi-sweet baking chocolate
1 1/2 c. flour
1/4 tsp. salt
1 1/2 tsp baking powder
1/2 tsp vanilla

Gradually stir sugar into the beaten egg; then stir in the coffee, butter, and melted chocolate. Sift together the flour, salt, baking powder and add to egg mixture. Add the vanilla. At this point you're supposed to place the batter in greased custard cups, but since we're going to dehydrate the pudding, there's no need. Just pour it all in a well-greased baking dish. Cover with foil and steam for half an hour in a 350 degree oven by setting the dish in a pan of hot water.

Spread over "Pammed," lined trays. Dry for 7 to 12 hours. Seal tightly in Ziploc bags, keep cool. (Keep the pudding cool too.) To reconstitute, moisten with some hot coffee or milk from powdered milk. Reheat and slosh down. If necessary grab partner by throat to prevent total consumption before you get a whack at it.

VARIATIONS:

For vanilla pudding, omit the melted chocolate and substitute milk for the coffee. Use one teaspoon vanilla.

For a fruit "flan," make the vanilla pudding and before dehydrating stir in four heaping tablespoons of stewed fruits or berries. Dry and rehydrate accordingly.

Trail Snacks

We are not going to teach you how to make gorp here. Anybody who can throw together in a bag any combination of raisins, nuts, sunflower seeds, granola, chopped dried apricots, chocolate chips and whatever else suits a nosher's fancy can make gorp. You've just done it. What you get here is something entirely different, beef and chicken/turkey jerky, and fruit leathers.

Jerky

We can almost hear the gnashing of old-time game-hunters' teeth when they contemplate the nambypamby methods of "jerking" beef these days—using commercial dryers and shovel loads of preservatives. "There's nothing complicated about making jerky," wrote a genuine Hudson's Bay outdoorsman 30 years ago, reminiscing about a better—a truer—age. "You cut lean deer, moose, elk, caribou, buffalo...into long strips about 1/2 inch thick. These you hang apart from one another in the sun, in the attic, or some other place where...they will gradually lose most of their water content. At the same time, they'll become hard, dry, black and, incidentally, both nourishing and tasty....Good? Friends of ours...jerk a deer or so a year in this fashion just for their own personal eating." (Bradford Angier, in *Wilderness Cookery*, pp. 87-88. Stackpole Books, Harrisburg, PA, 1961.)

That's a hard act to follow. We don't jerk no deer here. But Bradford was right. Jerky can be good, and it's simple to make.

Beef Jerky

1 1/2 lbs lean beef (the better the beef, the better the jerky:
  flank or round steak, and up from there)
Soy sauce, sesame oil, rice vinegar, honey, red wine as
  marinade
Fresh ground pepper to taste
Fresh grated ginger
Powdered mustard to taste

Either have the butcher slice the beef into ¼" slices or freeze the meat and slice it while just beginning to thaw, so you can get the blade through. The slices can be as long or short as you wish. Marinate in two parts soy sauce to one part other liquid ingredients, thoroughly mixed together with a wire whisk. Add pepper, ginger, mustard to taste. Marinate in fridge overnight.

Apply a liberal coating of Pam directly on the dryer trays; lay the beef strips on the trays and dry for 24 to 36 hours, until very dry, blackened, hard. Pack in airtight Ziploc bags and keep out of sun in camp. We try to make all our jerky the last week before a camping trip. High-powered commercial driers get more of the moisture out than our Model T, so we dry late and eat early.

Chicken / Turkey Jerky

Follow directions for *Beef Jerky*. Use the breast of the chicken or turkey for tenderest meat. Have the butcher slice it thin for you, or do same at home, partially frozen: it, not you. Try other marinades. Here are two that are great with poultry.

RECIPE 1:

1/2 c. olive oil
1 1/2 c. corn oil
7 cloves garlic
4 sprigs fresh thyme
4 sprigs rosemary
Ground pepper to taste

Mix thoroughly with a wire whisk. Spread on chicken/turkey slices. Refrigerate overnight.

RECIPE 2:

2/3 c. olive oil
1/3 c. tarragon vinegar
1/4 tsp. dry mustard
1 tsp. dry tarragon
Ground pepper to taste

Mix thoroughly with a wire whisk. Spread on chicken/turkey slices. Marinate overnight in fridge.

Fruit Leathers

Any fruit you can stew you can dry as a fruit leather too. The leather is intensely sweet, as the sugar gets concentrated, and in our opinion better than almost any other sweet we carry with us. There are two problems, however. One is that they're heavy. Made properly, they come off the dehydrator almost thin enough to see through yet concentrated with some moisture and lots of sugar to give them heft. You can't carry as much as you'd like unless willing to sacrifice that Dickens novel you've scheduled for the vacation. The second problem is they're popular. Ours lasted one day during a recent five-day trip. Now you seem 'em, now you don't. Plan accordingly.

Rhubarb and Strawberry Leather

2 lbs. rhubarb
1 1/2 c. water
2   boxes strawberries
2 c. sugar
Lemon juice

Wash and slice the rhubarb crosswise. Place in large enamel pan. Add water. (Rhubarb is loaded with water, so don't fret if it looks like there's not enough). Bring to slow boil, then lower heat to simmer. Add 1 cup of sugar. Stir very gently once during cooking to immerse top pieces in the boiling water. Slice strawberries and add just before the rhubarb begins to get soft. The whole process will only take 10 or 15 minutes. Near the end add the other cup of sugar to taste. Rhubarb is tart and usually takes more sugar than you'd like. When soft, it's done. Remove from heat. Squeeze half a lemon onto the mixture and adjust taste.

Spoon onto thoroughly "Pammed" and lined trays. Heavy aluminum foil works well here, as does plastic wrap. Dry for 12 to 24 hours. Peel off and store in airtight bags. That's the time to reduce the weight by eating more than you store. Enjoy.

Peach and Apricot Leather

2 lbs. ripe peaches
2 lbs. ripe apricots
1 1/2 c. sugar
2 c. water
Lemon juice

Slice peaches and apricots, remove pits, place in enamel pan. Add sugar and mix thoroughly till all slices are amply coated and the mixture begins to "sweat." Add water, bring to boil, keep heat moderately high, stir occasionally to prevent sticking. When the fruit mixture begins to thicken, in about 20 minutes, it's done. Remove from heat and add juice of half a lemon to taste.

Spoon onto lined, "Pammed" trays. Dry for 12 to 24 hours. Peel off and store in airtight bags. Eat more than you'll take if you're hiking; eat less than you'll take if you're car camping or canoeing.

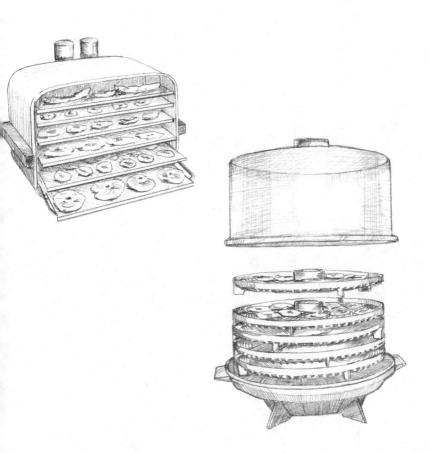

CHAPTER 9

Campsite Cooking:
Using the Imagination

Hidden Lake Soufflé

"Catch, clean and poach three to five small (7-9") trout taken
from a crystalline wilderness lake at 8,000 feet." Thus reads
the first sentence of our original recipe for Hidden Lake Souffle. "Remove and discard bones and skin. Set aside the flaked
meat in tent to protect from flies, bees and larger predators.
Over a low fire, prepare about a Sierra cup-and-a-half of white
sauce in the smallest of a set of three nested pots. Do not eat
ingredients halfway through. Assuage munchies or
lingering hunger with dried fruit, nuts, candy, whatever, thus
preserving the fish, cheese and eggs for the soufflé. Add flaked
fish to sauce, season well, and pour into a greased, two-quart
pot. Fold in egg whites which have been beaten stiff with the
trusty spring-loaded swizzle stick. Cover pot and bake in coals
until done. Cooking time: one chapter of *Huckleberry Finn*
read aloud. Eat at once. Bask in glow of self-congratulation.
Groan with pleasure."

We made up these directions one glorious morning in a remote campsite deep in the mountains. We'd planned the soufflé as a late brunch, but the project built slowly and turned into an early dinner. That didn't matter. We had all the time in the world. This wasn't survival, it was hedonism, like a day trip, a long nap, or an hour of fly-casting at sundown. After dinner, we revised the recipe, wrote it out, and then, the next day, left it in a cairn atop an unnamed peak in the mountains. We don't know if anyone ever found it or tried to use it. We were told later, however, by friends who did try, that they needed something a bit more specific, and in the following pages we will take you step-by-step through this recipe (poaching, making a sauce, and baking) as well as through others that have kept us fat and happy during long days in the mountains.

At the same time, though, we're trying to hook you on a general philosophy of backcountry cooking. Namely, that with some basic knowledge and ingredients, you can concoct masterpieces in the wilderness. If you don't have a home dehydrator, and arrive at your campsite with bindles of flour and bundles of sugar, beans and rice; if you've got time on your hands and a song on your lips; if you have a fired-up imagination and a fire on the hearth—you're in the right place. Recipes are fine in the beginning. You can jot some down in indelible ink on a few cards covered with plastic wrap that will fit into your map pouch, or you can tear out the ones in the Appendix. But the fact is, you don't need any. Now we show how to improvise, how to play variations on simple themes, how to work from the general to the specific: how to have your cake and eat it too!

Food Preparation Fundamentals

In Chapter 8 we assumed you knew all. Some wise old kitchen sage was just a phone call away. Here we assume you know naught. And can't get advice without hiking 13 miles to the nearest car phone. A few pages of basic training, then, and you'll be off on another adventure.

You'll be preparing food in one of five ways: boiling, baking, frying, grilling and poaching. Purists will insist that some of these are actually broiling, sautéing, wrap cooking and roasting, but this is not the Culinary Institute of America, and the fine points can be skipped.

Definitions

Boiling: Cooking in a liquid at its boiling point. Remember that the higher the altitude, the lower the temperature at which this occurs. That's the good news, because it takes less time to get the water bubbling. The bad news is that the lower boiling temperature means you have to cook the food longer than at sea level. The following chart indicates the differences:

Altitude	Boiling Point of Water	
	Fahr	*Cent*
Sea Level	212	100
2,000 ft.	208	98
5,000 ft.	203	95
7,500 ft.	198	92
10,000 ft.	194	90
15,000 ft.	185	85

Baking: Cooking in enclosed heat. At home this means using an oven. In the wilderness it means nesting a covered pot in coals. For best results, the pot is *not* set directly on top of the coals, but on a cleared spot in the middle of the ashes of a fire. It is then *surrounded* by the hot coals. Foil-wrapped food placed on or under coals (or both) is also "baked."

Frying: Cooking in fat over direct heat. The fat may be any cooking oil—vegetable, corn, peanut, canola, safflower, sesame—or vegetable shortenings like Crisco, Spry, etc. Margarine works too, if you keep it cool and in a tightly lidded container. Butter and olive oil spoil too rapidly to be practical. Bacon drippings are fine for frying, but bacon doesn't last much longer than butter. We travel with a plastic bottle of vegetable oil and several sticks of margarine in a small plastic container.

Grilling: Cooking over direct heat on a rack, grill or a stick, a.k.a. broiling or barbecuing. Backpacking grills are lightweight and small. Sticks, if used, should be pointed at one end, green so they don't burn, and long, so your hand doesn't cook along with the food. If the stick is big enough, it's called a spit, and if the food on it is rotated while cooking, this is known as roasting, a technique best left to Tudor kings with very large fireplaces.

Poaching: Cooking by simmering gently in just enough water to cover. Simmering describes what water does just below the boiling point: rather than bubble actively, it moves only slightly. This point is hard to maintain on an open fire, but happily it doesn't matter. Boiling works fine instead of poaching.

Practical Suggestions:

So much for theory. Practice is more rewarding. In getting started you should take the following into account:

Measurements: Our motto is "more or less." You won't have measuring spoons or cups and you don't need them. Approximations, guesses and tasting will suffice. In the following recipes, all of which make enough for two hungry adults, we try to keep quantities approximate. Where we use measures, they mean the following:

Spoonful: A standard camping-kit spoon, about soup-spoon size.

Cup: A Sierra-type cup, actually about a cup and a quarter by normal measurements. Sierra cups are lightweight, stack easily, and are less likely to burn your lips when drinking hot liquids than ordinary metal cups, because the rim is made of a heat-resistant alloy. They are available at all camping supply stores.

Handful: Just that, an average adult handful.

Pots: Our small one holds 4 cups, our medium 8 cups, and our large 12 cups.

Other Helpful Hints

Meal size: Camp cooking is cooking in miniature; i.e., a little goes a long way. Be prepared to scale down your normal at-home expectations as to how much you need. You don't want leftovers. Most are hard to store without attracting strange visitors. Plan meals with this in mind. If necessary, feed the last spoonful to the fire or the dogs.

Utensils: Pots and pans should be reasonably clean. Make sure the handles don't burn. If you have to stir something on the fire, lengthen your stirring spoon by tying on a stick. Garden gloves also work well to keep your hand from toasting.

Water: Have enough on hand for both cooking and cleaning up as you go. A dirty mixing pot often is needed for baking a few minutes later. Lids keep dirt and ashes out. Whenever you remove a pot top, set it on a clean rock or plate. Before replacing, check to be sure you won't be adding any unwanted twigs or leaves.

Fire: You want coals more than flame. A blaze burns rather than cooks. It also consumes a lot of fuel.

Fire Area: A fire requires a flat, cleared area, free of brush and clear of any overhanging branches. Don't put it too near your tent, or a slight wind may fill it with smoke. If the fire area is near some natural "chairs" (a big log will do) or "tables" (like a large flat rock), life is easier.

Ingredients: Keep them at hand. You don't want to run all over the campsite for garlic or soy sauce.

White or Wheat? We use unbleached white flour in all the recipes, but whole wheat works just as well.

Shade: Keep all food in the shade while you're in camp. You may need to move the food stash several times a day, but it's so little trouble, especially if you keep the perishables together, and so sensible it should become part of your daily routine. If you leave for the day, place the perishables somewhere out of the arc of the sun.

Tent: A veritable kitchen cabinet—use it. If there are several
stages to your food preparation and you need to put something aside, store it in the tent beyond the reach of flies,
bees and mosquitos. Make sure, however, that you don't
burn a hole in the tent floor with a hot pot. Feel the bottom of the pot, place it on a stone or plate if necessary, and
keep it away from sleeping bags and Ensolite pads. Don't
forget to zip the mosquito flap all the way. Also, be careful
of smelly spills. A tent reeking of raw fish or dried white
sauce is likely to attract unwanted guests, such as ants or
bears. If you have a spare poncho, spread that in the tent
before storing food inside. If you do spill anything on the
tent floor, wash it thoroughly before dark.

Covering Food: Foods you cook uncovered at home may need
to be covered over an open fire to keep out ash and dirt. In
such cases, set the lid on loosely and watch that the contents don't burn.

Washing Up: Make a wash-up area at the very edge of your
campsite so as not to attract insects and animals. Carry
water to the wash-up site rather than carrying dirty utensils to a lake or stream. Be sure any detergent, even "biodegradable" varieties, goes into the ground. Those bubbles
that you see more and more these days, even in the remotest wilderness areas, won't be going away. We usually
wash pots with no soap at all: a little hot water and a good
scrubber do fine. If you want to use soap, do so sparingly.
A few drops are enough.

When to Eat What? One hot meal a day usually suffices. Two
are sometimes essential. The hot-breakfast fanatic has to
be fed; there's no getting around it. The hot-dinner fanatic
also has to be fed. Now, if they're the same person....Don't
try to convert anyone to anything while out on the trail. If
you're a minimalist, cut back your own rations, but don't
force your partner the carboloader to abstain on your account. Just remember that there is no fixed order to
meals in the mountains, hot or cold. If you want nothing
but desserts for breakfast, enjoy. One day we made and
ate a chocolate cake with chocolate icing, a cherry pie and
a loaf of sweet sourdough nut bread. The next day roots
and grubs looked great. There's no accounting for the sud-

denness or strangeness of an attack of the munchies, so you might as well not fight it.

Invidious Comparisons: Whatever you cook in the wilderness won't be the same as what you make at home. The aim is not to duplicate what you can do seated at the controls of a 21st-century kitchen, but to make do with what you've got. The souffle you bake at 9,000 feet might fall flat. It might not even warrant the name you give it. But it will be full of eggs and cheese and trout and will taste at least as good as an omelet. So if you're a hotshot chef in the lowlands, don't despair when things turn out differently from what you think is "right." Hopefully, you'll enjoy the cooking as much as the eating.

KEYS AND SYMBOLS USED IN RECIPES:

❖	=	Can be prepared on camp stove or campfire
✳	=	Can be prepared only with campfire
c.	=	Sierra cupful
hfl.	=	Handful(s)
sp.	=	Camping kit spoonful

Pots:

small	=	4 cups
medium	=	8 cups
large	=	12 cups

Fish

Cleaning and Storing Fish

Unless you're a pelican or a down-at-the-heels samurai, you'll want to clean your fish before eating it—an easy task. Ideally you should do it as soon after your catch as possible, but that's often impossible. You may be on a day hike or out in the raft or too busy catching more to get far enough away from the lake to clean the one you've just caught. In those cases stow the fish is a Ziploc bag or a pot, or thread it on a stick. Try to keep the fish out of the sun.

Fish are easy to clean, but it's also easy to foul the environment while doing it. While floating on a pristine backcountry lake, nothing is more depressing than to look down and see fish entrails floating in the water. Always clean fish far from all fresh water sources—and from your campsite. And don't even begin to clean them until you've found a spot with soft soil or sand and have dug a hole or trench at least four or five inches deep with your heel or a cup. That's going to be your Dispose-All.

To clean a fish, you need a sharp knife and some rinse water. Hold the fish in your hand, belly up. Slit the belly from the vent (the small hole just in front of the back fin) to just behind the head. If you plan to cut off the head (lots of folks leave it on), do it now. Cut on a diagonal line from just behind the front fins through to the spinal column. The fish is going to be slippery; hold on tight. But that backbone is tough, so be careful you don't take your hand off along with the head as the sharp knife severs the bone.

The fish is now opened. Most of the entrails will spill out on their own (into the hole you've dug). Remove the remainder with your hand, scraping away the tissue along the backbone with a thumb nail or knife. That's all there is to it! Rinse out

Basic method of cleaning a fish: 1) Slit belly from anal vent to gills. 2) Sever lower junctions of gills. 3) Pull out innards and gills. 4) Run thumbnail along cavity to clean out dark matter.

the cavity, put the fish in a bag or pot, clean your knife and hands, pour out the dirty rinse water, cover up the hole and head for supper.

Fish are best cooked and eaten immediately after catching and cleaning. But this too is not always possible. To store the cleaned fish overnight, keep them in a plastic bag inside a pot. You don't need to use any water. Cover the pot and set a heavy rock on it to discourage late four-legged diners. The cold night air will preserve the fish and breakfast will be great.

Cooking Fish Without a Pan

You've bagged a couple rainbows and your partner has taken the required snapshot. The fish are fresh and cleaned; a feast is in order. There are many ways to cook fish: frying or poaching in a pan, stewing or baking in a pot, grilling or broiling over an open flame. For starters, let's say you left your frying pan in the car—at the time it seemed too heavy. The pot lids are too small and light to use as substitutes. The fish are biting on everything from hand-tied flies to Matzo balls, and the idea of one more fish stew palls. What to do? Go primitive. Use a stick, a rock, the flame or coals as your pan or oven. Here's how.

Primitive Trout Cooking

A lot of ink is spilled these days over such concepts as "back to basics," "less is more," "smaller is better." Well, here are several ways of putting theory into practice.

Trout on the Coals *

2 rainbow trout
1 campfire, flames low, coals just cooling
Pepper / hot sauce to taste
Lemon / lime juice

Toss fish in the coals! Honest. It works. If you were squeamish about ashes in your food, you wouldn't be here anyway.

The worst that'll happen is the fish will be charred beyond recognition. So who needs recognition? Extricate the blackened trout after three to five minutes (depending on the heat of the coals). Use a spare plate to scrape away the charred skin. The flesh will be fine and flaky. Add pepper/hot sauce and a squirt of lemon juice from the miniature plastic bottle. Make Neanderthal noises while eating.

Trout on a Stick ✱

Anybody who can roast a marshmallow can roast a trout on a stick too. And if that's all you've got by way of kitchen ware, use it.

2 rainbow trout
1 campfire, moderate flames, coals red hot
1 green, sharpened hardwood stick
Cooking oil
Pepper, salt to taste
Lemon / lime juice

Strictly speaking, this is a way to grill, not roast, fish. But the chances of dropping the fish into the fire are good, so you get the best of both techniques. Rub oil on the sharpened stick, lay the oiled part in the cleaned, open belly of the fish,

Trout on a stick.

poke the point of the stick into the head to secure it. Truss
the fish by poking twigs through one side of the belly, over
the stick, and through the other side of the belly. Season it
to taste and grill over red-hot coals. The smaller the fish,
the less time it takes: an 8" trout should be read in about 6-7
minutes. Check flesh with a fork or knife (or your fingers, if
you've lost the cutlery too). If it flakes easily, it's ready to eat.

Trout on a Rock ✳

OK, we've never done this, but others have. If a highly selective bear makes off with all your gear except a fishing line,
three matches, and some oil, you too can get dinner.

2 *rainbow trout*
1 *campfire, very hot*
1 *big, flat rock*
Cooking oil

Heat the rock in the fire. Work it to the edge of the fire
ring, oil the fish, set it on the flat face of the rock, turning
once during the cooking. No utensils? Gather round the rock
and eat with your hands. Incoherent Cro Magnon grunting
appropriate here.

Grilling Fish

There must be a word for people who hate fish: fishogonists?
fishophobes? They're the ones who catch a fish and then go
to elaborate lengths to disguise its taste by PO (Preparation
Overkill). Grilling is not one of their strong suits. Grilling is
simple, direct, honest: a tribute to the noble creature that
gave you such a good fight.

Grilled Trout ✳

2 *freshly caught small trout*
Cooking oil
Soy sauce / tamari
Rice vinegar / lemon juice

1 campfire, red hot coals
1 lightweight, wire-mesh grill or 3-pronged
* backpacking grill*

Oil the grill to prevent the fish from sticking. Set it about 5"
above the coals. Let the grill get very hot before it receives
the trout. Sprinkle cavity with soy sauce and rice vinegar,
also a light coat of same on the trout's skin. Toss on grill. (If
using a three-pronged grill, set the fish on it gently. Otherwise it'll end up in the fire.) After about 5 minutes, turn the
fish. A small spatula is useful for this, though chopsticks or a
knife and fork will do as well. Use the flake test for doneness:
that is, with a fork pry up a piece; if is flakes off easily, the
fish is finished, and you've just begun to eat. It will remind
you of that great Japanese restaurant you went to last year.

Baked Trout

One of the best and easiest ways to cook fish without a pan is
to wrap it in aluminum foil, set it on a bed of hot coals, and
cover it with another bed of coals. As the recipes below show,
there are endless variations to this way of cooking. We carry
enough foil for at least one meal made this way. About two-
and-a-half feet can be folded small and tucked inconspicuously
in a pack pouch. It's usable only once. And remember, foil
doesn't burn, so pack out the remains with your other non-organic garbage.

You can either wrap the fish individually or fashion a flat
"oven pan." First, crimp the edges up on all sides so the juices
won't spill out. Second, keep the "lid" opening toward you and
not the fire; that way you can open the foil with a minimum of
movement when the baking is done, without losing the juices.

Foil-Baked Trout ✳

2 10" trout
Rosemary / tarragon
Salt, pepper to taste
1 clove garlic, sliced thin
Small dab of margarine

Hot coals
1 - 2 1/2 ft. length heavy aluminum foil

Rub the cavity with the margarine, then season it with the herbs and garlic. Foil-wrap the fish tightly and place on a bed of coals. Cover with hot coals. Note: coals have a habit of cooling, so expect the fish to take about 15 minutes to bake. You may need to add fresh coals if the originals lose a lot of their heat along the way. If you get good at it, you can test for doneness by poking a fork through the foil, while the fish are cooking. If the fork slides in and out easily, meeting little resistance, dinner is done. Or take the whole shmeer out of the fire, open, check, eat, or return for a little more cooking.

VARIATIONS ON FOIL-BAKED TROUT:

- Bake in soy sauce, garlic, ginger and Chinese sesame oil.
- Stuff the fish with finely chopped nuts and prunes soaked for an hour or so in brandy and warm water. Add a dash of sesame oil.
- Lay the fish on a bed of cooked rice, add a mixture of chopped nuts and cut-up dried fruits (apricots, raisins, apples, prunes), salt, curry powder and lemon juice.
- If you find any roe (fish eggs) when cleaning the fish save them. Put the roe back in the cavity with whatever else strikes your fancy and bake.

Pan-Fried Fish

If you carry a cast-iron frying pan into the mountains, you'll develop very strong calf muscles but you won't get too far. If, however, you bring a lightweight, teflon-coated pan, the slight increment in weight will be repaid many times over in versatility and pleasure. You can't cook a pancake on a stick, and it's hell to fry a fish without a pan.

Pan-fried trout are so easy and satisfying that you may not get beyond them in a week in the mountains. Small lake or stream trout are tender, cook fast and need almost nothing to enhance their flavor. A pan, lightly greased and set on a grill or nestled between rocks about four to five inches above a bed of coals, and a string of cleaned, lightly seasoned trout are all you need for a first-rate meal. The oil should be hot before you add the fish. Turn them over after about four or five minutes (sooner if they're small or the fire is very hot) and cook for another four or five minutes. Sprinkle generously with lemon juice. That's all, folks.

As soon as the flesh flakes with a fork, it's done. Be careful at this stage; an overcooked fish loses a lot of flavor. When in doubt, take the fish off the fire sooner rather than later. You can always put it back, but you can't reverse a burn-out. All our suggestions for minutes per side are approximate. We don't wear watches in the wilderness. It's better to feel for doneness, following the clock in your head, than to put a stop watch on the food in your pan.

One other precaution: make sure the oil doesn't burn. It starts to smoke and turns black if it gets too hot. At the smoking stage, add more oil to the pan to reduce the temperature. By experimenting with the heat of the fire and the height of the pan above it, you'll soon get the right combination and the fish will cook to perfection.

Pan-Fried Trout ❖

4 8" trout, cleaned, with heads left on
Cooking oil / margarine
Salt, pepper to taste
Lemon juice

Heat a mixture of oil and margarine if you can spare them; otherwise one or the other. Brown the trout on one side, about 4 minutes; turn and finish cooking. Salt and pepper to taste. Test for doneness by flaking. Turn out on plate, pour the cooking oils over fish, add a dash of lemon juice.

Trout Amandine 1 (Trout with almonds) ❖

Prepare as Pan-Fried Trout. Add a handful of chopped almonds to the pan after you have removed the cooked fish. Brown the almonds quickly in the cooking oils. Do not burn. Spread almonds over the trout and the juices over all. This is simple and elegant, maybe the best of all ways to prepare a freshly caught small trout. Don't worry if you only have peanuts or cashews. It'll taste just as good, and Escoffier is not likely to pop out from behind a tree to point an accusing finger.

Trout Amandine 2 ❖

Dust the fish with a handful of seasoned flour. To season flour add any combination of spices to it and mix: pepper, rosemary, tarragon, basil, ginger. Prepare as per Trout Amandine #1.

Trout Meunière (Flour-dipped, Pan-Fried Trout) ❖

"Meunière" means a miller, someone who grinds grain to make flour. This is one of the classic ways of preparing fresh whole trout. Note that "sp." here means "spoon," as in "mess-kit" spoon. Quantities are not important. Not to worry.

4 fresh, cleaned trout, with heads left on
2-4 sp. margarine / cooking oil
2 sp. flour
Salt, pepper to taste
Lemon / lime juice

Dip the trout in flour to coat. Heat oils—a mix of the two is great—and add fish. Season to taste. Brown on one side, about 4 minutes. Turn and complete cooking. Add a dash of lemon juice. Serve. Why leave the head on in these recipes? For both taste and style. The cheek meat on a fish is the tenderest of all. Why give it to the scavengers? And a whole cooked trout is beautiful. That's reason enough.

TROUT MEUNIÈRE VARIATIONS:

- Prepare as per Trout Meunière, but use a mixture of flour and cornmeal. Some old timers put the flour-cornmeal mixture in a bag, drop in the fish, shake, and fry.
- Make a small cup of milk with instant powdered milk and water, dip the fish into the milk, then the flour or flour- cornmeal mixture. Cook as for Trout Meunière.

- Substitute an egg for the milk. Crack it into a pot lid and beat lightly with a fork. To make it go farther, add a spoonful of water or milk to the egg. Dip the fish into the egg and then into the seasoned flour.

- Suppose you run out of flour and cornmeal and still want to coat the fish? Crush a couple of RyKrisp or whatever other crackers you have between a plate and your Sierra cup. Using this coarse meal, proceed with or without egg or milk.

- A piece of stale bread or biscuit can also replace flour or cornmeal. Just make a fine layer of crumbs by rubbing the bread between your hands. Ground up nuts, seeds, left-over rice—almost anything'll do. Use your imagination.

Trout Flambé ❖

Plan to serve this spectacular dish after dark for best effect. Prepare as in any of the pan fried recipes. Just before eating, pour a little brandy in a Sierra cup, hold it over the fire until it's warm to the touch and light it with a match. As the brandy catches fire, pour it over the trout. A soft blue flame will dance over and around the trout for up to half a minute and will add another delicate flavor to the dish.

Poaching

We've noticed on camping trips that we often crave rib-sticking foods, the kind that even in small quantities make us feel full. This may be a genuine physiological need: to replenish bodies that have worked abnormally hard over two or three days. Or it may be all in the mind: a need to eat a lot when there isn't a lot to eat. Whatever the cause, the consequence is either to eat everything in one sitting and then go home, or devise ways of making hearty, bulky meals with what you've got. We prefer the latter. That's where poaching comes in.

If you want a thick stew, curry, trout in white sauce, soufflé, or crepes, you won't want to pick bones and skin out of them. To remove these beforehand, simply poach the fish. This leaves the flesh tender and ready to eat; the rest is disposable. Here's how.

Poached Trout ❖

A poached fish is a finished product. Seasoned well and not over-cooked, it's as tender as you'll get a trout. But a poached fish is also part of a process that involves other methods of cooking. The six recipes following this one will show you how to combine several methods of preparing fish in order to end up with something definitely more than the sum of its parts.

2 fresh, cleaned trout
Seasonings to taste: pepper, Italian herbs
Lemon juice
Fry pan filled with boiling water

Put enough water in your frying pan to barely cover the fish. Season it with salt and herbs to taste. Place the pan over the fire and let the water come to a slight boil. The fish will curl up. That's all right. There's also no need to turn the fish over. It's done when the skin peels off easily, and the flesh has lost its "transparent" look and comes off the bone at a nod and beckon. This takes about 10 minutes from the time the water begins to boil.

Remove the pan from the heat, the fish from the pan, and then with fork, knife or fingers peel off the skin and flake the flesh from the bones. Ideally, the backbone comes off in one piece, taking most of the skeleton and leaving you with a simple mop-up operation close to the fins. It's simple, but work fast or you'll end up wearing a halo of flies and other airborne participants. When finished, place the fish in the tent until ready to use and go bury the skin and bones. If you won't be using the poaching water (see *Trout in Curried Sauce, Fried Rice Chinese Style,* or *Hidden Lake Soufflé* for possibilities), throw it out far from both your living area and the lake or stream.

Trout Tandouri ❖

This is a curry dish, filling and fiery. Eat it, and you'll find the rainbow at the end of the pot. hfl. = Handful(s).

3 small rainbow trout, cleaned and poached
2 hfl. rice, boiled
Assorted chopped nuts, dried fruits, about a small dishful
Chopped dried onion, as much as you like
Cooking oil
2-3 large pinches garam masala to taste
Cayenne pepper (optional)
Lemon / lime juice (optional)

Heat up just enough oil to cover the bottom of your frying pan. Toss in the poached fish, rice, nuts and fruit. Season with garam masala and cayenne to taste. Add a dash of lime juice. Stir frequently. Done when hot. Serve with a Campground Chutney (pg.257). Guaranteed to warm whatever in you is not.

Trout in Curried Sauce ❖

Ingredients are the same as for Trout Tandouri. Add the poached trout to a cup of white sauce made with the poaching liquid, and flavored with garam masala and cayenne. Serve over boiled rice with nuts and fruits on the side, and a big helping of chutney (pg. 257).

Fried Rice Chinese Style ❖

3 small trout, cleaned and poached
2 hfl. rice, boiled
2+ cloves garlic, chopped
Chinese sesame oil / peanut oil / cooking oil
Powdered ginger
Dry mustard
Black pepper
Soy sauce

Heat oils (a mixture is desirable but not necessary) in frying pan. Add poached trout, rice and spices. Fry, stirring, till hot. Then add soy sauce to taste, and stir thoroughly. Note: the soy sauce provides all the salt you'll need. The Chinese have a saying: Chinese food doesn't taste good unless you use chopsticks. You have now been warned.

Hidden Lake Soufflé ✳

A soufflé is a concoction made by putting cooked food—in this case, poached trout—into a sauce, pumping it up with air provided by beaten egg whites, and baking. This definition may not satisfy the cognoscenti, and our methods will probably plunge them into a deep culinary depression, but they work, and the results are unspeakably good.

A soufflé is a three-stage affair: poaching the fish, making a white sauce with the poaching liquid, and folding in beaten egg whites before baking. Note: "c." = Sierra cup(s). Here are the instructions:

2-4 small (8") trout, cleaned and poached (pg. 219)
1 1/2 c. thick white sauce (pg. 225)
1-2 eggs, separated
Salt, pepper to taste

Never separated egg whites from yolks? Crack the egg in half gently against the side of a pot, or strike a knife against the shell. Hold half the shell in each hand. Most of the white will drool into the container by itself. Help the rest by moving the yolk back and forth between the shell halves. Don't kill yourself to get all the white. It's OK if a little yolk stays along.

After separating the eggs, mix a spoonful of the cooked sauce into the yolks so they won't hard-boil, then add to the sauce to make it thicker and richer. Now toss in the poached fish and seasonings. Stir and remove sauce from heat. Reserve (in tent if there are flies).

Beat egg whites with the spring-loaded swizzle stick or a wire whisk. (If you can spare two eggs, all the better, but one will do too.) The idea is to get them stiff but not dry. Out here in the wilderness this isn't always possible or necessary. Basically you're trying to whip air into them. The bigger the pot and the more you agitate the egg whites, the better your chances of ending up with the right product. We've tried to use forks as beaters with little luck. Our trusty swizzle stick was just the ticket until it finally broke down this past year and seems irreplaceable. (Try some old bar or kitchen-supply stores.) A miniature wire whisk works OK.

Fold the beaten egg whites into the sauce, gently as she goes. Just turn the sauce over on the whites with a spoon till they're pretty thoroughly incorporated. Lose their air and the soufflé will end up with a specific gravity close to that of lead.

Now grease and lightly flour the middle-sized pot (even if you have to do some dish washing and pot juggling to get it free and clean), and pour in the soufflé mixture. It should come about one-third of the way up the pot, depending on how much fish you have. Cover and bake.

You've already got a fire going (to poach and thicken the sauce) so by now the coals are glowing red. Scoop out a pot-sized depression in the ashes near the front of the fire and set the pot down—not on the coals, but on the cleared ground or warm ashes. With a heavy stick, pile coals around the pot until it's nestled up to its lid in heat. If the coals are too hot, the souffle will burn. If they're too cool, it'll take ages to cook and you'll do a slow burn with it. Ideally, the coals should have lost their most intense heat; the fiery red glare should be going out of them. Baking time will be about 20-30 minutes, or a chapter from a good book. You may need to add coals to the pile to keep its warmth constant.

It's permissible to peek but be careful not to knock everything awry or get ashes in the pot. Don't worry if the outside of the soufflé is slightly burned; the inside will be as tasty as promised. The soufflé *will* actually rise, to almost double its bulk, and will look spectacular. Savor it quickly, however, for it deflates rapidly after taken off the heat. But by then, appetite will take over from aesthetics. Tuck in, eat up.

Trout Crepes ❖

Once you can poach a fish and prepare a sauce, you also have the makings of the filling for crepes.

2-3 fresh trout, cleaned and poached
1 1/2 c. thick white sauce, made with poaching liquid
Seasonings to taste
2 c. crepe batter (pg. 237)

Crepes are made with eggs, so you don't need any in the sauce. Keep the sauce warm, near the fire, and covered while you make the crepes. It's neither easy nor necessary to make all the crepes at once, so eat them in turns as they come off the fire. Put a crepe on a plate, spoon sauce into it, wrap and eat. Then let your partner(s) follow suit.

Trout, Rice and Bean Salad ❖

Here's another use of poached trout, especially if you've had an abundance of luck on the lake. Take the leftover poached, flaked trout and add it to our famous *Bean and Rice Salad* (pg. 232).

Sashimi (Japanese-style Raw Fish)

This book does not aim at conversions. If the idea of eating raw fish turns you green, move on to sauces. But if you like *sashimi*, learn how to prepare it, because you'll never have fresher fish than the ones you catch. Here are some important facts about preparing *sashimi* in the wilderness:

Raw Trout

- The fish must be absolutely fresh. They can't sit around for a couple hours in a pot, even cleaned. You need to eat them soon after catching or keep them alive until you have enough (say, four or five 8" trout) for a meal. Incidentally, if you're fishing near a snowfield, you can pack your catch in snow immediately, and have them as iced as your local fishmonger's.

- There's not much flesh on a small trout. Some is also lost in skinning and boning. Don't expect a filling meal, but *sashimi* is a perfect lunch snack.

- There are two ways to prepare it. For both, clean the fish thoroughly. In the first, skin it and peel the flesh from the bones. To skin a fish, begin by cutting under the fins and yanking them toward the head. Then slice along the backbone from head to tail. With your knife, loosen the skin around the gills. Now work your fingers, the knife, or both, under the skin at the head and strip it back toward the tail. Once the fish is skinned, cut away the flesh, beginning at the backbone and working down. Toward the end, fingers work better than a knife. Place the raw fish in a Sierra cup.

- In the second method, bone the fish first, then remove the skin. Spread open the cleaned and beheaded fish, gutted side facing you. With your knife cut gently along one side of the backbone from top to tail. Do the same on the other side. This severs the spine from the skeletal bones or ribs, and it can be pulled out, working from neck to tail. Last, get the skeletal bones out. Starting from the tail, work your blade under the bones gently toward the neck, turn the knife around, and then come back toward the tail. Starting from the neck, lift the bones away. This leaves a whole, flat, boned fish with the skin still on the "under" side. You can now remove the flesh from the skin by working your blade under the flesh and scraping it away. Start at the tail which you can grasp for leverage, and move up. You'll have the fish in one piece this way. Again put it into a Sierra cup.

- One word of caution. All this boning and skinning tends to draw flies. Unless you're fast, you may want to do it in your tent. If so, spread a poncho on the floor so the tent will stay clean even if you're messy.

- You need a spicy condiment with your *sashimi*, as well as some soy sauce. The Japanese use a fiery green horseradish called *wasabi*. This comes in powdered form. You add enough water to make a paste, which is then added to the soy sauce. The fish is dipped into it and eaten straight away. You needn't carry a packet of dried *wasabi*. Dry mustard, particularly the good hot kind, will do just as well and is, frankly, more functional, since you can use it in many other dishes. Either way, *sashimi* is great! Give it a try.

Sauces

You've been in the mountains eight days and are low on supplies. You have some RyKrisp left, a lump of degenerating cheese, a few spoonfuls of flour, some oil that looks like it came from a crank case and a handful of milk powder. The prospects of catching a trout are dim. You want a hot meal. Not to worry! If you know how to make a sauce you're in business. A combination of oil, flour, milk powder and water will give you a base for the cheese and whatever spices you have left. When it's all melted, thick and steaming hot, you've got yourself a kind of rarebit which can be eaten on the crackers for a filling, hearty meal.

This kind of sauce, practically a meal in itself, can also stretch other foods far and in many directions. It has almost as many names as uses: cream sauce, white sauce, bechamel. It's basically equal parts shortening (usually butter) and flour, which are heated for a few minutes before you slowly add liquid (usually milk or the stock with which you've been cooking). That's it. Some seasonings, cheese, perhaps an egg yolk give you sauce thick enough to eat alone or use in a soufflé, crepes, curry or cream soup.

At home, you'd use real butter and whole milk. Over an open fire and with neither on hand, the technique changes a bit, but the principle is the same.

White Sauce ❖

3 sp. margarine/shortening/oil
3 sp. flour
1-2 c. poaching liquid, or
1-2+ c. water
1 sp. milk powder
Salt, pepper, curry powder, nutmeg, paprika to taste

In a small pot melt the margarine (or, in descending order of preference, shortening or oil: they all work). Add equal amount of flour (heaping spoonfuls if a very thick sauce is desired). Stir this mixture over the heat for a minute or two to kill the taste of the raw flour. In your kitchen you'd use a low flame. At a campfire, that isn't so easy; alternate the pan on and off the heat to prevent the sauce from burning. If you are using the poaching liquid from the fish, add this a little at a time, stirring. If you are using the milk powder and water, add the milk powder to the mixture, then the water a little at a time, stirring. The mixture will thicken almost instantly. Continue to add liquid slowly. By the time you've added a cupful or more, the sauce will have thinned out, much to the relief of anyone who thought they were being conned into making kindergarten paste. Keep stirring till smooth. Add seasonings to taste. The sauce is done when reasonably thick and smooth. Don't lose heart if the flour and milk powder aren't completely absorbed by the liquid. It'll still be hot, filling and delicious. When done, add whatever else you want: poached fish, crushed biscuits, cheese, cooked rice, noodles.

United Nations Rarebit ❖

It would be an insult to the Welsh to call this by its conventional name, so we'll let the Security Council decide its provenance. Anyway, it'll stick to more than ribs and keep you fat and happy.

3 c. white sauce
3-4+ sp. sliced cheese
1 egg (optional)
Hot sauce
Brandy

Add as much sliced cheese as you can spare to the completed white sauce. If you have an unaccounted for egg, beat it well and add. Continue to stir till cheese is melted. Season with hot sauce to taste and a dash of brandy from the medicine kit. Serve on crackers, boiled rice, or fresh baked bread.

If the sauce is too thick or pasty, keep adding liquid till you get the right consistency. If it's too thin, either let the sauce boil down while stirring, or in a pot lid, make 5 or 6 marble-sized balls of dough from flour and shortening or oil. Drop these into the sauce and stir. They'll thicken the sauce without leaving it filled with lumps of unabsorbed flour which would happen if you added flour alone to the sauce.

Tomato Sauce ❖

Here is the stripped-down fighting version of the homemade sauce (pg. 192) you weren't able to dehydrate this year. As long as you have some dried tomatoes and onions, perhaps some dried mushrooms and jerky, you're in business. You'll use this sauce for pasta and for the pizza (pg. 248) you can't live without.

1 lg hfl. dehydrated tomatoes
1 hfl. dehydrated onions
1 clove garlic, sliced
1 hfl. dehydrated mushrooms
2 sp. sliced or diced jerky (optional)
Mixed Italian spices
Salt, pepper to taste
Water

Cover the tomatoes with twice their volume of water. Bring to boil and stir frequently while the tomatoes are rehydrating. Add water as necessary. The tomatoes will not completely transform into a sauce, but enough to give a first-rate illusion of same, about 20 minutes. About half way through the cooking, add the onions, mushrooms, garlic, jerky and spices. Continue to cook till the ingredients absorb most of the water and become saucy. Adjust seasonings. Ta Da!

Note: If this is going to be the base of your pizza, omit the onions, mushrooms and jerky, as they'll go on separately.

Rice, Noodles, and Beans

You can't always count on catching fish, but you can always count on a hot and filling meal if you have any of these great staples of backpacking. They can be eaten alone, hot or cold (though cooked), in stews and soups, in freeze-dried dinners to add bulk and a little real taste, in puddings, salads, omelets and a thousand other dishes. Their only drawback is that they're heavy, so you need to limit the amounts you take and make do with what you can sensibly carry.

Rice

Put two generous handfuls of white rice in the medium pot with a pinch of salt. Add enough water to come up to just below the middle knuckle of your forefinger. This is enough rice for two adults. We can't explain the knuckle measure. It was taught to us years ago and for reasons that are still mysterious, is invariably correct. Neither the size of the finger nor the size of the hand nor the size pot seem to matter. Remember: the water will boil faster in the mountains than at sea level. Thus the knuckle measure will give you more water to start off with than you'd use for a good fluffy rice at home.

White rice cooks in about 10 to 15 minutes, depending on the heat of the fire. Brown rice requires more water, to about the middle of the knuckle, and more time to cook. Allow about 25 minutes. To make the pot easier to clean, pour water in it immediately after you've spooned out the rice, and keep it warm near the fire. By wash-up time, the pot almost cleans itself!

Fried Rice With Vegetables & Chicken ❖

This joins *Trout Tandouri* and *Fried Rice Chinese Style* in the fried-rice repertoire.

2 hfl. boiled rice
1 c. mixed dried vegetables, rehydrated in water to cover
1 hfl. chopped nuts
Sliced / diced chicken jerky (optional)
1 clove garlic, sliced
Cooking oil
Hot sauce, spices to taste

Heat the oil in the frying pan, add garlic and nuts till just turning brown, then vegies and spices. Stir and sauté till done; add cooked rice, stir till thoroughly mixed. Adjust seasonings.

Rice Pudding ✳

This can be a meal in itself—dessert and main course combined. Seem like too many ingredients? Maybe, but check that food list (Table 1) back in Chapter 4. You have all the makings well within your weight limit.

2 hfl. cooked rice
1 sp. milk powder
1/2 c. water
2+ sp. sugar
Pinch of salt
Cinnamon to taste
1 egg
Dash lemon/lime juice
1/2 sp. margarine
1 hfl. chopped dried fruit
Dash of brandy (your basic vanilla substitute)
1 hfl. crushed ginger snaps/crackers

Oil or grease a medium pot. Line it with crushed ginger snaps or crackers. Mix the rice, milk powder, water, sugar, salt, cinnamon, egg, lemon juice, margarine, fruit, and brandy thoroughly and add to the lined pot. Cover with more crushed ginger snaps. Cover and bake in coals until the pudding is set, about 20 minutes. Eat hot or cold.

If you're out of some ingredients, improvise. No spare egg? You can still make the pudding. It may not be as rich, but no one's measuring on a taste meter. Substitute a spoon of flour or cornmeal and a little more water. No margarine? Use oil. Ditto for the seasonings—not everyone carries lemon juice or even cinnamon (although no backpacker carrying cinnamon has ever been known to starve in the wilderness). Maybe throw in some Swiss Miss powdered chocolate drink instead of sugar and cinnamon. Fine. And of course the cookie crumbs can be left out. Experiment. Enjoy.

Noodles

If pasta palls, go East. Chinese wheat or rice noodles, Japanese buckwheat noodles (*soba*) are great boiled, fried, baked. They can substitute for almost all the rice recipes: *Trout Tandouri, Fried Rice Chinese Style, Trout, Rice and Bean Salad,* or *Fried Rice with Vegetables and Chicken.*

Cooking Noodles ❖

Noodles don't double in bulk when cooked, but the more water you use the less they stick together and to the pot. Use the large pot, half to three-quarters full of water, add salt, boil, and throw in the noodles. Two very generous handfuls will get two of you through a meal. The water should boil rapidly as they cook. They taste done in about 10-12 minutes (at moderate to high altitudes). If you plan to use them in another dish you need time to put together, just drain the noodles, add fresh cold water to cover and let them stand. This prevents them from sticking together. When everything is ready, drain them again, and away you go. If you make a sauce, use the noodle water as the liquid base. It's already hot and flavorful.

Cold Noodle Salad ❖

1/2 packet Japanese buckwheat noodles (soba), cooked
and drained
Sesame oil / regular cooking oil
Rice vinegar / regular vinegar
1 hfl. dried mixed vegetables, rehydrated
Sprinkling of mung bean sprouts (optional)
Salt, pepper to taste

Mix all ingredients in a pot. Adjust seasonings. Serve.

Beans ❖

Beans are so good, nutritious and easily prepared that it's a pity they weigh so much. Nevertheless, they are definitely worth taking along, in limited amounts. And it doesn't matter what kinds you bring. Red, kidney, white, black beans can all be used with equal ease. Put a couple handfuls in a pot, cover with cold water, cover the pot and soak overnight or for four to five hours during the day. Empty the old water, cover again with fresh water, and cook until the beans are tender, 25-40 minutes, depending on the amount and kind of beans and the heat of the fire. That's all there is to it. Use the cooking liquid for making sauces.

Lentils and split peas may be substituted for beans in most of these recipes. *Note*: Watch your fuel supply if cooking beans on a camp stove. It may cost you other meals down the line.

Fried Rice and Beans ❖

As any Mexican cook will tell you, the combination of rice and beans is a nutritional powerhouse. It's also plain good eating. Spice it up with chili powder, cayenne or hot sauce and you've got a ready-made fiesta. To the recipe *Fried Rice with Vegetables and Chicken* add cooked beans and fry till done. If spicy, make sure you've got a full water bottle within reach.

Baked Rice and Beans in Cheese Sauce ✻

1 hfl. boiled rice
1 hfl. cooked beans
2 c. white sauce
3 sp. sliced cheese
Cayenne, chili powder, hot sauce

To the white sauce, add the cheese and stir till melted. Add the rice and beans, mix. Bake in coals 10 to 15 minutes till set. Serve with mariachi music and plenty of water.

Refried Beans ❖

2 hfl. cooked beans and the cooking liquid
Cooking oil
Hot sauce, pepper
Sliced cheese

Drain the beans but reserve the liquid. Heat oil in the frying pan. Mash the beans with a fork or spatula as they're frying. If the beans get too dry, add some of the reserved liquid. Fry slowly, season with pepper and hot sauce. Slice cheese to taste over them. Eat with biscuits and you get a great Tex-Mex meal.

Ranch Omelet ❖

For two adults, scramble three eggs with refried beans and some dried tomatoes. Serve with plenty of hot sauce.

Bean and Rice Salad ❖

2 hfl. beans, cooked, drained, cooled.
2 hfl. cooked rice
1 poached trout (optional)
1 hfl. bean sprouts
Salt, pepper, lemon juice, sesame oil, mustard powder.

Mix all ingredients together. Season to taste. This is a wonderful meal, even without the trout.

Bean and Sprouts Salad ❖

Same as above, though without the rice. Use half beans and half mung-bean sprouts. Season as above.

Bean Sprouts

We always bring some dry mung beans to sprout on the trail. They're a great snack, excellent in soups, fried rice, sauces, souffles, and salads. The first night, soak a handful in a plastic bag. In the morning, drain the water, close the bag and keep in a dark place. While hiking, we carry them in the smallest nested pot; at camp, they're stored in the backpack. Rinse once or twice a day to keep moist, but not wet. They'll sprout in about three days. They don't need to be cooked, but do get moldy fast, so when they're ready, use them. Then begin a new batch.

Drinking Your Dinner: Soups and Stews

The dry soup mixes that you buy in the local market taste all right, but they're not very filling. If they're going to be your supper, you need to jack them up, give them some body and thus a bit of soul. A handful of uncooked rice or noodles, as much cooked rice and beans as you want, a clove of garlic, a slice of onion, vegetables from your home dehydrator, broken crackers, poached fish, cheese—whatever seems to fit your soup mix will thicken the pot. Starting from scratch is easy too. Here are a couple examples.

Fish Stew or Chowder ❖

Clean two or three fish, but save the heads. Toss fish and heads into the big pot, cover with water and poach. Save the liquid in another pot, remove and bury the bones, heads and skin, then combine the fish and liquid. If necessary, add water. Toss in two handfuls of rice (less for more fish), and as much chopped onion and garlic as you can spare. Season with salt, pepper, herbs, even a dash of hot sauce. Boil slowly until the rice is done. The thicker the better, so a packet of dry soup mix, especially leek, helps immeasurably. Ignore the packet's directions, and keep tinkering with the seasonings until it tastes just right.

VARIATIONS:
- For Chinese-style "hot-and-sour" soup, add a good dash of vinegar and considerable black pepper.

- For New England chowder, add a spoonful of milk powder just before it comes off the fire.

Black Bean Soup ❖

Soak overnight and cook two handfuls of black beans in the big pot. If you've got a packet of chicken or beef soup stock, add that, as much dried chopped onion as you can spare, some chips of jerky, lots of garlic, salt, pepper and cayenne. Bring to a boil and let simmer for an hour if you've got the time and the coals are working right. Long cooking gives it more flavor, but even 20 minutes is fine since all the ingredients have already been cooked. Just before serving, add a dash of lemon juice or vinegar and a good hit of brandy. That's it. You'll want seconds, guaranteed. And if you don't have black beans, use what you have and just call it by a different name.

Lentil or Pea Soups ❖

If you prefer lentils or dried peas to beans and noodles, take them to use as you would for bean soup. Like beans, lentils and peas need two- to three-hours' soaking before cooking.

Pancakes and Crepes

There's something about the cold morning air, a warm fire, a hot griddle and real maple syrup that makes pancakes almost a ritual necessity on a backpacking trip. Here's how to make them.

Ready-made pancake mixes are available in supermarkets. Natural ones are available in some health food and whole grain stores. They're adequate. The only problem is you can't unmix them. All you can do with them is make pancakes. If you try using it as a flour supplement or substitute in breads and cakes, you'll end up with something that tastes and looks like a pancake with elephantiasis. The same goes for sauces. You get a warm pancake batter (with cheese), edible only in life-threatening situations. As long as you're taking flour, eggs and milk powder anyway, why not start from scratch?

Pancake batter is made of flour, eggs and milk, to which some shortening and a leavening agent such as baking powder are added. Change the proportions and you get different kinds of pancakes: crepes, for example. There are only a few general rules:

- Always add the liquid ingredients to the dry. This is a conservation principle: if you start with too much liquid, you'll waste a lot of flour thickening the batter. But starting with flour, you can add the liquid gradually until the batter is just right. Water is usually expendable.

- You don't need to grease your pan if the batter is made right. The oil or shortening goes in the batter, not in the pan. A thin film of oil won't hurt, but with a decent pan—it doesn't even have to be teflon coated—it won't be necessary. Crepes need a little oil in the pan, but not much.

- Heat the pan before you pour batter in. Test by splashing a few drops of water into the pan. If they dance, sizzle and evaporate, you're ready to go.

- The first pancake is a test run. If it sticks to the pan or isn't golden brown, the pan isn't "tempered" yet. Scrape it off. The second won't stick. If the first one tastes like a sodden brick, you need more liquid. A runny mess means you need more flour. With a little refining, the rest of the pancakes will be just fine.

Basic Pancakes ❖

At home, the usual proportion for pancakes is roughly 2:2:2— two cups flour, two cups milk and two eggs. In the wilderness, the proportions are the same, though the quantity is reduced. A Sierra cup holds around 6 heaping spoonfuls of flour, which makes way too many pancakes for two adults. Our recipes make from 10 to 12 inflated "silver dollar" pancakes, more than enough for two. The cakes are thick, light and filling. You could write home about them. Except there isn't a post office within 3-days' walk.

4 heaping sp. flour
1 sp. milk powder
Dash of salt
1/2 sp. sugar (optional)
1 egg, beaten
2 sp. oil/melted margarine
1/2 c. water

In a small pot mix the flour, milk powder, salt, and, if you like, the sugar and leavening agent. Not to worry if you don't have baking powder or soda; they're not necessary, and frankly we rarely use them for pancakes at any altitude, home or away. Add the beaten egg and oil to the dry ingredients and stir quickly. To hell with any lumps! Now add the water gradually, stirring. The batter will be thick. So you may need to add a bit more water, just enough to keep it thick but still smooth enough to flow off a spoon, like a thick velvet ribbon. Don't worry about getting a perfectly smooth batter. Lumps will disappear in the cooking.

To cook, drop a large spoonful of batter in the middle of the heated pan. If it looks pitifully small, add a dollop more. The cake is ready to flip (only once) when bubbles begin to form on the surface. Flip and let cook another few minutes. The second side never takes as long as the first. That's it. Eat! Or, if the first one is good, make 3 or 4 pancakes at one time so that one of you can have a decent breakfast. Then trade places.

VARIATIONS:

- Use the same proportions, but separate the egg and use only the yolk. After the batter is ready, beat the white until it's stiff but not dry, exactly as you would for a soufflé. Fold the beaten white into the batter gently, to preserve as much of the air as possible. Cook as above. The result will be so light that you'll seriously rethink the theory of gravity.

- Chop apricots, apples, banana chips into tiny pieces and add to the batter.

- Add a half-spoonful of sourdough starter to the dry ingredients and omit the baking powder (See Starting the Sourdough, pg. 240). Whole wheat or buckwheat flour, a mixture of flour and cornmeal work well and make great pancakes. So do flour with ground up RyKrisp, ginger snaps or vanilla wafers. Just remember that each kind of flour has a different moisture content, so adjust the liquid accordingly.

Crepes ❖

Crepes are French pancakes. They should be paper thin, to wrap other foods in. To achieve the thinness, change the proportions of flour to liquid to eggs. At home, it would be roughly 2:2:4 (two cups flour, two cups milk and four eggs). At 9,000 feet, you're unlikely to have that many eggs to spare. So stick with one egg and follow the basic pancake recipe with the following changes:

- Omit the baking powder or soda. Instead of a spoonful of milk powder, use a ½ spoonful and increase the water to make a thin batter—thin enough to look drinkable, like a homemade smoothie.

- No self-respecting crepe recipe includes oil in the batter. If tradition counts with you, leave it out and spread a thin film of oil on the pan for each crepe. We, however, are not so self-respecting, and after making sure the Academie Francaise is not meeting in the nearest bog, we throw in a spoonful anyway.

- If you have time to fish before breakfast, set the crepe batter aside, covered, in a cool spot. Crepe batter is happier if it sits a while. When you get back, poach your fish, crank up a sauce, and savor trout crepes.

COOKING THE CREPES:

Pour two or three spoons of batter into a sizzling pan. Tilt the pan away from you, then to the side, then toward you so the batter spreads out roughly in a circle as thin as you can get it. The more you practice, the easier it gets and the rounder and thinner the crepes will be. They'll only take a minute or so to cook and are ready to turn when the center looks almost, but not quite, dry. Either work a spatula underneath to turn it, or pick it up in your hand and flip it over. The second side takes less time than the first. The result should be cooked but also pliable, so it can be wrapped around food.

CREPE FILLINGS:

- For trout crepes see pg. 222
- For cheese crepes see pg. 226

Fruit Crepes

Simmer a handful or so of mixed dried fruits in water to cover. Add a spoonful or two of sugar. Stir and simmer till a thick stewed fruit is formed. Stuff crepes with the fruit, sprinkle sugar and cinnamon on top and serve. These can also be flambéd after dark, as homage to the inventor of Crepes Suzette.

Breads

Anybody who can make pancakes can make pan-fried bread. And anybody who can make the dough for pan-fried breads can add some yeast and bake the bread in a pot in the coals. And anybody who can do that can just as easily make a cake. No excuses.

For pancakes, the liquid ingredients outnumber the dry and you end up with batter. In bread, the opposite is true and you end up with dough. The dough can be picked up without running down your sleeve and dripping all over your shoe. It can be folded or spindled without harm. A cake is somewhere in between: in other words a stiff sweet batter and the promise of dessert.

There's considerable lore about campfire breads and cakes, such as bannock, the basic pan bread, so basic it consists of little more than flour and water with a little baking powder and salt tossed in for luck; sourdough, the old-time, home-made substitute for yeast once carried around in pots hung from the saddle in gold country. But lore's a bore when you're hungry. Here are some of our favorite mountain breads.

Pan-Fried Breads ❖

This recipe is so uncompromisingly basic that it has little to recommend it except to give you an idea of how simple bread-making is. Try it once for experience, then move on to the tastier variations.

In the medium-sized pot mix together four heaping spoonfuls of flour, a ¼ spoonful of baking powder, and a pinch of salt. Add enough water to make a stiff but smooth dough you can pick up and handle without half of it sticking to your fingers. Have the flour sack handy so you can keep both hands floured, and if necessary, add small increments of flour to the dough to get the right consistency. Put a layer of oil in the frypan to preheat, and form six to eight small patties of dough, about the size of a muffin and ½-¾ inches thick. (If you like flipping them in the air, cook one at a time.) Let them brown slowly over a moderate bed of coals. If the fire is too hot, the crust will cook too fast, leaving the insides half raw. Flip or use a spatula to turn them, as often as you like. They're done when they sound hollow to the tap of a finger, roughly 15 minutes, and are more than enough for two ravenous adults.

Corn-meal Muffins ❖

In the medium pot, mix together two heaping spoonfuls of flour and two of cornmeal. Add a pinch of salt, a spoonful of sugar and one of oil, a half spoonful of milk powder, and a quarter spoonful of baking powder. Mix thoroughly, then add enough water to make a smooth dough, easy to handle but not sticky. Keeping your hands lightly floured, form the dough into whatever shape suits you. Cook as above. The result is indecently good, a cross between English muffins and old-fashioned corn fritters, or something like famous Southern hush puppies. Eat plain, with a sprinkling of sugar, or split open and cover with maple syrup. They're also great with grilled or foil-baked fish.

- For part of the cornmeal or flour, substitute a packet of dry instant oatmeal.
- Dust the muffins with cornmeal before you fry them.

- Season with pepper, nutmeg, cinnamon, sesame seeds, or a small amount of crushed nuts.

Baked Breads

Baked breads involve one more step than pan-fried, and a lot more time. The extra step is mixing a leavening agent into the dough to lighten it—to puff it up with a myriad of tiny bubbles, making it rise before it's baked. The mixing must be thorough, so you have to punch and push—or "knead"—the dough fully. There are a number of leavening agents. Yeast is the most famous, sourdough starter is another. We carry several packets of store-bought dry yeast with us, and take along a small plastic bottle with sourdough starter. Baking powder and soda work only under extreme heat (in the act of baking itself) and can't be used for pre-bake rising.

STARTING THE YEAST:

All leavening agents work by slowly releasing gas, which gets trapped in the dough and which, in trying to get out, forces it to expand. Yeast needs warmth to produce the gas. In the wilderness, the sun is your warmth. It's also possible to use the warmth of dying coals, but the sun is always your best bet. Don't plan to let your bread rise at night.

Yeast is also activated by warm water and sugar; it's inert until this is done. Sometimes it gets too inert or stale. Check the date on your yeast packets. It should read at least a couple of months ahead. To activate, sprinkle the amount of yeast you need, usually a packet or less, over a half cup of water that's only warm enough to keep your finger in. Add a couple generous pinches of sugar, mix thoroughly, cover and set aside in a warm place until you're ready to add it to the dough. When the yeast is frothy and expanding, it's ready to use.

STARTING THE SOURDOUGH:

Sourdough is exactly that: a dough made of flour and water that has begun fermenting, thus growing microscopic organisms that give off carbon-dioxide gas and a characteristic sour smell as they feed. In its working form this is called a "starter" because, like yeast, it initiates the leavening process. Having carried it into the mountains and hung it in a tree to get warm and smelly, you're ready to use it freely in breads, pancakes, etc.

In theory, sourdough starter is a complete substitute for yeast. In frontier days it was impossible to keep yeast fresh, but sourdough could be replenished every time it was used, thus keeping it alive and ready indefinitely. The best starter comes from the sourdough pot of a friend whose family has kept it, along with great-grandad's Klondike nugget, for a hundred years. Or you can buy dried starter in a health food outlet. But if great-grandad took his starter (and nugget) to the grave, and the store is out, here is a basic starter recipe to make at home before beginning your trip.

Heat a cup of milk, add a cup of water and cool to luke-warm. Thoroughly mix one tablespoonful of sugar, a teaspoonful of salt and two cups of flour in a large bowl—it's going to expand. Cover the bowl with a towel and leave in a warm place for four or five days or until it looks and smells frothy. Now add a package of yeast. Re-cover the bowl, and let sit at room temperature for another week. Stir it down each day and don't worry how it smells or looks: the badder the better. Store in a jar in the fridge until you're ready to use it.

Sourdough starter alone was fine for Yukon prospectors, but frankly it takes so long for dough to rise that it often dries out, leaving you with a loaf that looks and feels like a gold brick. We always add yeast to the sourdough starter, hedging our bets. Things move along at a fine pace and the bread tastes better, too.

Basic Mountain Loaf *

A loaf of bread will be as big or small as you have flour to spare. Everything else is secondary. If you have nothing but flour, water and yeast, you can make bread. It might not win prizes at the Happy Valley bake-athon, but it will beat dried-out Triscuits. And with any additional ingredients like salt, milk powder, sugar, oil, sourdough, raisins, nuts, cornmeal, oatmeal, a spare egg, onion, garlic, cinnamon, nutmeg, sesame, poppy or sunflower seeds, to name a few, your breads will become a hedonist camper's dream-come-true.

The following recipe makes about the smallest loaf that is practical and still plentiful for two people. To double it, use twice as much flour, the same amount of yeast, salt and milk. Smaller pots bake better, though a bigger bread will require a larger pot.

Your basic utensils are: two pots, a plate, a Sierra cup, a spoon and eventually, a bed of hot coals.

To ½ a Sierra cup of warm water, add a packet of yeast and a couple pinches of sugar. Cover and set in a warm place. In the medium pot mix together a Sierra cup of flour, a dash of salt, one spoonful each of milk powder and oil or melted margarine. Mix the bubbly yeast into the pot thoroughly. The result will be lumpish, perhaps soggy. Never mind. If a lot of the flour is still dry, add a bit more water, not much. You want a fairly stiff dough, not a batter.

Now turn this out onto a floured plate or flat, clean floured rock. Flour your hands and keep the bag nearby. The aim is to turn this sodden stuff into smooth, springy, velvety dough. You do this by kneading—that is, by folding the dough over and over on itself. Use the heel of your palm to push the dough away from you, fold it back on itself, give it a quarter turn, repeat, turn, repeat, and so on. If the flour on your hands and the plate doesn't suffice, add flour in very small amounts, and knead thoroughly before adding any more. As you knead, the dough will take shape, becoming firm and springy. Conversely, if it gets too hard to knead (or is hard at the outset), you have too much flour and need a little more liquid, either water or oil, the latter being easier to work in at this stage. Soon, the consistency will be just right. The dough is easy and pleasurable to work. You may find yourself spacing out and kneading just because it feels good. It can't hurt, so enjoy it. No harm if you want to go on for a half hour, though five or 10 minutes should suffice. The finished dough will spring slowly back when you poke a finger into it. Don't be dismayed if the dough takes on the hue of your pot-blackened hands or picks up small pieces of dirt. You won't taste or see it, nor contract some dread mountain disease.

When the dough is kneaded to perfection, it's ready to rise. Grease or oil the small pot, bottom and sides, and drop in the dough ball. Roll it around so its surface gets fully coated with oil. Now remove the dough, re-oil the pot and dust it with a little flour, a process to help prevent the baked bread from sticking. Set the dough back in, cover, put in a warm place and go off to fish, read, sleep, whatever, for an hour or so while the dough rises to double its original bulk.

What's a warm place? Any sun-exposed spot is ideal, unless the sun is searing; then warmth in the shade will be fine. A tent in the sun works. Sometimes we stow the pot in a sleeping bag if the day isn't too warm. Avoid setting the pot near the fire. It may get too hot and bake the bread.

What if it clouds over and gets cold? Not to worry, the rising just takes longer—all day is all right. If it's not ready before bedtime, wait till morning, knead the dough some more to bring the spring back, and let it rise again. It's ready to bake when it's doubled in bulk. Incidentally, if you have time, breads are lighter and tastier if you let them rise twice, punching down the dough after the first rising and allowing it to double again. Literally, make a fist and jab the dough in midsection. It will deflate. Then cover it and let the rising continue.

It's perfectly kosher to peek at the working dough. But it isn't an elevator; you won't be able to see it rise. If things go right, it will rise even if it takes time. If everything goes wrong and it won't rise, just turn the mess into a cake (see *Getting a Rise Out of a Dud*, pg. 246). What if it doesn't rise and you don't want a cake? Pretend it's fully risen and bake anyway. The fire's heat gives a last lift to the dough, so the finished loaf will be fine; somewhat heavy but just as tasty.

Let's assume, however, that the dough did double, it didn't rain, the coals are still hot, and you're ready to bake. If you wish, gently spread a light film of oil or melted shortening over the top of the dough with your fingers or the underside of a spoon. The oil will give a beautiful brown color to the top crust.

Oven-baked bread is usually started at a high temperature (400 degrees or higher); then after about 10 minutes the heat is reduced to 350 or 375 degrees to finish the baking, normally about 50 minutes. To reproduce those conditions in a bed of coals isn't easy, though as anyone who has ever made "coffee can bread" at summer camp knows, it's possible. The basic notion is to nestle the pot in a clearing in the warm ash or dirt, pile hot coals around it, then let them cool as the bread bakes. As more coals are needed to maintain the heat, rake them around the pot. On windy days, when the fire burns hot to windward and cool to leeward, rotate the pot 180 degrees every 15 minutes to assure an even distribution of heat.

Baking time differs according to the heat of the fire (which burns slower with wet, faster with dry, and hotter with soft wood), the size of the loaf and its ingredients. The basic mountain loaf should take between 20 and 30 minutes. It varies; keep checking. If the loaf sounds hollow when you tap it sharply, it's done. Remove the pot from the coals and set it to cool for 10-15 minutes. Under the best circumstances, when nothing has stuck to the sides, the loaf will come out when you turn the pot over and give it a couple of sharp raps on the bottom and top edges. Normally, though, you have to run a knife blade around the edges. In the worst of cases, so much will stick to the sides and bottom that you may have to saw the loaf in half and dig it out in sections. Usually, however, patience, cooling, deft use of the knife and a sharp knock of the pot against a rock brings forth a gorgeous golden loaf. Let it cool, then be prepared to defend your share against invaders from outer space—or your partner—intent on scarfing it down in one megabite!

No doubt about it, the Basic Mountain Loaf is a taste of camping heaven. Using the rough ratio of a generous cup of flour to an ungenerous half-cup of liquid, a packet of yeast and kneading until you get a smooth, unsticky, springy dough, you can overcome all but the most exotic forms of munchies. But the variations are better, and within each variation are other endless permutations.

Sourdough Bread ✳

Use the same proportions and ingredients as above, but add a spoonful of sourdough starter when you add the yeast. Depending on the starter's thickness, you may have to add a little more water or flour to the dough.

Raisin-Nut Loaf ✳

Also known as cinnamon-nut loaf, apricot-nut loaf, banana-nut loaf, mango-nut loaf, prune-nut loaf, nut-nut loaf. This one's sweet. Double the sugar, and add some cinnamon along with a good dash of baking powder or soda, which help enormously when fruit is involved. At the kneading stage, add half a handful of mixed raisins or finely chopped dried fruits and nuts. Proceed as above. Before baking, sprinkle the top with cinnamon, sugar and more chopped nuts.

Jelly-Roll Bread ✳

While the bread is rising, boil some dried fruit, sugar and water into a thick jelly. Punch down the dough and pat it out on a floured plate. Spread the jelly mixture on top of the flattened dough, roll it up and plop it back into the greased pot for a second rising. You can do the same sort of thing with a sugar-cinnamon-nut paste, using enough margarine to hold it together, and come up with the camping equivalent of a morning Danish.

Oatmeal Bread ✳

Prepare a packet of instant oatmeal as though you're making breakfast, let it cool while you put together the dry ingredients (omitting the sugar) and start the yeast. Add the oatmeal along with the yeast and mix thoroughly. Continue as above.

Onion and Garlic Bread ✳

Fry a large spoonful of chopped onion and garlic until they're translucent. Mix them into the dry ingredients of the Basic Mountain Loaf.

Egg Breads ✴

An egg in any of the above recipes enriches the bread and adds more taste. If you use one, you may need more flour.

Mountain Challah ✴

When you add the yeast, throw in an egg or two. Mix thoroughly. You may need more flour than usual to absorb the extra liquid. If possible, let this loaf rise twice. If you have eggs to spare, use a third, separated, as follows: Throw the white into the dough at the outset along with the other ingredients, but save the yolk. Then, just before baking, beat $\frac{1}{2}$ spoonful of water into the yolk, and brush the top of the loaf with the egg and water mixture. It will produce a burnished golden finish that will drive neighboring backpackers into a near frenzy.

Getting a Rise Out of a Dud

What happens if the dough doesn't rise? You did everything right. The yeast bubbled and frothed, the dough kneaded nicely, the sun has been shining for hours. But by mid-afternoon, you have an inert gray mass of dough that looks near death. This happened to us on a recent trip. Our options were to toss it or change it. Rick started to reason, like Marie Antoinette, that if you couldn't give them bread, let them eat cake. What wouldn't rise with yeast might with baking powder and whipped egg white. So we added enough water and milk powder to turn the dough into a batter, threw in some baking powder, and came up with a great nut-and-raisin cake.

Some research gave us clues as to why that particular dough didn't rise. Experts have countless reasons to explain failure. Humidity and air temperature affect yeast. Too much sweetener slows down or stops the process. Too much salt also inhibits rising. And too little white or whole wheat flour makes matters worse. That's because wheat flour contains a magic substance, gluten, which gives dough the necessary elasticity it needs to trap the yeast-produced bubbles of gas, allowing the dough to rise. Corn meal, rye and rice flour, etc.

have less or no gluten. The dough is made more porous as these are added, and the gas escapes, leaving you with a mound of play dough.

In our case, the dough had too much maple syrup and corn-meal, relative to the amount of white flour. It's hard to give exact proportions, especially as you may run out of important ingredients on the trail. But as a rough rule of thumb, try these:

First, half a spoonful of sugar or a full spoonful of honey or syrup is plenty for starting the yeast. If you want a sweeter bread, add the rest of the sugar to the dough, but remember that the sweeter the dough, the longer the rising time.

Second, use at least half white or whole wheat flour relative to all the other dry ingredients. If you're running too low on flour for that ratio, consider making cake instead of yeast bread.

Cornbreads

Yeast Cornbread ✹

If you like cornbreads which rise, substitute cornmeal for half the flour in the Basic Mountain Loaf recipe (pg. 241). Add a healthy hit of baking powder or soda and proceed as above.

Baking Powder Cornbread ✹

If you're low on yeast, use a ratio of four spoonfuls of cornmeal to two of flour and forget the yeast. Add a spoonful of baking powder, a shot of salt, a heaping spoonful of milk powder, two or three spoonfuls of sugar, a beaten egg or two and enough water to make a thick batter, similar in consistency to a thick pancake batter. Turn this into a well-greased pot. Bake at once for about a half-hour. Since cornbread won't sound hollow to the tap, you'll know it's done when the top splits open a bit, and when a knife blade inserted in the middle comes out clean.

Pizza

Ranger Ron said it couldn't be done west of Chicago. It's all very well, he argued, to bake bread in a pot, but pizza has to be flat, and the oven has to be hotter than you can get in the wilderness. We showed him something. Pizza is just an open-baked hot bread with lots of good things piled on top. If you have a frying pan with a removable handle, or a pie plate and a piece of aluminum foil, you can bake a gorgeous pizza in the wilderness.

Hal & Rick's South Side Pizza ✳

1 packet yeast
1/2 c. warm water
Couple pinches of sugar
1 1/2 c. flour
Dash of salt
1 sp. oil
1/2 c. tomato sauce (see recipes in this chapter)
Mixed dried vegetables, slightly rehydrated: mushrooms, zucchini, onion, peppers
2 cloves garlic, sliced
Sliced salami or jerky (optional)
4-5 sp. sliced cheese
Pepper to taste
Hearty sprinkling of dried oregano
Cooking oil
Aluminum foil

In a Sierra cup mix the warm water, yeast and sugar. Set aside covered in a warm place. When "proofed" (that is, bubbly) add it to the flour, salt and oil in a pot. Mix thoroughly with a spoon, adding more oil and water as necessary to make a workable dough. Knead on a plate till smooth. If it's slightly sticky, that's OK. Set in a warm place to rise in a covered, oiled pot. While the dough is rising, make the tomato sauce and rehydrate the vegies slightly by soaking in hot water barely to cover till partially soft. Drain and set aside.

When the dough has risen, turn out on a plate and begin to work it into a round, flat shape with your fingers, pushing out from the center in all directions. You can even pick it up and toss it into the air with a spiral motion, like they do at Mama Mia's. It's helpful to catch it. You may need a little flour on your hands for this. When the dough has become a nice, even circle, fit it into a well-oiled frying pan. It should extend part or all the way up the sides. Then spread the tomato sauce over the dough and pile on the vegetables (and salami/jerky). Sprinkle on the cheese, garlic, pepper and oregano. Then drip a very thin layer of oil over the finished product, and cover the pan with foil. Alternatively, place a large tin plate over the pizza and seal it to the frying pan with the foil.

Ranger Ron was right in one respect. The idea is to bake the dough fast, before you burn everything on top. Pizza ovens are extremely hot (about 500 degrees Fahrenheit). But if you put your frying pan on a bed of red hot coals, you'll end up with something you might have to call cheese-n-charcoal. Instead set the pan on cleared ground, surround it with hot coals, and slide coals on top of the foil too. Let it bake about 15 minutes. Then work some moderately warm coals under the pan and push others around it and on top. In another 10 minutes or so, the pizza is done. The dough will be crusty, the cheese melted, and mouths watering. Overlook his chagrin and give Ranger Ron a piece. Tell him it's crow!

How to bake pizza.

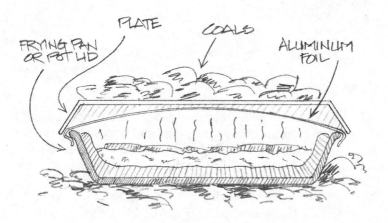

Cakes

Making cake on a camping trip is sort of like sex on Wednesday afternoon: gratuitous but a lot of fun. It has nothing to do with survival, nor your ability to read a compass, has not one ounce of redeeming moral, social or nutritional value. But as long as you have semi-sweet baking chocolate with you anyway (also great for eating plain because it's unlikely to melt in your pack), some margarine, sugar, eggs, flour, baking powder and powdered milk; and as long as it's Wednesday afternoon and the sun is high, you might as well hunker down, bake a cake, make an icing, slap the two together, lay back and pig out. It really is a piece of cake.

Basic Ground-Level Two-Step Cake ✸

Pancakes are the result of frying batter. Cakes are the result of baking batter—batter which contains more sugar and eggs. Here's everything you ever needed to know about the unadorned, ultra-simple, starter cake loved by 93% of humankind.

1 c. flour
1 sp. milk powder
1/2 sp. baking powder
Dash of salt
1 sp. margarine
3 sp. sugar
1 egg
Dash of brandy
Water
Oil for greasing pot

In a medium pot mix together the dry ingredients. In the pot lid, cream together the margarine and sugar, using the underside of a spoon to mix. (If you're out of margarine, oil will work.) Break the egg into the sugar mixture and beat till the glop is smooth. Add the brandy as a substitute for vanilla. Combine both mixtures with enough extra water to make a smooth, thick batter that will pour like a ribbon into a well-greased and floured small baking pot.

Bake the cake in coals cooler than for bread. At home, you'd use a moderate oven (350-375 degrees). Out here, start with coals just beginning to turn black and try to keep any you add roughly the same color. If you can't, don't worry. Betty Crocker won't be around, peeking over your shoulder. Baking time will vary, as usual, but should run about 25 minutes to half an hour. Test for doneness by inserting a knife blade into the center of the cake. If it comes out clean, the cake is done. When cool remove from pot. Eat or ice.

VARIATIONS:

Basic Man Eatin' Cake *

Follow the preceeding recipe, only separate the egg, reserve the white, and add the yolk to the sugar and butter mixture. When the batter is ready to pour into the baking pot, gently fold in the egg whites, beaten stiff but not dry. This makes the cake even lighter, a cruel blow to weight watchers and lifters alike.

Advanced Man-Eatin' Cake *

For a moister, richer cake, use two eggs, separate both and proceed as above. Add other things to the batter: cinnamon, Kahlua in addition to or instead of the brandy, several squares of chocolate shaved with a knife, or assorted dried fruits and nuts.

Chocolate Cake *

Set up as for Man Eatin' Cake (Basic or Advanced). In a pot lid place two squares of semi-sweet baking chocolate or two rows of German Sweet chocolate. Add about a $\frac{1}{4}$ cup water. Stir and melt over the fire, being careful not to burn the chocolate. When melted, add to the egg and sugar mixture along with a little brandy. Proceed as in Man Eatin' Cake, folding in egg whites last. *Note*: it is not necessary in any of these recipes to separate the eggs, so if you left the wire whisk at home, proceed as for Basic Two-Step Cake. No one will notice the difference.

Surprise-Delight Cake ✳

Suppose you don't have all the ingredients and still want to make a chocolate cake. Use what you have. Substitute carob for chocolate; scrape the carob off a Tiger Milk Bar to melt in water. Or melt the whole bar and add it to the egg and sugar mixture. Or use powdered Swiss Miss. If you don't have anything to beat the egg whites with, leave them whole. No baking powder? Use beaten egg whites as a rising agent. No brandy? Forget it. No sugar? Double the amount of chocolate, or use both chocolate and instant cocoa, which has plenty of sugar in it. Stretch your mind. Just keep the proportions of wet and dry about the same so the batter stays the proper consistency.

Chocolate Icing ❖

2-3 *squares semi-sweet baking chocolate, or*
3-4 *rows German Sweet chocolate*
1 sp. *margarine*
$^1/_4$ c. *water*
Dash of brandy

In a pot lid melt the chocolate (you can use a combination of the two kinds) in the water. *Note:* the more chocolate you use, the more water you need, but add it moderately. The idea is to have a fairly thick, smooth melt. Add margarine, stir till melted and thoroughly mixed with the chocolate. Remove from heat. Add brandy. Cool till icing begins to thicken. This will take some time, especially on a hot day. To hasten, set icing container in a larger container of cold water. Don't fret, it will harden. In fact, if left too long, it will suddenly harden so much that you may have to warm it slightly to turn it back into spreading consistency. When thickened to that consistency, ice the cake with a spoon or knife. The result is so good you'll have difficulty waiting for your partners to return from a day hike, or wherever they're spending Wednesday afternoon.

To store the iced cake, place the large pot over the cake till time to eat. If there's any left over at night, remove from plate and double bag in Ziplocs.

Note: Icing can be made without a cake. Hardened, it is the perfect nosh, the equivalent of that box of Bartons you were supposed to bring your Great Aunt Emily on her birthday, but ate first. Softened and thickened with a spoon each of milk powder and flour, and a cup or two of water, it transmutes into Chocolate Pudding!

Fruit Cake *

This is a mixture of fruits and nuts held together with a mixture of eggs, sugar and flour. It's a snap to make and a great way to use up nuts and fruit before packing out. In a medium or large pot lid, put as much cut up fruit and nuts as you wish. For the smallest fruit cake, about three large handfuls will do. To this add a beaten egg, three spoonfuls of sugar and a hit of brandy. Mix thoroughly. Now add a dash of salt, a spoonful of baking powder and enough flour (about three spoonfuls) to hold the mixture together. Pour into a well-greased small pot, cover and bake very slowly in moderately hot coals. At home, you'd bake at only 300 degrees, so these coals will be the coolest you've used. Allow an hour or so to cook, and don't expect it to rise much. You'll know when it's done by looking at the top—which should be brown—and testing with a knife for firmness. Run the knife around the edge, turn the pot over and bang it sharply on a rock to get the cake out. If it won't come out whole, cut it in pieces or eat it right from the pot. When the cake is cool, pour some brandy over it and let it sit for as long as you like. It'll keep for days. Incidentally, if it comes out of the pot whole, the cake will be very beautiful.

Cookies

The hardest part of mountain cookie baking is deciding
on the ingredients. Chocolate chip, cinnamon-nut, oatmeal,
lemon only begin the possibilities. The ratio of ingredients
should be 4:2:1, that's four flour (including oatmeal) to two
sugar to one margarine. Begin by "creaming" half a Sierra cup
of sugar and two spoonfuls of margarine into a paste. Add an
egg and a splash of brandy. To a Sierra cup of flour (or
flour/oatmeal) add half a spoonful of baking powder, a pinch
of salt, and a spoonful of powdered milk. Combine this with
the butter and egg mixture. Then add your special ingredients—shredded chocolate bars, raisins, coconut, chopped nuts,
dried fruit, cinnamon, nutmeg, ginger, etc. Add flour or water
as necessary to get the right consistency, halfway between
pancake batter and bread dough. The finished mixture should
be thick and chunky. Taste it for sweetness. If it doesn't taste
really sweet, your cookies will be more like biscuits.

Cookies are baked in a greased pan exactly like pizza
(pg. 249). If you have a plate or lid that fits over your frying
pan, you can use it instead of foil to hold the top coals. A few
coals below will keep the bottom of the pan warm. You can
only bake three or four at a time, so filling the cookie jar is an
all-day project. In a pinch, you can make them like pan-fried
bread. They may burn a bit on the top or bottom, but if you
dip them in coffee or hot chocolate, you'll hardly notice.

Quiche

One of the best things about the kind of improvisational cooking we've been discussing is that you're never quite sure
what's going to happen next. For more than five years we'd
been baking breads, inventing variations of chocolate cake, ig-
niting brandy and generally congratulating ourselves on the
smooth workings of our unbridled imaginations. But we'd
never made a pie. Too much trouble, we argued. Too hard. Anyway, what would we fill it with? The answer came from Polly,
a doctor who'd lived in the Andes, floated down the Amazon,

and survived 20 years in the jungle of Chicago. Five days into the high Sierras in the midst of a hail storm and high winds, she announced she'd make supper that night for six: quiche.

Quiche is a pie, similar to custard pie but with vegetables and cheese as the main ingredients. We wished her luck and set her up in the tent to get out of the wind (it's not easy to work with flour in a gale). Every so often we'd hear a muffled cry for spices, powdered milk or water and we finally put the entire food pack into the tent so she could work in peace. By sundown, the storm had blown itself out and we were all sitting around the campfire complimenting the chef on her work of art.

Quiche Improvisation *

The first thing to do is to make a pie crust of pastry dough, which is different from bread dough. It consists of a mixture of flour and shortening, with just enough water to hold the two together. Here's what you'll need to make a crust in an 8" fry pan:

A large pot
A spoon
Water
5 heaping spoonfuls of flour
Dash of salt
4 sp. margarine or shortening

Mix the flour and salt together. Add the margarine, and knead until the dough has the texture of cornmeal. Don't worry if there are some pea-sized globules. Now add two or three spoonfuls of cold water to the mixture, one at a time, blending it in with the spoon or two forks. Only add enough water to hold the dough loosely together. One way to tell if it's right is to form the dough into a lightly packed ball. If it falls apart, you need more water. If it holds together, set the ball on an ungreased fry pan or pie plate, and press the dough down with the heel of your hand, working it to cover the bottom and sides of the pan. It should be very thin, not more than an eighth of an inch thick. But don't worry if it's thicker. It will bake well and taste great.

If you're camping in France go ahead and follow the national custom. Partially bake the pie crust next. If you're not in France, skip it. Just go ahead and fill the uncooked crust with quiche goodies:

Eggs
Milk
Cheese
Jerky
Diced dried vegetables: mushrooms,
*   peppers, zucchini, etc. (rehydrated if possible).*
Onion (dried and crumbled or chopped)
3 sp. milk powder + water to make 1 cup
2 eggs, well beaten
Salt and pepper to taste
Dash of nutmeg
1 sp. flour

In a pot mix together the cup of milk, beaten eggs, salt, pepper and nutmeg. Add the rehydrated vegetables and onion. (*Note*: If you can't rehydrate the vegies, don't worry. They'll soften in the baking.) To thicken the pot, add the flour and mix well. Pour the mixture into the pie shell. Sprinkle on as much finely shredded cheese as you can spare. Any cheese will do. The quiche is ready to bake.

If you have another pie pan or tin plate of the right size, invert it to cover the quiche. If not, cover it with aluminum foil like a pizza, and bake exactly as in the pizza recipe (pg. 249). Set hot coals around and on top. After about 20 minutes, when it's half-done, work some moderately hot coals underneath. The quiche is finished when the filling is firm and slightly browned. The reason it takes up to 40 minutes to bake is that the pan is shallow, making the transfer of heat a slower process. You'll be ravenous by the time it's ready, so you'll eat it hot. But it's possible to eat quiche cold, too.

Campground Chutney

Summer-fruit Chutney

If you haven't eaten all the dried fruit by now, and you've just turned out a fabulous Indian meal (*Trout Tandouri, Trout in Curried Sauce*, or *Fried Rice with Vegetables and Chicken*), garnish it with chutney. Stew a handful of fruit in water to cover, stirring till softened and thickened. Add an immodest squirt of vinegar or lemon juice (or both!), a spoon of sugar, and continue to stir till thick. Voilà! Chutney.

Snow Cones

The Instant High Mountain Popsicle

Whenever you're above 7,000 feet, you're likely to come on a snowfield or remaining patches of last winter's snow hidden from the mid-summer sun. If you're hiking, pull over and make snow cones—they're so refreshing it's like finding a soda fountain along the trail. Fill your Sierra cup halfway with snow and add any or all of the following: instant chocolate, cinnamon and sugar, lemon or lime juice and sugar, Kahlua, brandy, nutmeg, ginger, etc. Eat with a spoon. They're the *real* treasure of the Sierra, madre!

Cooking in the Rain

Several years ago we were settled into a campsite when it began to rain. Forty-eight hours later it was still raining. Then it began to snow. Though our sleeping bags got soggy, our spirits didn't even dampen. We kept warm and full. When it's raining or cold outside, we like to keep our insides full of hot foods.

You can't make elaborate meals in the rain. Baking is out—you can't keep wet coals hot. Frying is possible, but unless your fire is protected from the rain or you fry fast, the food gets wet on top while it cooks on the bottom. Also, if the pan fills with water, you'll be poaching, which *is* a practical method. Another good technique in the rain is grilling (a rack will not fill with water). A third choice is cooking in a covered pot, which is our usual choice. Soups and stews are great: hot, easy, filling and needing little tending, so you can stay dry under a tree or tarp as they cook. You're likely to catch fish in the rain, and it's simple to grill them quickly or poach them and add to your pot.

Keep the stored food and matches in waterproof containers inside covered packs. When the sun comes out again, dry any damp food or packets to prevent spoilage. And don't go without at least one hot meal a day in the rain. Even a steaming cup of cocoa and some biscuits, or a bowl of oatmeal will keep the spirits up.

Stove Cooking Hints

- Conserve fuel, cook fast.
- When frying remember that the circumference of heat over a camp stove is smaller than at home or over an open fire. Thus that large pan of frying fish will stay cooler on the edges than in the middle.
- Ignore suggestions for long, slow simmer in all recipes. Boiling time for half a small pot of water is five to 10 minutes. A few more minutes and soup's on.
- Stove safety: Use in a sheltered spot, out of the wind and rain. Unless an emergency requires it, don't cook in the tent, even in the rain. Fuel can spill, fumes can make you sick, tents can burn. Use your ingenuity to cook outside instead.

Eating on the Trail

When we're camped, deeply immersed in cooking, two meals a day are adequate. Hiking, our eating patterns change. A light, fast, early breakfast gives us a fresh start and enough energy to make that long haul to the pass without cardiac arrest from undigested pancakes in the gut. Eating on the trail is part of a pattern of rest and recovery, necessary to put strength back in the muscles and energy back in the system.

Some backpackers eat continually while hiking. They carry a pouch of gorp, and munch away throughout the day on their mixed dried fruits, nuts, candy, coconut, or whatever. Others prefer to snack at rest stops and have a more substantial lunch at a point where tired muscles, sore feet and spectacular scenery call for a longer break. It's amazing how a good meal makes the body willing to go on, and able to do so.

Keep trail food easily accessible. Why empty your pack every time you want a raisin cookie or a lemon drop? And it should be nourishing. Make sure you have on hand dried fruit, chocolate, cookies, crackers, etc. for energy, as well as salami, nuts, jerky, etc. for strength (protein for muscle restoration) to keep you fit. You also need to replace liquid frequently. Be sure you have enough water to drink often, though not necessarily in great quantity. If you're sure of water sources along the trail, you needn't carry much. Water is heavy. But if you're doubtful, keep your canteen full.

Our style includes frequent stops. Often we're more thirsty than hungry, but we also make sure to get some quick energy by sharing something sweet. We lunch at the top of a pass if the weather is as good as the view. We make cheese and salami sandwiches on crackers, eat nuts and dried fruits, a few bean sprouts and plenty of water. If there's a snowfield nearby, we make snow cones for dessert. Otherwise, it's raisin cookies or the last part of yesterday's cake. We take our time; this is a rest stop. Then we set off toward our destination, often crosscountry. We try to arrive by mid-afternoon, but not at the expense of as many rest and snack stops as necessary to keep our spirits up and our legs moving. If we need to make camp before our destination, we give ourselves a simple but hot supper. Dehydrated dinners and a backpacking stove are handy at such times.

Some backpackers have a saying about emergency situations, "When in doubt, sit it out." We have no objections to that, but we've added a few words of our own. When we come to a crossroads, a roaring creek or a mountain pass, our saying is "When in doubt, the food comes out." Friends say that ours are the only camping trips they've ever heard of on which the backpackers invariably *gain* weight. Right. What better vacation could you have, staying full of great food and drink, and coming home rock hard from all the hiking, climbing and packing? Those visions of sugar plums and all the delicacies will embellish every tale you tell, all winter long. Give it a try. You'll love it.

CHAPTER 10

Hanging Out

The Fine Art of Spending Time, Filling Space

Doing nothing is an art—and an oxymoron. *Doing* nothing?
Maybe Zen masters and 143-year-old yogis can manage it.
And yuppie CEOs who work 100-hour weeks and then just sit
still, breathe, and wonder how big the universe is for days at
a time in the backcountry. Or crane operators whose idea of
heaven is to hand tie the most intricate fishing flies. Small
children can spend hours squatting wisely in a tide pool watching. Just watching. Adults can wake full of energetic intentions and crash into sullen boredom five minutes after the
pancakes and brew. But we've also known fanatic hikers who
think nothing of 15-mile day trips, or solo backpackers who
need to contrive detailed daily schedules while in camp to
keep the lonely-blues away.

Hanging out is thus a subjective thing. It depends on what
you like to do. Rick breathes quicker if there's a handy peak
to climb. Karen fishes for approximately 27 hours a day and
is reluctant to permit the sun to set. She is sublimely happy

to hear an 800-page novel read aloud while she casts. Sarah, who affects High Photographic Sensibility, takes pictures of wildflowers. Not trees, not wildlife. Certainly not the human relics she travels with. Just flowers. The smaller the better. We've known birders to abandon small children and all responsibilities in quest of the western tanager; mountain bikers to return at dusk bruised and besotted with pleasure after a day on the trail; canoeists who spend long hours on minor and gratuitous repairs, lovingly touching up the lacquer, masking the dent—erecting campsite body shops just for the hell of it. We began this book hanging out one day years ago. Turn back to the tale of the fabled Hidden Lake Soufflé, and you'll see the first words we put down on paper. Active or passive, intro- or extrovert, gregarious or a loner, the possibilities for finding pleasure in hanging out are endless. You've come a long way. Now's the time to enjoy.

Secrets of the Hammock and other Lounging Devices

Lots of people get to a campsite and don't want to move. Now or forever. "Wake me when it's time to go home," is the cry from the heart. Up goes the hammock between two sturdy birches; up goes the *Do Not Disturb* sign. Then the trouble begins.

The next time you pull into a car campground, check out the hammocks and their occupants. Looks like the entire melon section of the supermarket encased in individual string bags, doesn't it? People stretched out end-to-end, sinking pathetically in the middle until they look like human nutcrackers. Head and feet high, tush low—a painful, humiliating, miserably uncomfortable position. You can't get a lot of rest that way, and if your back doesn't go out, your dreams of bucolic ease will. You'll enlist on the next day hike and never return.

It's true: an awful lot of people don't know how to lie in a hammock! There's a physics to it, and you should be the first to know. Lie *diagonally*. That creates just enough countervailing forces to maintain you in a horizontal position. It minimizes sag and rests your back. You can lie there for hours, whiling away the time watching clouds and daydreaming. You won't miss the activists. You won't join the potato sack race. Keep a mosquito net hat in the hammock, a stuff sack filled with a few clothes as a pillow, a book and the snack of your choice, and you won't have to touch down till the cows come home.

Other lounging machines are Ensolite pads dragged out of the tent, propped against a rock in the sunlight or shade, air mattresses afloat on the lake or cast on a summer meadow, or the canoe floating at anchor lined with sleeping pads. (Though not a sleeping bag unless you're awfully good at boarding and alighting dry. Pads dry fast; bags don't.) Lawn chairs, inflated inner tubes, re-sited dome tents, even a smooth, sun-drenched granite rock overlooking the lake— all are outdoor sofa substitutes. Deep-six the alarm clock. We'll wake you for dinner.

Stop Your Ramblin', Stop Your Gamblin'...

Tom Stienstra, a great wilderness camper and author (see Book List), tells a fine story about cutthroat, penny-candy-ante poker high in the backcountry, where money doesn't count but a steely-eyed bluff's still a bluff. He pulled an inside straight on the last deal in a seven-card stud game 11,000 feet above the nearest gaming table, and backed down at the prospect of losing his last five M & Ms. A man who knows his priorities.

A camping trip in the county park or in the high Canadian Rockies calls for portable amusements, and if you can't spring granny's soapstone mah-jongg set loose, a pack of cards will do. We have watched two seasoned couples in a drive-in camp-site playing pinochle through a hurricane warning, oblivious to the rising wind, collapsing tents, overturned food hampers and the first heavy drops of rain. You can't tell us they weren't having a glorious camping trip.

The farther you go on foot, the lighter your games will need to be. Miniature, plastic chess, checkers or backgammon sets, *si*; Monopoly or croquet, *non*. A cribbage board, dice, Trivial Pursuit cards travel well in a backpack. Hang gliders and bowling balls don't. What fits and what's light is what counts.

...Stop Stayin' Out Late at Night

You say you wanna keep shuffling cards till the wee hours, that one more deal is gonna win the pot. You say your end game against your partner's Indian defense takes time to develop: you're not playing chess against a clock out here. True, but you *are* playing against a huge drain on the flashlight batteries. Unless you're carrying one of those six or twelve-volt floodlight batteries or a powerful fuel-fed camping lantern, you'll have to close down the house and continue in the morning. That, or agree to watch the stars the following nights and brush your teeth in the dark. Even hanging out comes with finite options. And sometimes they're non-negotiable.

The Library

One of our own personal camping pleasures is reading aloud. We find so much time for it—during a rest break on the trail, while preparing one of our elaborate meals, while one of us is fishing, or just while hanging out—that over the years we've gotten through some of the world's longest books. As we read we burn, so that we don't have to carry the book's weight out. This may seem barbarous, but there's a silver lining (of the authors' pockets) too. When we get home, we go out and buy the book again, a treasure on our shelves and increased royalties in the writer's money-market account.

The most satisfactory kinds of books for this kind of reading are those long, episodic novels where it doesn't matter if you miss a paragraph or even a whole chapter. Great dialogue counts a lot. So does the ability to tell a good story. Among our favorites have been Mark Twain's *Huckleberry Finn* and *A Connecticut Yankee at King Arthur's Court*, Robertson Davies' *Deptford Trilogy* and his equally wonderful *Salterton Trilogy*, John Barth's *The Sotweed Factor*, *Bleak House* by Charles Dickens (over 900 pages!), Henry Fielding's *Tom Jones* (a lot funnier and longer than the movie), the short stories of P.G. Wodehouse and Ring Lardner, the mystery novels of Dashiell Hammett and a good collection of ghost stories. Jon Carroll, the columnist for the San Francisco *Chronicle* and a fine old gonzo backpacker, once rebuked us for not including the novels of Anthony Trollope on our list. OK, they're in. And your favorites will be too if you let us know before the next edition comes out. In short, bring anything you enjoy reading—magazines, comic books, joke books, box tops—and any other printed material which you won't mind burning or packing out—crosswords, puzzles, games, mantras, amulets, recipes: whatever tickles your fancy. And *at least one book per child*, however old or young. More if you can manage it. Read and burn. It's the best of cheap thrills.

Music

We're a plugged-in generation, so there's no use complaining that the quality of silence in the great outdoors has changed for the worse. In fact, that isn't so. The Walkman has come to the rescue of purists like you and us. It's now possible to bring the baddest neo-punk jam into the wilderness without causing damage to more than two eardrums, a net gain no matter how you figure it. There's no further need for a boom box in a campground. There should be no further need for a radio without earplugs. There's nothing wrong with amplified sound except when it's unleashed. Kept inside the brain case, it's an acceptable part of the modern camper's gear.

If you're in a crowded campground similar consideration for the neighbors in the next tent requires the guitar, mouth organ, and group sing-a-long to be muted and closed down before the third watch. Make it soft, low, and early.

You can no doubt fit a drum set into a canoe, carry a Fender bass on a pack mule, but backpackers and long-distance hikers who play music have to weigh things in the balance. The manufacturers have. They've come out with a backpacking guitar, a lightweight instrument that looks like a stretch ukelele. It's long, thin, light, reasonably durable, and produces a sound good enough to keep even a member of the Seattle string band Who's Driving? happy in the wild woods.

Our friend Jules plays a mandolin while hiking and fashions percussion instruments out of hollow logs. Peter the Headwaiter plays the spoons. Penny whistles. Kazoos, comb-and-paper, harmonicas are light, easy, fun and cheap: a child's delight. There's no need to deprive anyone of music if it soothes the soul. Just make sure that it soothes others' too. Otherwise take a hike and soothe solo.

Using Ranger Ron

Campers at county, state, and national parks should check out the free entertainment offered by the park services. Local naturalists know their turf, and have an affection for it. A guided nature hike or a nighttime illustrated talk by Ranger Ron probably won't be like those awful didactic affairs you remember so well from summer camp and other forced-march jamborees. Take advantage of their sense of place and of the patient pleasures of spotting a real Big Bird, identifying a meadow of ephemeral wildflowers, or geologically reading the terrain. If you can't stand the scholarship, you can always go hang glide off Half Dome, but a snail's pace is often just right: lovely and unimportant, surprising, revealing. What's the hurry?

Day Trips

Hikers, fishers, climbers, and bikers itch to get going. To them hanging out is filled with motion. An unexplored off-trail route, a first-time trail, a nearby stream to fish, a peak to bag: these trigger the imagination, get the blood churning. Anticipation quickens the pulse. A daypack stuffed with food, flashlight, water bottle, maps and compass, warm clothes and rain gear, a minimum first-aid kit, sun screen and lip balm, and, if on bike, a repair kit, is featherweight compared with the big frame pack that got you to camp. You can make good time, cover a fair amount of ground, and get back to home base before dark. Good planning and common sense make the day safe and filled with satisfactions.

Easiest is a hike along a trail to a ridge, pass, peak or lake that you would otherwise miss if held to the original itinerary. Fishing a remote, shaded stream may bring you thrills and a late dinner. Lake fishing is less likely to be successful, because you invariably end up fishing in the glare of the sun, when the fish are lying low. It's nearly noon when you get there, and you have to leave around 2 or 3 o'clock to return to camp by sundown. As long as you don't mind a slow few hours of fishing, it can be a scenic and relaxing day. If you're fishing from a canoe, then all bets are on. You can get an early start, stay along the shaded shoreline, check out the inlets, fish from land, have a ball.

And before you set off, secure your campsite. Prepare for hot sun, heavy rain or a ripping wind; any or all could happen while you're gone. Keep food in the shade, leave a rainfly over the tent, and batten down the hatches just in case.

Bagging Peaks

We're not mountain climbers—as in K-2, El Capitan, the Jungfrau. But when we're out in the high country and spot a peak in the middle distance, we often take a day trip to climb it. No ropes and crampons, no technical climbing, but careful scrambling and steady going. Planned right, it's safe. Executed right it's exhilarating, exciting, exhausting. Gazing out over the crest of a 12,000-footer is worth every hard step and passing terror. The heart in your mouth is your own. It's the best place for it as you look down and around from the top of the world, astounded by your audacity and courage. It can become an addiction.

At the top of major peaks you'll find a register to sign and log your comments. On less important peaks the equivalent is often a small tin can buried under a cairn of rocks, in which you'll find a small note pad with room for your signature and a remark or two about the state of the union, the view, the weather or the climb.

Preparation and planning are the keys to successful peak bagging. Plan your route early, the day before the climb if possible. Use the topo map. The easiest way to the top is across the widest spaces between the altitude lines on the map. That's where you should trace your route. If your camp is close to the peak, trace the route up the peak with your eyes, looking for rock slides or impenetrable brush which might not show up on the map.

Start the climb early in the morning. We usually eat a quick cold breakfast, pack our daypack, and leave close to dawn. Mountain weather is always unpredictable and more so in the afternoon, and the only thing worse than getting caught at the top of a peak in an afternoon hail storm is getting caught there in a lightning-and-hail storm. An electric storm on the trail in the forest is impressive enough. On an exposed peak it's positively terrifying. To avoid this nasty business try to bag the peak early in the day.

Your supplies for a peak-bagging expedition will be the same as those above for any day trip. If you don't have a light daypack, rig a stuffsack to one of the straps off your backpack, and sling it over your shoulder.

Dark glasses are *required*, not optional. If you plan to hike over snow fields, you'll also need "blinders" on the sides of your glasses to protect your eyes from reflected glare. Don't have them? Make some the night before with cardboard cutouts from the cookie or biscuit box, and adhesive tape, or rig up a "foreign-legion" side shade from a T-shirt or bandanna, which will also protect the back of your neck from sunburn.

Elementary climbing rules should be followed scrupulously:

Beginners never go alone. Partnered climbing is always preferred whatever the level of experience. Some prefer a minimum of three.

Don't climb directly below the person above you. Stay off to one side. It's easy to dislodge a large rock or boulder and start a rock slide. Wherever possible, climbers should spread out horizontally or diagonally across the mountain. If you must be in the line of fire of the person above you, wait till she/he has stopped climbing before you head up.

If you get into an area with rocks jutting above your head, be sure to turn your visor around (like a baseball catcher) before you crack your head on an unseen crag.

Don't exceed your physical limits and climbing skills. If in doubt, or if you become scared, go back. You get no medals for false valor. Macho man doesn't live long on the mountain.

If the going gets too hard, too dangerous, *everyone* turns back together. This is a group effort all the way.

Topo maps are helpful, but look closely and make decisions as you climb. Rock can be solid or loose. Snow is hard in the mornings and soft in the afternoons. Brush can be full of narrow deer paths or completely impenetrable. Alter your route accordingly, and mark it with trail ducks if you expect to retrace your steps.

The higher you climb, the more often you need to rest. Altitude thins the air and deprives lungs and muscles of oxygen. Short breath and sore muscles result and require immediate attention. R & R is mandatory.

Don't trust the topo map completely. A 30-foot cliff may not show up within 40-foot contour intervals (see *How to Read a Topo Map*, pg. 137). The "peak" you saw from your camp may not be the true top of the mountain, which may require another half-hour (or half-day) of climbing.

Don't expect to find an easier way back down the far side of the mountain. You may come upon a sheer drop from the top and find it too dangerous to descend *and* too far to ascend again. It's safer to mark your trail on the way up and follow that same trail back.

As you get more interested in climbing, you'll want to refer to a "mountaineer's guide" (see Book List for these Sierra Club guides) for a specific mountain range. This set of small *Tote Books* lists specific climbing routes and "difficulty" ratings for each route and peak in a given area. There's a guide to the High Sierra in California, a guide to the Cascade Range in Oregon and Washington, another for the Wind River Range in Wyoming, one for the Great Basin Desert, etc. Match your ability to the difficulty of various climbs, from Class 1 ("hiking") and Class 2 ("hands are occasionally used for balance") to Class 3 ("handholds and footholds are used...some climbers may wish to be belayed") and even higher classes. Beginners should stick to Classes 1 and 2; advanced climbers can choose more difficult peaks and routes. These *Tote Books* also include cross-country "knapsack routes," which can help you plan off-trail hiking through areas which might otherwise seem inaccessable with a full pack. Once you get hooked on bagging peaks, guidebooks like these are indispensable.

Mountain Biking

Bikers go faster and farther. A day trip to them may cover twice or three times the distance of a day hiker. Trail biking in the high country challenges stamina and skill and offers solitude and scenery. With a light pack on the back, tools included, the biker is unfettered. If, however, the trail is obstructed by fallen trees or is filled with granite scree, if it climbs or descends too steeply, if it disappears into dense brush, the mountain biker will have to dismount, schlep and haul, or turn around and go home. Expecting the unexpected is a cardinal rule for the trail biker. So is expecting the expected—hikers and backpackers on foot; minor spills and falls; mechanical failures; fatigue. Be, you should pardon the expression, prepared.

Some mountain bikers carry a strap so they can shoulder their bikes up impossible grades. Others grab the handlebars, flip the front wheel up, and roll the bike ahead on the rear wheel. All have to dismount to get over tree trunks and logs. This is hard work, and at high altitude it's sometimes exhausting too. Rest. Swig some water, nosh on a piece of chocolate. Get out the compass and topo map and triangulate your position, even if you know where you are! Anything that takes time and forces you to rest and relax. Take a siesta even though it's only 10 a.m.

When injured, rest some more. Walter Mitty made it across the Channel at the helm with an unset broken arm, but you won't and shouldn't. He's a fiction. You're a fact. And the fact is that cycling, especially rough trail riding—draws injuries like flies to a feast. Knees and elbows, even encased in long pants and sleeves, are vulnerable, and when scraped and strained require attention and a rest break. Elevate the injury (above the heart). Treat it with the ever-present first-aid kit—a cold pack, disinfectant, ace bandage—and don't get back on the bike till the swelling's down. No sense sending yourself to the trauma ward when all you want to do is hang out.

Hanging Out with Children

Everything can be a wonderment—or a bore—to small chidren, and it's up to you to help make it the first, not the second. If you decide to hang around camp for the day, follow their lead. It could take you (and them) no further than the nearest inch worm. Call it nature study. It may take hours. After all, the worm takes hours doing what it does. Young children may need direction around rather than through the still warm fire or caution before diving into space, or preferably your arms, from the high scarp overlooking the kitchen. But exploring children are usually happy children, which makes your job that of a benign overseer. As long as they don't get lost or hurt (remember the whistle around their necks?) they can keep busy longer than you may care to imagine. If you're baking bread, give them some dough to knead or feed to the ants. If you're fishing, let them cast, even if the bubble or lure never quite make it into the water. (Keep baby brother out of the range of the hook.) If you're off on a day hike, make sure the five and six year olds have lots to do on the trail—hiding, eating, staring breathlessly at a deer, hearing a story told or telling one.

Water play is as theraputic for children as adults. They don't need a wading pool or San Simeon to be happy. A puddle or stream, a lake or tide pool will enhance their day and yours. If old enough, they can float in the current of the stream near the canoe or raft. If too young, they can paddle around at the shoreline. For reasons known only to physiologists and low-temperature physicists, toddlers and five year olds never seem to get cold. Lips turn blue, goose flesh appears, yet on they go, insisting on one more splash, one more dunk, one more handful of mud before surrendering to a warm blanket in the sunshine. Yes, we know about the dangers of chill, and so do you, but let them dawdle in the water while the sun is high and they're discovering the joys of the aquatic life. Tide pools are the top of the line in water ware, and entire families can spend whole afternoons wading about touching, watching, feeling, collecting. Shells and stones weigh down packs the next day, but sometimes you have to pay the price.

Rick is one of the world's great grasshopper catchers. He uses them as fishing bait. Now he uses them for Sheri bait. His five-year-old daughter took to the chase as if born to it. Probably some genetic explanation there. Anyway, with the single mindedness of the true believer, she chased and caught them for the better part of an August day on her third back-packing trip. We're talking hours here, endless pleasure-filled hours, over rocks, along the lake front, through the tall grass. Hal and Rick took turns monitoring the hunt, holding the Zip-loc bag. They got tired long before she did. And at the end of the day, she let them loose (hoppers and adults). It seems to have been as much fun watching them depart as it was getting them to arrive.

If you know your edible wild plants, let the kids taste-test them. They seem to love it. And older children often like to use the tree finder—one of those little guides that send you to page 4 if the needles come in threes, then to page 17 if the bark smells like a pineapple. All children appear to like to draw, and we know parents who always take along blank books for the inevitable art projects.

There's a message here. It's simple. If you bring the kids along, allow them the fun they seek, and help them get it. You may have to sacrifice the hammock or the mountain bike, but you'll be repaid in kind down the road when they offer to take *you* backpacking or camping in their favorite wilderness. In the meantime, they can get scrubbed and clean next week at home, and you can burn the clothes in the incinerator.

The Stars at Night

The day trippers are back, the children are changed, warm and dry, Uncle Zeke is out of the hammock, and James Fenimore Cooper has left the canoe in the dry dock. Supper is warm and filling, dusk is settling over the camp, and the first star is in the evening sky. The last great arena of the hang-out artist is straight above you, and it's worth a look. Chapter 12 will show you how.

CHAPTER 11

Fishing

The sky is cloudless, a deep indigo. The sun has already set. It's surprising how fast the warmth vanishes when the sun goes down. A cool breeze blows from the west. Time for parka and knit cap.

We've been fishing from the shore of the lake for about an hour without a bite. Almost in a trance, Rick casts a lure into the depths of the lake and reels it back slowly: twitching it, stopping it, speeding it up; casting left, then right; trying to run it deep, then shallow. Hal goes on reading *Catch 22* aloud. Milo Minderbinder has cornered the world market on guns and is moving in on butter.

A slight tug on Rick's line brings his thoughts back to the lake. Is it a fish nibbling at the lure or just a snag on some undergrowth? To find out he slows down the lure, twitches it a little, keeps it moving very slowly. Another tug, and Rick says, "Hey, I think I've got one!"

Half a ton of live, angry fish breaks the surface to our left. The body completely leaves the water, a full 6 inches above the ripples, then splashes back under the surface. That's when Rick notices his line peeling off the reel. The monster fish is the one on his line.

Rick tightens up on the drag. Not too much, though; that fellow could easily snap his light line. His heart pounds; his hands tremble. This is one big fish.

Reel it in; let it run out on the drag. Reel it in; let it go out again. The fish is getting tired. Rick's getting tired too. The line gets shorter as man coaxes fish toward the shore. Now we can see it: weary, slightly over on its side. It's in about three feet of water below the rock we stand on. But it's too heavy to yank out, and we have no net.

Like walking a dog, Rick slowly leads the fish along the rocky bank to a muddy inlet about 15 feet away. Every three or four feet, the fish twitches. But it's exhausted and hurt. Rick drags it closer to the muddy incline. Now it is in only four inches of water. Then, with a steady pull, he lands the fish. It flops a few times on the beach, but the line holds. Rick reaches down, unhooks it and puts it in our pot: a 16-inch golden trout.

Rick starts to speak, but nothing comes out. His heart is still pounding; he feels a little dizzy. Ten minutes of play has felt like an hour's work. He sits down. Leaning against a rock, eyes closed, it takes 10 minutes more to get back to normal. And then in only an hour, Rick and Hal sit down to the finest, freshest trout amandine dinner they've ever eaten.

Someone once described an airline pilot's job as hours and hours of utter boredom punctuated by a few moments of sheer terror. We could describe mountain fishing as hours and hours of pure relaxation punctuated by a few moments of wild excitement. The most enjoyable part of high mountain fishing is the relaxation: the scenery, the weather, the routine of casting, retrieving and playing the lure or fly.

The picture hanging above Rick's desk at work is not of a string of 14-inch trout. Rather, it's a shot of him casting into a mountain lake at sunset. The peaks above are nearly orange; you can see their reflection in the lake. Standing on a spit of land, his figure is a silhouette against the pale sky. More than anything else, we recommend high-country fishing for the beauty and quiet pleasure it brings. The tasty trout are but an additional bonus.

Mountain Trout: A Fish's Eye View

Winter

If you've never fished for trout before, a good place to begin learning is to experience the lake as the fish does—in the mind's eye of a high-mountain lake trout. During the winter the lake surface is covered with snow and ice. The water below is close to freezing, and only a little nourishment flows through. The trout, being cold-blooded, respond appropriately: as the temperature descends, so does their metabolism. Though they continue feeding all winter, they need very little food. If you could get into high country in the dead of winter, you'd work very hard for your fish, first to get through the ice, second to get it to bite.

In early spring, which in the mountains means late May and early June, the fishing is also often lean. Occasionally we've camped at a high lake just as spring is breaking. Parts of the lake are still frozen. And just five or 10 feet from shore, huge trout swim slowly along, evidently there for the taking. But nothing seems to work. Flies, lures, moving bait are universally ignored. Sometimes the fish will feed on a small worm or grub buried in the mud. But basically they're just out sunning, warming themselves in the water's upper layers. There's not much to eat yet and the fish aren't hungry. Neither the spawning cycle (which produces lots of yummy eggs) nor the insect hatching cycle (which produces a living feast) have yet begun. As Br'er Rabbit would observe, "They're layin' low."

Spring: June and Early July

The longer, warmer days of June and early July melt the snow rapidly. Suddenly there is water everywhere. Lakes are overflowing. Meadows turn emerald with lush growth and are dappled with wild flowers. The insect hatch begins. From tiny eggs, insect larvae appear—little white worms called grubs or nymphs which live in the shallows of lakes or streams.

As the lake begins warming, and the body temperature of fish rises, the trout start moving faster. They quickly get hungry. And as the snow melts in the mountain meadows, it washes small grubs down through the lake, so the fish don't have to look far for food. They congregate at the places in the lake where they can find shelter, comfort, and nourishment.

Where are these spots? Shelter could mean deep water. However, trout aren't too comfortable in the deepest part of the lake: there's little food, less oxygen, and the cold temperatures make them sluggish. In the spring, as the ice melts, the upper 40 feet of the lake will have a good supply of oxygen and water of the right temperature. Shelter in this region might be available under a bank or beneath a rock overhang.

To trout, like the rest of us, the food question is simple: how to get the most food for the least energy? In the springtime, they do this by finding a quiet place next to a food-bearing flow of water. This allows them to watch the current passively, then dart into it only when a tasty morsel appears. In mountain lakes, these quiet spots are usually found where the shallows drop off rapidly into deep water near where a feeder stream enters the lake. They are often called "holding" areas by fisherfolk.

Another important factor in finding food has to do with the trouts' ability to see. Too little (or too much) light makes it difficult for them to distinguish a moving grub from a twig or pine needle. So fish will usually lurk at the depth of water that offers the right amount of light. They'll feed in shallow water in the early morning, then move deeper during the day, and feed again in the shallows at dusk.

What kind of food do trout look for in the spring? Mainly, grubs. Some grubs float free; some squirm in the mud; many are encased in little "houses" of bark and sand. Open the stomach of a trout and you'll usually find a few partially digested grubs along with lots of dirt, twigs, and mud.

Occasionally the fish in these holding areas get a special treat: a batch of trout eggs or roe. Springtime marks spawning season for trout. Many trout swim up into the feeder streams, the females to deposit eggs in warm, shallow water, and the males to fertilize them. Sometimes a batch of eggs is washed from its sandy bed and floats down to the lake. Lake trout are always watching for eggs in the springtime.

How should you fish mountain lakes in the spring? We usually cast fairly deep, near the inlet of a feeder stream, baiting with salmon eggs. Try to find the "drop-off" point and get your eggs just over the ledge. Late in the day, when the water is still warm and the light is losing its glare, those hungry fish will move toward your bait. Chances of a nibble are good.

If you're stream fishing, you can sometimes catch spawners in the shallow creek beds by drawing a lure in front of them— slowly, as if it were an intruder to their nesting area. The fish won't be hungry, but may grow angry and snap at it in order to protect their turf.

Summer: July and August

In early and mid-summer, the days turn long and hot in the mountains. The snow is gone. The creeks have slowed. The biggest change from springtime is the proliferation of insect life. Larvae emerge from their twig and sand houses, crawl into the sun on top of a rock, and metamorphose into small flies and bugs. Grasshoppers emerge from eggs and begin hopping through the grassy meadows.

The rushing, running water of the spring is gone. Insect life centers on and around the mountain lakes. Their surfaces become breeding grounds for insects too tiny to see. These in turn become food for larger flying insects which dance along the surface of the water whenever it is calm, eating the smaller ones. From the fish's eye view, the livin' is easy.

Trout continue to spawn during the early summer, with females swimming up feeder streams to lay. Many of the eggs laid earlier in spring now hatch. Shallow waters are filled with tiny trout, or minnows, which provide excellent nourishment for larger fish. The minnows soon learn the importance of remaining near shelter at all times.

In summer, the lake divides into three layers of water: an upper warm layer, a lower cold layer, and a combined middle layer. In the morning, the trout come into the shallows to feed on nymphs and minnows. The water here is cooler then and the low sun makes it easier to see the nymphs (larval flies which swim several inches below the surface of the water) and minnows, which hang out in nooks and crannies for protection.

During midday, the trout move lower, to cooler water. The brighter it gets, the deeper they go. They spend most of these hours nosing around the lake bottom for grubs, larval flies which live in the mud. Occasionally the fish come across some tasty fish eggs or a small worm. Then in the afternoon, they go back to the shallower areas to feed, primarily in the shade, where it is easier for them to see the surface.

During late afternoon, when the cold-blooded insects are most active on the water and sunlight strikes the lake at an angle, the trout will rise to work the surface. This is when you'll see them jumping. They wait below the still surface for a fly to land and feed. Then they come up—so fast that they just keep going, often completely out of the water. It's always a thrill to see and usually signifies prime time to catch dinner.

Yet trout fishing any hour of the summertime day can be a real pleasure. In the morning we often fish with lures. Lures spin bright and silvery in the water, imitating minnows darting through the upper layers of the lake. During the middle of the day, the fish often seem to "stop biting." They've gone to the cooler depths to forage for grubs. Sometimes they can be caught with salmon eggs, but catching a tan is a better bet, or a nap in the shade after a swim while the old fishing rod, secured by a few sturdy rocks, takes care of itself. If the salmon eggs get soggy, so what?

Afternoons are the most productive times to fish. Everything seems to work. We fish flies when the trout are jumping. We fish lures along the steep drop-offs, often following the shadow line along the shore, as the fish do underwater. We also fish with grasshoppers near the shore in shady places under overhanging bushes. These are the likely spots where grasshoppers may accidentally fall into the lake, spots where the fish will be waiting for them. This time of day usually gives us our best fish memories and stories, and if things work out, a pan full of the freshest supper you could ever want.

Fall: September and Early October

In the fall, the water level is the year's lowest. The days get shorter, nights colder, food scarcer. The creeks and streams feeding the lakes have all but dried up. There isn't much insect life flowing through the lake. The temperature layers of the lake water begin to equalize. As the surface water cools, it's easier for the trout to spend time in it.

At this time of year there are fewer but larger fish in the lakes. They are the survivors, and they want to fatten up for the winter cold spell. They feed on grubs and nymphs, now more plentiful in the shallower stretches, and on insects, which still land on the lake's surface in the late afternoon. Grasshoppers are fewer but fatter and still choice bait. Everything seems more tempting to the hungry fish.

Fishing in the fall is thus similar to fishing in the summer—with one big exception: with the fish bigger and hungrier, and the action near or on the surface most of the day, it's even easier! There are a couple of other bonuses as well. The weather is better and the wilderness less crowded. Now if you could only arrange vacation time then....

Rivers and Streams

Stream fishing, like lake fishing, has its unique pleasures and problems. It promises more solitude—a chance to get off by yourself even near the trail. And while it's hard work it's often productive, and usually satisfying whether you bag a fish or not.

Stream fishing means a lot of hiking for a little angling. It often requires hopping on rocks, or holding onto overhanging branches for dear life or taking off your pants and putting on your boots, or getting your line tangled in thickets of brush, or all the above. Yet the angler who is willing to fish a mountain stream often will return to camp with a string of trout, having discovered the right tackle and baits and the best places to fish only a spit and a holler from the well-worn path.

Many hiking trails parallel streams, dipping down occasionally to cross them at fordable points. At those points are often
located well-used (and sometimes populated) campsites. But
just a few hundred yards in either direction up or down
stream you'll find no sign of human life and often many signs
of underwater life. A little scrambling gets you a lot of fishing.
And if the fish aren't biting, you can retrace your steps, hike
along the trail, leave it again where it approaches the stream,
and continue for a whole day, covering long stretches of running water. Along the way you'll often discover several natural, picture-perfect campsites, too remote for the casual hiker.
There you can set up shop for a couple of days of fine early-
morning and late-afternoon fishing.

Stream trout eat the same things as lake trout, but they
tend to secure their food in a different way. By knowing what,
how, and where they eat, you can usually find and often catch
them. Larvae, grubs, insects, eggs and minnows thrive in
streams as well as lakes and fill up the "market basket" of
hungry river fish. Your job is to figure out just what the fish
are feeding on—you may have to try several riggings and
baits before you get the right one—and then go after them.
Here's how.

Lake trout, you remember, move around looking for food.
River trout, conversely, stay in one place. That's the major difference between the two and makes for a different kind of fishing. As the river water flows, it carries insects, eggs, and
larvae with it. A fish needn't move to get the food when food is
moving to it. This is ecological efficiency at work, and by tap-
ping into its logic, you can imitate nature with your bait and
catch a fish.

The fish knows where the food is coming from and where to
be to get it. Obviously it'll come from upstream. The place to
be, if you're a stream trout, is in a quiet, well protected pool,
just off the mainstream which carries the goodies along. Such
pools may be under an overhanging boulder, bank, or branch,
beneath a rotted log, or at the bend of the river where the flow
eddies wide, leaving a quiet spot near one bank. They may be
at the far end of a rapids or beneath a miniature waterfall or
cascade, all of which act as natural conveyor belts for the food
that fish fancy.

Stream trout "hold" in these pools (hence the angling term,"holding pools"), and watch the rapidly flowing main current without having to swim against it. When a morsel flows by, they dart out and grab it. Then it's back to the safety of the shadowed pool to watch and wait for more of the same. Like the fish, you can also trace the path of the food. Toss a leaf into the flowing stream or over the cascade. See how it's taken by the current into a calmer spot: that's the pool. Now try to cast your baited hook in such a way that it does the same thing as the leaf. Throw your bait into the current. The eggs, if that's what you're using, will sink slightly, then be carried into the pool below. If you've done your homework and fish are waiting, you'll get a quick bite. River fish are not likely to mouth the bait and spit it out several times as lake fish often do. River fish must get their food on the first bite or watch it disappear downstream.

Sneak up on stream trout from behind. They're facing upstream; you should be hiking and casting upstream also. Cast your bait or lure just above where you suspect they're holding. Let the bait float naturally through the area, as if it just hatched or fell into the water. As the bait floats back to you,

Stream eddies and holding pools.

reel in just enough line to take up the slack and keep it from snagging—easier said than done!

Several such casts, allowing the bait to flow into the pool, are all you need. Look around for other likely holding pools upstream. Perhaps there's a log blocking the current, or a large rock in the middle of the stream. A fish might lurk behind it, observing the water flow by. Let your bait or lure drift past. Still no bites? Then it's time to move on.

Moving on takes some care. You need to be quiet and cautious at the same time—quiet in order to sneak up on fish which are often just inches below the surface, and cautious to keep from slipping, tripping and falling along overgrown banks and slippery rocks. River trout are easily spooked. Be careful of your shadow dancing on the water. Plan your moves so your shadow falls on the bank instead. That might mean hunching over, even crawling in spots. Keep your casting motion short and low; the sudden movement of your arm and rod can startle fish. Once they sense your motion or are alerted by rocks and gravel you dislodge as you scramble down a bank, they're likely to duck into a safe hiding place for hours.

Once you manage to get to the holding pools without sending all the fish to the local fright-recovery unit, and if you have the right bait, your chances of landing a trout are greatly enhanced if you fish early or late in the day. When there's little light on the water, the fish see the surface better and, like their lake cousins, go for living foods on or just below it. At midday, they go as deep as they can, still watching the flowing water for an easy lunch in the deep shade. You might try it yourself.

One last thing. To quiet and caution, add patience. Stream fishing can be frustrating. Your line can get snagged on an overhanging branch, the hook or lure can get hung up on a submerged rock or log, the trout on your line can free itself by taking your line under a rock and snapping it. But the rewards of solitude, beauty, challenge, and good eating more than make up for the hard parts. Take it slow, easy, and enjoy.

Fishing in the Rain

When rain clouds roll in on summer afternoons, many campers head into their tents. We put on ponchos and parkas, and head out to fish. Some of our most memorable fishing has been on rainy afternoons.

One theory has it that fish can't possibly conceive of any other creature, especially an over-coddled human, who might prefer to be as wet as they are. Thus, when they see a shiny lure dancing through the rain-splashed water, they figure it's the real thing. Our own theory doesn't attribute quite so much intelligence to the trout. We've found that as the storm moves in, the fish stop biting. They sense the air pressure decreasing—what weather forecasters mean by the barometer falling. Fish—and most other living things—seek shelter.

Once the storm is in full splendor, the barometer steadies, then begins to rise. As the air pressure increases, the rain may still be falling, but the fish sense that the worst is over, and out they go to see what fresh food has entered the lake. The rain washes the surface of the lake clean. New bugs appearing on the surface are likely to be alive. Minnows darting below the surface are likely to be real. And anglers' shadows broken by the rain-mottled surface are likely to go unnoticed. While all this is conjecture, the fact is that if you don't mind the wet, fishing in the rain can be highly successful and a lot more fun than huddling in the tent.

Gear

Mountain trout are usually small. Most range from 8-12 inches in length and weigh a little under a pound. A two to three pounder in the high country is a monster. And even these require very little in the way of gear to bait, hook, and reel into your frying pan.

First, you need a rod and reel. We leave fancy fly fishing, with its graphite rods, hand-tied flies and special line, to the purists. Instead, we use a simple telescoping spinning rod. It telescopes down to a two-foot length short enough to stick in the backpack, though it's also long and stiff enough to give a good cast. Inexpensive models can even be found in some drugstores. But treat them gently and pack them carefully: expensive or cheap, they're fragile.

Reels come in all shapes and sizes. A look at *Consumer Reports* might be in order before you put your money down. The more expensive reels have better machinery inside—bearings, gears and levers—that last longer and take more abuse. The cheaper "backpacking" reels are lighter, less substantial and more likely to jam up after you drop them onto the ground or into the sand a couple of times. We usually compromise—the best combination of inexpensive and lightweight that our discount sports store has in stock when we're buying.

If you're left-handed, you might want a left-handed reel which permits you to wind in with your right hand while holding the rod and reel in your left. On the other hand (!), you might want to learn to fish with a righty's reel. It isn't hard and saves bringing extra gear if you don't mind sharing.

It's a good idea to practice taking the cover off the reel and lubricating the inside mechanism. It won't take many trips before your reel falls into the water or sand for one reason or another. If you don't lubricate it soon afterwards, certainly before your next outing, it will get sticky and much harder to cast properly. For this purpose, you can either buy a special reel lubricant or use any light gear-and-bearing grease.

You'll need fishing line on the reel. We usually deposit our reels at a local bait and tackle shop a few days before each out-

Winding a reel.

ing and have them wound with four pound monofilament line. The shop has a special winding machine which lays the line on evenly and regularly.

If you prefer, you can wind the line onto the spool yourself. Set up the rod and reel as if you were going fishing. Thread the line through the rod's eyelets and tie it to the spool of the reel with the bail open. Drop the spool of fresh line into a clean waste basket. Grasp the line and rod with your right hand about a foot up from the reel. Snap the bail shut and reel the new line in with your left hand. Keep a slight drag on the line with your right hand, and watch the reel as you wind. If you see stray loops or uneven winding, vary the drag until you get it right. Don't allow any lumps, clumps, twirls or snags to grow on the spool. Be sure the line lays down in even symmetrical rows.

Why do you need fresh line each outing? The monofilament tends to shape itself to the spool on which it's wound. Line which has been on your reel for several months tends to lie in the water in hundreds of little curlicues. As you reel in these curls, they quickly form hundreds of small knots. Then you spend your fishing time untangling knots instead of casting— a disheartening task.

The rest of your backpacking fishing tackle, except for a net, should fit easily into a large Ziploc bag. In that bag, supplies should be divided into smaller bags or plastic boxes. It's important both to save weight when backpacking and to save space in the pack. Don't fill your fishing bag with empty space. Pack lightly but efficiently.

Basically, you'll need the following items:

Bubble: About a dozen clear and torpedo-shaped if available. These are used mainly for casting weight. A large bubble will get your fly farther into the middle of the lake than a small one.

Flies: A dozen small flies will fit into a tiny bag, box, or foam-lined case. Buy various colors and shapes, with hook sizes between 8 and 14. Most of our flies are on #10 or #12 hooks. They cost between 50 cents and a dollar each, though hand-tied flies will set you back a lot more.

Hooks: One package each of hooks already tied to a small piece of leader, sizes 8, 10, 12, 14. The leaders have a loop at the other end and can be clipped easily onto a snap or swivel in your rigging.

Spare Line: We usually bring 100 yards of four-pound test monofilament on a spool. This can be wound directly onto your reel if you run completely out (as a result, for example, of having consecutively cut away tangled sections). Spare line can also be used as "leader"—line tied directly to a fly or bait. Some people bring 25 yards of two-pound test monofilament to use as leader.

Snaps: About 30 of the smallest you can find. These are used at the end of the line to attach bubbles, lures and other riggings.

Swivels: About 10, all small. These attach weights or hooks in the middle of a rigging. They can be two- or three-way swivels. They are helpful in dreaming up new ways to rig your bait.

Weights: One package (20 weights) of $\frac{1}{8}$-ounce "egg sinkers." These are sliding weights with a hole down the middle. One package of $\frac{1}{16}$-ounce "split shot," small weights which clamp to a single spot on the line. If you plan long, deep water casts, add a package of $\frac{1}{4}$-ounce egg sinkers.

Fishing tackle.

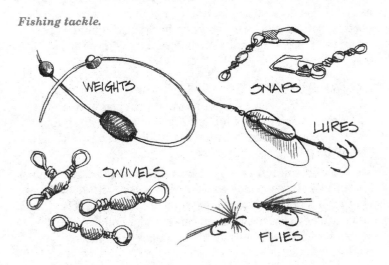

Lures: About a dozen lures with treble (triple) hooks, sizes 8, 10, 12. This will allow you to lose a few and still have a reserve. Lures have a habit of snagging; you'll donate quite a number to the lake or stream bottom. The larger, heavier lures can be cast farther. Smaller, lighter lures work better in mountain streams. They don't sink as fast so they're less likely to snag on sunken trees and branches. Check with your favorite expert about his or her special lure before you shop—lures are expensive. We've had the most success with 1 ½" Super Dupers and ½-ounce # 6 Panther Martins.

Salmon Eggs: Two small bottles of Pautchke's "Balls of Fire," green label. This brand is slightly more expensive but comes highly recommended. Keep the eggs in their glass bottles despite the excess weight. Also keep them cool and in the shade or they'll start to spoil.

Net: Get the smallest, lightest net available from a tackle shop. Pack it with the pots, pans and plates and it'll add very little weight and take up hardly any space. It helps a lot in landing fish, especially from a steep, rocky shore.

License: You might never meet a ranger or game warden in the backcountry who wants to see your license, but you need one anyway. The fee is steep but worth it, and your money goes to a good cause. It's used by your state's Fish and Game people to restock lakes, maintain hatcheries, and keep streams and rivers clear. Don't travel without one. And make sure when you get one to pick up a free copy of your state's fishing regulations. It explains what kind of fishing is legal in which areas at what times of year. Read carefully.

Bait and Rigging

The best way to find out if "they're biting" and "what to use" is to ask those who are there or who you meet on the trail coming from your lake. If they tell you, "Salmon eggs toward the lake inlet," go to it with salmon eggs. If they tell you, "Lures by the steep north wall," don't use flies by the inlet.

That's simple enough.

Of course, this presumes the presence of people with information. The farther off the beaten track, the fewer ready-made answers. Alone at a lake, deciding what and where to fish becomes a wonderful challenge. Size up the lake closely for a few moments. Where does the water come in? Where does it leave? Where are the deepest spots? Where are the shady overhangs? Consider the season, the weather, and the time of day to figure out where the fish might be.

If you prepare wisely, you're ready in advance for any kind of fishing, deep or shallow, lures or bait. Your lures, fastened to a cork so they won't tangle, can clip easily onto the snap at the end of the line. Your salmon-egg rigging is tied up inside a small plastic bag, available for instant use. If the fish are jumping in the shady section of the lake, you can quickly switch from eggs to a bubble and fly. Or perhaps you feel like putting a grasshopper in the water near the shrubs by the base of a steep cliff, then reading another chapter of your book as you wait for a tug on the line. It's fun and easy to experiment when you've put your riggings together in advance. It's frustrating when that big cahoonga is right there laughing at you, as you try to tie new knots, re-rig a line, and catch a grasshopper all at the same time.

Fishing Knots, Swivels and Clips

Like Boy Scouts, anglers often wallow lovingly in the intricacy of knotsmanship. "Lark's-head loops" and "Bimini twists" are often cited as prerequisites to catching large fish. Fortunately this is not the case. Everything in your fishing arsenal can be tied strongly and securely with a simple square knot, and confusion about the fancier systems of connecting line and tackle won't prevent you from catching a single trout. Nevertheless, for the precision angler and other fine-tuners, we include on the next few pages a few simple knots and tying instructions. We often use the clinch knot.

Swivels are used to tie one piece of tackle to another so they don't slip or come apart. For example, when you fish with salmon eggs, you may want two groups of eggs suspended above the bottom of the lake. A couple of three-way swivels allow you to connect two short "drop" leaders to the main line with a minimum of fuss.

A snap at the end of the line is a must; it'll save you a lot of time when you're making up and changing riggings. You can clip a lure onto the end of your line for fishing deep. Then, if the fish start feeding on surface insects, you can easily detach that lure to clip on a bubble-and-fly rigging. Snaps save you from cutting the line and retying whenever you change tackle. Remember, early morning and evening are the times when it

Improved clinch knot.

Lark's head knot.

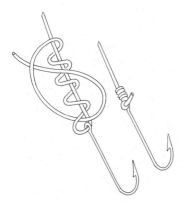

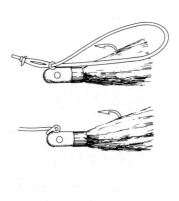

Bimini twist knot.

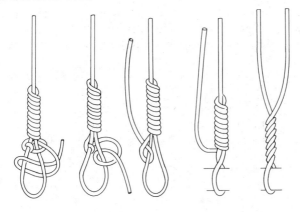

will be most difficult for you to see the line to tie or untangle it, yet those are the times of the most fishing action. If you have a supply of snaps and swivels in your tackle bag, you'll be ready for those quick changes when time counts.

Salmon Egg Riggings

Trout lay their eggs in shallow rock beds near the headwaters of rivers and streams. These eggs occasionally get jarred loose and float downstream on the streambed, finally settling on the bottoms of lakes. Mountain trout love 'em.

To fish a stream, you need to gauge the amount of weight necessary to keep the egg low in the water. Without any weights at all, salmon egg riggings float near the surface. Too much weight will get your line snagged on the first branch. You should also know the depth and speed of the water to guess the right amount of weight, in the form of split shot(s). Clamp them onto your line about 12" to 16" above the hook. The traditional way to squeeze the split shot tight on the line is to bite down on it with your molars. Your dentist would probably prefer that you use a small pliers or vise-grips for the job. If the split shot is clamped too loosely, it will slide down the line and settle near the hook, making the bait look unnatural. With a couple of salmon eggs on the hook and a couple of split shot tight on the line, you're ready to sneak up and cast it into the nearest holding pool.

On a lake, salmon eggs are usually rigged deep for fishing at times when no fish surface to feed. These riggings are also good for any other bait which isn't supposed to be alive: a bit

Rigging for three-way swivel.

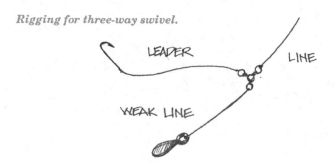

of salami or scrap of cheese, for example. You want to get these bits of food to where the fish are—along the bottom looking for food that has been washed into the lake. Trout lay eggs in clusters; if they wash away from the shallow stream in which they were laid, they remain clustered as they're carried down into the lake. We usually stick three or four salmon eggs on a #8 hook to simulate nature. One hint on getting them to stay hooked: lay them in the sun about 15 minutes before you use them. This hardens the outside skin and makes them less likely to float off the hook.

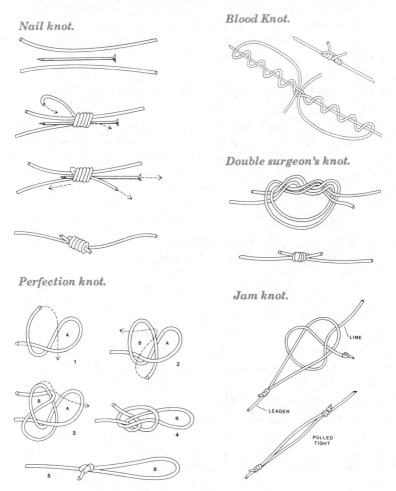

Nail knot.

Blood Knot.

Double surgeon's knot.

Perfection knot.

Jam knot.

When a lake trout spots a cluster of salmon eggs, it will often mouth them, not swallowing them completely at first. It's testing for weirdness, like a hook lurking in its Sunday brunch. Our first suggested rigging is called the Long Lake Rigging (after the lake where two old-timers taught it to us). It suspends two clusters of eggs several inches above the lake bottom. When you feel a slight tug on the line, wait just a moment, then "set" the hook in the trout's mouth by pulling up slightly on the rod. The point is to try to snag the fish's lip as it's drawing the bait in for a second mouthing. If you don't wait, you'll pull up empty, for the fish will have let the bait go before taking another taste. With this rigging, you need to hold the line fairly taut at all times so you're sensitive to what's happening at the other end.

Our other suggestion is called the Grizzly Lake Rigging. It rests the bait down on the lake bed and depends on a hungry trout to gobble it up completely. The fish won't know the eggs are on a hook until they're in its stomach. It's a perfect rigging for reading, sunning, napping, even cooking. You cast, lean the rod against a rock or your leg, and wait. The line goes slack. The fish feels no resistance as it mouths the bait and pulls back, because the line feeds freely through the doughnut weight. When you feel or see a tug on the slack line, the hook is already set, and the fish is ready to be reeled in.

With either rigging, the weight should be only as heavy as necessary to get the hook(s) and salmon eggs where you want them. Heavy weights may cast farther, but as soon as a fish bites, that heavier weight gives the trout an advantage. All it has to do is go rapidly in one direction—up, for example—then switch directions with a snap of its head. If the weight is heavy enough, the line will break. Though the fish still has a hook in its mouth, you'll reel in an empty line. We usually start with ⅛ or ¼ ounce sinkers and # 8 hooks, whatever the rigging.

Any rigging meant to lie on the lake bottom tends to snag as you reel it in. Leave the rigging motionless for several minutes after you cast, so it can settle free of an obstruction that might otherwise snag it immediately. After that, a twitch every few minutes won't hurt and might attract a fish to the moving eggs. When you're ready to cast from a different rock

Bubble and fly rigging.

Long Lake rigging.

Grizzly Lake rigging.

or in another direction, pick up the line quickly from the lake bottom by reeling it in fast. *Keep* reeling fast so the hooks and sinker stay above sharp rocks and dead tree trunks on the bottom of the lake.

Bubble-and-Fly Rigging

The evening is warm, the air still, the lake calm, the surface of the water broken only by the fish jumping for insects. If you're equipped to simulate the insects you'll almost certainly get a fish. That's where the bubble-and-fly comes in.

This rigging consists of a fly tied onto one end of several feet of leader, either four-pound or two-pound test line, and a teardrop bubble tied on the other. The bubble's weight lets you cast the fly where the fish are feeding. Once the bubble-and-fly lands, the object is to make the fly seem like all those other surface bugs. Watch how the real flies behave, scooting across the water close to shore. Reel in the line with quick short bursts so the fly seems to dart along like its real-life cousins.

The best thing about bubble-and-fly fishing is that you rarely have to worry about snags. You can spend your time casting and retrieving rather than losing masses of tackle on underwater branches. Once in a while you'll snag a fly on a bush when fishing near shore. Also, be careful of trees and shrubs on your backswing. But if you develop good casting habits, you'll while away the hours snagging fish rather than unsnagging line.

Flies come in a wide variety of shapes, sizes and colors. When the fish are jumping in those out-of-the-way backcountry lakes, neither shape nor color seem to matter. Size, however, is important. The fish are small; so are the bugs they eat. Try sizes 10 or 12. We've also noticed that flies produce the best results when they're first cast. They hit the water dry, and sit on the surface for the first several casts. Thereafter they ride slightly below the surface, and the fish are a little less likely to go after them. Sometimes we whip the fly through the air several times between casts in order to dry it off.

Keep moving as you fish bubble-and-fly. After a half-dozen casts in one area or direction, walk on. You can cover a whole lake this way, perfecting your casting technique, seeing the site from startling new perspectives and, if the fish are feeding, bagging dinner into the bargain. We backpack with a number of fanatics who don't care if they ever catch a fish. They just love the feel of casting, and over the years have become expert at placing the fly a micrometer's distance from an overhanging branch, an inaccessible inlet, a rocky spit. Now, if we could just get them to move where the fish are...

Fishing With Lures

The bigger the trout, the more likely it is to feed on small fish. From the backpacker's point of view, a lure is the closest thing to fishing with small fish; it often gets you the biggest trout. A lure is bright, shiny, silvery, often spoon-shaped. It dances and flashes through the water, reflecting light much like a minnow. Lure fishing requires a technique simulating the movements of a tiny fish—darting quickly, stopping momentarily, darting again. The art is in the play of the line, not in the distance of the cast, which can be quite short. As in bubble-and-fly fishing, you have to keep moving—your lure and yourself.

If you're fishing a stream, don't let the lure sink very far or you'll end up with a rock on the end of your line. The art of fishing a lure in a stream is to pick one that's not too heavy, then reel it through the water at a speed which will keep it just off the bottom. If you reel too fast or jerk it too hard, it will pop up to the surface. If you hesitate, it will sink to the bottom and tangle in the first branch or log. You'll definitely want a few spare lures while you're getting the hang of it. Think of the snagged lures as offerings to the spirit of the stream.

The lure simulates the motion of a small fish. If a trout wants to catch a minnow, it has to move fast. The speedy minnow will try to hide instantly, if it senses danger. It can dart into areas too shallow for the big guys, or it can escape under logs or into holes beneath banks. Thus, quickness is essential, for both minnow and trout; as soon as a trout sees the minnow flashing in the water, it strikes. The lure is below the surface.

You can't see what's happening. If you feel a nibble, you've usually hooked the fish, because it hits the triple-barbed hook with mouth wide open, intent on swallowing the small fish whole. One minute you're reeling in the lure, the next you've got a big trout solid on the line.

Suppose the large fish aren't feeding on minnows. They may still be attracted by the lure. They often swim up and seem to check it out, following it toward shore. If they're cautious, their senses will alert them that the lure doesn't sound or smell like a minnow, and they'll move away. It's an angler's nightmare to watch the big one follow a lure up to shore without biting. But frustration goes with the franchise, just as excitement does, and if that fish lives to savor a real minnow today, he'll be there for the taking tomorrow.

Another problem with lures is that they're made to fish deeper than flies. They ride somewhere between six and 24 inches below the surface as you reel them in. You can't see what's happening so it's harder to direct their path. Most lures have a three-pronged hook, which is more likely to catch a trout's mouth, but also more likely to snag underwater weeds or branches. Furthermore, if you have a problem with your equipment while the lure is in the water, the moment you stop reeling the treble hook drifts downward to catch on whatever lies there. By the time you fix the reel or untangle the line, the lure is hopelessly hooked on the lake bottom. One thing about lure fishing: it's never dull.

Fishing with Grasshoppers

An old saying goes, "You can catch any fish if you've got the right bait." Natural bait stimulates all the fish's senses. It's the r-e-e-l thing. Grasshoppers are a special treat to lake trout, and depending on the time of day and year, fish will be attuned to the possibility of a large hopper falling onto the lake's surface. Not only will a trout go after one without hesitation, it will often encounter fierce competition from kindred fish for the tasty tidbit.

The challenge of capturing the grasshoppers themselves, however, more than makes up for the ease of landing the fish that bites the hopper that feeds it. There are books on the subject; well, chapters anyway. One suggests chasing hoppers onto a blanket: they get stuck in the blanket hairs and are easy pickin'. That's plausible, but not many backpackers carry wool blankets into the high country anymore. Another expert calls for an insect net, also a great idea if you're not backpacking. We have our own methods, summed up by the rueful phrase, "going to great lengths." The bare-handed stab is the classiest technique, though it helps if you're The Flash. Those bugs move fast! The pot-lid slam is inelegant, often resulting in a dented pot lid and a handful of meadow, while the hopper easily eludes this oafish lunge. Our favorite exercise in futility, however, is the "long-distance pole press" invented one morning by Rick as he wandered forlornly through an Eden of grasshoppers with a fishing rod in hand. The long, narrow pole, he noticed, casts only a thin shadow which hoppers don't seem to notice. Once the pole is directly over its victim, you bring it down suddenly, pinning the hopper on the ground. Sometimes instead of pinning the hopper, this artful action stuns it, so you can pick it up while it's still dazed from the blow. Sometimes, instead of stunning the bug, you kill it, which is great if you're fighting a plague of locusts but not so good if you're trying to look like an expert. And sometimes— often, in Hal's case—you miss the grasshopper altogether. That pole is limber, and requires a modicum of hand-eye coordination. No matter how you try, it ain't easy.

Spring meadows are often literally covered with baby grasshoppers, and the catching's easier. As the year moves on, the hopper population decreases and the adults have more savvy. Like all insects, grasshoppers are cold-blooded. Dependent on the sun's warmth for their energy, they are least active in the morning, and thus theoretically there for the picking, right off leaves and grasses with your fingers. The only trouble in practice is that you can't see them till they flee, always just out of reach, and then you're back to square one: cunning strategies.

Some hoppers have wings and fly each time they take off, while others just hop. The key to catching them is to sneak up from behind, thus avoiding their field of vision, which extends roughly from the middle of their right side to the middle of their left. They'll jump just as your hand comes even with their heads, but not before. Try to move your hand slowly into position, perhaps one inch behind the hopper. Be careful not to cast a shadow on it as you move. Then suddenly slap down your open palm. Come down hard, quick and flat! Splat! Usually, you won't kill the hopper, but even if you do the fish won't care. Twelve-year-olds have an uncanny ability to catch grasshoppers this way.

Once you catch enough hoppers, you can keep them alive for as long as two days in a sealed plastic bag. Store them in the shade and be careful not to crush them at the bottom of your pack.

Hopper fishing is done with a rigging similar to a bubble-and-fly. The only difference is that the hook is empty. When you're ready to cast, poke the sharp point of the hook into the underside of the hopper's neck and out again at the belly-button. The hopper will stay alive for a short while because its head hasn't been damaged. It may even flutter its wings in the water, attracting the fish.

The best place to fish hoppers is under the overhanging limb of a bush or tree where a hopper would be likely to fall in, or where the fish are already jumping. Sometimes when all else fails—the flies and lures and eggs—a hopper will save the day and provide your evening's dining pleasure. They're worth the scramble.

Hooking a grasshopper.
To set a hook in a grasshopper, first insert the point of the hook into the head or the upper body under the head. Next, push the hook through the body and turn it so that the point of the hook emerges from the bottom of the grasshopper. Try to leave as little of the hook exposed as possible.

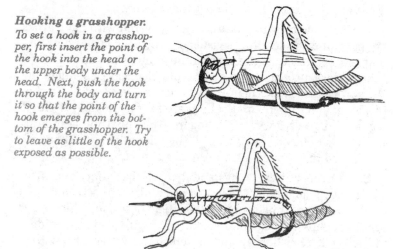

Fishing with Other Natural Bait

Rick's grandfather Harry wasn't exactly a fitness fanatic. Fifty pounds overweight, his favorite meal was a can of corned beef hash washed down with a shot of Jack Daniels. Harry's idea of a vacation was shooting craps at a Nevada casino till the wee hours. But one or two mornings afterwards, he'd get up at 7 a.m., grab his old bamboo fishing pole, and head out to the local trout stream. Harry would fish from a cement bank, not more than a few feet from his car. Invariably, he'd return with a string of six or eight fish, while others in the same area would leave empty-handed.

Harry's secret? He fished with natural bait. He told Rick that his favorite bait was a "prairie wrinkle." (A "periwinkle" is actually a small sea snail which lives on rocks or pilings along the ocean shore. Don't tell Grandpa.) Oblivious of the malapropism, he'd go on to describe a large fly larva usually called a hellgrammite. Just before dinner, Harry would go down to a shallow stream behind the hotel. He'd stir up the bottom and use an old window screen to catch these one- to two-inch-long worm-like creatures. Whether they were hellgrammites, dragon fly larvae or may-fly pupa didn't matter. As long as they were fat, wet and slimy, the fish loved them.

Most mountain insects develop from larvae (a.k.a. grubs) which grow in shallow pockets in the mud and under stream rocks. There they build a small nest or shell around themselves made up of whatever materials are on hand—bits of gravel, bark, leaves. When they finally mature, they crawl out of their "cocoon" into the warm sun on top of a nearby rock, and within hours fly away.

On a camping trip, the best time to become a grub hunter is in the middle of the day, with the sun hanging high and the fish lying low. You can comb the shore of a lake, stir up the bed of a trickling stream, or probe the underside of the bark on a rotting log. Anything that's soft, fat and wiggly (your partner excepted) will work as trout bait. Try rigging your mosquito netting with a wire loop and hold it in a stream just below a large rock. Pick up the rock and see what you catch. Teach the kids. They'll love it.

You can fish with these larvae either in their cocoons or out of them, depending on the size of the larvae and your hooks. Insect larvae are usually fished on the bottom, like salmon eggs, but you can also fish them from a bubble as you would a grasshopper.

Casting and Reeling

Nothing is more satisfying than catching trout in the wilderness. Nothing is more peaceful and relaxing than the routine of casting and retrieving a lure or fly, working the lake surface in the late afternoon while the fish feed. And nothing is more frustrating than snagging a lure or tangling your line because of improper reeling. The sun is setting, the fish are jumping, and there you are on your hands and knees trying to untangle a seemingly endless number of knots while your lure drifts slowly toward the lake floor to snag on a hidden log or brush. It makes you want to cry.

Prevent this by developing good casting habits. Practice in the local park at home or at the campsite using only a bubble

Casting; hold the line with your forefinger, raise the rod just past vertical, then cast. As the tip passes "10 o'clock," let go of the line.

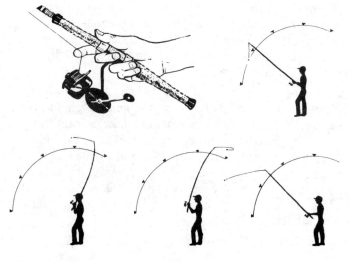

on the line. Grip the rod as shown in the illustration. Point it in the direction you intend to cast. Catch the line on the ball of your forefinger. Then open the bail. With one smooth motion, bring the tip of the rod up, just past vertical, then back down. As the rod passes the "10-o'clock" position in front of you, straighten your forefinger. The line will spin off the reel as it follows the bubble across the lake. Once the bubble or lure is in the water, give the handle on the reel a quick turn to snap the bail back into position. As you continue turning the handle, the line reels regularly and neatly onto the spool, ready to peel off with little resistance on the next cast.

Reeling in the line seems simple, but requires some vigilance at the beginning. Most backpacking reels are small and light; the line is wound in very small loops around a narrow spool. When the line shoots out over the water, it pulls straighter at the bubble end than it does near the reel. The line on the water near you will be twirled and curled, and when you begin to reel in, it might tangle itself into a knot. Even a small knot on the line will foul up smooth casting.

To prevent these tangles, you need to watch the line as you reel in the first 10 or 15 feet. This is distracting: your attention is usually focused where the fish are. Force yourself. Watch for knots and tangles until the line is straight in the water.

Another way to defend against tangles is to grasp the rod and line with your rod hand about a foot in front of the reel as you begin to haul in. As the line slips through your hand, you'll feel any knots and can untangle them on the spot.

What if you reel in a tangle or knot without noticing it? The first indication will be a sudden halt to your lure or bubble as you cast. Knots and tangles catch in the eyelets through which the line passes along the rod. This will stop your cast dead. Then you'll have to decide whether to untangle the mess or just cut it off and continue with the fresh line still on your spool. Most spools contain about three times the amount of line you actually use when casting. If you cut off a length of tangled mess, you'll still have enough for an afternoon's fishing. If you have to cut again, however, you'll be approaching the end of what line is on the reel. Once you hit the bottom of the spool, you'll need to wind on new line, either from the extra four-pound monofilament in your fishing bag, or from another reel (See previous instructions on winding line onto an empty spool).

What happens if you're in a wooded area where branches are too close to permit an overhead cast? Use a side-arm cast. Practice casting *from* either side *to* either side. That way, you'll be prepared to fight your way through brush and cast from a muddy bank overgrown with dense bushes. You can still put the lure or bubble wherever you want it.

Underwater Snags

Try as you might, the line will occasionally snag on a rock or branch under water. First make sure you haven't actually caught a large fish! The big ones sometimes move so slowly that you might mistake them for a rock. Watch the line carefully in the water as you hold it tight. If it moves at all, it's a fish! Otherwise, you've got a snag. Don't just snap a snagged line. Try loosening its tension and pulling again from all directions. Walk back and forth along the bank, hop around the rocks. You may get lucky and dislodge it. If the weather is warm and the water not too cold, you can swim out to free it. Sometimes we cut the line and tie it somewhere on shore, and in the heat of the following day we'll screw up our nerve, jump in, and retrieve the lure.

If you decide to sacrifice the lure or rigging, be careful not to break your rod in the process of snapping the line. Point the rod in the direction of the snagged lure. Wrap the line two or three times around your hand between the reel and the first eyelet on the rod. (If your skin cuts easily, wrap the line around your shirtsleeve near your wrist. The line, when taut, is knife-like.) Then start walking backward. The line will normally break near the lure, though sometimes the extra pressure will free the lure from the snag. Either way, when the line suddenly goes limp, reel it in. Never snap a line by raising the tip of the pole. That's a guaranteed way to break the pole instead.

Playing and Landing a Trout: What's a Drag?

When a fish takes your hook, it reacts like any animal with something sharp and painful in its mouth—it runs away. It swims as rapidly and strongly as it can away from the danger it has encountered, toward a secure hiding place. At this point, it's up to the angler to "play" the fish, to let it run against a constant resistance, to tire it out.

If your line is taut, the fish can snap it with a few quick maneuvers. How can a fish which weighs only one pound snap a "four-pound test" line? Easy. The "four-pound" figure indicates only the amount of dead, motionless weight the line can lift vertically off the ground. Even a one-pound fish moving rapidly can exert more than four pounds of force on a taut line. If it does, the line will snap.

Spinning reels are equipped with a "drag" to prevent this. This drag adjustment allows the line to unwind when it is pulled hard by a fish; that is, it unwinds rather than snaps. You should check and adjust the drag each time you fish. Don't wait till the fish hits your lure or bait. You may not have time.

The drag is adjusted with the same screw mechanism that holds the spool in position on the reel. Most light, inexpensive

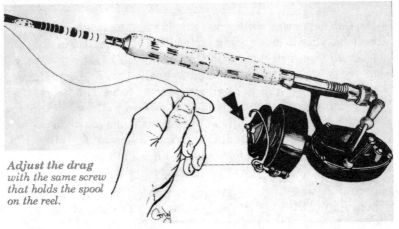

Adjust the drag with the same screw that holds the spool on the reel.

backpacking reels are equipped with cheap drag fittings. The vibration of the reel winding and unwinding, the snapping of the bail, even the bouncing of your pack as you hike along the trail can disturb the drag mechanism, and you'll need to fiddle with it from time to time.

First check the adjustment. Grab the line below the closed reel and pull. The line should go taut, and then the spool should begin to revolve, allowing line to peel off. If you can pull hard enough to snap the line without it unwinding, the drag is too tight. If you feel no resistance, it's too loose. When it's adjusted right, a solid tug will unwind the line slowly against a constant resistance. Remember that a very small movement in the adjustment nut—⅛ or ¼ of a turn—will make all the difference in the drag. Make sure to check it each time you begin to fish.

If, when you set out to test the drag, the handle and bail revolve, permitting line to come easily off the spool, the reel's one-way-only ratcheting mechanism is not engaged. It's controlled by a little lever or switch on the reel. It should always be engaged when you fish, so that the reel makes a soft clicking sound as you wind the line in.

Landing Fish

If a fish gets away while you're trying to land it, it's usually because your heart is going faster than your head. Finally, after all that waiting and all that work, you've got a live, very angry animal on the end of a pathetically thin line, and there are too many things to do all at the same time. The rod is bobbing and weaving, your friends are cheering, whooping and being useless with a million suggestions, none of which you can hear for all the pounding inside your ears. It feels like you're waltzing with a tiger and he knows all the steps.

OK. You're supposed to remain cool and collected. That's part of the challenge. Anyway, you want to land that thunder bolt. Adjust the drag as you begin to play the fish. Bring it closer to you. Make it work, pulling against the drag, taking the line slowly out again. Then increase the drag just a touch and reel it in again. The fish is now close enough to see. It's a big one! Dinner for four! Better repeat the process. Let it go out again; reel it in again. Is it still fighting mad? Do it again! Don't try to land a biggy until it's tired. Otherwise you're going to end up talking about dinner rather than eating it.

The big ones are the heart stoppers, but the small ones are fun and exhilarating too. And most of the fish you'll catch in the mountains are going to be small—in the 8- to 10-inch bracket: great eating and easy to store. Bring the small fry close to shore, then lift it out of the water and away from the lake all in one fluid motion. If you decide to release the fish— it may be too small or you may only be fishing for sport—get the hook out of the fish's mouth as quickly and gently as possible. Then hold it lightly in your hand and place it under the surface of the water. If it has enough strength to survive, it will dart quickly out of your hand with a sudden, swift motion. If it's nearly dead, it will float motionless in your hand. Don't leave the fish floating there if it doesn't have the strength to swim away. It's as good as dead, and there's no sense polluting the lake with it. Keep it and eat it.

Be careful also about regulations on fish size. In some lakes and streams, there's a legal minimum limit on the size of fish you can keep; smaller fish must be returned to the water. Check in your regulation manual for this information.

The most efficient way to land a larger fish is with a net. This is absolutely imperative if, like us, you enjoy wading out into the lake up to your hips as you fish. Trying to grab a trout with bare hands is more difficult than catching the proverbial greased pig. Net your catch head first so that it will move into the net while trying to escape. Once it's in, lift the net clean out of the water. Then, with your other hand, grab the fish and webbing from the outside with a firm grip around the middle of the fish. Now remove the hook (while holding your rod out of the water, if necessary; it can be done) and release the fish or store it for later eating.

What if you don't have a net? You'll have to beach the fish. Keep in mind when you do this that fish fight harder as the water gets shallower. Play the fish till it's tired, then lead it up to a sandy stretch of shore. With a single, continuous motion, guide the fish onto the beach. Don't jerk the line or it may break. Just pull steadily and the trout will follow the line. The fish might try to twitch and jump when it feels the sand, but if it's tired and your motion is swift and smooth, it won't realize what is happening until it's too late.

What if you have no net and no shore? When fishing from a rocky bank, you'll have to use the "clean-and-jerk" method. If the fish is very tired and the water is shallow, you can use the same motion that you'd use to beach a fish to pull it up out of the water toward land. Once it's airborne and moving in your direction, it may arch its body rapidly, wriggle frantically, or in some other way unhook itself or snap the line. Hopefully it will have enough inertia at this point to continue on its shoreward flight and land on the rocky bank—flipping, flopping and unhooked, but far enough away from the water to prevent a last-minute leap from the frying pan to the watery deep.

You've landed your fish and, like Rick with his 16-inch golden trout, you need time to "come down." Savor the moment and the future bragging rights. Then put the gear in order (the line may be a mess), pack up the plastic bags, and head for the campsite with your catch and a gleam in your eye that spells baked trout and a loaf of bread hot out of the "oven" for supper.

CHAPTER 12

Star Gazing

Basic Sky

Being in the backcountry changes your nightlife dramatically.
You're a million light years from Main Street, far beyond the
reach of the entertainment section, even if you could read it in
the failing light. Dinner has been cleaned up and the evening
fishing is over; the wind dies down and the clouds disappear. A
chill slides into the air. Time for parkas and wool hats, a fire,
maybe a ghost story or the lament of a harmonica. You can try
to read until the flashlight begins to flicker. You can follow
Ben Franklin's "early-to-bed" advice. Or you can stroll down
by the lake and watch the moon rise. It's never too late for another cup of hot chocolate and brandy. But in the end, eyes invariably drift upwards toward the Great White Way—the
stars in the nighttime sky.

You start to look for the Big Dipper, maybe Scorpio or the
Pleaides. Though this is where most non-stargazers' knowledge of the sky ends, we've found that almost everyone has
a natural curiosity about the stars and their groupings. If
you've packed in a star chart, you'll almost certainly reach

for it and try to distinguish Cygnus, the giant swan, from Draco, the great dragon. If you don't have a chart, or have never studied the stars, this chapter will introduce you to one of the greatest pleasures of long summer nights, that of stargazing.

It's an exciting, challenging process to identify planets and constellations. It takes concentration and some patience. Like anything else, the more often you try, the easier and more familiar it gets. At first, however, you're lying on your back, staring into a giant half-dome but the star map is flat, distorting the sky in order to get it down on paper. Also, the sky moves as the earth rotates, so what you see at 7 p.m. will not be the same as what you see at two or three in the morning. The stars also change with the seasons; the June sky is not the same as September's. Trees, clouds, mountains can block your view. A bright moon obscures many stars in its part of the sky. Nonetheless, with a little time and effort, you can slowly find planets, sort out constellations, even identify individual stars. And while you're at it, you're bound to see flashes of shooting stars, blinking satellites, high-flying aircraft and, depending how far north you are, maybe even a glimpse of the aurora borealis—the northern lights.

Star charts throw half the sky at you at once, far too many stars to see or sort out. In this chapter, we show you one small section of the sky at a time. We describe each with pictures, instructions and stories. But before you begin, it's good to know a little basic astronomy.

Astronomy 101

Everything—the moon, Earth and planets, sun and stars— is moving in space. Astronomical distances are so great, however, that aside from shooting stars, nothing seems to move very fast or very much. Most of the "motion" you observe during the night (or day) is the result of Earth turning. If you picture a spinning ball inside a stationary, star-speckled globe, you'll begin to get the picture. But, from an observational viewpoint, it appears as if all the heavenly bodies do move across the sky. So for expedience's sake, we'll refer to the sun, moon and constellations as the moving entities.

Only the star that happens to sit above the North Pole appears not to move as Earth turns; all the rest do appear to move. During the daytime, the sun moves across the midsection of the sky from east to west. During the night, the moon follows a similar path. Trace the same arc that the sun and moon describe across the sky and look for very bright stars: the brightest are probably planets. The sun, moon and planets are close to being on the same plane, which paints a wide stripe inside our star-studded globe. They spin in circles, but they travel across the sky within that stripe.

Divide that stripe into 12 pieces and you have the 12 "houses" of the Zodiac. Each house refers to a specific group of stars, or a constellation. Ancient astronomers used these 12 houses to keep track of the seasonal and relative positions of the sun, moon and planets, which appear to be stationed

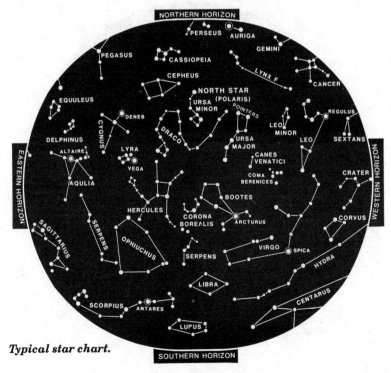

Typical star chart.

"in front" of any given house at any time of month or year. The naked eye may trick you into thinking that the sun, moon and planets are traveling in a high arc "overhead" while the Zodiac is on the horizon, but they are all in that wide stripe running round the equator, just about in the same plane.

It takes the stars in a constellation many millions of years to move in relation to one another. To us, it appears as if they never change position (even though the constellation itself appears to move during the night, due to the spinning of Earth). The sun, moon and planets do move very slowly against the backdrop of the Zodiac constellations. It takes the sun a year to travel slowly through the 12 houses of the Zodiac, remaining in each Zodiac house for a month. The moon travels the same path in only a month, and is in each house for three or four days, though even this short passage of time across the constellations is too slow for our eyes to see. On any night, the moon seems locked into its Zodiacal house. However fast it

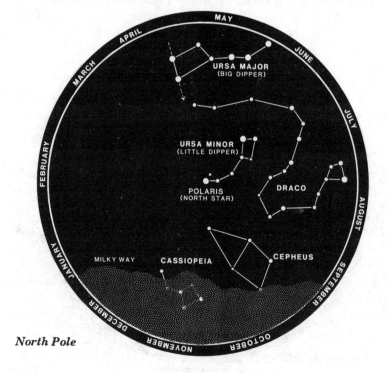

North Pole

seems to rise and set, it never seems to leave "home." What's happening is that the whole nighttime sky, with the moon in front of a Zodiac constellation, is moving overhead during the night. Saying that the moon is in Virgo means the moon is in that section of the sky occupied by the constellation Virgo. If the sun is in Scorpio, then Scorpio is behind the sun during the day. During an eclipse of the sun, the stars of Scorpio would be visible in that section of the sky.

Of course you don't *need* to know any of this to enjoy the night sky. If you couldn't care less that the Mars Bar overhead is really the Milky Way, then make up your own constellations. Rewrite the sky! (See pg. 327 for proof it can be done.) If, on the other hand, you'd like to get a handle on the "classic" sky, the rest of this chapter shows you how. We'll tell you where the constellations are, what they look like, and how to find them.

Go slow at first. The constellations won't go away. If you find one star group a night, you'll be doing well, and the odds are strong that you'll never forget where it is. Tomorrow night it may be in a slightly different place, but not by much. With a little practice, you'll spot it in September as easily as in July, at 11 o'clock as well as at 9 o'clock.

We start you off with the major constellations—the easy, circumpolar ones, which revolve in a tight ring around the North Star. Then we proceed to describe the smaller, more distant, and more difficult or obscure ones.

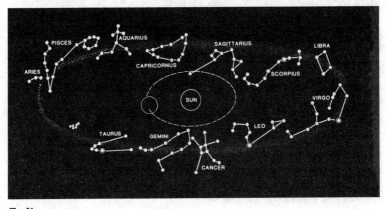

Zodiac.

We use several arbitrary devices to clarify directions and relationships between and among the constellations. First, compass directions (east, southwest, etc.) refer to the earthly horizon. Thus if you're lying on your back looking at the North Star and we send you southwest toward a constellation, trace the direction as you would on a compass: toward southwest on the ground. This may sound obvious, but it isn't when you realize that *all* stars are located literally south of the North Star. Secondly, we assume in our directions that you're facing the sky, holding your star map above you—looking *up* at it—and that it's oriented correctly toward the earthly horizon. Thirdly, we show you the sky at a theoretical 9 p.m. To figure out where things are earlier, turn your star map clockwise; later, turn it counterclockwise. A good star map or chart will allow you to adjust for the month. Our theoretical June should not upset your own calculations, whatever the time of year.

Ursa Major (Big Dipper), Ursa Minor (Little Dipper), Draco (Dragon)

Almost everyone can locate the Big Dipper: seven bright stars, visible even in the city, a clear constellation in winter as well as summer. Draw a line through the two stars on the end of the Big Dipper's bowl, then follow that line three times its length to reach Polaris, the North Star. During the night, all

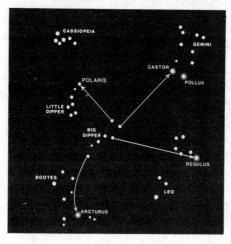

the other stars in the sky will seem to move, while the North Star will remain in place. You can check that you have the right star with your compass, as long as you realize that magnetic north, toward which your compass needle points, is not quite the same as true north, where Polaris sits.

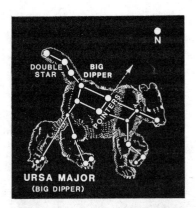

URSA MAJOR
(BIG DIPPER)

The Big Dipper is actually the hind quarters and tail of Ursa Major, the Big Bear. If you look closely, you can find the bear's paws and outline, but it's not easy. Housatonic Indians saw the four bowl stars as a bear and the three handle stars as a hunter with two dogs in pursuit. The middle handle star is really a double star; the hunter carried a pot in which to cook the bear. The hunter chased the bear from spring until autumn, and when the animal was wounded in the fall, its blood was visible in the leaves of the forest.

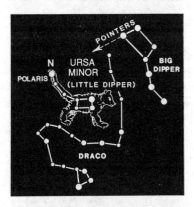

For centuries the Big Dipper has guided people to the North Star which, seemingly "fixed" in the sky, has in turn guided mariners and land navigators in their travels. The North Star acts as the tip of the handle of the seven-star Little Dipper, also known as Ursa Minor. The Persians saw the Little Dipper as a Date Palm. It was a Jackal in Egypt. Ancient Norsemen called it the Hill of Heaven,

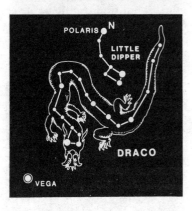

abode of the guardian of the rainbow bridge connecting heaven and earth. It certainly doesn't look much like a small bear.

Beginning between the North Star and the two "pointer" stars of the Big Dipper is a long winding string of stars that goes southeast around the Little Dipper, then back northwest, encircling the Little Dipper on three sides. Then it goes southwest again, ending in a rectangle of four stars. This is the constellation Draco, the Dragon. The Hindus called it an Alligator and the Egyptians a Crocodile. To the Greeks, it was the Monster Serpent killed by Hercules. Its teeth were sown on the earth to become a crop of armed men.

Cassiopeia, Cephus

From the double star in the Big Dipper's handle, draw a line through Polaris. There, bend the line slightly to the right and keep going the same distance as from the pointers. You'll be in the middle of a five-star "W"-shaped constellation, Cassiopeia. Cassiopeia was the Queen of Ethiopia until she offended the sea nymphs, who bound her to this seat in the sky. The same five stars looked to the early Arabs like a giant hand, each one marking a fingertip.

Between Cassiopeia and Draco's head (the four-star rectangle), you'll find the five-star constellation Cepheus. It's not as bright as Cassiopeia or the Big Dipper. The Greeks saw it as the "sky father", King of Ethiopia and husband of Cassiopeia.

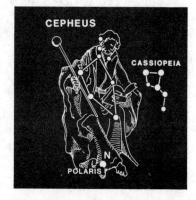

It looks somewhat like a large, A-frame tent, pointing toward Polaris.

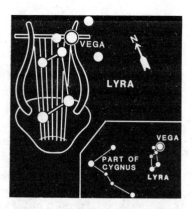

Lyra (Lyre), Cignus (Swan), Hercules

A line from Polaris through the brightest star in the head of Draco points to Vega. Vega is one of the brightest stars in the sky, only 26 light years distant, and part of the five-star constellation Lyra, the lyre or harp. It's said that this harp was invented by Hermes and given to his half-brother Apollo. The Arabs thought of the same constellation as a swooping Stone Eagle of the Desert, with half-closed wings tucked as it dove for a kill.

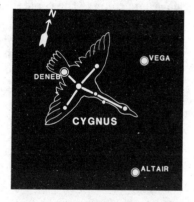

A line from Polaris through the brightest star of Cepheus (skirting the back of Cepheus' throne) goes to the star Deneb, the head of the giant swan Cignus. Cignus is a large cross in the sky, four bright stars long and three wide. It was known in Arabia as a giant bird called a "Roc" made famous by its conflicts with Sinbad the Sailor. Find the Milky Way stretching across the sky and you'll find Cignus in full flight along it.

Finally, a line from Polaris skirting west of Draco's head takes you to Hercules. A four-star rectangle forms his body, with different numbers of stars for his arms, legs and weapons. The rectangle is the key to finding Hercules, but none of its stars are exceptionally bright. It's sometimes hard to find. It's usually nearly straight overhead on summer evenings. Moving from east to west, Cygnus, Lyra and Hercules are all about the same distance from the North Star.

Bootes (Herdsman), Corona Borealis (Northern Crown)

Follow the curve of the Big Dipper's handle away from the bowl. It leads to another very bright star, Arcturus. Stretching toward the North Star from Arcturus, in the shape of a kite or ice cream cone, is the constellation Bootes, the Herdsman. The kite shape is the body; the two legs meet at Arcturus. The Arabs called him the Shepherd, with the idea that the stars around the North Pole resembled a flock of sheep, and he was always going in circles to herd them. He has also been seen as a hunter in pursuit of Ursa Major, the Great Bear.

Between Bootes and Hercules, about the same distance from Polaris, is a seven-star half-circle. This is the Corona Borealis, or Northern Crown. (A similar one lies in the southern sky near the South Pole.) To the Shawnee Indians these seven stars were the Celestial Sisters, the fairest (brightest) of them the wife of the hunter White Hawk, Arcturus.

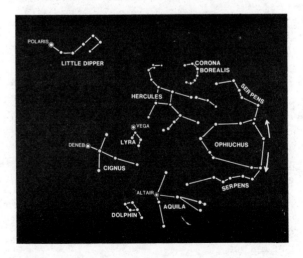

Aquila *(Eagle)*,
Delphinus *(Dolphin)*,
Ophiuchus *(Serpent Holder)*,
Serpens *(Serpent)*

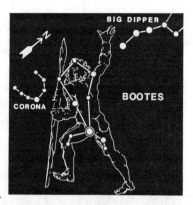

A line from Polaris through the tail of Cygnus the Swan takes you to Altair, the bright head of the eagle Aquila. Altair is only 16 light years away, bright enough to be seen even through city smog. Aquila the Eagle, cruciform in shape, is about the same size as Cygnus, and it's easy to imagine Aquila chasing Cygnus along the Milky Way, always a little behind and to the east of its prey.

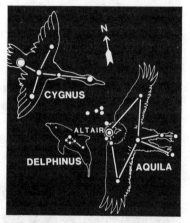

The Koreans saw Altair and its two bright neighbors not as the head and shoulders of an eagle, but as a prince and his servants, banished across the Milky Way by an irate father-in-law. The Prince's bride is our Lyra. Only once a year, on the seventh day of the seventh moon, could the two lovers meet by crossing a bridge of magpies over the Milky Way.

Just northeast of the eagle is Delphinus, the five-star dolphin. It's a small constellation on the edge of the Milky Way, on a direct line from Polaris through Deneb, the head of Cygnus.

A large area of the sky south of Hercules is taken up by a vague constellation, Ophiuchus and his two serpents, Serpens

Caput and Serpens Cauda. The head of Serpens Caput is a bright triangle just south of the Corona Borealis (Northern Crown). The rest of the serpent stretches south, then east towards the Milky Way. The key to this constellation is figuring out what it is not. Once you find Hercules and Corona Borealis to the north and Scorpio to the south, you can find Ophiuchus with his two serpents in between.

In Greek legend, Ophiuchus was the ship's surgeon for Jason and the Argonauts. He became so skilled that he could restore the dead to life. This caused Pluto to fear for his kingdom of the dead and Ophiuchus was struck with a thunderbolt by Jove and placed among the constellations.

Virgo *(Virgin),* Leo *(Lion)*

Remember the pointer stars of the Big Dipper? If you point in the opposite direction from Polaris, past the bottom of the dipper, you come to the bright star Regulus, head of Leo. The Lion's mane looks like a backwards question mark running east and then north from Regulus, and a triangle of stars to the southeast represents the lion's back legs and tail. The Greeks called it the Nemean Lion, placed in the heavens at

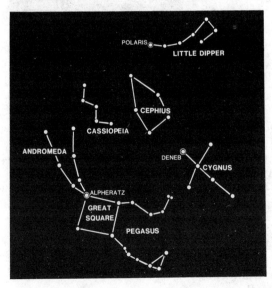

the same time as Hercules, the lion's slayer.

Virgo is a dim constellation, difficult to find. Start with the Big Dipper's handle and follow it through Arcturus at the base of Bootes. The next bright star on that arc is Spica in the constellation Virgo. The constellation itself is shaped like a distorted Y, with Spica representing an ear of wheat in the maiden's left hand.

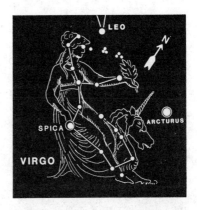

Pegasus (Horse), Andromeda

A line from Polaris passing just east of Cassiopeia goes to a large bright square of stars. The star in the northwest corner of the square is part of a small bright triangle. This is Pegasus, the horse. The square represents the horse's body; the triangle is the horse's rear legs. Pegasus is always near the horizon, "upside down" with its head away from Polaris. In Greek mythology, Pegasus sprang from the blood of Medusa after she was slain by Perseus. Later, Bellerophon attempted to ride Pegasus to heaven, but Jupiter, incensed by such boldness, caused an insect to sting the horse. Pegasus threw his rider and then rose alone to his permanent place among the stars.

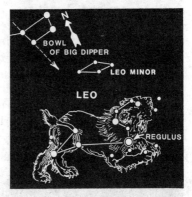

The bright triangle of stars at one corner of Pegasus is also the end of the constellation Andromeda, the Woman Chained. Alpheratz, the brightest star in the "Great Square" of Pegasus, is the last star in Andromeda. It's the meeting point for two lines of stars (four stars in each line) that represent Andromeda, the daughter of Cepheus and Cassiopeia, chained in exposure to the sea monsters as punishment for Cassiopeia's boasts of her own beauty.

Sagittarius *(Archer)*, Scorpio *(Scorpion)*, Libra *(Scales)*

These three Zodiac constellations are usually close to the southern horizon. Sometimes you can't see them at all; sometimes you see only their northernmost stars. Remember that if Polaris is the head, the Zodiac ring of constellations is a giant belt around the waist of the sky. As Earth tilts during seasonal changes and Polaris moves closer to the northern horizon, this ring moves up from the southern horizon. During the winter months, with Polaris higher in the sky, these constellations move below the horizon and cannot be seen.

Scorpio is the most spectacular. A line from Polaris through the Corona Borealis and on through the serpent's head on

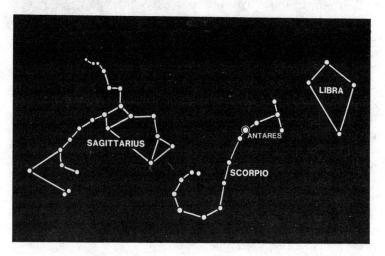

Ophiuchus passes through three very bright stars near the southern horizon. This is the head and the two claws of the scorpion. The rest of the scorpion's body winds south, through Antares, a bright star, and continues to a curlicue tail. Legend has it that this scorpion killed Orion, the hunter. They were placed in the sky so that Orion, still fearful, sinks below the northern horizon as Scorpio rises in the south. Antares, the heart of the scorpion, was known to the Chinese as the Fire Star.

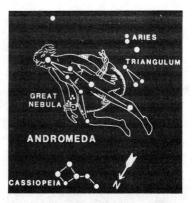

Sagittarius follows Scorpio across the sky. Four stars represent a bow and arrow; another five are the archer's body. The arrow points towards Scorpio. Ancient Arabs saw this constellation as two sets of ostriches, passing to and from the celestial river of the Milky Way.

The four stars of Libra lie between Scorpio and Virgo, in a roughly rectangular shape. The Greeks considered these stars the claws of Scorpio. Later they became known as separate constellations.

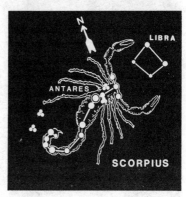

Perseus (Winged Warrior), *Auriga (Charioteer)*

Follow the Milky Way from Cygnus through Cassiopeia. The next constellation is Perseus, a warrior wearing winged sandals. He is holding the head of Medusa in his hand, which he later used to rescue Andromeda from the sea monsters. Perses, the son of Perseus and Andromeda, gave Persia its name. Algol, a bright star in Perseus, was called the "De-mon's Head" by the Arabians.

Continuing along the Milky Way, from Cassiopeia through Perseus, you'll come to Auriga. It contains seven stars in a rough circle, including Capella, called the Goat Star in ancient Greece and the Shepherd's Star in Peru.

Taurus (Bull), *Gemini (Twins)*, *Cancer (Crab)*

Follow the last three stars in Perseus away from Polaris and you see seven twinkling stars in a very small cluster. These are the Seven Sisters, the Pleiades (pronounced "Plee-a-dees"). They are also the shoulder of the bull, Taurus. The head of the bull is a bright star, Aldebaran, in the midst of another cluster, and the bull's horns extend into the Milky Way, nearly to Auriga.

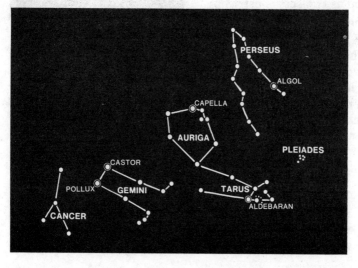

Pleiades were seen by Australian aborigines as young girls playing music to young men dancing (Orion's belt). The Finns called this cluster a little sieve. The second cluster next to Aldebaran, the bull's head, is called Hyades (Hie-a-dees). These were seen by the Greeks as half-sisters to the Pleiades. The whole of Taurus was seen as a bull with huge horns even by ancient South American tribes, and as the jaw of an Ox by natives in the Amazon region.

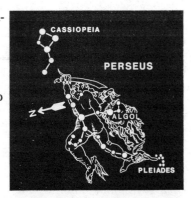

Gemini is a big rectangle. Two stars are inside the Milky Way, just beyond Auriga. The other end of the constellation consists of two bright stars, Castor and Pollux, the twins' heads. To the Phoenicians, the constellation represented two gazelles, to the Arabians, two peacocks. In India it was two horsemen.

Cancer is the most inconspicuous of the Zodiac constellations. Its stars are so dim that it is impossible to see them close to a bright horizon. Cancer lies between Gemini and Leo and is roughly in the shape of an upside-down Y with its tail pointing toward the North Star. Greek myths say it is the crab that was crushed by Hercules in his contest with the Hydra, then raised to the sky by Juno. The Egyptians saw it as a scarab, the Chinese as a quail's head.

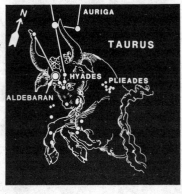

Triangulum, Aries (Ram), Pisces (Fishes), Cetus (Whale)

A line from Polaris through the easternmost star in Casseopeia takes you through the end of Andromeda's chain, then through a small three star constellation, Triangulum, to one of the two bright stars in Aries, the ram. This ram was sacrificed after helping Phrixus escape the wrath of his stepmother, Ino. Its fleece was placed in the Grove of Ares (Mars), where it turned to gold and became the object of the Argonauts' quest.

Pisces, the fishes, is a huge V-shaped constellation stretching from one leg near Andromeda to a point south of Aries, then back along another long leg toward Aquarius. Most of the stars in Pisces are dim. Star finders are vague about its shape since it is usually "falling off" the edge of the map and badly distorted. It rarely comes above the horizon and what parts of it do are usually obscured by mountains or trees since it is always so low in the sky. If you can see a fairly straight line of stars south of Pegasus, you've found half of Pisces.

Cetus, as large as Pisces and lower in the sky, is also rarely seen in the Northern Hemisphere. This is another huge, rambling constellation. The four stars in Cetus' head are just south of Aries. It represents a whale or sea monster, fabled to be the monster sent to devour chained Andromeda, but turned to stone at the sight of Medusa's head in the hand of Perseus.

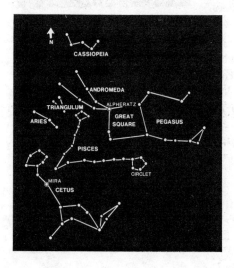

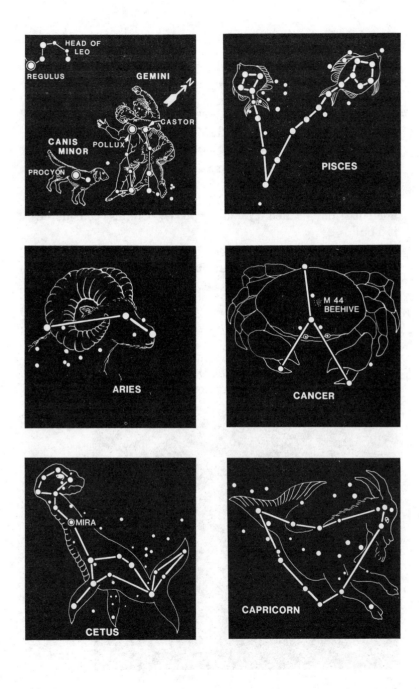

Aquarius (Waterbearer), Equuleus (Colt), Capricorn (Goat)

Follow the triangle of Pegasus (his head) to the south, and you come to Aquarius. The sun tends to be in Aquarius during the rainy season, hence the relationship with water. In Babylon, the constellation was an overflowing water jar, in ancient Arabia a well-bucket, in Rome a peacock.

Capricorn, between Aquarius and Sagittarius, is generally depicted with the head and body of a goat ending in a fish's tail. It is another one that is tough to make out in the sky. The ancient Hindus called it an antelope. The Chinese considered it a bull.

Equuleus, the colt, is between Delphinus (Dolphin) and Pegasus on the north and Aquarius on the south. It is a small constellation (five stars) representing the brother of Pegasus.

Orion (Hunter), Canis Major (Greater Dog)

South of Taurus lies Orion, the hunter. It has three bright stars for a belt, two more representing a sword. The tip of the sword is the star Rigel; Orion's head is the star Betelgeuse.

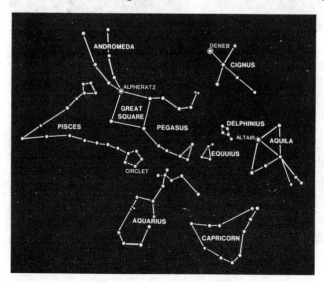

Both are very bright. Orion can be seen from most of Earth, north and south, at one time of the year or other. Mythology holds that he was inflicted with a scorpion sting because of his boastfulness. Then he was placed in the sky in such a way that he could escape whenever his slayer, Scorpio, rose in the east.

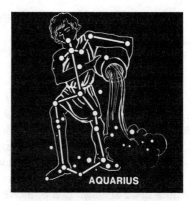

Canis Major is a southern-sky constellation, just southeast of Orion. Sirius, its brightest star, lies just on the edge of the Milky Way. From the earliest times, it has been the dog of Orion, shown sitting up and watching his master. The Hindus knew it as the Deer Slayer, who shot an arrow, which is our belt of Orion. The rest of Orion represented to them a prince, stopped by the arrow from pursuing his daughter, Aldebaran (the bright star in the head of Taurus).

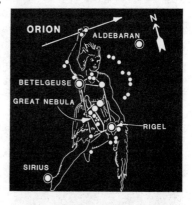

The Great Horned Wyoming Jackalope and Other Do-It-Yourselfers

If you stand on your head, squeeze your eyes real tight, count to ten and don't pass out or fall asleep, you'll awaken to see the Great Horned Wyoming Jackalope. It's seen especially clearly when reflected in high Rocky Mountain lakes. If you

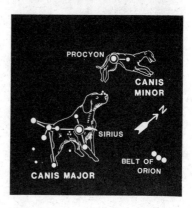

happen to be in Northern California, you might see the Giant Hot Tub, with its pointer stars directing you to a local Zen master. And of course, twinkling through the smog of Southern California comes the Spiraling Red Camaro, complete with sooty black exhaust.

We've picked out everything from grapefruits to beer bottles in the sky, depending on our moods. Rather than getting all strung out making exact identifications, or getting frustrated by not seeing the shapes that the constellations are supposed to be, the important thing is to have fun with the process of discovering the stars. When asked what he liked most about backpacking, a five-year-old friend of ours replied, "I get to eat a lot of cookies and I can stay up as late as I want." On those nights that *you* stay up late, the stars can be enjoyable and agreeable companions, along with a slow-burning fire and some brandy and hot chocolate.

If you really do get turned on by all of this and want more see the suggested readings in the Book List.

Looking Ahead

Wilderness camping, like anything else that is complicated and beautiful, is never quite finished. There is always more to learn, about yourself and the wilderness, about technique and enjoyment. There is rarely one way to do things, which means that both common sense and uncommon sensibilities need to be brought to bear on problems and projects. If you accept that as a reasonable proposition, you'll remain open to the ideas, suggestions, and experience of others. And you'll tinker, fiddle and improvise until you've got a camping trip down to where you want it, rather than the way friends, salesmen, old-timers, or experts say it should be done. It's at such a point that our book will have served its purpose.

The wilderness is growing smaller. If you want to get a feel for the majesty of the backcountry, you'll have to act fast and with knowledge. The better prepared you are to deal with impassive nature—its demands and your perception of them— the faster you'll be able to get farther into the wilderness. And if your aim in part is to leave the masses behind, if only for a day or two, being able to negotiate the backcountry is a useful skill to have.

Solitude is perhaps our most rapidly dwindling personal resource. Its natural habitat is in the mountains and on the lakes and rivers. In a real sense, then, *we* are the endangered species. If our capacity to be awed by nature is blunted, if we lose the ability to be modest—to be participants in the wilderness rather than masters of it—we diminish ourselves. Wilderness campers are no more high-minded than anyone else, but the very nature of their work—or rather, their play—requires that they stay attuned to the possibilities inherent in the relationship between an individual and the world beyond roads.

If you are high up on a sun-soaked peak one day, enjoying the view and reflecting that the hard, off-trail hike ended at the second most beautiful campsite in the world, that the bubble-and-fly bagged a panful of trout, that the bread rose, the souffle scored a hit, and the chocolate cake was the best you ever tasted, write a note about it and stick it in the message cairn. Whoever comes along and reads it will treasure your mood and want to make it their own. And who knows? Maybe even we'll come across it sometime down the line. And then we'll know for sure that our book has accomplished its goal.

Book List

This list is selective and is meant to be used in conjunction with the resources listed in Chapter 2.

Camping and Backpacking Books

A select selection of "how-to" books:

Fletcher, Colin. *The Complete Walker*. Alfred Knopf, 1989.

Hart, John. *Walking Softly in the Wilderness*. Sierra Club, 1984.

Hampton, Bruce. *Soft Paths: How to Enjoy the Wilderness Without Harming It*. National Outdoor Leadership School, 1988.

Manning, Harvey. *Backpacking One Step at a Time*. Vintage, 1986.

Silverman, Goldie. *Backpacking With Babies and Small Children*. Wilderness Press, 1986.

Winnett, Thomas. *Backpacking Basics*. Wilderness Press, 1988.

Wood, Robert. *Pleasure Packing for the '80's*. Ten Speed Press, 1980.

Guides to Trails, Mountains and Campgrounds

"Where-to-Go" and "How-to-Get-There" guides:

High Sierra Hiking Guides. Wilderness Press, 2440 Bancroft
Way, Berkeley, CA 94704.
A series of nine expert little guides, each based on one of the quad-
rangles established by the U.S. Geological Survey. Small and
light enough to carry with you. The same press publishes guides
to other wilderness areas, high-mountain trails, and desert hiking
in the western United States. Camping stores will have similar
guides to other regions.

The Complete Western Campground Guides. Foghorn Press,
PO Box 77845, San Francisco, CA 94107.
A series of three big books: *California Camping* (1,500 campgrounds), *Rocky Mountain Camping* (1,400 campgrounds) and
Pacific Northwest Camping (1,400 campgrounds) all written by
outdoorsman Tom Stienstra. Camping stores will have similar
guides to other states and regions.

Sierra Club Mountaineers' Guides. Sierra Club Books, distributed by Random House.
A series of 21 *Tote Books*, pocket-size climbing guides to virtually
all the major mountain ranges in the United States.

Reading Maps and Compass

Orienteering, by the godfather of the sport:

Kjellstrom, Bjorn. *Be Expert with Map and Compass.* Charles
Scribner's Sons, 1976.

Backpack Cooking

Pale imitations of what you have just read, but honorable:

Axcell, Claudia. *Simple Foods for the Pack.* Sierra Club, 1986.

Fleming, June. *The Well-Fed Backpacker.* Vintage Books, 1986.

McHugh, Gretchen. *Hungry Hikers Book of Good Cooking.*
Alfred Knopf, 1989.

MacManiman, Gen. *Dry It, You'll Like It.* MacManiman, Inc.,
1983.

Outdoor Epicure, An REI Cookbook. REI, 1979.

Yaffe, Linda. *High Trail Cookery.* Chicago Review Press, 1989.

Outdoor Medicine

Words of wisdom from the body shop:

Darvill, Fred, Jr., MD. *Mountain Medicine*. Wilderness Press, 1989.

Forgey, Wm., MD. *Wilderness Medicine*. ICS Books, 1987.

Lentz, Marth, Ph.D., RN. *Mountaineering First Aid*. The Mountaineers, 1985.

Witherson, James, MD. *Medicine for Mountaineering*. The Mountaineers, 1985.

Canoeing

Essentials of the craft:

American National Red Cross. *Canoeing*. Doubleday & Co., 1977.

Jacobson, Cliff. *Basic Essentials of Canoeing*. ICS Books, 1988.

McNair, Robert. *Basic Canoeing*. American Camping Association, 1985.

Mason, Bill. *Path of the Paddle*. NorthWord Press, 1984.

Bicycling

Touring and cycle repair information:

Bridge, R.. *Bicycle Touring*. Sierra Club, 1979.

Cuthbertson, Tom. *Anybody's Bike Book*. Ten Speed Press, 1990.

Savage, Barbara. *Miles From Nowhere*. The Mountaineers, 1983.

Sloane, Eugene A.. *Eugene A. Sloane's Book of All-Terrain Bicycles*. Simon & Schuster 1985.

The Complete Book of Bicycling. Simon & Schuster, 1988.

Van der Plas, R.. *The Bicycle Touring Manual*. Bicycle Books, 1987.

Winning, Robert. *Bicycling Across America*. Wilderness Press, 1988.

The following are all written by the editors of *Bicycling Magazine* and published by Rodale Press, 33 E Minor Sreet, Emmaus, PA 18098. They are all short, small books (about 100 pages) and part of a series:

Basic Maintenance and Repair
Mountain Biking Skills
New Bike Owner's Guide
Mountain Bikes
Bicycle Touring
All-Terrain Bikes

Fishing

Two guides to charm you into fishing:

Holland, Dan. *The Trout Fisherman's Bible*. Doubleday, 1979.
Anderson, Sheridan. *The Curtis Creek Manifesto*. Frank Amato Publications, Portland, OR, 1988.

Children's Car Activities

Travel games, word games, string games, puzzles:

Anderson, Karen, ed.. *Kid's Big Book of Games*. Workman Publishing, 1990.
Are We There Yet? Rand McNally Travel Games, Puzzles and Quizzes, 1984.
Gryski, Camilla. *Many Stars and More String Games*. Wm. Morrow, 1985.
Price, Roger and Leonard Stern. *Mad Libs*. Price Stern Sloan. This is a series of three packaged word games. The individual titles are *The Original # 1, Monster*, and *Off-the-Wall*.

Stars

Reliable introductions to astronomy:

Baker, David. *The Henry Holt Guide to Astronomy*. Henry Holt Co., 1990.
Moore, Patrick. *The Pocket Guide to Astronomy*. Simon & Schuster, 1983.

The Miller Planisphere. Datalizer Slide Charts, Inc., 501 West Gate Street, Addison, Illinois 60101-4524. 1-800 837-9675. Indispensible rotating disc showing principal stars visible for every hour in the year at 42 degrees N. A compact star map. Comes in two sizes, the smaller of which fits easily into a backpack pouch.

Index

A

A-frame tent: 57

ABLEDATA, Adaptive Equipment Center: 36

Access America, An Atlas and Guide to the National Parks for Visitors with Disabilities: 35

Access to Recreation: Adaptive Recreational Equipment for the Physically Challenged: 36

accessories: group 104; clothing 48-49

acclimated: 123-24

advocacy organizations for outdoors: 41-42

alcohol stoves: see stoves

Aldebaran, star: 323, 327

Algol, star: 322

Alpheratz, star: 320

Alpine Club of Canada: 41

Altair, star: 317

altitude: acclimating to 123-24; effect on boiling temperature

205; high altitude clothing 108 (also see weather)

American Alpine Club: 41

American Canoe Association: 39

American Hiking Society: 41

American Red Cross: 39

American Walkers Association: 41

American Whitewater Affiliation: 39

Andromeda, constellation: 319-320

Antares, star: 321

Appalachian Mountain Club: 41

Appalachian Trail Conference: 41

Aquarius, constellation: 326

Aquila, constellation: 317-18

Archer, constellation: See Sagittarius

Arcturus, star: 316

Aries, constellation: 324-25

aspirin: 80, 123 (also see first aid)

E

Eagle, constellation: see Aquila

Eastern Mountain Sports: story 2; resource info 32

eggs: packing 97; separating 221 (see recipes)

emergencies: food 90, 260 (also see first aid)

Environmental Traveling Companions: 34

equipment: 32-33, 45-83; disabled 36, 77; rental 47; repair list 110; for rain 166-67; before leaving home list 101, climbing 268, fishing 283-87 (also see specific activity)

Equuleus, constellation: 326

ethics: what to leave at home 106; cutting corners on trails 143; drainage ditch around tent 156; choosing a campsite 153; fires 157, 159-61; washing up 167-69; low impact camping 169; cleaning fish 210

F

fears: 134-35

fires: starting 159-61; ethics of 157; for cooking or baking 158, 207

fireplace: fuel 157-59; building 158; clean up 169; low impact 169, 207 (also see fires)

first aid: prevention of blisters 62; kit 80-81; for serious injuries 81-82; list 109; aspirin 80, 123: salt 123

fish: cleaning and storing 209-211 (also see fishing, trout, food, recipes)

Fishes, constellation: see Pisces

fishing: 273-306; list 112; lakes 275-79; streams 279-282, 295; time of day 278; during rain 283; gear 283-87; catching trout 303-06; casting 281-82, snags 302; 300-02; net 305-06;

drag 303-04; flies 285, 294-95; lures 278, 295-96; bait 272, 281, 287-88, 299-300; riggings 287-295, with children 271-72; license 287; (also see bait, trout, cooking, recipes)

flashlights: see equipment

food: planning 85-96; food planning table 89; in emergencies 90; for dogs 90, 95; in bulk 91, 94; freeze-dried 91, 93; Japanese 94; weighing 82-83, 95-96; packing 96; packaging and transporting 96-98; caching 98; organizing 97-98; hanging 98; shopping list 112-13; storage 98, 161-62; bear-proofing 163-65; dehydrated 172-76; for trail 97, 124, 197-201, 259-60; sheltering from sun 162; meal size 207; when to eat what 208 (also see cooking, recipes, trout)

footwear: see boots, socks

fressers: 87, 171

Friends of the River: 40

fruit: filling for crepes 175, 238; cake 175; chutney 175; leathers 199-201

frying: definition of 201

fuel: estimating 71-75 (also see stoves)

fun and games: list 111

G

games: list and types of 111, 263

garbage bag: 59; uses of: in rain 167; food storage 98; toilet 168-69

garlic onion bread: see bread

gas stoves: see stoves

Gemini, constellation: 322-23, 325

geodesic tent: 57 (also see tents)

Geological Survey maps: see maps

giardia: 155

Goat, constellation: see
    Capricorn
Goretex: 129
Greater Dog, constellation: see
    Canis Major
Green Mountain Club Inc., The:
    41
grilling: definition of 206; fish
    213-14
grizzly bears: see bears
groups: traveling with 18-22,
    packing for 118; lists 104-05
    (also see fears, ethics)

H

hammocks: 262-63
hanging out: 261-272; games
    263-64; music 265-66; books
    264-65; day trips 266; park
    entertainment 266
Harp, constellation: see Lyra
heights, fear of: 135 (also see
    fears)
Hercules, constellation: 315-16
Herdsman, constellation: see
    Bootes
hiking: pacing 18-19, 123-24;
    distance rules 17-18; solo 19;
    group rules 21-22; with dogs
    21; trail guides 27; topo maps
    29; permits 30; snacks 124, 197-
    201; in rain 128-29; in mud and
    snow 130-31; protecting
    against mosquitos 136; short
    cuts 144; losing a trail 144-45;
    off-trail 146-52 (also see off-
    trail hiking)
hip belt for backpacking: adjust-
    ment of 65
hooks for fishing: 286
Horse, constellation: see Pegasus
horses: see pack animals
hostels, youth: 39
houses of Zodiac: see Zodiac
Hunter, constellation: see Orion
Hyades, constellation: 323
hypothermia: 129

I

icing: see cakes
injuries: mountain bike 270 (see
    first aid)
insects: 136
International Bicycle Touring
    Society: 37
International Directory of
    Recreation-Oriented Assistance
    Devises: 36
International Mountain
    Bicycling Association: 37

J

Japanese foods: 94
Japanese raw trout (sashimi):
    223-25; mustard condiment 224

K

Kevlar canoes: 45
kerosene stoves: see stoves
kids: see children
kindling: see fireplace
knots, for fishing: 288-90 (also
    see fishing)

L

lake fishing: 275-79
laundry washing: 51-52
layering: 49 (see clothing)
League of American
    Wheelmen: 37
Leo, constellation: 318-19
Libra, constellation: 320-21
library: see books
license, for fishing: 287
life jacket, for canoeing: 71
Lion, constellation: see Leo
lists: see Chapter 5 for lists 99-
    114; for cut-out lists see
    Appendix; list of lists 100;

Y

Z

APPENDIX

Clip-Out Lists
and Recipes

As promised, *The Camper's Companion* clip-out and take-it-with-you section. The best wilderness books have pages missing. Somebody has spotted a hint too good to pass up, lifted the information and stowed it in the pack along with the maps and cookies. That's how to treat this book. You'll find each of the packing lists duplicated here, the makings of your very own master list. We've also rerun most of the recipes, which can be used and then incorporated into your campfire. Tear away. If you want to dismantle the fishing or stargazing sections as well, feel free, it's *your* book.

List of Lists:

☐ The Before-Leaving-Home-Did-I-Turn-Off-the-Gas Check List

☐ Bicycle Touring/Mountain Bike List

☐ Canoeing List

☐ Group Accessories, Individual Needs, Optionals

☐ Backpacking List: Equipment

☐ Backpacking List: Clothing, Boots

☐ First Aid and Medicines

☐ Repair Kit

☐ Maps and Permits

☐ Kiddy List: For Babies and the Very Young

☐ Fun and Games

☐ Traveling with a Dog

☐ Fishing List

☐ Food Planning for Two Six Day Trips

☐ Food Shopping List

☐ Your Master List
  - *Select from the following lists those appropriate for your trip.*
  - *Eliminate duplicated items.*
  - *Tear out and combine into a handy packet (you may want to seal your lists in plastic or some other protective covering so they last longer).*

The Before-Leaving-Home-Did-I-Turn-Off-the-Gas Checklist

☐ Leave a schedule/map/itinerary with someone to call out the Mounties if you don't return on time. Include name and phone number of nearest ranger station.

☐ Get neighbor to watch the house and take in newspapers, take out garbage, feed the pets.

☐ Leave written instructions on plant care.

☐ Leave adequate pet food, and name and phone number of the vet. Alternatively, take pets to the boarding kennel.

☐

☐

☐ Camping equipment:
  ☐ Lubricate all zippers—on tents, sleeping bags, packs—with silicone lube or a light oil (WD-40).
  ☐ Waterproof boots. Use only recommended agent for your particular footwear.
  ☐ Repair/replace damaged or missing parts.

  ☐
  ☐
  ☐
  ☐

☐ Check car:
  ☐ Tires, belts, hoses, and battery cables

☐ Wiper blades. Fill windshield washer reservoir with a mix.ture of Windex and water

☐ Vital fluids: gas, oil, automatic transmission fluid, brake fluid, coolant

☐ Tire-changing equipment: jack, lug wrench, spare tire

☐ Roof rack: All parts present?

☐

☐ In car:
  ☐ License and car registration
  ☐ Credit cards and cash on board
  ☐ Fire/wilderness permits, fishing licenses
  ☐ Road maps and directions to trailhead or campground
  ☐ Ranger station address and telephone number
  ☐ Sunglasses
  ☐ Accessible rain gear
  ☐ Cooler/ice chest with perishable foods
  ☐ Car meals and snacks
  ☐ Drinking water
  ☐ Dog food and water bowl
  ☐ Litter bag
  ☐ Games, toys, stuffed animals, books, distractions
  ☐ Personal needs: music/story tapes, Walkman, pencil, paper
  ☐ Clean clothes for return drive home
  ☐

☐ Did I leave the gas on, the toilet running?

Group Accessories, Individual Needs, Optionals

Group Accessories:

- ☐ Toilet paper
- ☐ Maps and permits
- ☐ Compass
- ☐ Star chart
- ☐ Tree guide/bird book/wild-flower guide
- ☐ Two boxes kitchen matches with sulphur heads (strike anywhere). Everyone carries some in Ziploc bag.
- ☐ First-aid kit
- ☐ Drugs and medicines
- ☐ Repair kit
- ☐ Tooth paste, dental floss
- ☐ Small towel
- ☐ Liquid (biodegradable) dish soap and pot scrubber
- ☐ Mosquito repellent (two bottles)
- ☐ Plastic spade (to bury human waste)
- ☐ Paper and pencil
- ☐ Camera, film, extra battery
- ☐ Extra pack straps
- ☐ Garbage bags (one for each member of the party)
- ☐ Extra Ziploc bags (10-12)
- ☐ Extra tent pegs
- ☐ Extra ground cloths/ponchos (one for each tent)
- ☐ Backpacking (Sven) saw
- ☐ Book for reading aloud

- ☐ Two-person inflatable backpacking raft plus paddles (when other weight considerations permit)
- ☐ Lantern (car/canoe/horse camping only)

Individual Needs:

- ☐ Pocket knife
- ☐ Sunglasses (in hard case)
- ☐ Matches
- ☐ Flashlight

Optionals:

- ☐ Ring clip to carry the car keys
- ☐ Fishing license
- ☐ Camera and film
- ☐ Binoculars
- ☐ Paperback book
- ☐ Toothbrush, toothpaste, comb, barrettes, ponytail bands
- ☐ Towel and bar of (biodegradable) soap
- ☐ Sanitary napkins, tampons, sponges, etc.
- ☐ Birth control devices
- ☐ Glasses case and extra glasses
- ☐ Contact lens solution
- ☐ Personal medications or prescriptions
- ☐ Nail clippers
- ☐ Playing cards, chess set, etc.

Bicycle Touring/Mountain Bike List

- [ ] Bicycle in top running order
- [ ] Cycling shorts
- [ ] Helmet
- [ ] Cycling shoes
- [ ] Shoe covers
- [ ] Cycling gloves
- [ ] Rain gear
- [ ] Sunglasses (shield type)
- [ ] Safety glasses (for mountain biking)
- [ ] Shoulder strap
- [ ] Rear-view mirror
- [ ] Horn/bell
- [ ] Panniers
- [ ] Pannier rain covers. Alternatively, plastic garbage bags in which all gear is stowed.
- [ ] Lock
- [ ] Headlamp plus extra batteries
- [ ] Fold-up reflective triangle
- [ ] Water bottle(s)
- [ ] Litter bag
- [ ] Talcum powder (for saddle sores & flat tires)
- [ ] Optional (for high-tech cycling):
  - [ ] Small radio (for weather reports)
  - [ ] Cyclometer (indicates speed, distance traveled, etc.)
  - [ ] Two-way radio that fits in helmet
  - [ ]

- [ ] Tool and Repair Kit
  - [ ] 6" crescent wrench
  - [ ] Folding Allen wrench set (metric/standard)
  - [ ] 2 four-way cone wrenches (metric/standard)
  - [ ] Small vise-grips with wire-cutter built in
  - [ ] Swiss Army knife
  - [ ] Paper towels and hand cleaner
  - [ ] Pump (does it fit your tire valve?)
  - [ ] Spare tube (right size?)
  - [ ] Talcum powder (to dust spare tube before wrapping in a plastic bag)
  - [ ] Plastic bag
  - [ ] Patch kit: fresh, unopened tube of glue plus several patches in a plastic bag
  - [ ] 2-3 tire irons (plastic, aluminum or steel)
  - [ ] Duct tape
  - [ ] Pocket vise
  - [ ] Spoke wrench
  - [ ] 3-4 extra spokes taped to frame
  - [ ] Chain tool
  - [ ] 4 spare chain links
  - [ ] Chain lube
  - [ ] Extra rear brake cable (cut off one end)
  - [ ] Extra derailleur cable (cut off one end)
  - [ ] Extra nuts and bolts (for all-purpose emergencies)
  - [ ]
  - [ ]
  - [ ]
  - [ ]
  - [ ]

Canoeing List

- ☐ Canoe
- ☐ Roof rack and tie-down line
- ☐ Paddles and one spare
- ☐ Personal Floatation Device: one per person
- ☐ Dry sacks. Alternatively, duffels lined with plastic garbage bags.
- ☐ Waterproof map case. Alternatively, large Ziploc bag.
- ☐ Portage harnesses (to convert duffels, sacks into carrying packs)
- ☐ Knee pads plus cushions for children
- ☐ 50-foot length of 3/8" line: one per multi-canoe party (for rescue, etc.) *Note: Plastic lines float.*
- ☐ Two 15-foot end lines (bow and stern), 3/8" diameter
- ☐ Foul-weather gear
- ☐ Sneakers with drainage holes cut in them

- ☐ Watertight food containers
- ☐ Large sponge (your handy "bilge pump")
- ☐ Bailer
- ☐ Portaging yoke (if required)
- ☐ Optional
  - ☐ Extra flotation (styrofoam inserts)
  - ☐ Thigh straps
  - ☐ Extra tie-down straps
  - ☐ Spray skirt
- ☐ Repair kit
  - ☐ Duct tape
  - ☐ Patch material (appropriate to canoe-type, e.g., epoxy plus glass cloth scraps)
  - ☐ Swiss Army knife (with scissors, sharp blades)
  - ☐ Small putty knife
  - ☐ Sandpaper
  - ☐ Paper towels
  - ☐ Lacquer thinner
  - ☐ Small paint brush
- ☐
- ☐
- ☐

Backpacking List: Equipment

Tent and Sleeping Gear:
- ☐ Sleeping bags
- ☐ Ensolite, Ridge Rest, or Therm-A-Rest pads
- ☐ Tent, rainfly, stakes, poles. (*Note*: a two-person tent will not sleep three. Add another tent, rainfly, etc.)
- ☐ Spare tent stakes
- ☐ Ground tarps/ponchos: one per tent

Packs and Protection:
- ☐ Backpacks
- ☐ Four straps per pack
- ☐ Four extra pack straps
- ☐ Large green garbage bags. Alternatively, pack covers.
- ☐ Ponchos/tarps (as rain gear in addition to ground tarp for tent)
- ☐ Stuff sacks for clothes and personals
- ☐ Day-pack. Alternatively, a strap-rigged stuff-sack to double as day-pack.
- ☐ Flashlights plus new batteries and bulbs
- ☐ Dog packs, as necessary
- ☐ Child carrier, as necessary

Cooking, Fire, Water Gear:
- ☐ Three nested pots and lids
- ☐ Sierra cups

- ☐ Tin plates
- ☐ Spatula
- ☐ Forks and spoons. Alternatively, chopsticks.
- ☐ Frypan
- ☐ Backpack grill
- ☐ Camp stove plus fuel and funnel
- ☐ Matches (two plus boxes; strike-anywhere type)
- ☐ Lighter fluid/fire starter paste in tube or cubes
- ☐ Candle
- ☐ Scouring pad/sponge
- ☐ Aluminum foil (two folded sheets for baking)
- ☐ Light mesh bag (as dish drainer, suspended from tree)
- ☐ Pair of garden gloves (for cooking, wood gathering)
- ☐ Sven saw (for gathering dead wood)
- ☐ Canteens/water bottles
- ☐ Water-purifier system
- ☐ Food storage:
  - ☐ plastic egg carton (half dozen or one dozen sizes)
  - ☐ plastic pill box (as "spice rack")
  - ☐ plastic bottles, jars (as condiment, syrup, oil, margarine containers)
  - ☐ spare Ziploc bags (10 each small & large)
- ☐
- ☐

Backpacking List: Clothing, Boots

For high altitude temperatures: 90s-20s Fahrenheit

- ☐ One pair pants
  (jeans or cotton/canvas)

- ☐ One pair shorts
  (light weight; doubles as
  swim suit)

- ☐ Three pair socks
  (inner and outer)

- ☐ Three underwear

- ☐ Two cotton shirts
  (one long-sleeved,
  one short)

- ☐ Long johns
  (cotton/polypropy-
  lene/wool)

- ☐ One sweater or
  sweatshirt

- ☐ Down parka.
  Alternatively,
  Gore-Tex shell and
  layered sweaters.

- ☐ Baseball cap or sun visor

- ☐ Wool (ski) hat

- ☐ Sunglasses
  (with UV protection)

- ☐ Boots

- ☐ Moccasins/tennies/
  reef slippers
  (for stream crossings,
  fishing, in camp)

- ☐ Mosquito-netting "hat"
  (slips over visor; indispensable for "that" time
  of year)

- ☐ Pocket knife

- ☐ Personal toiletries:
  (mandatory)

  - ☐ toothbrush
  - ☐ toothpaste, dental floss
    (Group Accessory)
  - ☐ toilet paper
    (Group Accessory)

- ☐ Personal toiletries:
  (optional)

  - ☐ comb/brush
  - ☐ barrettes/ponytail bands
  - ☐ razor
  - ☐ glasses case
  - ☐ small towel (share)
  - ☐ birth control devices
  - ☐ contact lens solution
  - ☐ nail clippers
    (Group Accessory)

- ☐
- ☐
- ☐
- ☐
- ☐
- ☐

First Aid and Medicines

Quantities for Four-Person Trip

First Aid:

- ☐ Moleskin
  (one or two packets)

- ☐ Adhesive tape
  (one small half-inch roll)

- ☐ Band-Aids
  (12 assorted sizes)

- ☐ Gauze pads
  (six assorted sizes)

- ☐ Ace bandage (one)

- ☐ Butterfly bandages (four)
  (Attention: mountain bikers)

- ☐ Hydrogen peroxide
  (Attention: mountain bikers)

- ☐ Instant cold pack
  (Attention: mountain bikers)

- ☐ Tweezers/surgical locking hemostat (one)

- ☐ Small mirror
  (for shaving, inspecting eyes, signaling)

- ☐ Baby-wipes or similar "dry washes" (four unless there's a baby aboard, in which case thousands!)

Drugs and Medicines:

- ☐ Aspirin or its equivalent

- ☐ Mosquito repellent
  (two for four people)

- ☐ Sunscreen

- ☐ Lip balm

- ☐ Hand lotion

- ☐ Optional:
  - ☐ Vitamins
  - ☐ Neosporin/Bacitracin (first-aid ointment)
  - ☐ Caladryl itching lotion
  - ☐ Antacid pills
  - ☐ Snake-bite kit
  - ☐ Aspirin with codeine
  - ☐ Lomotil diarrhea medicine
  - ☐ Athlete's-foot treatment
  - ☐ Desitin/Zinc ointment
  - ☐ Talcum powder
    (Attention: cyclists)

☐

☐

☐

☐

☐

☐

Repair Kit

- ☐ Swiss Army knife
- ☐ 50-foot length of nylon rope
- ☐ Small vise-grips
- ☐ Heavy duty ("carpet") thread plus two large needles
- ☐ Light nylon thread plus two small needles
- ☐ Nylon patch material (called "ripstop" tape)
- ☐ Patch kit for rubber raft

- ☐ Extra flashlight bulb(s) plus batteries (two per flashlight)
- ☐ Safety pins
- ☐ Spare clevis pins and key wires for backpacks
- ☐ Roll of half-inch adhesive tape *(see First Aid and Medicine List)*
- ☐
- ☐
- ☐

Maps and Permits

- ☐ Spare change for phone call
- ☐ Campsite reservation
- ☐ Fire permit
- ☐ Wilderness permit
- ☐ Fishing license
- ☐ Driver's license
- ☐ Automobile registration
- ☐ Road map

- ☐ Trail map
- ☐ Topo map
- ☐ Sea chart
- ☐ Waterproof map pouch or Ziploc bag
- ☐ Compass
- ☐ Star chart
- ☐
- ☐

Kiddy List: For Babies and the Very Young

- ☐ Whistle
  (hang a loud one around
  child's neck)

- ☐ Extra clothes
  four pair of pants, three
  shirts, four pair of socks
  for one-week trip

- ☐ Diapers

- ☐ Diaper-washing gear:
  two plastic buckets,
  biodegradable soap,
  clothes line

- ☐ Baby-wipes

- ☐ Tie-on hat

- ☐ Rain suit
  (for use at meals as well)

- ☐ Plastic bags as "outer"
  socks (quart/gallon size
  depending on size of foot)

- ☐ Life jacket
  (for swimming, boating,
  canoeing)

- ☐ Syrup of Ipecac
  (induces vomiting)

- ☐ Fever-scan forehead-type
  thermometer

- ☐ Zinc oxide/Desitin

- ☐ Games

- ☐ Books

- ☐ Favorite toys

- ☐ Comforters:
  stuffed animal, favorite
  blanket, etc.

- ☐ Edible hiking incentives!

- ☐

- ☐

Fun and Games

- ☐ Paper and Pencil
- ☐ Playing cards
- ☐ Star chart
- ☐ Tree guide
- ☐ Wildflower guide
- ☐ Bird book
- ☐ Binoculars
- ☐ Books

- ☐ Camera, including extra
  battery and film
- ☐ Musical instruments
- ☐ Pocket chess/checkers
- ☐ Lightweight games
- ☐ Frisbee
- ☐
- ☐

Traveling with a Dog

☐ Check that dogs are permitted in your camping venue

☐ Dog pack

☐ Dog food (minimum two packets moist food per day)

☐ Leash

☐ Flea collar

☐ Name tag with address, phone number

☐ Water bowl for car

☐ Extra food for car

☐ Tweezers/hemostat

☐

☐

☐

Fishing List

Quantities for Two Anglers, Five-day Trip; Spinning Tackle Only

☐ Fishing license

☐ Telescoping rod

☐ Rod case

☐ Spinning reel, lubricated and in good working order

☐ Fresh 4 lb. test monofilament line on reel

☐ Spare 4 lb. test line (one small spool)

☐ Spare 2 lb. test line (one small spool)

☐ Six bubbles

☐ Eight flies

☐ 10 lures (vary by weight, size, color)

☐ Two bottle corks

☐ Eight snap swivels

☐ Two packets No. 12 hooks (six per packet), for 8"-15" fish

☐ One packet No. 14 hooks (six per packet), for 8"-12" fish

☐ Eight weights: split shot, egg sinkers (vary in size, weight)

☐ Bait (bottled salmon eggs; power bait; cheese; worms)

☐ Worm threader *(optional)*

☐ Net

☐ Large Ziploc bags

☐ Swiss Army knife

☐

☐

☐

☐

☐

Food Planning for Two Six-Day Trips

	Trip One Min. Cooking	Trip Two Max. Cooking	Weight Difference (2nd trip)
	(weight = lbs.)		
Ready-to-Eat Foods:			
Dried fruit, Raisins	3.0	3.0	
Chicken/Beef Jerky	1.8	1.8	
Dried Vegetables	1.5	1.0	0.5 less
Cheese	3.5	2.5	1.0 less
Nuts	0.8	0.5	0.3 less
Cookies	1.5	1.5	
Crackers	1.5	1.5	
Chocolate	2.0	2.0	
Granola and Coconut	0.8	0.5	0.3 less
Sprouts	0.1	0.1	
Rice, Pasta, Soups:			
Minute Rice	1.0	0.7	0.3 less
Dried Minestrone	0.8	0.8	
Dried Pea Soup	0.8	0.0	0.8 less
Spaghetti Sauce	0.8	0.8	
Spaghetti and Ramen	1.2	1.0	0.2 less
Flour, Sugar, Cereals:			
Instant Oatmeal	0.4	0.0	0.4 less
Flour	1.5	3.0	1.5 more
Yeast, Baking Powder	0.0	0.3	0.3 more
Cornmeal	0.3	0.3	
Sugar	0.5	1.0	0.5 more
Dairy, Oils, Spices:			
Powdered Milk	0.5	0.8	0.3 more
Eggs	1.0	1.7	0.7 more
Hot Chocolate	1.5	1.5	
Tea/Coffee	0.2	0.2	
Cooking Oil	0.0	0.5	0.5 more
Margarine	0.5	0.5	
Spices, Condiments, Syrup	2.5	2.5	
Total Weight	30.0	30.0	

Food Shopping List

No quantities given here.
If drying food at home, purchase fresh fruit and vegetables up to a month in advance of trip; purchase meat and poultry no more than a week before trip.

- ☐ Flour
- ☐ Cornmeal
- ☐ Sugar
- ☐ Yeast
- ☐ Baking powder
- ☐ Baking soda
- ☐ Powdered milk
- ☐ Semi-sweet baking chocolate
- ☐ German sweet baking chocolate
- ☐ Instant hot chocolate
- ☐ Tea
- ☐ Coffee
- ☐ Rice
- ☐ Beans
- ☐ Mung beans
- ☐ Pasta: spaghetti
- ☐ Soba
- ☐ Instant ramen
- ☐ Chinese noodles
- ☐ Nori *(Japanese seaweed)*
- ☐ Raisin cookies
- ☐ Ginger snaps
- ☐ Ak-Mak crackers
- ☐ Saltines
- ☐ Instant soups
- ☐ Instant oatmeal
- ☐ Cooking oil
- ☐ Sesame oil
- ☐ Rice vinegar
- ☐ Soy sauce
- ☐ Maple syrup
- ☐ Brandy
- ☐ Hot sauce
- ☐ Lemon/lime juice
- ☐ Salami

- ☐ Cheese
- ☐ Margarine
- ☐ Dried fruit/fresh fruit for drying
- ☐ Vegetables for drying
- ☐ Dried meat (jerky) or turkey/chicken for drying
- ☐ Nuts: almonds, cashews, filberts
- ☐ Eggs/powdered eggs
- ☐ Raisins
- ☐ Powdered ginger
- ☐ Garlic
- ☐ Cinnamon
- ☐ Cayenne
- ☐ Paprika
- ☐ Tarragon
- ☐ Basil
- ☐ Thyme
- ☐ Curry powder/Garam Masala (pepper, cumin, cinnamon, cardamom, coriander, cloves, mace, nutmeg)
- ☐ Salt
- ☐ Pepper
- ☐ Car food
- ☐ Chicken
- ☐ Salad stuff
- ☐ French bread
- ☐ Cheese
- ☐ Juices
- ☐ Fresh fruit
- ☐ Dog food
- ☐ Baby food
- ☐
- ☐
- ☐

Food Preparation Fundamentals

Definitions

You'll be preparing food in one of five ways: boiling, baking, frying, grilling and poaching.

Boiling: Cooking in a liquid at its boiling point. Remember that the higher the altitude, the lower the temperature at which this occurs. That's the good news, because it takes less time to get the water bubbling. The bad news is that the lower boiling temperature means you have to cook the food longer than at sea level. The following chart indicates the differences:

Altitude	Boiling Point of Water	
	Fahr	Cent
Sea Level	212	100
2,000 ft.	208	98
5,000 ft.	203	95
7,500 ft.	198	92
10,000 ft.	194	90
15,000 ft.	185	85

Baking: Cooking in enclosed heat. At home this means using an oven. In the wilderness it means nesting a covered pot in coals. For best results, the pot is *not* set directly on top of the coals, but on a cleared spot in the middle of the ashes of a fire. It is then *surrounded* by the hot coals. Foil-wrapped food placed on or under coals (or both) is also "baked."

Frying: Cooking in fat over direct heat. The fat may be any cooking oil—vegetable, corn, peanut, canola, safflower, sesame—or vegetable shortenings like Crisco, Spry, etc. Margarine works too, if you keep it cool and in a tightly lidded container. Butter and olive oil spoil too rapidly to be practical. Bacon drippings are fine for frying, but bacon doesn't last much longer than butter. We travel with a plastic bottle of vegetable oil and several sticks of margarine in a small plastic container.

Grilling: Cooking over direct heat on a rack, grill or a stick, a.k.a. broiling or barbecuing. Backpacking grills are lightweight and small. Sticks, if used, should be pointed at one end, green so they don't burn, and long, so your hand doesn't cook along with the food. If the stick is big enough, it's called a spit, and if the food on it is rotated while cooking, this is known as roasting, a technique best left to Tudor kings with very large fireplaces.

Poaching: Cooking by simmering gently in just enough water to cover. Simmering describes what water does just below the boiling point: rather than bubble actively, it moves only slightly. This point is hard to maintain on an open fire, but happily it doesn't matter. Boiling works fine instead of poaching.

Practical Measurements:

KEYS AND SYMBOLS USED IN RECIPES:

❖ = Can be prepared on camp stove or campfire

✳ = Can be prepared only with campfire

c. = Sierra cupful

hfl. = Handful(s)

sp. = Camping kit spoonful

Pots:

small = 4 cups

medium = 8 cups

large = 12 cups

Measurements: Our motto is "more or less." You won't have measuring spoons or cups and you don't need them. Approximations, guesses and tasting will suffice. In the following recipes, all of which make enough for two hungry adults, we try to keep quantities approximate. Where we use measures, they mean the following:

Spoonful: A standard camping-kit spoon, about soup-spoon size.

Cup: A Sierra-type cup, actually about a cup and a quarter by normal measurements. Sierra cups are lightweight, stack easily, and are less likely to burn your lips when drinking hot liquids than ordinary metal cups, because the rim is made of a heat-resistant alloy. They are available at all camping supply stores.

Handful: Just that, an average adult handful.

Pots: Our small one holds 4 cups, our medium 8 cups, and our large 12 cups.

Cooking in the Rain

You can't make elaborate meals in the rain. Baking is out—you can't keep wet coals hot. Frying is possible, but unless your fire is protected from the rain or you fry fast, the food gets wet on top while it cooks on the bottom. Also, if the pan fills with water, you'll be poaching, which *is* a practical method. Another good technique in the rain is grilling (a rack will not fill with water). A third choice is cooking in a covered pot, which is our usual choice. Soups and stews are great: hot, easy, filling and needing little tending, so you can stay dry under a tree or tarp as they cook. You're likely to catch fish in the rain, and it's simple to grill them quickly or poach them and add to your pot.

Keep the stored food and matches in waterproof containers inside covered packs. When the sun comes out again, dry any damp food or packets to prevent spoilage. And don't go without at least one hot meal a day in the rain. Even a steaming cup of cocoa and some biscuits, or a bowl of oatmeal will keep the spirits up.

Stove Cooking Hints

Conserve fuel, cook fast.

- When frying remember that the circumference of heat over a camp stove is smaller than at home or over an open fire. Thus that large pan of frying fish will stay cooler on the edges than in the middle.
- Ignore suggestions for long, slow simmer in all recipes. Boiling time for half a small pot of water is five to 10 minutes. A few more minutes and soup's on.
- Stove safety: Use in a sheltered spot, out of the wind and rain. Unless an emergency requires it, don't cook in the tent, even in the rain. Fuel can spill, fumes can make you sick, tents can burn. Use your ingenuity to cook outside instead.

Other Helpful Hints

Meal size: Camp cooking is cooking in miniature; i.e., a little goes a long way. Be prepared to scale down your normal at-home expectations as to how much you need. You don't want leftovers. Most are hard to store without attracting strange visitors. Plan meals with this in mind. If necessary, feed the last spoonful to the fire or the dogs.

Utensils: Pots and pans should be reasonably clean. Make sure the handles don't burn. If you have to stir something on the fire, lengthen your stirring spoon by tying on a stick. Garden gloves also work well to keep your hand from toasting.

Water: Have enough on hand for both cooking and cleaning up as you go. A dirty mixing pot often is needed for baking a few minutes later. Lids keep dirt and ashes out. Whenever you remove a pot top, set it on a clean rock or plate. Before replacing, check to be sure you won't be adding any unwanted twigs or leaves.

Fire: You want coals more than flame. A blaze burns rather than cooks. It also consumes a lot of fuel.

Fire Area: A fire requires a flat, cleared area, free of brush and clear of any overhanging branches. Don't put it too near your tent, or a slight wind may fill it with smoke. If the fire area is near some natural "chairs" (a big log will do) or "tables" (like a large flat rock), life is easier.

Ingredients: Keep them at hand. You don't want to run all over the campsite for garlic or soy sauce.

White or Wheat? We use unbleached white flour in all the recipes, but whole wheat works just as well.

Shade: Keep all food in the shade while you're in camp. You may need to move the food stash several times a day, but it's so little trouble, especially if you keep the perishables together, and so sensible it should become part of your daily routine. If you leave for the day, place the perishables somewhere out of the arc of the sun.

Tent: A veritable kitchen cabinet—use it. If there are several stages to your food preparation and you need to put something aside, store it in the tent beyond the reach of flies, bees and mosquitos. Make sure, however, that you don't burn a hole in the tent floor with a hot pot. Feel the bottom of the pot, place it on a stone or plate if necessary, and keep it away from sleeping bags and Ensolite pads. Don't forget to zip the mosquito flap all the way. Also, be careful of smelly spills. A tent reeking of raw fish or dried white sauce is likely to attract unwanted guests, such as ants or bears. If you have a spare poncho, spread that in the tent before storing food inside. If you do spill anything on the tent floor, wash it thoroughly before dark.

Covering Food: Foods you cook uncovered at home may need to be covered over an open fire to keep out ash and dirt. In such cases, set the lid on loosely and watch that the contents don't burn.

Washing Up: Make a wash-up area at the very edge of your campsite so as not to attract insects and animals. Carry water to the wash-up site rather than carrying dirty utensils to a lake or stream. Be sure any detergent, even "biodegradable" varieties, goes into the ground. Those bubbles that you see more and more these days, even in the remotest wilderness areas, won't be going away. We usually wash pots with no soap at all: a little hot water and a good scrubber do fine. If you want to use soap, do so sparingly. A few drops are enough.

Invidious Comparisons: Whatever you cook in the wilderness won't be the same as what you make at home. The aim is not to duplicate what you can do seated at the controls of a 21st-century kitchen, but to make do with what you've got. The souffle you bake at 9,000 feet might fall flat. It might not even warrant the name you give it. But it will be full of eggs and cheese and trout and will taste at least as good as an omelet. So if you're a hotshot chef in the lowlands, don't despair when things turn out differently from what you think is "right." Hopefully, you'll enjoy the cooking as much as the eating.

Cleaning and Storing Fish

Unless you're a pelican or a down-at-the-heels samurai, you'll want to clean your fish before eating it—an easy task. Ideally you should do it as soon after your catch as possible, but that's often impossible. You may be on a day hike or out in the raft or too busy catching more to get far enough away from the lake to clean the one you've just caught. In those cases stow the fish is a Ziploc bag or a pot, or thread it on a stick. Try to keep the fish out of the sun.

Fish are easy to clean, but it's also easy to foul the environment while doing it. While floating on a pristine backcountry lake, nothing is more depressing than to look down and see fish entrails floating in the water. Always clean fish far from all fresh water sources—and from your campsite. And don't even begin to clean them until you've found a spot with soft soil or sand and have dug a hole or trench at least four or five inches deep with your heel or a cup. That's going to be your Dispose-All.

To clean a fish, you need a sharp knife and some rinse water. Hold the fish in your hand, belly up. Slit the belly from the vent (the small hole just in front of the back fin) to just behind the head. If you plan to cut off the head (lots of folks leave it on), do it now. Cut on a diagonal line from just behind the front fins through to the spinal column. The fish is going to be slippery; hold on tight. But that backbone is tough, so be careful you don't take your hand off along with the head as the sharp knife severs the bone.

The fish is now opened. Most of the entrails will spill out on their own (into the hole you've dug). Remove the remainder with your hand, scraping away the tissue along the backbone with a thumb nail or knife. That's all there is to it! Rinse out the cavity, put the fish in a bag or pot, clean your knife and hands, pour out the dirty rinse water, cover up the hole and head for supper.

Fish are best cooked and eaten immediately after catching and cleaning. But this too is not always possible. To store the cleaned fish overnight, keep them in a plastic bag inside a pot. You don't need to use any water. Cover the pot and set a heavy rock on it to discourage late four-legged diners. The cold night air will preserve the fish and breakfast will be great.

Cooking Fish Without a Pan

There are many ways to cook fish: frying or poaching in a pan, stewing or baking in a pot, grilling or broiling over an open flame. For starters, let's say you left your frying pan in the car—at the time it seemed too heavy. The pot lids are too small and light to use as substitutes. What to do? Go primitive. Use a stick, a rock,

---

c. = Sierra cupful, *hfl.* = Handful, *sp.* = Camping kit spoonful

the flame or coals as your pan or oven. Here's how.

Trout on the Coals ✳

2 rainbow trout
1 campfire, flames low, coals
   just cooling

Pepper/hot sauce to taste
Lemon/lime juice

Toss fish in the coals! Honest. It works. If you were squeamish about ashes in your food, you wouldn't be here anyway. The worst that'll happen is the fish will be charred beyond recognition. So who needs recognition? Extricate the blackened trout after three to five minutes (depending on the heat of the coals). Use a spare plate to scrape away the charred skin. The flesh will be fine and flaky. Add pepper/hot sauce and a squirt of lemon juice from the miniature plastic bottle. Make Neanderthal noises while eating.

Trout on a Stick ✳

2 rainbow trout
1 campfire, moderate flames,
   coals red hot
1 green, sharpened hardwood
   stick

Cooking oil
Pepper, salt to taste
Lemon/lime juice

Strictly speaking, this is a way to grill, not roast, fish. But the chances of dropping the fish into the fire are good, so you get the best of both techniques. Rub oil on the sharpened stick, lay the oiled part in the cleaned, open belly of the fish, poke the point of the stick into the head to secure it. Truss the fish by poking twigs through one side of the belly, over the stick, and through the other side of the belly. Season it to taste and grill over red-hot coals. The smaller the fish, the less time it takes: an 8" trout should be read in about 6-7 minutes. Check flesh with a fork or knife (or your fingers, if you've lost the cutlery too). If it flakes easily, it's ready to eat.

Trout on a Rock ✳

2 rainbow trout
1 campfire, very hot

1 big, flat rock
Cooking oil

Heat the rock in the fire. Work it to the edge of the fire ring, oil the fish, set it on the flat face of the rock, turning once during the cooking. No utensils? Gather round the rock and eat with your hands. Incoherent Cro Magnon grunting appropriate here.

Grilled Trout ✳

2 freshly caught small trout	1 campfire, red hot coals
Cooking oil	1 lightweight, wire-mesh grill or
Soy sauce / tamari	3-pronged
Rice vinegar / lemon juice	backpacking grill

Oil the grill to prevent the fish from sticking. Set it about 5"above the coals. Let the grill get very hot before it receives the trout. Sprinkle cavity with soy sauce and rice vinegar, also a light coat of same on the trout's skin. Toss on grill. (If using a three-pronged grill, set the fish on it gently. Otherwise it'll end up in the fire.) After about five minutes, turn the fish. A small spatula is useful for this, though chopsticks or a knife and fork will do as well. Use the flake test for doneness: that is, with a fork pry up a piece; if is flakes off easily, the fish is finished, and you've just begun to eat. It will remind you of that great Japanese restaurant you went to last year.

Foil-Baked Trout ✳

One of the best and easiest ways to cook fish without a pan is to wrap it in aluminum foil, set it on a bed of hot coals, and cover it with another bed of coals. Remember, foil doesn't burn, so pack out the remains with your other non-organic garbage. You can either wrap the fish individually or fashion a flat "oven pan." First, crimp the edges up on all sides so the juices won't spill out. Second, keep the "lid" opening toward you and not the fire; that way you can open the foil with a minimum of movement when the baking is done, without losing the juices.

2 10" trout	Small dab of margarine
Rosemary / tarragon	Hot coals
Salt, pepper to taste	1 - 2 $^1/_2$ ft. length heavy
1 clove garlic, sliced thin	aluminum foil

Rub the cavity with the margarine, then season it with the herbs and garlic. Foil-wrap the fish tightly and place on a bed of coals. Cover with hot coals. Note: coals have a habit of cooling, so expect the fish to take about 15 minutes to bake. You may need to add fresh coals if the originals lose a lot of their heat along the way. If you get good at it, you can test for doneness by poking a fork through the foil, while the fish are cooking. If the fork slides in and out easily, meeting little resistance, dinner is done. Or take the whole shmeer out of the fire, open, check, eat, or return for a little more cooking.

Pan-Fried Fish

Pan-fried trout are so easy and satisfying that you may not get beyond them in a week in the mountains. Small lake or stream trout are tender, cook fast and need almost nothing to enhance their flavor. A pan, lightly greased and set on a grill or nestled between rocks about four to five inches above a bed of coals, and a string of cleaned, lightly seasoned trout are all you need for a first-rate meal. The oil should be hot before you add the fish. Turn them over after about four or five minutes (sooner if they're small or the fire is very hot) and cook for another four or five minutes. Sprinkle generously with lemon juice. That's all, folks.

As soon as the flesh flakes with a fork, it's done. Be careful at this stage; an overcooked fish loses a lot of flavor. When in doubt, take the fish off the fire sooner rather than later. You can always put it back, but you can't reverse a burn-out. All our suggestions for minutes per side are approximate. We don't wear watches in the wilderness. It's better to feel for doneness, following the clock in your head, than to put a stop watch on the food in your pan.

One other precaution: make sure the oil doesn't burn. It starts to smoke and turns black if it gets too hot. At the smoking stage, add more oil to the pan to reduce the temperature. By experimenting with the heat of the fire and the height of the pan above it, you'll soon get the right combination and the fish will cook to perfection.

Pan-Fried Trout ❖

*4 8" trout, cleaned, with
  heads left on
Cooking oil/margarine*

*Salt, pepper to taste
Lemon juice*

Heat a mixture of oil and margarine if you can spare them; otherwise one or the other. Brown the trout on one side, about 4 minutes; turn and finish cooking. Salt and pepper to taste. Test for doneness by flaking. Turn out on plate, pour the cooking oils over fish, add a dash of lemon juice.

Trout Amandine 1 (Trout with almonds) ❖

Prepare as Pan-Fried Trout. Add a handful of chopped almonds to the pan after you have removed the cooked fish. Brown the almonds quickly in the cooking oils. Do not burn. Spread almonds over the trout and the juices over all. This is simple and elegant, maybe the best of all ways to prepare a freshly caught small trout. Don't worry if you only have peanuts or cashews. It'll taste just as good, and Escoffier is not likely to pop out from behind a tree to point an accusing finger.

❖ = Prepare on stove or campfire, ✳ = Prepare only with campfire

Trout Amandine 2 ❖

Dust the fish with a handful of seasoned flour. To season flour add any combination of spices to it and mix: pepper, rosemary, tarragon, basil, ginger. Prepare as per Trout Amandine #1.

Trout Meunière (Flour-dipped, Pan-Fried Trout) ❖

4 fresh, cleaned trout, with
heads left on
2-4 sp. margarine / cooking oil
2 sp. flour

Salt, pepper to taste
Lemon / lime juice

Dip the trout in flour to coat. Heat oils—a mix of the two is great—and add fish. Season to taste. Brown on one side, about 4 minutes. Turn and complete cooking. Add a dash of lemon juice. Serve. Why leave the head on in these recipes? For both taste and style. The cheek meat on a fish is the tenderest of all. Why give it to the scavengers? And a whole cooked trout is beautiful.

TROUT MEUNIÈRE VARIATIONS:

- Prepare as per Trout Meunière, but use a mixture of flour and cornmeal. Some old timers put the flour-cornmeal mixture in a bag, drop in the fish, shake, and fry.
- Make a small cup of milk with instant powdered milk and water, dip the fish into the milk, then the flour or flour- cornmeal mixture. Cook as for Trout Meunière.
- Substitute an egg for the milk. Crack it into a pot lid and beat lightly with a fork. To make it go farther, add a spoonful of water or milk to the egg. Dip the fish into the egg and then into the seasoned flour.
- Suppose you run out of flour and cornmeal and still want to coat the fish? Crush a couple of RyKrisp or whatever other crackers you have between a plate and your Sierra cup. Using this coarse meal, proceed with or without egg or milk. A piece of stale bread or biscuit can also replace flour or cornmeal. Just make a fine layer of crumbs by rubbing the bread between your hands. Ground up nuts, seeds, left-over rice—almost anything'll do. Use your imagination.

Trout Flambé ❖

Plan to serve this spectacular dish after dark for best effect. Prepare as in any of the pan fried recipes. Just before eating, pour a little brandy in a Sierra cup, hold it over the fire until it's warm to the touch and light it with a match. As the brandy catches fire, pour it over the trout. A soft blue flame will dance over and around the trout for up to half a minute and will add another delicate flavor to the dish.

---

c. = Sierra cupful, *h/l.* = Handful, *sp.* = Camping kit spoonful

Poached Trout ❖

If you want a thick stew, curry, trout in white sauce, soufflé, or crepes, you won't want to pick bones and skin out of them. To remove these beforehand, simply poach the fish. This leaves the flesh tender and ready to eat; the rest is disposable. Here's how.

A poached fish is a finished product. Seasoned well and not over-cooked, it's as tender as you'll get a trout. But a poached fish is also part of a process that involves other methods of cooking. The six recipes following this one will show you how to combine several methods of preparing fish in order to end up with something definitely more than the sum of its parts.

2 fresh, cleaned trout	*Lemon juice*
Seasonings to taste: pepper,	*Fry pan filled with boiling water*
Italian herbs	

Put enough water in your frying pan to barely cover the fish. Season it with salt and herbs to taste. Place the pan over the fire and let the water come to a slight boil. The fish will curl up. That's all right. There's also no need to turn the fish over. It's done when the skin peels off easily, and the flesh has lost its "transparent" look and comes off the bone at a nod and beckon. This takes about 10 minutes from the time the water begins to boil.

Remove the pan from the heat, the fish from the pan, and then with fork, knife or fingers peel off the skin and flake the flesh from the bones. Ideally, the backbone comes off in one piece, taking most of the skeleton and leaving you with a simple mop-up operation close to the fins. It's simple, but work fast or you'll end up wearing a halo of flies and other airborne participants. When finished, place the fish in the tent until ready to use and go bury the skin and bones. If you won't be using the poaching water (see *Trout in Curried Sauce, Fried Rice Chinese Style,* or *Hidden Lake Soufflé* for possibilities), throw it out far from both your living area and the lake or stream.

Trout Crepes ❖

2-3 fresh trout, cleaned and	*Seasonings to taste*
poached	*2 c. crepe batter*
1 ¹/₂ c. thick white sauce, made	
with poaching liquid	

Crepes are made with eggs, so you don't need any in the sauce. Keep the sauce warm, near the fire, and covered while you make the crepes. It's neither easy nor necessary to make all the crepes at once, so eat them in turns as they come off the fire. Put a crepe on a plate, spoon sauce into it, wrap and eat. Then let your partner(s) follow suit.

❖ = Prepare on stove or campfire, ✳ = Prepare only with campfire

Fried Rice Chinese Style ❖

3 small trout, cleaned and
  poached
2 hfl. rice, boiled
2+ cloves garlic, chopped
Chinese sesame oil/peanut
  oil/cooking oil

Powdered ginger
Dry mustard
Black pepper
Soy sauce

Heat oils (a mixture is desirable but not necessary) in frying pan. Add poached trout, rice and spices. Fry, stirring, till hot. Then add soy sauce to taste, and stir thoroughly. Note: the soy sauce provides all the salt you'll need. The Chinese have a saying: Chinese food doesn't taste good unless you use chopsticks. You have now been warned.

Hidden Lake Soufflé ✳

A soufflé is a three-stage affair: poaching the fish, making a white sauce with the poaching liquid, and folding in beaten egg whites before baking. Here are the instructions:

2-4 small (8") trout, cleaned
  and poached
1 1/2 c. thick white sauce

1-2 eggs, separated
Salt, pepper to taste

After separating the eggs, mix a spoonful of the cooked sauce into the yolks so they won't hard-boil, then add to the sauce to make it thicker and richer. Now toss in the poached fish and seasonings. Stir and remove sauce from heat. Reserve (in tent if there are flies).

Beat egg whites with the spring-loaded swizzle stick or a wire whisk. (If you can spare two eggs, all the better, but one will do too.) The idea is to get them stiff but not dry. Out here in the wilderness this isn't always possible or necessary. Basically you're trying to whip air into them. The bigger the pot and the more you agitate the egg whites, the better your chances of ending up with the right product. We've tried to use forks as beaters with little luck.

Fold the beaten egg whites into the sauce, gently as she goes. Just turn the sauce over on the whites with a spoon till they're pretty thoroughly incorporated. Lose their air and the soufflé will end up with a specific gravity close to that of lead.

Now grease and lightly flour the middle-sized pot (even if you have to do some dish washing and pot juggling to get it free and clean), and pour in the soufflé mixture. It should come about one-third of the way up the pot, depending on how much fish you have. Cover and bake.

You've already got a fire going (to poach and thicken the sauce) so by now the coals are glowing red. Scoop out a pot-sized depres-

---

c. = Sierra cupful, *hfl.* = Handful, *sp.* = Camping kit spoonful

sion in the ashes near the front of the fire and set the pot down—not on the coals, but on the cleared ground or warm ashes. With a heavy stick, pile coals around the pot until it's nestled up to its lid in heat. If the coals are too hot, the souffle will burn. If they're too cool, it'll take ages to cook and you'll do a slow burn with it. Ideally, the coals should have lost their most intense heat; the fiery red glare should be going out of them. Baking time will be about 20-30 minutes, or a chapter from a good book. You may need to add coals to the pile to keep its warmth constant.

It's permissible to peek but be careful not to knock everything awry or get ashes in the pot. Don't worry if the outside of the souf-flé is slightly burned; the inside will be as tasty as promised. The soufflé *will* actually rise, to almost double its bulk, and will look spectacular. Savor it quickly, however, for it deflates rapidly after taken off the heat. But by then, appetite will take over from aesthetics. Tuck in, eat up.

Trout Tandouri ❖

This is a curry dish, filling and fiery. Eat it, and you'll find the rainbow at the end of the pot.

3 small rainbow trout, cleaned
  and poached
2 hfl. rice, boiled
Assorted chopped nuts, dried
  fruits, about a small dishful
Chopped dried onion, as much
  as you like

Cooking oil
2-3 large pinches garam masala
  to taste
Cayenne pepper (optional)
Lemon / lime juice (optional)

Heat up just enough oil to cover the bottom of your frying pan. Toss in the poached fish, rice, nuts and fruit. Season with garam masala and cayenne to taste. Add a dash of lime juice. Stir frequently. Done when hot. Serve with a Summer-fruit Chutney. Guaranteed to warm whatever in you is not.

Trout in Curried Sauce ❖

Ingredients are the same as for Trout Tandouri. Add the poached trout to a cup of white sauce made with the poaching liquid, and flavored with garam masala and cayenne. Serve over boiled rice with nuts and fruits on the side, and a big helping of chutney.

Summer-fruit Chutney ❖

Stew a handful of fruit in water to cover, stirring till softened and thickened. Add an immodest squirt of vinegar or lemon juice (or both!), a spoon of sugar, and continue to stir till thick. Voila! Chutney.

❖ = Prepare on stove or campfire, ✳ = Prepare only with campfire

Sauces

You've been in the mountains eight days and are low on supplies. You have some RyKrisp left, a lump of degenerating cheese, a few spoonfuls of flour, some oil that looks like it came from a crank case and a handful of milk powder. The prospects of catching a trout are dim. You want a hot meal. Not to worry! If you know how to make a sauce you're in business. A combination of oil, flour, milk powder and water will give you a base for the cheese and whatever spices you have left. When it's all melted, thick and steaming hot, you've got yourself a kind of rarebit which can be eaten on the crackers for a filling, hearty meal.

This kind of sauce, practically a meal in itself, can also stretch other foods far and in many directions. It's basically equal parts shortening (usually butter) and flour, which are heated for a few minutes before you slowly add liquid (usually milk or the stock with which you've been cooking). That's it. Some seasonings, cheese, perhaps an egg yolk give you sauce thick enough to eat alone or use in a soufflé, crepes, curry or cream soup.

At home, you'd use real butter and whole milk. Over an open fire and with neither on hand, the technique changes a bit, but the principle is the same.

White Sauce ❖

3 sp. margarine / shortening / oil
3 sp. flour
1-2 c. poaching liquid, or
1-2+ c. water

1 sp. milk powder
Salt, pepper, curry powder,
    nutmeg, paprika to taste

In a small pot melt the margarine (or, in descending order of preference, shortening or oil: they all work). Add equal amount of flour (heaping spoonfuls if a very thick sauce is desired). Stir this mixture over the heat for a minute or two to kill the taste of the raw flour. In your kitchen you'd use a low flame. At a campfire, that isn't so easy; alternate the pan on and off the heat to prevent the sauce from burning. If you are using the poaching liquid from the fish, add this a little at a time, stirring. If you are using the milk powder and water, add the milk powder to the mixture, then the water a little at a time, stirring. The mixture will thicken almost instantly. Continue to add liquid slowly. By the time you've added a cupful or more, the sauce will have thinned out, much to the relief of anyone who thought they were being conned into making kindergarten paste. Keep stirring till smooth. Add seasonings to taste. The sauce is done when reasonably thick and smooth. Don't lose heart if the flour and milk powder aren't completely absorbed by the liquid. It'll still be hot, filling and delicious. When done, add whatever else you want: poached fish, crushed biscuits, cheese, cooked rice, noodles.

---

c. = Sierra cupful, *hfl.* = Handful, *sp.* = Camping kit spoonful

United Nations Rarebit ❖

It would be an insult to the Welsh to call this by its conventional name, so we'll let the Security Council decide its provenance. Anyway, it'll stick to more than ribs and keep you fat and happy.

3 c. white sauce	Hot sauce
3-4+ sp. sliced cheese	Brandy
1 egg (optional)	

Add as much sliced cheese as you can spare to the completed white sauce. If you have an unaccounted for egg, beat it well and add. Continue to stir till cheese is melted. Season with hot sauce to taste and a dash of brandy from the medicine kit. Serve on crackers, boiled rice, or fresh baked bread.

If the sauce is too thick or pasty, keep adding liquid till you get the right consistency. If it's too thin, either let the sauce boil down while stirring, or in a pot lid, make 5 or 6 marble-sized balls of dough from flour and shortening or oil. Drop these into the sauce and stir. They'll thicken the sauce without leaving it filled with lumps of unabsorbed flour which would happen if you added flour alone to the sauce.

Tomato Sauce ❖

Here is the stripped-down fighting version of the homemade sauce you weren't able to dehydrate this year. As long as you have some dried tomatoes and onions, perhaps some dried mushrooms and jerky, you're in business. You'll use this sauce for pasta and for the pizza you can't live without.

1 lg hfl. dehydrated tomatoes	2 sp. sliced or diced jerky
1 hfl. dehydrated onions	(optional)
1 clove garlic, sliced	Mixed Italian spices
1 hfl. dehydrated mushrooms	Salt, pepper to taste

Cover the tomatoes with twice their volume of water. Bring to boil and stir frequently while the tomatoes are rehydrating. Add water as necessary. The tomatoes will not completely transform into a sauce, but enough to give a first-rate illusion of same, about 20 minutes. About half way through the cooking, add the onions, mushrooms, garlic, jerky and spices. Continue to cook till the ingredients absorb most of the water and become saucy. Adjust seasonings. Ta Da!

Note: If this is going to be the base of your pizza, omit the onions, mushrooms and jerky, as they'll go on separately.

❖ = Prepare on stove or campfire, ✳ = Prepare only with campfire

Rice, Noodles, and Beans

You can't always count on catching fish, but you can always count on a hot and filling meal if you have any of these great staples of backpacking. They can be eaten alone, hot or cold (though cooked), in stews and soups, in freeze-dried dinners to add bulk and a little real taste, in puddings, salads, omelets and a thousand other dishes. Their only drawback is that they're heavy, so you need to limit the amounts you take and make do with what you can sensibly carry.

Rice

Put two generous handfuls of white rice in the medium pot with a pinch of salt. Add enough water to come up to just below the middle knuckle of your forefinger. This is enough rice for two adults. We can't explain the knuckle measure. It was taught to us years ago and for reasons that are still mysterious, is invariably correct. Neither the size of the finger nor the size of the hand nor the size pot seem to matter. Remember: the water will boil faster in the mountains than at sea level. Thus the knuckle measure will give you more water to start off with than you'd use for a good fluffy rice at home.

White rice cooks in about 10 to 15 minutes, depending on the heat of the fire. Brown rice requires more water, to about the middle of the knuckle, and more time to cook. Allow about 25 minutes. To make the pot easier to clean, pour water in it immediately after you've spooned out the rice, and keep it warm near the fire. By wash-up time, the pot almost cleans itself!

Fried Rice With Vegetables & Chicken ❖

This joins *Trout Tandouri* and *Fried Rice Chinese Style* in the fried-rice repertoire.

2 hfl. boiled rice
1 c. mixed dried vegetables, rehydrated in water to cover
1 hfl. chopped nuts
Sliced / diced chicken jerky
(optional)

1 clove garlic, sliced
Cooking oil
Hot sauce, spices to taste

Heat the oil in the frying pan, add garlic and nuts till just turning brown, then vegies and spices. Stir and sauté till done; add cooked rice, stir till thoroughly mixed. Adjust seasonings.

---

c. = Sierra cupful, *hfl.* = Handful, *sp.* = Camping kit spoonful

Rice Pudding ✳

2 hfl. cooked rice	Dash lemon / lime juice
1 sp. milk powder	$^1/_2$ sp. margarine
$^1/_2$ c. water	1 hfl. chopped dried fruit
2+ sp. sugar	Dash of brandy (your basic
Pinch of salt	vanilla substitute)
Cinnamon to taste	1 hfl. crushed ginger
1 egg	snaps / crackers

This can be a meal in itself—dessert and main course combined.
Seem like too many ingredients? Maybe, but check that food list
(Table 1) back in Chapter 4. You have all the makings well
within your weight limit.

Oil or grease a medium pot. Line it with crushed ginger snaps
or crackers. Mix the rice, milk powder, water, sugar, salt, cinnamon, egg, lemon juice, margarine, fruit, and brandy thoroughly
and add to the lined pot. Cover with more crushed ginger snaps.
Cover and bake in coals until the pudding is set, about 20 minutes. Eat hot or cold.

If you're out of some ingredients, improvise. No spare egg?
You can still make the pudding. It may not be as rich, but no
one's measuring on a taste meter. Substitute a spoon of flour or
cornmeal and a little more water. No margarine? Use oil. Ditto
for the seasonings—not everyone carries lemon juice or even cinnamon (although no backpacker carrying cinnamon has ever
been known to starve in the wilderness). Maybe throw in some
Swiss Miss powdered chocolate drink instead of sugar and cinnamon. Fine. And of course the cookie crumbs can be left out. Experiment. Enjoy.

Fried Rice and Beans ❖

As any Mexican cook will tell you, the combination of rice and
beans is a nutritional powerhouse. It's also plain good eating.
Spice it up with chili powder, cayenne or hot sauce and you've got
a ready-made fiesta. To the recipe *Fried Rice with Vegetables and
Chicken* add cooked beans and fry till done. If spicy, make sure
you've got a full water bottle within reach.

Beans

Beans are so good, nutritious and easily prepared that it's a pity they weigh so much. Nevertheless, they are definitely worth taking along, in limited amounts. And it doesn't matter what kinds you bring. Red, kidney, white, black beans can all be used with equal ease. Put a couple handfuls in a pot, cover with cold water, cover the pot and soak overnight or for four to five hours during the day. Empty the old water, cover again with fresh water, and cook until the beans are tender, 25-40 minutes, depending on the amount and kind of beans and the heat of the fire. That's all there is to it. Use the cooking liquid for making sauces.

Lentils and split peas may be substituted for beans in most of these recipes. *Note*: Watch your fuel supply if cooking beans on a camp stove. It may cost you other meals down the line.

Baked Rice and Beans in Cheese Sauce ✴

1 hfl. boiled rice　　　　　　*3 sp. sliced cheese*
1 hfl. cooked beans　　　　　*Cayenne, chili powder, hot sauce*
2 c. white sauce

To the white sauce, add the cheese and stir till melted. Add the rice and beans, mix. Bake in coals 10 to 15 minutes till set. Serve with mariachi music and plenty of water.

Refried Beans ❖

2 hfl. cooked beans and the cook-　　*Hot sauce, pepper*
ing liquid　　　　　　　　　　　　*Sliced cheese*
Cooking oil

Drain the beans but reserve the liquid. Heat oil in the frying pan. Mash the beans with a fork or spatula as they're frying. If the beans get too dry, add some of the reserved liquid. Fry slowly, season with pepper and hot sauce. Slice cheese to taste over them. Eat with biscuits and you get a great Tex- Mex meal.

Ranch Omelet ❖

For two adults, scramble three eggs with refried beans and some dried tomatoes. Serve with plenty of hot sauce.

---

c. = Sierra cupful, *hfl.* = Handful, *sp.* = Camping kit spoonful

Bean and Rice Salad ❖

2 hfl. beans, cooked, drained,
   and cooled.
2 hfl. cooked rice
1 poached trout (optional)

1 hfl. bean sprouts
Salt, pepper, lemon juice,
   sesame oil, mustard powder.

   Mix all ingredients together. Season to taste. This is a wonderful meal, even without the trout.

Noodles

If pasta palls, go East. Chinese wheat or rice noodles, Japanese buckwheat noodles (*soba*) are great boiled, fried, baked. They can substitute for almost all the rice recipes: *Trout Tandouri, Fried Rice Chinese Style, Trout Rice and Bean Salad,* or *Fried Rice with Vegetables and Chicken.*

Cooking Noodles ❖

Noodles don't double in bulk when cooked, but the more water you use the less they stick together and to the pot. Use the large pot, half to three-quarters full of water, add salt, boil, and throw in the noodles. Two very generous handfuls will get two of you through a meal. The water should boil rapidly as they cook. They taste done in about 10-12 minutes (at moderate to high altitudes). If you plan to use them in another dish you need time to put together, just drain the noodles, add fresh cold water to cover and let them stand. This prevents them from sticking together. When everything is ready, drain them again, and away you go. If you make a sauce, use the noodle water as the liquid base. It's already hot and flavorful.

Cold Noodle Salad ❖

1/2 packet Japanese buckwheat
   noodles (soba), cooked
   and drained
Sesame oil/regular cooking oil
Rice vinegar/regular vinegar

1 hfl. dried mixed vegetables,
   rehydrated
Sprinkling of mung bean sprouts
   (optional)
Salt, pepper to taste

   Mix all ingredients in a pot. Adjust seasonings. Serve.

❖ = Prepare on stove or campfire, ✹ = Prepare only with campfire

Soups

Fish Stew or Chowder ❖

Clean two or three fish, but save the heads. Toss fish and heads into the big pot, cover with water and poach. Save the liquid in another pot, remove and bury the bones, heads and skin, then combine the fish and liquid. If necessary, add water. Toss in two handfuls of rice (less for more fish), and as much chopped onion and garlic as you can spare. Season with salt, pepper, herbs, even a dash of hot sauce. Boil slowly until the rice is done. The thicker the better, so a packet of dry soup mix, especially leek, helps immeasurably. Ignore the packet's directions, and keep tinkering with the seasonings until it tastes just right.

VARIATIONS:

- For Chinese-style "hot-and-sour" soup, add a good dash of vinegar and considerable black pepper.
- For New England chowder, add a spoonful of milk powder just before it comes off the fire.

Black Bean Soup ❖

Soak overnight and cook two handfuls of black beans in the big pot. If you've got a packet of chicken or beef soup stock, add that, as much dried chopped onion as you can spare, some chips of jerky, lots of garlic, salt, pepper and cayenne. Bring to a boil and let simmer for an hour if you've got the time and the coals are working right. Long cooking gives it more flavor, but even 20 minutes is fine since all the ingredients have already been cooked. Just before serving, add a dash of lemon juice or vinegar and a good hit of brandy. That's it. You'll want seconds, guaranteed. And if you don't have black beans, use what you have and just call it by a different name.

Lentil or Pea Soups ❖

If you prefer lentils or dried peas to beans and noodles, take them to use as you would for bean soup. Like beans, lentils and peas need two- to three-hours' soaking before cooking.

---

c. = Sierra cupful, *hfl.* = Handful, *sp.* = Camping kit spoonful

Hal & Rick's South Side Pizza ✹

1 packet yeast	2 cloves garlic, sliced
1/2 c. warm water	Sliced salami or jerky (optional)
Couple pinches of sugar	4-5 sp. sliced cheese
1 1/2 c. flour	Pepper to taste
Dash of salt	Hearty sprinkling of dried
1 sp. oil	oregano
1/2 c. tomato sauce	Cooking oil
Mixed dried vegetables, slightly	Aluminum foil
rehydrated: mushrooms,	
zucchini, onion, peppers	

In a Sierra cup mix the warm water, yeast and sugar. Set aside covered in a warm place. When "proofed" (that is, bubbly) add it to the flour, salt and oil in a pot. Mix thoroughly with a spoon, adding more oil and water as necessary to make a workable dough. Knead on a plate till smooth. If it's slightly sticky, that's OK. Set in a warm place to rise in a covered, oiled pot. While the dough is rising, make the tomato sauce and rehydrate the vegies slightly by soaking in hot water barely to cover till partially soft. Drain and set aside.

When the dough has risen, turn out on a plate and begin to work it into a round, flat shape with your fingers, pushing out from the center in all directions. You can even pick it up and toss it into the air with a spiral motion, like they do at Mama Mia's. It's helpful to catch it. You may need a little flour on your hands for this. When the dough has become a nice, even circle, fit it into a well-oiled frying pan. It should extend part or all the way up the sides. Then spread the tomato sauce over the dough and pile on the vegetables (and salami/jerky). Sprinkle on the cheese, garlic, pepper and oregano. Then drip a very thin layer of oil over the finished product, and cover the pan with foil. Alternatively, place a large tin plate over the pizza and seal it to the frying pan with the foil.

The idea is to bake the dough fast, before you burn everything on top. Pizza ovens are extremely hot (about 500 degrees Fahrenheit). But if you put your frying pan on a bed of red hot coals, you'll end up with something you might have to call cheese-n-charcoal. Instead set the pan on cleared ground, surround it with hot coals, and slide coals on top of the foil too. Let it bake about 15 minutes. Then work some moderately warm coals under the pan and push others around it and on top. In another 10 minutes or so, the pizza is done. The dough will be crusty, the cheese melted, and mouths watering.

❖ = Prepare on stove or campfire, ✹ = Prepare only with campfire

Basic Pancakes ❖

At home, the usual proportion for pancakes is roughly 2:2:2—two cups flour, two cups milk and two eggs. In the wilderness, the proportions are the same, though the quantity is reduced. A Sierra cup holds around 6 heaping spoonfuls of flour, which makes way too many pancakes for two adults. Our recipes make from 10 to 12 inflated "silver dollar" pancakes, more than enough for two. The cakes are thick, light and filling. You could write home about them. Except there isn't a post office within 3-days' walk.

4 heaping sp. flour
1 sp. milk powder
Dash of salt
$^1/_2$ sp. sugar (optional)

1 egg, beaten
2 sp. oil/melted margarine
$^1/_2$ c. water

In a small pot mix the flour, milk powder, salt, and, if you like, the sugar and leavening agent. Not to worry if you don't have baking powder or soda; they're not necessary, and frankly we rarely use them for pancakes at any altitude, home or away. Add the beaten egg and oil to the dry ingredients and stir quickly. To hell with any lumps! Now add the water gradually, stirring. The batter will be thick. So you may need to add a bit more water, just enough to keep it thick but still smooth enough to flow off a spoon, like a thick velvet ribbon. Don't worry about getting a perfectly smooth batter. Lumps will disappear in the cooking.

To cook, drop a large spoonful of batter in the middle of the heated pan. If it looks pitifully small, add a dollop more. The cake is ready to flip (only once) when bubbles begin to form on the surface. Flip and let cook another few minutes. The second side never takes as long as the first. That's it. Eat! Or, if the first one is good, make 3 or 4 pancakes at one time so that one of you can have a decent breakfast. Then trade places.

VARIATIONS:

• Use the same proportions, but separate the egg and use only the yolk. After the batter is ready, beat the white until it's stiff but not dry, exactly as you would for a soufflé. Fold the beaten white into the batter gently, to preserve as much of the air as possible. Cook as above. The result will be so light that you'll seriously rethink the theory of gravity.

• Chop apricots, apples, banana chips into tiny pieces and add to the batter.

• Add a half-spoonful of sourdough starter to the dry ingredients and omit the baking powder. Whole wheat or buckwheat flour, a mixture of flour and cornmeal work well and make great pancakes. So do flour with ground up RyKrisp, ginger snaps or vanilla wafers. Just remember that each kindof flour has a different moisture content, so adjust the liquid accordingly.

---

c. = Sierra cupful, *hfl.* = Handful, *sp.* = Camping kit spoonful

Crepes ❖

Crepes are French pancakes. They should be paper thin, to wrap other foods in. To achieve the thinness, change the proportions of flour to liquid to eggs. At home, it would be roughly 2:2:4 (two cups flour, two cups milk and four eggs). At 9,000 feet, you're unlikely to have that many eggs to spare. So stick with one egg and follow the basic pancake recipe with the following changes:

- Omit the baking powder or soda. Instead of a spoonful of milk powder, use a ½ spoonful and increase the water to make a thin batter—thin enough to look drinkable, like a homemade smoothie.

- No self-respecting crepe recipe includes oil in the batter. If tradition counts with you, leave it out and spread a thin film of oil on the pan for each crepe. We, however, are not so self-respecting, and after making sure the Academie Francaise is not meeting in the nearest bog, we throw in a spoonful anyway.

- If you have time to fish before breakfast, set the crepe batter aside, covered, in a cool spot. Crepe batter is happier if it sits a while. When you get back, poach your fish, crank up a sauce, and savor trout crepes.

COOKING THE CREPES:

Pour two or three spoons of batter into a sizzling pan. Tilt the pan away from you, then to the side, then toward you so the batter spreads out roughly in a circle as thin as you can get it. The more you practice, the easier it gets and the rounder and thinner the crepes will be. They'll only take a minute or so to cook and are ready to turn when the center looks almost, but not quite, dry. Either work a spatula underneath to turn it, or pick it up in your hand and flip it over. The second side takes less time than the first. The result should be cooked but also pliable, so it can be wrapped around food.

Fruit Crepes

Simmer a handful or so of mixed dried fruits in water to cover. Add a spoonful or two of sugar. Stir and simmer till a thick stewed fruit is formed. Stuff crepes with the fruit, sprinkle sugar and cinnamon on top and serve. These can also be flambéd after dark, as homage to the inventor of Crepes Suzette.

Breads

Anybody who can make pancakes can make pan-fried bread. And anybody who can make the dough for pan-fried breads can add some yeast and bake the bread in a pot in the coals. And anybody who can do that can just as easily make a cake. No excuses.

For pancakes, the liquid ingredients outnumber the dry and you end up with batter. In bread, the opposite is true and you end up with dough. The dough can be picked up without running down your sleeve and dripping all over your shoe. It can be folded or spindled without harm. A cake is somewhere in between: in other words a stiff sweet batter and the promise of dessert.

There's considerable lore about campfire breads and cakes, such as bannock, the basic pan bread, so basic it consists of little more than flour and water with a little baking powder and salt tossed in for luck; sourdough, the old-time, home-made substitute for yeast once carried around in pots hung from the saddle in gold country. But lore's a bore when you're hungry. Here are some of our favorite mountain breads.

Pan-Fried Breads ❖

This recipe is so uncompromisingly basic that it has little to recommend it except to give you an idea of how simple bread-making is. Try it once for experience, then move on to the tastier variations.

In the medium-sized pot mix together four heaping spoonfuls of flour, a ¼ spoonful of baking powder, and a pinch of salt. Add enough water to make a stiff but smooth dough you can pick up and handle without half of it sticking to your fingers. Have the flour sack handy so you can keep both hands floured, and if necessary, add small increments of flour to the dough to get the right consistency. Put a layer of oil in the frypan to preheat, and form six to eight small patties of dough, about the size of a muffin and ½-¾ inches thick. (If you like flipping them in the air, cook one at a time.) Let them brown slowly over a moderate bed of coals. If the fire is too hot, the crust will cook too fast, leaving the insides half raw. Flip or use a spatula to turn them, as often as you like. They're done when they sound hollow to the tap of a finger, roughly 15 minutes, and are more than enough for two ravenous adults.

Corn-meal Muffins ❖

In the medium pot, mix together two heaping spoonfuls of flour and two of cornmeal. Add a pinch of salt, a spoonful of sugar and one of oil, a half spoonful of milk powder, and a quarter spoonful

---

c. = Sierra cupful, *hfl.* = Handful, *sp.* = Camping kit spoonful

of baking powder. Mix thoroughly, then add enough water to make a smooth dough, easy to handle but not sticky. Keeping your hands lightly floured, form the dough into whatever shape suits you. Cook as above. The result is indecently good, a cross between English muffins and old-fashioned corn fritters, or something like famous Southern hush puppies. Eat plain, with a sprinkling of sugar, or split open and cover with maple syrup. They're also great with grilled or foil-baked fish.

- For part of the cornmeal or flour, substitute a packet of dry instant oatmeal.
- Dust the muffins with cornmeal before you fry them.
- Season with pepper, nutmeg, cinnamon, sesame seeds, or a small amount of crushed nuts.

Baked Breads

Baked breads involve one more step than pan-fried, and a lot more time. The extra step is mixing a leavening agent into the dough to lighten it—to puff it up with a myriad of tiny bubbles, making it rise before it's baked. The mixing must be thorough, so you have to punch and push—or "knead"—the dough fully. There are a number of leavening agents. Yeast is the most famous, sourdough starter is another. We carry several packets of storebought dry yeast with us, and take along a small plastic bottle with sourdough starter. Baking powder and soda work only under extreme heat (in the act of baking itself) and can't be used for prebake rising.

STARTING THE YEAST:

All leavening agents work by slowly releasing gas, which gets trapped in the dough and which, in trying to get out, forces it to expand. Yeast needs warmth to produce the gas. In the wilderness, the sun is your warmth. It's also possible to use the warmth of dying coals, but the sun is always your best bet. Don't plan to let your bread rise at night.

Yeast is also activated by warm water and sugar; it's inert until this is done. Sometimes it gets too inert or stale. Check the date on your yeast packets. It should read at least a couple of months ahead. To activate, sprinkle the amount of yeast you need, usually a packet or less, over a half cup of water that's only warm enough to keep your finger in. Add a couple generous pinches of sugar, mix thoroughly, cover and set aside in a warm place until you're ready to add it to the dough. When the yeast is frothy and expanding, it's ready to use.

❖ = Prepare on stove or campfire, ✳ = Prepare only with campfire

Basic Mountain Loaf ✳

A loaf of bread will be as big or small as you have flour to spare. Everything else is secondary. If you have nothing but flour, water and yeast, you can make bread. It might not win prizes at the Happy Valley bake-athon, but it will beat dried-out Triscuits. And with any additional ingredients like salt, milk powder, sugar, oil, sourdough, raisins, nuts, cornmeal, oatmeal, a spare egg, onion, garlic, cinnamon, nutmeg, sesame, poppy or sunflower seeds, to name a few, your breads will become a hedonist camper's dream-come-true.

The following recipe makes about the smallest loaf that is practical and still plentiful for two people. To double it, use twice as much flour, the same amount of yeast, salt and milk. Smaller pots bake better, though a bigger bread will require a larger pot.

Your basic utensils are: two pots, a plate, a Sierra cup, a spoon and eventually, a bed of hot coals.

To ½ a Sierra cup of warm water, add a packet of yeast and a couple pinches of sugar. Cover and set in a warm place. In the medium pot mix together a Sierra cup of flour, a dash of salt, one spoonful each of milk powder and oil or melted margarine. Mix the bubbly yeast into the pot thoroughly. The result will be lumpish, perhaps soggy. Never mind. If a lot of the flour is still dry, add a bit more water, not much. You want a fairly stiff dough, not a batter.

Now turn this out onto a floured plate or flat, clean floured rock. Flour your hands and keep the bag nearby. The aim is to turn this sodden stuff into smooth, springy, velvety dough. You do this by kneading—that is, by folding the dough over and over on itself. Use the heel of your palm to push the dough away from you, fold it back on itself, give it a quarter turn, repeat, turn, repeat, and so on. If the flour on your hands and the plate doesn't suffice, add flour in very small amounts, and knead thoroughly before adding any more. As you knead, the dough will take shape, becoming firm and springy. Conversely, if it gets too hard to knead (or is hard at the outset), you have too much flour and need a little more liquid, either water or oil, the latter being easier to work in at this stage. Soon, the consistency will be just right. The dough is easy and pleasurable to work. You may find yourself spacing out and kneading just because it feels good. It can't hurt, so enjoy it. No harm if you want to go on for a half hour, though five or 10 minutes should suffice. The finished dough will spring slowly back when you poke a finger into it. Don't be dismayed if the dough takes on the hue of your pot-blackened hands or picks up small pieces of dirt. You won't taste or see it, nor contract some dread mountain disease.

When the dough is kneaded to perfection, it's ready to rise. Grease or oil the small pot, bottom and sides, and drop in the dough ball. Roll it around so its surface gets fully coated with oil. Now remove the dough, re-oil the pot and dust it with a little flour, a process to help prevent the baked bread from sticking. Set the dough back in, cover, put in a warm place and go off to fish, read, sleep, whatever, for an hour or so while the dough rises to double its original bulk.

What's a warm place? Any sun-exposed spot is ideal, unless the sun is searing; then warmth in the shade will be fine. A tent in the sun works. Sometimes we stow the pot in a sleeping bag if the day

---

c. = Sierra cupful, *h/l.* = Handful, *sp.* = Camping kit spoonful isn't too warm. Avoid setting the pot near the fire. It may get too hot and bake the bread.

What if it clouds over and gets cold? Not to worry, the rising just takes longer—all day is all right. If it's not ready before bedtime, wait till morning, knead the dough some more to bring the spring back, and let it rise again. It's ready to bake when it's doubled in bulk. Incidentally, if you have time, breads are lighter and tastier if you let them rise twice, punching down the dough after the first rising and allowing it to double again. Literally, make a fist and jab the dough in mid-section. It will deflate. Then cover it and let the rising continue.

It's perfectly kosher to peek at the working dough. But it isn't an elevator; you won't be able to see it rise. If things go right, it will rise even if it takes time. If everything goes wrong and it won't rise, just turn the mess into a cake. What if it doesn't rise and you don't want a cake? Pretend it's fully risen and bake anyway. The fire's heat gives a last lift to the dough, so the finished loaf will be fine; somewhat heavy but just as tasty.

Let's assume, however, that the dough did double, it didn't rain, the coals are still hot, and you're ready to bake. If you wish, gently spread a light film of oil or melted shortening over the top of the dough with your fingers or the underside of a spoon. The oil will give a beautiful brown color to the top crust.

Oven-baked bread is usually started at a high temperature (400 degrees or higher); then after about 10 minutes the heat is reduced to 350 or 375 degrees to finish the baking, normally about 50 minutes. To reproduce those conditions in a bed of coals isn't easy, though as anyone who has ever made "coffee can bread" at summer camp knows, it's possible. The basic notion is to nestle the pot in a clearing in the warm ash or dirt, pile hot coals around it, then let them cool as the bread bakes. As more coals are needed to maintain the heat, rake them around the pot. On windy days, when the fire burns hot to windward and cool to leeward, rotate the pot 180 degrees every 15 minutes to assure an even distribution of heat.

Baking time differs according to the heat of the fire (which burns slower with wet, faster with dry, and hotter with soft wood), the size of the loaf and its ingredients. The basic mountain loaf should take between 20 and 30 minutes. It varies; keep checking. If the loaf sounds hollow when you tap it sharply, it's done. Remove the pot from the coals and set it to cool for 10-15 minutes. Under the best circumstances, when nothing has stuck to the sides, the loaf will come out when you turn the pot over and give it a couple of sharp raps on the bottom and top edges. Normally, though, you have to run a knife blade around the edges. In the worst of cases, so much will stick to the sides and bottom that you may have to saw the loaf in half and dig it out in sections. Usually, however, patience, cooling, deft use of the knife and a sharp knock of the pot against a rock brings forth a gorgeous golden loaf. Let it cool, then be prepared to defend your share against invaders from outer space—or your partner—intent on scarfing it down in one megabite!

❖ = Prepare on stove or campfire, ✳ = Prepare only with campfire

Sourdough Bread ✳

Use the same proportions and ingredients as Basic Mountain Loaf, but add a spoonful of sourdough starter when you add the yeast. Depending on the starter's thickness, you may have to add a little more water or flour to the dough.

Raisin-Nut Loaf ✳

Also known as cinnamon-nut loaf, apricot-nut loaf, banana-nut loaf, mango-nut loaf, prune-nut loaf, nut-nut loaf. This one's sweet. Double the sugar, and add some cinnamon along with a good dash of baking powder or soda, which help enormously when fruit is involved. At the kneading stage, add half a handful of mixed raisins or finely chopped dried fruits and nuts. Proceed as above. Before baking, sprinkle the top with cinnamon, sugar and more chopped nuts.

Jelly-Roll Bread ✳

While the bread is rising, boil some dried fruit, sugar and water into a thick jelly. Punch down the dough and pat it out on a floured plate. Spread the jelly mixture on top of the flattened dough, roll it up and plop it back into the greased pot for a second rising. You can do the same sort of thing with a sugar-cinnamon-nut paste, using enough margarine to hold it together, and come up with the camping equivalent of a morning Danish.

Oatmeal Bread ✳

Prepare a packet of instant oatmeal as though you're making breakfast, let it cool while you put together the dry ingredients (omitting the sugar) and start the yeast. Add the oatmeal along with the yeast and mix thoroughly. Continue as above.

Onion and Garlic Bread ✳

Fry a large spoonful of chopped onion and garlic until they're translucent. Mix them into the dry ingredients of the Basic Mountain Loaf.

---

c. = Sierra cupful, *hfl.* = Handful, *sp.* = Camping kit spoonful

Egg Breads ✻

An egg in any of the above recipes enriches the bread and adds more taste. If you use one, you may need more flour.

Mountain Challah ✻

When you add the yeast, throw in an egg or two. Mix thoroughly. You may need more flour than usual to absorb the extra liquid. If possible, let this loaf rise twice. If you have eggs to spare, use a third, separated, as follows: Throw the white into the dough at the outset along with the other ingredients, but save the yolk. Then, just before baking, beat ½ spoonful of water into the yolk, and brush the top of the loaf with the egg and water mixture. It will produce a burnished golden finish that will drive neighboring backpackers into a near frenzy.

Cornbreads

Yeast Cornbread ✻

If you like cornbreads which rise, substitute cornmeal for half the flour in the Basic Mountain Loaf recipe. Add a healthy hit of baking powder or soda and proceed as above.

Baking Powder Cornbread ✻

If you're low on yeast, use a ratio of four spoonfuls of cornmeal to two of flour and forget the yeast. Add a spoonful of baking powder, a shot of salt, a heaping spoonful of milk powder, two or three spoonfuls of sugar, a beaten egg or two and enough water to make a thick batter, similar in consistency to a thick pancake batter. Turn this into a well-greased pot. Bake at once for about a half-hour. Since cornbread won't sound hollow to the tap, you'll know it's done when the top splits open a bit, and when a knife blade inserted in the middle comes out clean.

Cakes

Basic Ground-Level Two-Step Cake ✱

Pancakes are the result of frying batter. Cakes are the result of baking batter—batter which contains more sugar and eggs. Here's everything you ever needed to know about the unadorned, ultra-simple, starter cake loved by 93% of humankind.

1 c. flour
1 sp. milk powder
$^1/_2$ sp. baking powder
Dash of salt
1 sp. margarine

3 sp. sugar
1 egg
Dash of brandy
Water
Oil for greasing pot

In a medium pot mix together the dry ingredients. In the pot lid, cream together the margarine and sugar, using the underside of a spoon to mix. (If you're out of margarine, oil will work.) Break the egg into the sugar mixture and beat till the glop is smooth. Add the brandy as a substitute for vanilla. Combine both mixtures with enough extra water to make a smooth, thick batter that will pour like a ribbon into a well-greased and floured small baking pot.

Bake the cake in coals cooler than for bread. At home, you'd use a moderate oven (350-375 degrees). Out here, start with coals just beginning to turn black and try to keep any you add roughly the same color. If you can't, don't worry. Betty Crocker won't be around, peeking over your shoulder. Baking time will vary, as usual, but should run about 25 minutes to half an hour. Test for doneness by inserting a knife blade into the center of the cake. If it comes out clean, the cake is done. When cool remove from pot. Eat or ice.

Basic Man Eatin' Cake ✱

Follow the preceeding recipe , only separate the egg, reserve the white, and add the yolk to the sugar and butter mixture. When the batter is ready to pour into the baking pot, gently fold in the egg whites, beaten stiff but not dry. This makes the cake even lighter, a cruel blow to weight watchers and lifters alike.

Advanced Man-Eatin' Cake ✱

For a moister, richer cake, use two eggs, separate both and proceed as above. Add other things to the batter: cinnamon, Kahlua in addition to or instead of the brandy, several squares of chocolate shaved with a knife, or assorted dried fruits and nuts.

---

c. = Sierra cupful, *hfl.* = Handful, *sp.* = Camping kit spoonful

Chocolate Cake ✳

Set up as for Man Eatin' Cake (Basic or Advanced). In a pot lid place two squares of semi-sweet baking chocolate or two rows of German Sweet chocolate. Add about a ¼ cup water. Stir and melt over the fire, being careful not to burn the chocolate. When melted, add to the egg and sugar mixture along with a little brandy. Proceed as in Man Eatin' Cake, folding in egg whites last. *Note*: it is not necessary in any of these recipes to separate the eggs, so if you left the wire whisk at home, proceed as for Basic Two-Step Cake. No one will notice the difference.

Surprise-Delight Cake ✳

Suppose you don't have all the ingredients and still want to make a chocolate cake. Use what you have. Substitute carob for chocolate; scrape the carob off a Tiger Milk Bar to melt in water. Or melt the whole bar and add it to the egg and sugar mixture. Or use powdered Swiss Miss. If you don't have anything to beat the egg whites with, leave them whole. No baking powder? Use beaten egg whites as a rising agent. No brandy? Forget it. No sugar? Double the amount of chocolate, or use both chocolate and instant cocoa, which has plenty of sugar in it. Stretch your mind. Just keep the proportions of wet and dry about the same so the batter stays the proper consistency.

Chocolate Icing ❖

2-3 squares semi-sweet baking chocolate, or	1 sp. margarine
3-4 rows German Sweet chocolate	¼ c. water
	Dash of brandy

In a pot lid melt the chocolate (you can use a combination of the two kinds) in the water. *Note*: the more chocolate you use, the more water you need, but add it moderately. The idea is to have a fairly thick, smooth melt. Add margarine, stir till melted and thoroughly mixed with the chocolate. Remove from heat. Add brandy. Cool till icing begins to thicken. This will take some time, especially on a hot day. To hasten, set icing container in a larger container of cold water. Don't fret, it will harden. In fact, if left too long, it will suddenly harden so much that you may have to warm it slightly to turn it back into spreading consistency. When thickened to that consistency, ice the cake with a spoon or knife. The result is so good you'll have difficulty waiting for your partners to return from a day hike, or wherever they're spending Wednesday afternoon.

To store the iced cake, place the large pot over the cake till time to eat. If there's any left over at night, remove from plate and double bag in Ziplocs.

Note: Icing can be made without a cake. Hardened, it is the perfect nosh, the equivalent of that box of Bartons you were supposed to bring your Great Aunt Emily on her birthday, but ate first. Softened and thickened with a spoon each of milk powder and flour, and a cup or two of water, it transmutes into Chocolate Pudding!

❖ = Prepare on stove or campfire, ✳ = Prepare only with campfire

Fruit Cake ✳

This is a mixture of fruits and nuts held together with a mixture of eggs, sugar and flour. It's a snap to make and a great way to use up nuts and fruit before packing out. In a medium or large pot lid, put as much cut up fruit and nuts as you wish. For the smallest fruit cake, about three large handfuls will do. To this add a beaten egg, three spoonfuls of sugar and a hit of brandy. Mix thoroughly. Now add a dash of salt, a spoonful of baking powder and enough flour (about three spoonfuls) to hold the mixture together. Pour into a well-greased small pot, cover and bake very slowly in moderately hot coals. At home, you'd bake at only 300 degrees, so these coals will be the coolest you've used. Allow an hour or so to cook, and don't expect it to rise much. You'll know when it's done by looking at the top— which should be brown—and testing with a knife for firmness. Run the knife around the edge, turn the pot over and bang it sharply on a rock to get the cake out. If it won't come out whole, cut it in pieces or eat it right from the pot. When the cake is cool, pour some brandy over it and let it sit for as long as you like. It'll keep for days. Incidentally, if it comes out of the pot whole, the cake will be very beautiful.

Cookies

The hardest part of mountain cookie baking is deciding on the ingredients. Chocolate chip, cinnamon-nut, oatmeal, lemon only begin the possibilities. The ratio of ingredients should be 4:2:1, that's four flour (including oatmeal) to two sugar to one margarine. Begin by "creaming" half a Sierra cup of sugar and two spoonfuls of margarine into a paste. Add an egg and a splash of brandy. To a Sierra cup of flour (or flour/oatmeal) add half a spoonful of baking powder, a pinch of salt, and a spoonful of powdered milk. Combine this with the butter and egg mixture. Then add your special ingredients—shredded chocolate bars, raisins, coconut, chopped nuts, dried fruit, cinnamon, nutmeg, ginger, etc. Add flour or water as necessary to get the right consistency, halfway between pancake batter and bread dough. The finished mixture should be thick and chunky. Taste it for sweetness. If it doesn't taste really sweet, your cookies will be more like biscuits.

Cookies are baked in a greased pan exactly like pizza. If you have a plate or lid that fits over your frying pan, you can use it instead of foil to hold the top coals. A few coals below will keep the bottom of the pan warm. You can only bake three or four at a time, so filling the cookie jar is an all-day project. In a pinch, you can make them like pan-fried bread. They may burn a bit on the top or bottom, but if you dip them in coffee or hot chocolate, you'll hardly notice.

---

c. = Sierra cupful, *hfl.* = Handful, *sp.* = Camping kit spoonful